LAW & GOSPEL IN ACTION

LAW & GOSPEL

IN ACTION

FOUNDATIONS
ETHICS
CHURCH

ESSAYS BY

MARK MATTES

EDITED BY RICK RITCHIE

FOREWORD BY JOHN T. PLESS

Law and Gospel in Action: Foundations, Ethics, Church

Published by:
1517 Publishing
PO Box 54032
Irvine, CA 92619-4032

Publisher's Cataloging-In-Publication Data
(Prepared by The Donohue Group, Inc.)

Names: Mattes, Mark C. | Ritchie, Rick, 1966– editor.
Title: Law and gospel in action : foundations, ethics, Church / essays by Mark C. Mattes ; edited by Rick Ritchie.
Description: Irvine, CA : 1517 Publishing, [2018] | Includes bibliographical references and index.
Identifiers: ISBN 9781948969239 | ISBN 9781948969079 (softcover) | ISBN 9781948969086 (hardcover) | ISBN 9781948969093 (ebook)
Subjects: LCSH: Law and gospel. | Law and gospel—Biblical teaching. | Lutheran Church—Doctrines. | Christian ethics—Lutheran authors.
Classification: LCC BT79 .M38 2018 (print) | LCC BT79 (ebook) | DDC 241/.2—dc23

Printed in the United States of America

Cover design by Brenton Clarke Little.

In honor of the decision to bequeath its legacy to the Grand View University Theology Department, this book is dedicated, with profound gratitude, to the board of trustees of the Lutheran Bible Institute in California.

Mark 9:8
Lamentations 3:22–23
Revelation 2:10

Contents

Foreword

"Theology is for proclamation" was the rallying cry of Dr. Mark C. Mattes's esteemed teacher, Gerhard Forde. These essays and sermons demonstrate how theology is for the proclamation of Christ Jesus. While shaped by the legacy of Forde, Mattes is no mere clone of his mentor. In his appropriation of Forde's agenda for contemporary Lutheran theology, he has the freedom to criticize and correct. Classic biblical and Lutheran themes such as the distinction of the law from the gospel, the theology of the cross, and vocation are given robust treatment and are brought to speak with evangelical clarity and biblical substance to the life of the church in our day. As the title of this book suggests, law and gospel are not static categories but God's two-fold action of killing and making alive, of condemning sin and consoling sinners. The law is to be preached not to make people better but to expose sin for what it is—the failure to fear, love, and trust in God above all things. The law does order human life in creation, revealing how God wills His human creatures to live, but the law is not Christ, and it is powerless to reconcile sinners to their Creator. Mattes has learned from Luther and Walther that the ability to distinguish these two words of God from each other is the highest art of the theologian.

Hermann Sasse recognized that the way of the Lutheran church is a "lonely way," for authentic Lutheranism is under attack from all sides. To paraphrase Adolf Koeberle, Lutherans are accused of being "too free" and "not free enough." For some, Lutherans appear to play fast and loose with commandments and tradition, leaving the door open for moral laxity and undercutting the catholic vision. Others would see Lutherans as clutching too tightly to the words of Jesus and holding to a static understanding of life within the orders of creation. Mattes demonstrates that confessional Lutherans are neither libertarians nor traditionalists but those made free by the gospel to live *accurate assessment?*

outside of the self by faith while at the <u>same time living in creation</u> <u>by love according to God's commandments.</u> Mattes is a sure-footed guide to Sasse's lonely way as he navigates readers on the journey that begins, continues, and ends with faith in Christ's promises.

One of the essays that exemplifies Mattes's approach is "Discipleship in Lutheran Perspective." Mattes makes it clear that authentic Lutheranism is at home neither in the socially conservative world of American evangelicalism nor in the socially liberal world of mainline liberal Protestantism. Discipleship is, therefore, not an attempt to fine-tune the missional effectiveness of the church by transforming individual believers any more than it is an effort to renovate this fallen creation into a new world order of peace, justice, and ecological harmony. Mattes is too much of a realist to settle for anything less than an understanding of discipleship geared to repentance and faith, death and resurrection.

Confessional Lutherans are often scored as inherently weak in regards to ethics. This charge will not stick with Mattes. Several of the essays deal concretely with ethics giving evidence that the Lutheran theology has the resources to address moral issues with clarity without abandoning the doctrine of justification by faith alone. <u>In fact, Mattes makes the case</u> that the Lutheran confession of justification *Agree* by faith alone actually frees Christians from the quest for ~~salvation~~ so that they can devote their attention to attending to the needs of the neighbor in the world. Rather than fixating on the law to the point that the gospel is reduced to a remedy to restore a legal system, *melos:* Mattes recognizes that Christ is the end of the law for righteousness *a goal* to all who believe (Rom. 10:4). Christ, not the law, is the Lord of the Christian's conscience. <u>The law remains where it is necessary.</u> That is, in creation, where it continues to curb and guide but always accuses whatever is <u>not of</u> Christ. *? No constructive ELEMENT*

For Mattes, the theology of the cross is not simply one locus in a theological system. It is a lens and filter for focusing and connecting all the articles of faith and giving shape to the Christian life in the world. The theology of the cross guards ecclesiology from romanticism and keeps the church's mission centered on the proclamation of the word of the cross as the divinely mandated means of reconciling unbelievers to Christ. In an era when some Lutheran theologians seem to be embarrassed by evangelism and are in a state of denial of theology's proper apologetic task, Mattes offers a robust defense of both, anchored firmly in Lutheran categories governed by the first commandment. This is Lutheran pastoral theology at its best as it gives all glory to Christ alone as the Savior and full consolation to the broken sinner.

As we have already observed, "theology is for proclamation." For Luther, the university podium often became a pulpit, and the pulpit became a lectern for teaching the faithful. The same can be said for Mark Mattes; his teaching essays preach Christ, and his sermons teach the faithful. It is fitting that this anthology of Mattes's work includes several sermons that demonstrate once again that theology leads to sound and substantial proclamation. Mattes's homiletical work speaks to the mind and the heart of the hearer, always handing over Christ Jesus to those broken by sin and held captive to death. These sermons not only edify readers; they also carry the potential to stimulate good preaching in pastors who meditate on them.

A teaching theologian of the Evangelical Lutheran Church in America, Mattes's piety and thinking have been profoundly shaped by the former American Lutheran Church, especially such luminaries in that legacy as Wilhelm Löhe, J. Michel Reu, and Herman A. Preus. His scholarship is learned but accessible, comprehensive but clear. For those who have read Mattes's books, chapters, or journal essays, this volume will be a welcomed compendium of his rich contributions over the past quarter of a century. For others who might not be familiar with Mattes's work, *Law and Gospel in Action: Foundations, Ethics, Church* will be a fine a place to begin to explore one of the most significant confessional Lutheran theologians of our time. I look forward to using this volume in several of my courses, and I am delighted to commend it to pastors, teachers, and laity who seek to articulate God's word with accuracy and clarity.

John T. Pless
Assistant Professor of Pastoral Ministry and Missions /
Director of Field Education
Concordia Theological Seminary
Fort Wayne, Indiana
Pentecost 2018

Introduction

My institution, Grand View University, offers Nexus, a summer youth theology institute for high schoolers interested in a deeper exploration of their faith, including the question of whether or not they might be suited for a call to the preaching office or some other church vocation. Students explore the Bible, Christian doctrine, service learning, and, surprisingly enough, at least for Lutherans, apologetics—the defense of the faith—for which I am the teacher. The occasion that prompted the need to collect these seventeen essays and six sermons was the request from one of my Nexus students who, in the desire for further enrichment, asked for essays that I had written. I realized that I had no accessible go-to resource to put such essays into someone's hands. I am honored that 1517 Publishing took on this venture. It fits perfectly with its mission: "We promote the defense of the Christian faith, confessional Lutheran theology, vocation, and civil courage." With the leadership of 1517, I seek renewal for confessional Lutheranism. My prayer is that these essays and sermons can contribute to that revitalization by strengthening faithful pastors and teachers who will tend to the word in parishes and schools and thereby let the word impact the world as it deems fit.

Occasion and Purpose of This Project

In addition to six sermons, the following essays seek to apply the distinctively Reformational practice of distinguishing law and gospel to disputed topics in theology such as the question of authority and the nature of theology, theological ethics, and the mission and empowerment of the church and its ministry. There are many fine

resources that give a basic introduction to the art of distinguishing
law and gospel. One of the best is *Handling the Word of Truth: Law
and Gospel in the Church Today* by John Pless.[1] Very simply, the law
refers to the commands or expectations that God gives human creatures, all for the sake of advancing health in families and communities. Enjoying good order nurtured in creation, we as God's creatures
may live honorably and with integrity. In contrast, the gospel refers
to the promises that God gives to His creatures, particularly sinners.
Most people assume that if God gives laws, people must also be able
to fulfill them. In contrast, St. Paul teaches that the law is a custodian
that leads us to Christ (Gal. 3:24). That is, far from being doable, the
law, for sinners, proves to be just the opposite. The law causes sinners
to despair of themselves and so leads them to find no other recourse
for salvation or wholeness other than the mercy granted to them in
Jesus Christ.

Ultimately, for sinners, the law works death, undermining
every defense that sinners might erect to evade God's mercy. Sinners
are apt to seek the mercy found in the proclamation of Jesus Christ as
the forgiveness of sin only when every last ounce of their own
attempts at self-justification fails before the divine court of the law.
Of course, God uses the law to work order into the world and sustain His ongoing creation. But with respect to sinners, God speaks
through the law to condemn all who seek to live self-sufficiently,
apart from mercy, and so aim to establish a false humanity, and faux
humility, in rebellion against God's kindness and generosity. To live
from God's grace, to claim God's mercy, is to live freely: one's conscience is no longer bound by the law's condemnation but instead
claims the truth that "if God is for us, who can be against us?"
(Rom. 8:31).

Naturally, many North American theologians who write from
a law and gospel perspective tend to focus on the pastoral dimensions of the distinction between law and gospel, sometimes without
branching out into questions of specific ecumenical issues, apologetics, or contemporary voices in theological ethics. Overall, as helping
us to discern whether a conscience needs to be either alarmed or
comforted, they have done outstanding work. Sharing deep pastoral
concerns with these authors, the goal of these specific essays and sermons is to reclaim turf that both more liberal and more conservative

voices in the church concede all too quickly to secular agendas. Both rightist and leftist political stances assume that nothing is more ontologically prior than the individual. But this stance is inherently in conflict with the Scriptures. God gives gifts to individuals—the sacraments are given "for you"—but these gifts are mediated socially and linguistically through the body of Christ. Because Adam was not *underlined* created to live apart from Eve, community is prior to the individual. *Note* There never was a "state of nature," a primal situation in which individuals were ontologically primary and independent of each other. (The secular justification for government, as presented by Thomas Hobbes and John Locke, is that in a state of nature, individuals would be totally free but not safe. Individuals covenant to form a government whereby they exchange total freedom for a modicum of security.) Faithful Christians should challenge the individualism latent in all modern "liberal" political theories present on either side of the aisle.[2] This is not so as to favor any collectivist theories of government. Far from it! It is instead simply to acknowledge that humans are ever and only communal creatures. "Communitarian"

So these essays and sermons have been crafted with a distinctive apologetic and evangelistic texture, which is highlighted more prominently than is found in other contemporary law and gospel practitioners. Hailing not from a Midwestern Lutheran enclave but instead from the very pluralistic and secular environment of Seattle, which was nonchurchgoing even in my childhood in the late 1950s and early 1960s, when church membership was thriving elsewhere, I am sensitive to the corrosive effects that inevitably arise when faith is accommodated to secular agendas. For that reason, I'm especially interested in showing that law-and-gospel thinking should challenge mainline Protestantism when it sells out to secularism.

These essays seek to raise up and support pastors and laity who not only affirm faith as primarily a matter of the heart, resulting in gratitude to God and service to neighbors, but also honor the life of the mind, without which they cannot guard that faith from attack. Likewise, they are also written for scholars whose callings demand a pastor's heart. Increasingly, it would seem that whether in the church or the academy, such pastors or scholars are hard to find. Historically, Lutherans valued a learned clergy. This was not to promote learning for its own sake but instead because Lutherans acknowledged that clergy as confessors were guardians of others' souls and therefore beholden to sound doctrine. Pastors should seek sound doctrine not only to be faithful to the Scriptures but also to rightly guard peoples' consciences. After all, pastors are shepherds and guardians of souls.

At one time, most Lutheran-related church colleges prioritized the training of youth in preseminary studies. As the religion departments of these schools increasingly were colonized by ideologues of the American Academy of Religion and the Society of Biblical Literature, they lost their impetus to select and mentor budding pastors. Likewise, they fell short of their calling to urge a student to consider his or her life's work in light of the doctrine of vocation. With church colleges no longer serving as pipelines for pastoral candidacy, those seeking ordination increasingly have come out of either the Bible-camp milieu or those circles deeply influenced by the subculture of therapy. While the first conduit tends to be more doctrinally conservative and the second more liberal, both equally denigrate the life of the mind as integral to faith. Increasingly, the faith is dumbed down—and precisely by those who think they are quite bright based on whatever side of the aisle they vote for. But all this results in unfortunate consequences for parishes. Parishes need pastors who not only are warm and caring but also have smarts. After all, it takes a keen mind to effectively lead people, even when they are sheep!

Background

I am rostered in the Evangelical Lutheran Church in America (ELCA), called to teach theology at Grand View University. My family's spiritual roots were in the American Lutheran Church (1930), particularly that lineage known as the "Iowa Synod," indebted to the confessional and liturgical stances of the nineteenth-century Franconian mission-driven pastor Wilhelm Löhe. This heritage has profoundly influenced my life. In addition to this particular spiritual heritage, I have been equally formed by C. F. W. Walther's *The Proper Distinction Between Law and Gospel*, which I first read, quite by chance, as a teenager. My thinking was forever changed through reading Walther. Not only my reading of Walther but also family and in-law connections have provided me a long-standing rapport with many in those synods associated with the erstwhile Synodical Conference. Additionally, I have done much work in the thinking of both Gerhard Forde, my *ordinator*, and Oswald Bayer. While I do not agree with every aspect of how these faithful thinkers approach theology, I find their focus on the theology of the cross (as opposed to that of glory), the Christian walk as a daily return to baptism, the proper distinction between law and gospel, the performative nature of the word, the truth that theology is for proclamation, and that "for freedom Christ has set us free" (Gal. 5:1) to be most helpful and empowering. There is no question, however, that these essays, similar to Gerhard Forde, display a challenge to the directions in which many in the ELCA have moved since its inception in 1987 and that were already present in The American Lutheran Church (1960) and the Lutheran Church in America (1962). Many of the essays here were published in journals such as *Logia: A Journal of Lutheran Theology, Lutheran Quarterly*, and *Lutheran Forum* or *Forum Letter*. Often, readers of these journals do not overlap, and those aware of my essays in one journal are not likely to be aware of material I have written for the others. Collecting these essays into one volume will offer readers a fuller picture of how law and gospel bear on a wide range of topics.

General Overview

These essays and sermons were written over a sixteen-year span, the earliest in 2002 and the last in 2018. They are clustered around three themes: foundations, ethics, and church. The section "Foundations" presents essays dealing with the authority of Scripture, the theology of the cross and its impact on theological anthropology, and the role of reason in theology, both as it serves the explication of doctrine and as it allows itself to be critiqued when it oversteps its limits. Reason oversteps its limits when it fails to be accountable to the gospel and when it functions as a tool of humans' lust for power expressed in the goal of subduing nature or manipulating one's self and others. Law and gospel are in action when and where a theology of the cross is distinguished from a theology of glory and when and where God makes us people of faith in opposition to living artificial lives based on our own self-righteousness and self-justification.

The section "Ethics" challenges those Lutherans who accommodate to secular ethics, whether those of the deontological, duty-based "peace and justice" agendas, such as advocated by Cynthia Moe-Lobeda, or the utilitarian, happiness-based biotechnology, such as advanced by Ted Peters, both current among mainline Protestants. It also challenges nostalgic Neoplatonic attempts to recatholicize Protestant ethics, as found in the work of David Yeago or Roman Catholic convert Reinhard Hütter. In contrast, these essays propose that Christian ethics is a natural, even spontaneous, outflow of generosity from those graced by God's abundant forgiveness and mercy. God's forgiveness transforms sinners because, as people of faith, they can afford to entrust their destinies into the hands of their loving Father and thereby generously share of their wealth to those in need, dutifully exercise their vocations to help their families, assist at their work, contribute to civil society, and live as Christ's envoys in a world that valorizes the opposite of such altruism. Law and gospel are in action when works no longer have to do with securing one's eternal status before God or one's worldly value before the fickle evaluations of others but instead are done to help the neighbor in need.

The section "Church" advances a distinctively confessional identity for Lutherans as opposed to the need for fitting into either American evangelicalism or mainline Protestantism, positions that ultimately sell out the gospel.[3] Lutherans contribute the most to the wider public not by fitting into broader expressions of American religiosity but instead by cultivating those core theological convictions and spiritual practices that make them unique. No other function of the church needs more cultivation than that of parish ministry. Pastors should be loyal to one another and then, along with concerned laity, seek to raise up a new generation of pastors who not only care for individuals but also develop and support entire faith communities. Law and gospel are in action when the church realizes that its first mission, more important than anything else, is properly distinguishing law and gospel so that self-centered, insensitive sinners encounter the attack of the law on their self-righteousness, while sinners desperate from such attack can find refuge in God's promise. Thereby, men and women of faith find their hearts opened to others, a love for God blossoming, an appreciation for nature and the earth awakened, and a hunger to hear grace ever more satiate the soul.

Given the depth of criticism of ELCA-related theology present in these essays, one might ask, "Why stay?" Confessionally minded pastors and theologians who stay in the ELCA do so because they are called and they have not, at least yet, received orders to leave their posts. No doubt, they often feel like Elijah countering Ahab and Jezebel, hanging on only by the promise given in the still, small voice barely hearable in the wilderness. But such confessors of the faith also claim that they are surrounded and heartened by the assembly of angels, archangels, and all the hosts of heaven as their fellow confessors. Additionally, the ELCA is not monolithic. There are at least "seven thousand in Israel, all the knees that have not bowed to Baal, and every mouth that has not kissed him" (1 Kings 19:18): many faithful pastors, congregations, and laity abide in the ELCA. Mercifully, God provides daily community, "conversation and consolation of the brethren,"[4] which often makes the journey not only light but even joyous.

Section 1: Foundations

Chapter 1, "Standing on Scripture," was a convention lecture presented to The American Association of Lutheran Churches (TAALC) in June 2010. TAALC is a small synod composed of pastors and congregations, mostly from The American Lutheran Church (1960), which did not join the 1988 ELCA merger. This essay harkens to the events in the prophet Jeremiah's life where King Jehoiakim repeatedly cut away at Jeremiah's prophecies, written down by Baruch, in order to provide tinder to stoke his fire and keep himself warm in winter. Similarly, the tendency all too often among ELCA Churchwide Assembly voters has been to whittle away at the word in order to accommodate the church's life to various agendas in wider society, often in opposition to God's written word. This address urges listeners to follow the example of the Bereans in Acts 17, who searched the Scriptures and tested their ideas and behaviors in light of the Scriptures. Ultimately, Christians live, move, and have their beings in the Scriptures, which provide not only sound doctrine and a wholesome path for life but also a narrative from which life makes sense, a compass from which to interpret life in all its uncertainties, complexities, and mysteries.

Chapter 2, "The Theology of the Cross Speaks Today," was originally an address given to the Iowa Chapter of the Society of the Holy Trinity in May 2012. It was subsequently published in *Comfortable Words: Essays in Honor of Paul F. M. Zahl*.[5] Paul Zahl is an Episcopal priest, a personal friend, and the inspiration for Mockingbird Ministries.[6] Indebted to the thinking of Gerhard Forde, the essay challenges the misinterpretation of the theology of the cross at large in the ELCA, which views it as Christian solidarity with victims. In complete opposition to Luther, this misinterpretation actually results in feeding a form of self-righteousness: like God, I feel your pain. In contrast to this negative theology of glory,[7] we find that the suffering imposed upon us, our "suffering divine things," dislodges us from self-trust and self-security and so forces us to flee to God's mercy found in Jesus Christ. Living by grace does not result in a libertine lifestyle, but instead, as returning prodigals, we are ever eager to receive God's grace and to pay God's goodness forward to others. Christians do not concoct their own identity or define themselves but instead discover themselves as participants in Jesus' death and resurrection.

Expanding on the theology of the cross, chapter 3, "Theses on the Captivated and Liberated Will," originally published in 2007 in *Logia*, notes that a correct understanding of Lutheran anthropology argues that the will is never free on its own terms but instead is ever captivated by either God or, as Luther put it, the devil. The former is freedom—the latter bondage: being curved in on one's self. Neither an evangelicalism that privatizes Jesus as a means to cope with a run-amok economy nor a mainline Protestantism that seeks to tame the economy all for the sake of an individual's fetishes is compatible with Luther's stance on a liberated conscience. The office of preaching exists to liberate bound wills.

Chapter 4, "A Contemporary View of Faith and Reason in Luther," was originally an address given to the Luther-Akademie Ratzeburg in September 2012. It was subsequently translated into German by Oswald Bayer and published in *Glaube und Vernunft: Wie*

vernünftig ist die Vernunft?[8] In English it was published in the Daniel
Preus Festschrift, *Propter Christum: Christ at the Center.*[9] Counter to
longstanding claims that Luther was authoritarian and irrationalist,
now perpetrated by some of the "new atheists," Luther held reason
to be something "divine," appropriate not only for this-worldly matters such as ethical reasoning but also for evaluating doctrine, provided that such reasoning is grounded in and held accountable to the
grammar of faith. Naturally, Luther criticized reason when it sided
against God's grace in favor of works-righteousness. The content of
theology is not defined by reason; instead, reason's vocation is to test
truth claims employed to articulate and establish sound doctrine.
So with respect to divine matters, reason must comport with faith.
Genuine theology is to be contrasted with current secular thinking
in ethics. Contemporary secular ethics is highly unstable because,
although it assumes that truth must be reducible to quantifiable matters, it is then forced to import nonquantifiable ideals like freedom
and equality into its ranks in order to do its work. Secularism would
be advised to admit with Luther that, with respect to ultimate matters, all people must live from some kind of faith, whether it is in
God or some lesser matter—in Christian terms, an idol.

Chapter 5, "Toward a More Robust Lutheran Theology:
Response to Dennis Bielfeldt," was originally an address given to
the Word Alone Theological Conference in November 2006. At the
time, Word Alone was seeking to establish its own Lutheran House
of Studies as an alternative to ELCA seminaries. The project was
spearheaded by my predecessor at Grand View, Dennis Bielfeldt,
a longtime friend. Bielfeldt is opposed to existentialist interpretations of Luther that became prevalent among many ELCA theologians in the 1960s. The problem with such existentialism, at least for
Bielfeldt, is that by eschewing metaphysics—the attempt to ground
theological truth in reality in its most general, basic, or universal
terms—theology becomes wholly subjective. Ironically, the subjective approach to theology in existentialism is rooted in Immanuel
Kant's agnosticism about God's existence. For Kant, God is a reasonable "postulate" for ethics, or the ideal of the human potential to
ultimately know everything knowable, but as a metaphysical reality
is wholly unavailable or unknowable to us. Bielfeldt rightfully sees
that such a legacy disempowers the gospel. The gospel becomes

tantamount to *whatever* someone perceives as liberating, since it is grounded not in reality—nor even in the life, death, and resurrection of Jesus Christ—but instead in experience.

With respect to metaphysics, Bielfeldt advances a kind of "critical realism." What he means by "criticism" has nothing to do with jettisoning the Scriptures or the church's teaching for a more "rational" approach to faith. Instead, it is the conviction that the human mind is capable of knowing something about ultimate reality (although it cannot know everything about ultimate reality), even apart from revelation, based on the inferences it can draw from what is seen to what is unseen. In the "Commentary on Jonah," Luther highlighted the truth that the sailors in the midst of their peril called upon God—showing that they knew God exists—even though they were unclear about God's nature.[10] Those inferences lead to a "critical" realism because metaphysicians must constantly refine their proposals in light of new understandings of reality. For example, physicists change their views of the atom as new experiments yield new models of the atom. Metaphysicians then extrapolate truths about reality based on such inferences. My response to Bielfeldt is simply to suggest that descriptive, metaphysical claims about the cosmos can work in tandem with the Lutheran propensity to highlight the performative impact of the word—a word that does what it says and says what it does—paradigmatically expressed in the words of absolution or in the granting of the gospel as promise in preaching or consolation.

Concluding this section is chapter 6, "A Lutheran Case for Apologetics," a keynote address presented to the Lutheran Congregations in Mission for Christ (LCMC) in October 2014. The audience response of a standing ovation indicates the presentation struck a nerve. The perspective here does not reject the "evidentialist" approach so strongly favored by evangelicals. But it suggests that a better strategy in dealing with nonbelievers is less about arguing them into faith and more about reasoning with them about controverted topics from the perspective of faith. A major task of apologetics is to set the record straight with respect to mischaracterizations of faith promulgated by the Enlightenment. A good model to follow is that of Paul in his address on the Areopagus (Acts 17:22–34).

A mischaracterization of evidentialism

Section 2: Ethics

Section 2 deals with contemporary theological ethics. Chapter 7, "The Thomistic Turn in Evangelical Catholic Ethics," was published in *Lutheran Quarterly* in 2002. It hearkens to a lost era among ELCA Lutherans in which there were actually different, combative theological tribes in the church, in this case, Jensonites (followers of the thinking of the late Robert Jenson) and Fordeaner (followers of the thinking of the late Gerhard Forde). These two tribes have long since vanished from the ELCA. And the ELCA is much the worse for it because the skirmishes between these two groups kept those pastors who followed the debates theologically sharp. A portion of Fordeaner resides in the Augustana District of the LCMC, while one is apt to find Jensonites in the North American Lutheran Church. When these two tribes entered any fray, it forced pastors to keep up theologically so that they could defend their positions. The church of my adolescence and young adulthood had a cohort of pastors who took greater ownership in matters of theology than it currently does.

This essay challenges the work of two theologians influenced by Jenson, David Yeago and Reinhard Hütter, who have little place for the law and gospel distinction. I share their concerns about the rise of contemporary antinomianism among mainline Protestants, but I disagree with their constructive proposals. In their way of thinking, both freedom and law must be configured in light of humanity's ultimate teleology in God. Otherwise, freedom is no longer one's ability to discipline one's own behavior but instead is misinterpreted as self-exploration based on arbitrarily self-chosen values. All the while, positive law is seen, like Kant, as something external or heteronomous, a threat to one's ethical maturation, unless one is able rationally to commend it to themselves. In their "catholic" vision, freedom ultimately is a result of achieving human fulfillment through teleological self-expression, objectively grounded in God as one's final good. While this sounds promising, it does not square with Jesus Christ as both gift (*sacramentum*) and example (*exemplum*). Ultimately, being conformed to Jesus Christ is a result not of our self-actualization but instead of our fleeing to the mercy found in Jesus Christ by means of faith alone, resulting in a passive or receptive life, the outworking of God's "alien work" through the law to humble sinners and God's "proper work" to bring them to faith through the proclamation of the word. Humans accord with God not primarily through works but instead through complete trust in Christ and confidence in God's word to claim sinners. Thereby, Christ is the form of faith, and humans naturally and spontaneously live as Christs in the world. Christians are marked by a cruciform identity: dying and rising with Christ. Not through eudaimonistic self-development are humans conformed to Jesus Christ but instead by means of Spirit-bequeathed confidence in God's word. In the word, humans receive an identity granted through Jesus Christ that is wholly cruciform.

Chapter 8, "The Mystical-Political Luther," originally published in *Logia* in 2007, evaluates the ethical stance of Cynthia Moe-Lobeda, whose critique of global capitalism was for many years promoted by the ELCA. I characterize her interpretation of Luther as "mystical-political," since, based on the late Tuomo Mannermaa's work, she highlights Luther as a mystic and uses that characterization as a jumping board for a progressive, utopian agenda that is thoroughly opposed to global capitalism. Indeed, Luther had grave reservations about nascent capitalism and certainly would deplore the individualism at the center of modern, "liberal" political thinking, but he would never accept the utopian anticipations in Moe-Lobeda's ethics. Her theology is far more akin to Thomas Müntzer's than Luther's. Instead of so valuing individual self-expression, Luther would lead us to honor the family. With the well-being of the family as a standard, we can test proposed approaches to economics. The question at hand is: How well does the economy serve families?[11] Those economies that put tremendous strain on families should be reevaluated. Economics and politics exist to serve people and not vice versa.

I disagree with Moe-Lobeda's utopianism. But that does not mean that political theories that center on individualism accord with Luther's social ethics. Far from it! We should just as equally question the individualism and lack of appreciation for the family that is taken for granted in the political thinking of Thomas Hobbes and John Locke. Truth be told, there is no current economic and political structure in existence that wholly accords with Luther's thinking. That means that Lutheran ethicists are constantly forced to make compromises on matters they do not wish to compromise. Even so,

"Communitarianism"

the primary task of the church is the proclamation of the gospel. And correspondingly, the primary civic responsibility of all people, whether Christian or not, is to advance the common good. Whatever we make of justice or peace is accountable to the common good.

Chapter 9, "Discipleship in Lutheran Perspective," originally published in *Lutheran Quarterly* in 2012, seeks to claim a Lutheran stance for discipleship. After all, the gospels explore not only how sinners contribute to Jesus' death but also the various ways in which Jesus taught His disciples in words and deeds. The concept of discipleship should not be discarded by Lutherans as somehow pietistic. Nor should it be dominated by the social-justice concerns of mainline Protestantism. No doubt, there are pietistic versions of discipleship that are legalistic. But in a sense, as the gospels present it, God is taking a ragtag bunch of sinners and shaping them into a Christ-life, as He sees fit.

Chapter 10, "Bioethics and Honoring Humanity: A Christian Perspective," was an address for a conference, the Future of Lutheran Ethics, held in Hickory, North Carolina, in 2010. As a case study, the paper tackles the question of harvesting embryonic stem cells not only for the purpose of regenerative medicine but also for genetic enhancement, "designer babies." The essay challenges Ted Peters, who advocates the value of harvesting embryonic stem cells as a cost-effective measure, since embryos are not "persons." His stance represents not only the unquestioned conviction that the vocation of the human is to conquer nature and that technology is the means to achieve that end but also the privileging of the status of "person," as self-defining consciousness, over and against that of "human," as a being that has existed in many different phases, both conscious and nonconscious. Thereby, he makes the utilization of embryonic cells acceptable. Such a stance is wrong in multiple ways but most specifically in the privileging of the concept of "person" over "human."[12] After all, it is the human that is made in God's image, and this includes humanity in all stages of its development.

Closing out this section, chapter 11, "Rethinking Social Justice," is an opinion piece published in *Forum Letter* in August 2017. It summarizes several reasons the prioritizing of social justice in the ELCA is unfaithful to the witness and vision that should guide the church. In a democracy, Christians should, of course, be involved

in politics. But the church should not be reconfigured as a bureaucratic advocacy group.

Section 3: Church

Section 3 explores the nature and mission of the church. Chapter 12,
"Should Lutherans Be Mainline Protestants?," was originally published in *Logia* in 2015. Through a case study of the thinking
of the late William Streng, who had been a professor at Wartburg
Theological Seminary, I explore important shifts that developed in
the church in the 1960s and that transitioned the church from being
confessional to being mainline. Admittedly, Streng was not a major
figure. But as a seminary professor, he shaped hundreds of budding
preachers. He is paradigmatic for that generation for whom social
relevance as opposed to orthodox fidelity became all-important. The
chapter shows that the transition from confessionalism to mainline
Protestantism was grounded in the desire to transition the church
from a parochial, ethnic institution to a full-fledged "enlightened"
and "relevant" community. Long before Bishop John Shelby Spong,
"change or die" was at the forefront of such transitioning. The irony
is: the changes effectuated to enhance the church's relevance appear
to be killing the church.

Chapter 13, "A Confessional Response to North American
Lutheran-Reformed Ecumenism," was a presentation given in
November 2010 at the Lutherische Theologische Hochschule
in Oberursel, Germany. The essay was translated into German and
published in *Die Leuenberger Konkordie im innerlutherischen Streit:
Internationale Perspektiven aus drei Konfessionen*.[13] The English version of the essay was published in *Concordia Theological Quarterly* in
2011. I had been invited to represent an ELCA perspective. Chances
are, if the goal was to find an ecumenical advocate, I was the wrong
person to invite! The essay faults Lutheran-Reformed ecumenism
for undermining the historic doctrinal differences in Christology
and the Lord's Supper because progressive political perspectives
shared between the two communions outweigh traditional doctrinal differences. I propose that ecumenism is best achieved between
shared projects for social ministry at the congregational level and

not via denominational bureaucracies. Since traditional doctrinal differences have not been resolved but instead are merely set aside, there is no basis for full communion fellowship between the two communions.

Chapter 14, "Revival Time" (2008), and chapter 15, "Retrieving Confessional Identity" (2009), both written for *Forum Letter*, argue that Lutherans have the most to offer wider society and the church at large not when they conform to wider religious publics of either evangelicalism or mainline Protestantism but instead when they accentuate their unique doctrinal differences. Chapter 16, "A Brotherly Office," seeks to reclaim power for ministry by means of owning the confessional category of ministry as "office," as outlined in the Augsburg Confession, article V.[14] Again, counter to both evangelicalism and mainline Protestantism, pastors should base their ministry not on their own charm and charisma but instead by means of tending to the word. In doing the role to which they are called, they will experience freedom. Similarly, pastors should be loyal to others in the preaching office, just as family members at their best have each other's backs.

Finally, at least for the essays, chapter 17, "How to Cultivate Biblical, Confessional, Resilient, and Evangelistic Pastors," was originally published in *Lutheran Forum* in 2017. This article challenges the widespread assumption that Lutherans were never good at evangelism. That widespread supposition is just plain wrong. Indeed, Lutheran congregations grew even at a time when birth rates declined due to the decrease of the need for large farm families. Lutherans grew because they were committed to the gospel as the truth and because they had a cohort of pastors who had the skills to build communities of faith. Similarly, we need in today's world to support a similar cohort of confessionally solid builders. When I presented these ideas at the September 2017 Society of the Holy Trinity annual retreat, one young pastor approached me, saying, "I sure would like to be a builder. But how do I do it? I've never seen it done before." Caught off guard, I urged this thirtysomething pastor to be vigilant in visiting both members and potential members, advice that he found helpful. After all, I explained, pastors are perhaps the only profession designated to actually bless people. Such blessings are best done outside the parish office and inside peoples' residences.

But he raises exactly the right question, which needs further work and a new, young cohort who will put that work into action.

Section 4: Sermons

The last section includes sermons that attempt to model the theology embedded in the previous essays. All the sermons are based on Old Testament lessons. Hence I subtitle this section "Stranger Things from the Old Testament," echoing the popular Netflix series. The first three were delivered at the Cathedral Church of the Advent in Birmingham, Alabama, as part of its 2018 Lenten Preaching Series. It is a privilege to preach at that congregation! Not only is the pastoral staff solid with respect to Reformation teachings, but the laity are well versed biblically and theologically. It is an Episcopal church where Luther is well known, far better than at most Lutheran congregations. The other three sermons were preached on various Sundays as I do supply in the Southeastern Iowa Synod of the ELCA. My goal is that these sermons will serve to illustrate one way to preach that accords with the theology presented in the essays. Hopefully, these sermons can also be conduits of the gospel and build up people in faith.

Conclusion

Christians live from hope. Ultimately, we believe that Christ will return to judge the quick and the dead, and of His kingdom, there shall be no end. Ere the dawning of that new day, we pray to be faithful to our Lord in all our thoughts, words, and deeds. Renewal in the church comes not through gimmicks, sound bites, or programs. Rather, it comes through sound teaching and faithful practice. It lives from the apostolic hope and conviction of Christ's return.

This has always been the case. Renewal in the church, when it has happened, has only occurred through gospel-based preaching and fidelity to God's word. Lutherans offer the most when they adapt neither to the American religiosity of Charles Finney's revivalism nor to Thomas Jefferson's rationalistic deism. These religious options, no matter how popular, are dead-end paths. Each only feeds the bound will and can never liberate sinners from it. They lead us, in opposition to Paul, to be conformed to this world, instead of being transformed by the renewing of our minds (Rom. 12:2). Instead of these two versions of American religiosity, Lutherans offer their best when they proclaim God's judgment of sinners whose wills are curved in on themselves and God's mercy to all who repent and believe. In this way, the gospel liberates people from sin, self-righteousness, and death and secures their lives in Christ. People have a new path opened for them when they live "outside" themselves, in Christ and their neighbors. Thereby, their behaviors and their imaginations are governed by the word.

God is ever doing a new work, and the most amazing work that God does is bring mercy to sinners brought low by the accusations of the law. This mercy anticipates the creation of a new heaven and earth, a promise that God has already begun to make good on in the resurrection of Jesus Christ. It is my expectation that these essays and sermons will contribute to the renewal for which we all long and that the church needs today.

Essays in Law and Gospel

Foundations, Ethics, Church

Foundations

CHAPTER 1

Standing on Scripture

In Jeremiah we read of one of the last kings of Judah, Jehoiakim, and his response to the word of God. After Jeremiah dictated to his scribe Baruch the words of prophecy given to him by God, Jeremiah instructed him to read this document in the temple. Jeremiah himself was restricted and forbidden to enter the temple. When the king's officials heard these words, Baruch's document was taken and he and Jeremiah were told to hide. The official Jehudi was told to bring the book before the king and read it to him: "It was the ninth month and the king was sitting in the winter apartment, with a fire burning in the firepot in front of him. Whenever Jehudi had read three or four columns of the scroll, the king cut them off with a scribe's knife and threw them into the firepot, until the entire scroll was burned in the fire. The king and all his attendants who heard all these words showed no fear, nor did they tear their clothes. . . . Even though Elnathan, Delaiah, and Gemariah urged the king not to burn the scroll, he would not listen to them. Instead, the king commanded Jeahmeel, a son of the king, Seraiah son of Azriel and Shelemiah son of Abdeel to arrest Baruch the scribe and Jeremiah the prophet. But the LORD had hidden them" (Jer. 36:22–26).

Whittling the Word in the ELCA

This is one response to God's word: whittle it down, reject it, even burn it. At the 2009 Evangelical Lutheran Church in America (ELCA) Churchwide Assembly (CWA), major policy recommendations to allow for the blessing of same-sex unions and the rostering of pastors in same-sex, partnered relationships were affirmed. Some parties in the ELCA welcome these changes—indeed, believe that they are long overdue. Others who have misgivings about these changes believe that they are relatively harmless and won't affect their own congregations. Of course, there are others—including myself—who find these changes to be an affront to the Scriptures and reveal the ELCA to be heretical. In contrast, Richard Johnson, editor of *Forum Letter*, believes that to accuse the ELCA of heresy on account of this change is "a bit over the top." He goes on to say, "Heresy generally involves a specific and overt repudiation of some key doctrine of the Christian faith. What the ELCA has done is serious error, to be sure, but I don't think it rises to the status of heresy."[1] Can we agree with Richard Johnson? Not if we want to stand on the Word. The sixth commandment says, "You shall not commit adultery" (Exod. 20:14). Scripture sets firm, life-affirming boundaries to our behaviors. The sixth commandment expresses in words a law that is written into creation itself: "For this reason a man will leave his father and mother and be united to his wife, and they will become one flesh" (Gen. 2:24). God's requirements for marriage between a man and a woman are clear, built into the order of creation itself, and not to be revised! Prior to its vote on same-sex relations, the ELCA CWA passed by one vote—out of over a thousand total votes cast—a social statement on sexuality that admitted there was no consensus on the moral evaluation of homosexual conduct and offered no compelling biblical or theological reason to support the policies it later adopted. As Robert Benne, a strong voice in opposition to the changes in the ELCA, notes, "The Statement was firm and bold on issues that everyone agreed upon—the moral condemnation of promiscuity, pornography, sexual exploitation, etc.—but indecisive and vague about contested issues—co-habitation, premarital sex, the importance of the nuclear family, and, of course, homosexual conduct." Benne remarks that what the CWA of the ELCA did was "overturn the moral consensus of the one, holy, catholic, and apostolic church held throughout the ages and by 99% of the world's Christians."[2]

While this change of policy comes as a surprise to some laity, one wonders how that could be the case. If one has had any contact with the ELCA over the last decade, this vote is not all that surprising. This single issue has been pushed in synod assemblies year after year. No doubt, longtime members of The American Association of Lutheran Churches (TAALC) who refused to be a part of the ELCA merger over twenty years ago, due to their firm stance on the Bible as the word of God and not just as a vessel for the word of God, might respond, "I told you so!" And those of us who chose to stay in the ELCA definitely feel the sting of this criticism. Even though this specific agenda was pushed, no orthodox believer had the where-withal to believe the church could deviate so far from scriptural and apostolic practice—even if this agenda was pushed as long as it was. Increasingly, the ELCA has become a church of King Jehoiakims, whittling at the word of God and throwing it into the fire.

A Different Gospel

Already, prior to the merger, many in The American Lutheran Church (TALC) saw the church becoming more and more taken over by a "social gospel." Indeed, it is reported that one of the voting members at the 2009 CWA publicly claimed that "there is nothing but the social gospel." What was already in place in TALC and the Lutheran Church in America (LCA) has only increased rapidly in the ELCA such that virtually every institution of higher education, especially the seminaries, as well as the conference of bishops and the publishing house Augsburg Fortress, is guided by this "social gospel." What has become of the real gospel—that we are forgiven, are loved, are reborn for Jesus' sake because He bore our sin and its punishment on the cross, and have new life in His resurrection? Shockingly, ELCA leaders see this message as not equivalent to the gospel. In their estimation, this view addresses merely a "private matter"—our need for forgiveness and new life—and falls short of the political implications of the "real" gospel. Instead of forgiveness, they think that the gospel focuses on the quest for a just society. And since in their judgment, those engaged in same-sex partnering are oppressed minorities, they need justice rendered to them instead of the accusation of sin.

The "gospel" in the ELCA has been overtaken by specific ethical agendas: militant feminism, multiculturalism, antiracism, antihetero-sexism, anti-imperialism, and ecologism.[3] The mission of the ELCA sounds more like the ideals of the French Enlightenment—"liberty, equality, fraternity"—than the true gospel. Now, had God never given the gospel, it is hard to believe that anyone would ever have come up with such specific ideals as liberty, equality, and fraternity. The pagan world didn't acknowledge these three ideals. Instead, it accepted slavery, inequality, and violence. The French Revolution took genuine ideals of Christian truth—in Christ we are truly free (from sin, death, the devil, and the accusations of the law), have equal status before God (as created in God's image and as equally sinful before the cross), and have true brotherhood (fellowship)—and perverted them by reinterpreting them through the lens of humanism. Like the ancient Greek philosopher Protagoras, the French Enlightenment affirmed that "man is the measure of all things." But any Christian knows that this is foolishness! We are not our own creators. We are created. The source of our lives is in God, and we are only true to reality when we acknowledge that our lives are gifts and that God is our Creator.

In the ELCA, the true gospel is eclipsed. Perhaps the key test of this, in my mind, is to ask, whatever became of hell? If there's one teaching the majority of ELCA revisionists don't believe in, it is that sinners are destined to eternal torment—indeed, they partake of this torment even in this life. For an orthodox believer, Jesus saves us from hell. Jesus saves us from God's wrath against sin. For the majority of leaders in the ELCA, Jesus saves us from "injustice"—with accusation directed especially at we perpetrators of injustice. And the implication of that belief is that you ought to be as free as possible, provided you do no harm to anyone else. Hence we see the move toward license in sexual ethics.

How can such overturning of biblical teaching happen? We need to keep in mind that the ELCA is run by a quota system that skews every committee, council, task force, synod assembly, and national assembly toward the revisionist side.[4] All these venues must be composed of 60 percent laity, 50 percent women, 10 percent people of color or whose native language is other than English. Incidentally, bishops voted 44–14 to require a two-thirds majority for the enactment of the Sexuality Task Force's policy recommendations but were ignored by both the Church Council and the Assembly. Many of these bishops knew that it would be pastors and congregations who would have to face the aftermath of such radical changes. While orthodox pastors and laity appeal to the plain sense of Scripture, the revision-ists simply "contextualize" or "relativize" these texts. Repeatedly, I have heard professors of biblical studies at ELCA seminaries say that Paul believed that homosexual practices were sinful, but to be true to Paul today, we don't have to believe thus. After all, Paul was for freedom, and so we should be, too!

The Fate of the Apostate Church

What becomes of churches that adopt the "social gospel" and the revi-sionist agenda? We can examine the membership statistics of churches like the Episcopal Church USA, the United Church of Christ (UCC), and the Presbyterian Church (PC) USA.[5] The Episcopal Church has shrunk 10 percent in membership and 14 percent in average Sunday attendance since the consecration of Bishop Gene Robinson in 2003. At least ten dioceses have taken clear action in protest against their national church. Six remain in the Episcopal Church, but four dio-ceses have now departed, forming the new Anglican Church in North America, with seven hundred parishes and one hundred thousand members. The United Church of Christ declined 14 percent during the 1990s and has shrunk an astounding 19 percent in the first eight years of the current decade. They have barely 1.1 million members. It is likely the UCC will be nonexistent in about three decades. While local presbyteries of the Presbyterian Church USA have resisted the General Assembly's proposals to embrace revisionist sexual ethics and rename the Holy Trinity, the PC (USA) has suffered significant losses over the last several decades.[6]

The ELCA has thrown in its lot with such liberal, "mainline" denominations. And the consequences are increasingly visible. Visiting with the bishop of the Sierra Pacific Synod of the ELCA about two years ago, I was told that he could foresee about thirty to forty congregations closing in his synod within the next decade. All this was said without the good bishop even batting an eyelash. "Reconciling in Christ" congregations in the ELCA—those congre-gations that openly welcome practicing gay and lesbian persons—since 2001 have shrunk by 11 percent—twice as fast as the ELCA as a whole. Indeed, under the current Presiding Bishop, Mark Hanson, the ELCA has dropped from 5.1 million members to 4.7 million members.[7] This alone should call for an assessment. In higher education, we are expected to assess the effectiveness of our teaching on almost a semester-by-semester basis. At the forefront of our work are the questions: Where are we succeeding? Where are we failing? What can we do to improve? Business likewise needs such self-assessment. However, ELCA leadership continues its same liberal trajectory with nary a question raised. Since the ELCA was formed over twenty years ago, the number of annual new mission starts has declined by 50 percent, and the number of missionaries in the field has declined by more than 60 percent. Again, the kind of mantra we hear is what was said by an ELCA pastor on the floor of the Minneapolis Churchwide Assembly (quoting a former bishop): "Jesus would be passing out condoms." One wonders when and if the insanity will end. No doubt many ELCA leaders believe that the numerical decline is proof of the effectiveness of the ELCA's commitment to social justice initiatives. For many in the ELCA, the loss of members shows just how loyal the ELCA is to the gospel!

A Look Back

As I mentioned earlier, a lack of fidelity to the Scriptures was already in place in TALC prior to the merger. You folks knew this, and that's why you chose not to enter the merger. Many of our problems can be traced back to the 1950s and 1960s. During this time, the members of our churches were becoming less and less rural. While nostalgia has little place in the life of faith, it was not that long ago that we can remember powerful social forces that enhanced the life of faith. Whether in rural congregations or ethnic communities in cities, a synergy existed between church, school, and community that aided the retention of young people in the life of faith. Those youth who attended Bible camps and/or church-related colleges found their confirmation instructions strengthened and enhanced. Over forty years ago, church-related college religion departments were staffed by pastors who had served congregations. They modeled how the life of faith and the "life of the mind" need not be antithetical. Likewise, the public schools often reserved Wednesday evening as "church night." Soccer matches would never have been held on a Sunday morning. The national "Luther League" fostered a strong program of Bible study, in addition to what we today call "service learning."

How different things are today! Bible camps increasingly offer a simplistic approach to faith, where only a few verses of the Bible at most are learned. The Bible helps feed a high-energy, largely electronic, and highly emotional approach to faith. Now the Bible fuels feelings, rather than seeking to ground our feelings on the truth of the Scriptures. Likewise, college religion departments have virtually no pastors on staff. If anything, they are out to destroy "Sunday School faith," just as they have been for over thirty years. Several years ago, visiting with a teaching colleague at a prestigious Lutheran college in Minnesota, I heard him bemoan the fact that there were no more "fundies" for him to debate in class. I couldn't help but respond, "Well, that's what you have wanted these many years. Why is this troubling to you?" Now the Lutheran Youth Organization seems to be guided by political agendas, and when the Bible is mentioned at National Youth Gatherings, it is solely done in a way to legitimate some kind of "liberation." All in all, we have done a poor job of mentoring the faith for young people and for the unchurched. Study of the catechism, a daily exercise for Luther, is hardly deemed important. At best, it is a hoop to move through. More to the point, memory work is often seen as educationally harmful. Excising memory work from the confirmation program—making it "easier"—simply sends the message: "This isn't all that important." And what's not important is not worth the investment of one's life and calling. That attitude contributes to the decline in the ELCA.

The Authority of the Scriptures

Likewise, the theological training program of pastors in the ELCA believes that the Bible itself is merely a human document, driven by power struggles, and needs itself a thoroughgoing critique. But if we are going to critique the Bible, we can hardly look to it as a source for truth or as comfort for the anxious conscience or as power for ministry. One learns of Jesus Christ in the preached word that conveys Christ's very life. However, that preached word is intertwined with the written words of Scripture. It draws its life from the Scriptures, heard in the context of worship or contemplative study, and returns us back to the Scriptures. There is a kind of "exchange of attributes," one might say, between the preached word and the written word. Luther confirms this view when he writes,

> When you open the book containing the gospels and read or hear how Christ comes here or there, or how someone is brought to Him, you should therein perceive the sermon or the gospel through which He is coming to you, or you are being brought to Him. For the preaching of the gospel is nothing else than Christ coming to us, or we being brought to Him . . . if you believe that He benefits and helps you, then you really have it. Then Christ is yours, presented to you as a gift.[8]

If we are to take the Scriptures seriously as the true interpreters of our lives, we need to let them become dear friends. We need to spend time with the Scriptures, thoroughly ingest them, and keep them at the forefront of all that we say and do. The Scriptures thereby translate us outside of ourselves and into the promise of God so that the promise becomes definitive of our lives. As it opens us to God's promise, Scripture saves us from our own defensive tendencies to protect ourselves from others and from even challenges in life itself. Through the Scriptures, we are granted and can claim freedom. Hence Luther notes, "This is the reason why our theology is certain: it snatches us away from ourselves and places us outside ourselves, so that we do not depend on our own strength, conscience, experience, person, or works, but depend on that which is outside ourselves, that is, on the promise and truth of God, which cannot deceive."[9]

The Bible as authority is the sole authority—*sola scriptura*. It is not positioned by other authorities but maintains its own integrity in the face of all other contenders. This polemical doctrine was raised against the view of the Roman Catholic Church, which taught that it is the Roman episcopal hierarchy, embodied chiefly in the papal office, which is the proper interpreter of the Scriptures. Against this view, the *Formula of Concord* teaches that "the only rule and norm according to which all teachings, together with all teachers, should be evaluated and judged are the prophetic and apostolic Scriptures of the Old and New Testament alone."[10]

Ad Fontes

When we are in the thick of disputes, we sometimes forget that all disputes have a history. Let's face it: this is not the first time that the true church has been ignored or overwhelmed. We can recall that in the 1840s through the 1880s, fragmentation in the Lutheran church eventually led to strong orthodox and confessional leaders, such as Charles Porterfield Krauth and C. F. W. Walther. What turned things around? A return to the sources—*ad fontes*. What sources? The Scriptures, of course, and the Lutheran confessions, *The Book of Concord*. The ELCA claims to affirm the Scriptures as the word of God and the confessions as the true understanding of the Scriptures. But the issue today, as it was over a hundred years ago, is consistency of practice. It is one thing to claim the Scriptures as God's word, and it is another to allow them unconditionally to shape our lives, teachings, and even philosophy of life. This we must do if we are to be Jesus' disciples.

We can only affirm a growing dissatisfaction among laity with respect to ELCA leadership. Many informed laypeople have been patient with the ELCA, especially when they see that all too many intellectuals in the ELCA have been self-serving and speak only to their own. The fact that many laypeople are fed up is a sign of hope. The question that must continually be before us is, What do the Scriptures say? All too often, denominations get hung up on organizational structure and fail to live from the authority of the word. But let's face it: it's not a program that will save us but instead wisdom. That's why the study of God's word is so important. We need wisdom. We are not to be like King Jehoiakim and whittle away at the word. Rather, we are to treasure it, hold on to it, and live from its promises and guidance. In this regard, we are to be like King Solomon.

Our ministry needs to be true to the sources. So we need to keep in mind that we Lutherans talk of "formal" and "material" principles. What these fancy words mean is simple. The "formal" principle is nothing other than Scripture alone: Scripture is the source of our doctrine and life. The "material" principle is that we are justified by faith for Jesus' sake. Scripture is an inerrant word that always leads us to the Savior, and the Savior helps us live—as He did—from the Scriptures. The material and formal principles work in tandem.

Questions Are Your Friends

In Acts 17, we read of the Bereans. These believers need to be our role models: "As soon as it was night, the brothers sent Paul and Silas away to Berea. On arriving there, they went to the Jewish synagogue. Now, the Bereans were of more noble character than the Thessalonians, for they received the message with great eagerness and examined the Scriptures every day to see if what Paul said was true. Many of the Jews believed, as did also a number of prominent Greek women and many Greek men" (17:10–12). To examine the Scriptures in order to assess and test our thoughts, words, and deeds: that is the key. Are we allowing ourselves to be informed by and formed by God's word? Likewise, St. Paul writes in 2 Corinthians 13:5, "Examine yourselves to see whether you are in the faith; test yourselves. Do you not realize that Christ Jesus is in you—unless, of course, you fail the test?" And to quote one of my favorite passages of Scripture, it is written in 1 John 4:1: "Dear friends, do not believe every spirit, but test the spirits to see whether they are from God, because many false prophets have gone out into the world."

As a teacher, I get to teach some of the world's greatest literature. It is always a joy and privilege for me to teach Augustine's *Confessions*. Augustine lived in the late Roman Empire and was one of the greatest Christian teachers. In the *Confessions*, Augustine can ask on one page more questions than I can think in a year. When reading Augustine, I like to ask my students, "What's the connection between asking questions and being a disciple of Jesus?" It takes a while for the students to answer, but a light dawns: to be a disciple means that we must ask questions.

If we fail to ask questions of our leaders, then we fail in our responsibility as disciples. But by the same token, pastors, too, need to be asking questions of themselves and those under their charge, and they need to be open to questions. If they don't know the answer off the bat, they simply can respond that they'll search and then follow through with that promise. In this regard, pastors and laity together are a team, as both are guided by the Spirit of Truth promised to us by Jesus. The key is to be consistent as a disciple, who always seeks to follow his Master's directions.

Teach the Faith

Not only asking questions but teaching the faith and being taught the faith are crucial, if we are to be disciples. We've all memorized "The Small Catechism." But do you remember the occasion of Luther's writing of that great treatise? Luther made official visitations to congregations in Saxony from October 22, 1528, until January 9, 1529. He was appalled by the lack of knowledge that both pastors and laity had of the faith. If people didn't wish to learn Christian truth, Luther charged that they should "not be admitted to the sacrament, should not be sponsors for children at baptism, and should not exercise any aspect of Christian freedom, but instead should simply be sent back to the pope and his officials."[11] Luther acknowledged that

> although no one can or should force another person to believe, nevertheless one should insist upon and hold the masses to this: that they know what is right and wrong among those with whom they wish to reside, eat, and earn a living. For example, if people want to live in a particular city, they ought to know and abide by the laws of the city whose protection they enjoy, no matter whether they believe or are at heart scoundrels and villains.

In the church, we have the Scriptures and the Confessions. They provide the basic grammar of our faith and directives for our lives. They are grounded in truth—which is Jesus Christ Himself. And more than anything, Jesus raised from the dead is God's promise that delivers us from sin, death, and the devil and provides a new and abundant life.

Walk the Walk

The philosopher Søren Kierkegaard once gave a parable: On Sunday morning, all the ducks came into church, waddled down the aisle, waddled into their pews, and squatted. The duck minister came in, took his place behind the pulpit, opened his duck Bible, and read, "Ducks! You have wings, and with wings, you can fly like eagles, you can soar into the sky! Ducks! You have wings!" All the ducks yelled, "Amen!" and then they waddled home.

Friends, I think you can see the point of this. The word is not to be whittled away and burned. It is to be honored, treasured, and *lived*. Unlike the ducks mentioned above, we are the ones who "wait for the Lord" and have our strength "renewed"; we "shall mount up with wings like eagles" and shall "run and not be weary . . . shall walk and not be faint" (Isa. 40:31). God has given us an identity as sons and daughters of the king. Let us live according! Let us be true to this identity.

CHAPTER 2

Theology of the Cross Today

In today's world, Luther's theology of the cross (*theologia crucis*) is often badly misunderstood as our solidarity with victims. It becomes tantamount to "I feel your pain." As compassionate as many are, such sentiment is fraught with self-righteousness: "God feels your pain and, *like God*, I, too, can feel your pain." And whenever self-righteousness is involved, one is able to think, I'm better than others because I feel their pain. Such an interpretation of the theology of the cross offers a sentimental and codependent theology: Christ is a victim, and we can sympathize with Him and all other victims.

The context of Luther's development of a theology of the cross was that he was called by his mentor, Johann Staupitz, the vicar of the German Congregation of Augustinian Eremites, to explain his new approach to theology. This followed on the Indulgence Controversy in which Luther, on behalf of the spiritual and temporal well-being of common people, protested the sale of indulgences and, in the process, challenged Albrecht of Mainz, John Tetzel, and papal authority in general. Luther prepared twenty-eight theological and twelve philosophical theses for disputation during the Augustinian's meeting in Heidelberg on April 26, 1518. The resulting Heidelberg Disputation,[1] presenting Luther's theology of the cross, provides not only a research program opposed to the scholastic theology of the day, what Luther terms a *theology of glory*, but also an outlook in which the Christian life is not something that we do but instead something that is done to us. The Christian life is less about our progress in holiness and more about God's work of making us into people of faith.

Today's misreading is different from a genuine theology of the cross because the suffering described in the theology of the cross is due to our being at odds with God. The cross is God's work of breaking down our defenses so that we can freely live, sustained by God's forgiveness, mercy, and love. As Luther put it, the cross tests all things (*crux probat omnia*).[2] However, where there is brokenness, there is also grief. God's mercy provides a safe footing for us on which to grieve. And such grief cleanses us of the false illusions of old defenses and opens us to new life, changing us from the inside out. It leads us into life as God intends us to live—a full, abundant life (John 10:10). Gerhard Forde used to emphasize that the gospel is for those who are burnt out on religion. This truth has few witnesses better than the theses of the Heidelberg Disputation.

The Heidelberg Disputation

At its core, the Heidelberg Disputation is an assault on the late medieval view of salvation taught by Gabriel Biel, among others, which affirmed that God does not withhold His grace from those who do their very best (*facientibus quod in se est Deus non denegat gratiam*).[3] Biel's view is challenged directly in thesis 16: "The person who believes that he can obtain grace by doing what is in him adds sin to sin so that he becomes doubly guilty."[4] In Biel's theology, God has established a covenant (*pactum*) with humanity promising that He would give His saving grace to those who do their very best. In this perspective, the law and good works are understood to help the sinner become a pilgrim, or *viator*, who, trying his or her hardest in cooperation with God's grace, will eventually be a *comprehensor* in paradise—one enjoying the beatific vision of seeing God face to face.

In the most basic terms, Luther calls this theology a *theology of glory*, which is focused on the Christian life as an agenda that we do. In contrast, the theology of the cross is God's program to us. In order to remake us as people of faith, God smashes and destroys our most treasured defenses and convictions. Hence God reveals Himself, though paradoxically, as concealed in the cross: God's wisdom is granted in foolishness, His power in weakness, His glory in lowliness, and His life in the death of His Son. Not surprisingly Luther describes his theses as "theological paradoxes,"[5] carefully designed to "attack and vex scholastic theology."[6] In a word, the flip side of God's gracious generosity is our painful exposure to our own powerlessness and impotence, an experience that we want to neither admit nor endure. God's grace does not come to us therapeutically, like Carl Rogers's "unconditional positive regard." God's business is not in salvaging neurotics but in remaking sinners—sideswiping their quests for control and spaciously allowing them to trust God's promise and thus live.

More than anything, Luther believes that his theological approach is true to Scripture. Luther's attack on scholasticism was due less to his studies in humanism or the theology of St. Augustine and more to his intense work in the Bible. When Moses requested to see God's own glory, God granted Moses nothing other than God's own backside (*posteriora dei*; Exodus 33:18ff.), for no one can see God's glory and live. Similarly, following St. Paul in Romans 1:20ff., knowledge of God on the basis of God's works in nature does not catapult us into the inner workings of divine mystery but instead condemns us as self-centered, failing to give God His proper due. While sometimes seen (anachronistically—as if Luther were in league with the early Karl Barth of the *Römerbrief*) as a contribution to epistemology, offering a critique of "natural theology," the Heidelberg Disputation is primarily focused on soteriology—*where* (not how) do we find a gracious God?[7] And the answer lies: in the cross of Christ, in which God demonstrates His love for us by carrying away our sins and bestowing His favor on us sinners. That said, there is an epistemology embedded in the Heidelberg Disputation, one that, as you shall see below, thwarts analogical reasoning as a route into the divine life. Analogical reasoning, however, remains for Luther an important way of reasoning in temporal, penultimate matters, such as science and politics.

Structure of the Heidelberg Disputation

The theological theses move from a discussion about God's law (thesis 1) to one of God's love (thesis 28). The overall outline of the theses examines (a) the nature and worth of human works over against the

question of sin (theses 1–12), (b) the impotence of human free will
to avoid sin (theses 13–18), (c) the divide between the theologian of
the cross and the theologian of glory (theses 19–24), and (d) God's
love in Christ as a creative act that brings believers into being (theses 22–28).[8] In contrast to the widely held *pactum* theology, Luther
contended that sinners misunderstand the role of human works and
God's work. In our judgment, human works are splendid and good
(thesis 3), while God's works are deformed and bad (thesis 4). But
Luther asserts that, in truth, human works are "mortal sins" (thesis 3), while God's works are "immortal merits" (thesis 4). Hence
it is clear for Luther that appearance and reality do not correspond
with respect to our potentiality. In light of God's work, one's identity
is based not on actualizing one's potential *coram deo* but on God's
claiming the sinner, the ugly, the despised, and even (especially) the
one who is nothing. The paradox of God's love—in contrast to our
love—is that God loves the unlovable, is attracted to what is ugly, and
desires the worthless. As thesis 28 reads: "The love of God does not
find, but creates, that which is pleasing to it. The love of man comes
into being through that which is pleasing to it."[9]

Luther thus unmasks a theology of glory as suffering a severe
slippage between appearance and reality. God's law appears to be a
means to advancement but in reality threatens the viator (thesis 1).
Human works appear attractive but in reality are mortal sins
(thesis 3). The works of God appear unattractive but in reality are
eternal merits (thesis 4). The will appears to be free and potent but
in reality is mortal sin (thesis 13). It would appear that if God gives
us such directives as are enshrined in the law, then that must entail
that we are able to fulfill them. In reality, the law proves to be undo-
able in thought, word, and deed. It thwarts us. Hence righteousness in the presence of God is something that we cannot obtain
by doing righteous deeds. Instead, the righteousness that saves is
something we receive through the advocacy of our defender, our
Lord Jesus Christ.

Given that thesis 28 states that God's love creates that which is
pleasing to it, we are certainly dealing with a "passive righteousness"
coram deo (before God). Luther's contention is that his Reformation
discovery was that of a passive righteousness, in contrast to the
Aristotelian-inspired, scholastic views of righteousness in which

right deeds lead to righteous habits and thus ultimately produce a righteous character.[10] While such reasoning about an active righteousness is appropriate, beneficial, and necessary in civil matters, Luther claimed that it had no bearing on one's standing before God. Scholars debate about when Luther's evangelical breakthrough happened. While it is possible that a fully developed view of what the later Reformation tradition would term *forensic justification* is not present in the Heidelberg Disputation, there can be no question that Luther's argument here is a crucial step on the way to this insight. A brief reflection on Luther's mature view merits our review. Robert Kolb describes Luther's mature outlook on justification as grounded in the etymology of the German word *rechtfertigen*: "'Justify' or 'render righteous'—meant 'to do justice to': that is to inflict punishment, 'judicially' on the basis of a conviction, and thus 'to execute the law's demands,' or 'to conduct a legal process as an activity of a judge,' 'to execute, to kill.' From early on, Luther spoke of God's killing and making alive as he described justification, for he presumed that sinners must die (Rom. 6:23a) and be resurrected to life in Christ."[11]

Suffering and the cross would appear to be bad but are in fact the way that God breaks down self-centeredness so that we can actually rely on God for our lives and well-being. Gerhard Forde notes that the correlate of a theology of the cross is one of not glory but instead resurrection.[12] It is because God raises the dead that we can be confident in entrusting our lives to God's good care. Because God raises the dead, we are permitted to be completely honest with ourselves about ourselves in God's presence. Such complete honesty, and not a sanative approach to justification, is the best means for any healing from sin or pain that we can hope for in this life.

All this is premised on the great divide that Luther summarizes in theses 19–24 and that I will quote at length starting from thesis 18:

> 18. It is certain that man must utterly despair of his own ability before he is prepared to receive the grace of Christ.
> 19. That person does not deserve to be called a theologian who looks upon the invisible things of God as though they were clearly perceptible in those things which have actually happened. [Rom. 1:20]

20. He deserves to be called a theologian, however, who comprehends the visible and manifest things of God seen through suffering and the cross.
21. A theology of glory calls evil good and good evil. A theology of the cross calls the thing what it actually is.
22. That wisdom which sees the invisible things of God in works as perceived by man is completely puffed up, blinded, and hardened.
23. The law brings the wrath of God, kills, reviles, accuses, judges, and condemns everything that is not in Christ. [Rom. 4:15]
24. Yet that wisdom is not of itself evil, nor is the law to be evaded; but without the theology of the cross, man misuses the best in the worst manner.[13]

"Despairing of [our] own ability" (thesis 18) is nothing that our free will would ever choose. Instead, the will is captivated by its own power (theses 13–15). Few theologians have understood the dynamics of a bound will as well as has Paul Zahl. Zahl notes, "The point for theology is that we are not subjects; we are objects. We do not live; we are lived. To put it another way, our archaeology is our teleology. We are typically operating from drives and aspirations generated by our past. What ought to be free decisions in relation to love and service become un-free decisions anchored in retrospective deficits and grievances. This is the message of tragic literature. It is the message of diagnosis that sees into the animating engine of the unconscious."[14]

Zahl further states, "Free entities are subjects. Un-free entities are objects. Christ Jesus, the body of God on earth, was free. The world to which He came was un-free. It is un-free still. There is therefore only one subject in the world today, and He is surrounded by countless beleaguered objects."[15] As a sanative approach to justification would emphasize, there is a sense in which we are properly ordered to the divine, but it is not the path of exercising virtues that establishes habits leading to a good character and ultimately deifies us. Rather, it is the result of God's alien work (*opus alienum*), which breaks down our defenses such that we can live by faith and thus be opened (*ephphatha*[16]) to God as our good and be restored to this creation as created good. It is the foolishness of preaching that accomplishes this divine ordering.[17]

As Forde so rightly says, a theology of glory leaves the will in control.[18] Far from being free, the will is addicted to the self;[19] it seeks its *own* in all things, including "spirituality" or ethics.[20] So while we as theologians of glory believe that we are doing good deeds, fulfilling the law, acquiring merit, and the like, in fact, our good is less for our neighbor but is instead to secure our *own* status before God. Hence sinners do not seek God for God's own sake but instead seek God to fulfill their own needs.

What does it mean to be a theologian of the cross? Surely it means to be a believer. But can we be more specific about such saving faith? Paul Althaus notes that "to believe means to live in constant contradiction of empirical reality and to trust one's self to that which is hidden. Faith must endure being contradicted by reason and experience; and it must breakthrough the reality of this world by fixing its sights on the word of promise."[21] Here Luther's view is clearly more accurate with respect to the New Testament witness to the cross where Jesus suffered and died because *no one* identified with Him. Indeed, according to Scripture, He was crucified "outside the camp" (Heb. 13:13). Or as Marc Lienhard notes, the fact that God is strong in weakness, gives life by destroying, and grants grace by judgment is all tantamount to the fact that God imposes suffering on sinners in order to dislodge them from their own self-trust and let them live from trust in God[22]—to flee from God (as wrath) to God (as mercy).[23] Said colloquially, sinners must "hit bottom" before they can receive this grace. When we live by grace—apart from any manipulation of the law—we honor God for His own sake by letting God simply "be God." To be human is to live by faith. The question is whether we will place our trust in an idol or the true God.

Contradiction, Not Analogy

For Luther, the reality of God is given to humanity paradoxically, under the sign of its opposite.[24] As such, it is a threat to all analogical reasoning with respect to God as indicated in theses 19 and 22 and, thus, to theological reasoning as is usually done.[25] As Vítor Westhelle notes, the scholastics believed that reason provides an infrastructure for faith. They taught that faith fulfills reason and brings it to perfection by means of analogy.[26] By contrast, Luther provides an ironic deconstruction of analogy in theology and thereby frees theology from the dominant modes of rationality of his time, influenced primarily by Aristotle as they were. For Luther, Aristotle should not be the norm for theological reasoning, and analogy no longer is to rule in theology. Luther permits the use of analogy in philosophy and politics, insofar as they are limited to temporal, earthly matters, but reason should not be granted permission to dictate God's word.[27]

This is not to say that Luther was an irrationalist. One certainly reasons both outside theology as well as within it. But reasoning in theology is accountable to the incarnation and God's paradoxical work of redeeming sinners, claiming sinners as righteous. Reason is accountable to the gospel narrative in which God chooses "what is low and despised in the world, things that are not" (1 Cor. 1:28). Indeed, for the mature Luther, faith obtains a kind of knowledge, even if it is starkly different from knowledge that would accrue from the law: "But Christ is grasped, not by the law or by works but by a reason or an intellect that has been illumined by faith. And this grasping of Christ through faith is truly the 'speculative life,' about which the sophists chatter a great deal without knowing what they are saying."[28] But faith is not circumscribed *a priori* by the categories of what the Aristotelian tradition defines as rational. Indeed, the gospel transcends such circumscription.

It is true, as Denis Janz notes, that analogy builds into its structure both similarity and dissimilarity between the related matters (*relata*).[29] Christians, however, disagree on the nature of proposed analogous talk about God. Should we affirm Thomas Aquinas's "analogy of being," which adheres to the dissimilarity between God as uncreated and the world as created, in spite of God's imprint built into everything He has made? Or should we instead emphasize with Eberhard Jüngel that due to the incarnation, the gospel as analogous talk establishes a "still greater similarity" in the midst of such great dissimilarity between God and the world?[30]

Jüngel raises this question as a strategy to undermine the Roman Catholic scholar Erich Przywara's view of analogy developing the results of the Fourth Lateran Council of 1215: "Between the

Creator and the creature so great a likeness cannot be noted without the necessity of noting a greater dissimilarity between them." For Przywara, the relation between God and the world reflects a greater dissimilarity within so great a likeness between the Creator and the creature. For Jüngel, such a view is incompatible with the incarnation, God's "identifying" with the man Jesus. He proposes instead an "analogy of advent," in which God, as an "event," comes within language, incorporating parables such as the waiting father (Luke 15) that indicate the nature of God's love. God's mystery is not in the claim that God is unthinkable to the human but rather in the triune narrative of God's generosity to humanity.

Both views of analogy, either that of "being" (Aquinas, Przywara) or that of "advent" (Jüngel), are undermined by Luther's teaching. For one thing, if the incarnation is true, we would have to say that there is truly *univocal* talk about God: that God is a specific man, Jesus of Nazareth, is no analogy but univocally true. More to the question, while Janz is right to emphasize that analogy includes an element of dissimilarity, accentuated more in the Roman Catholic tradition of Przywara and the Fourth Lateran Council, and accentuated less in the Barthian tradition of Jüngel's "analogy of advent," paradox is based less on dissimilarity between two *relata* and more on the opposition between two propositional truths (which semantically refers to realities in Luther's way of thinking). That is, in analogous thinking, similarity parallels dissimilarity and vice versa, regardless of which of the two that we emphasize in the polarity. However, opposition, with which we deal in paradoxes, pits sameness against its opposite. The pairings aligned with the theology of the cross, "strength in weakness," "granting life through death," and "giving grace through judgment," present not merely dissimilarities but oppositions. Such oppositions, encountered in the gospel's claim of sinners, confound reason's ability to develop analogies and put reason on a different track as an instrument accountable to what God has actually done. Later, in his "Lectures on Galatians" (1535), Luther noted that law and gospel not only are distinct but are "separated as more than mutually contradictory."[31]

Now, the concept of "sameness" is a different matter than that of "dissimilarity." Sameness and its opposite incorporate conflict, even incompatibility, which the polarity of similarity and dissimilarity does not. The polarity of similarity and dissimilarity may transcend commensurability as one-to-one correspondences that can be compared and contrasted. But it carries a more neutral tone than that of sameness and difference.[32] In the latter case, we are dealing with matters that are incompatible. In the case of the theology of the cross, the incompatibility is between life and death, whose opposition thwarts any attempt at systematic synthesis, especially that of Hegel's. In a sense, seen abstractly, the same is the opposite of its opposite, while the opposite of the dissimilar is harder to establish since the similar includes an element of difference with respect to that to which it is compared, and vice versa. Here, there is more than mere incommensurability but instead an incompatibility built into the structure of the relationship itself. Only if God recreates new life out of death can some thread of a relationship be maintained. As Luther later put it in the *Bondage of the Will*, such opposition between God's proper work and alien work is so that faith will remain faith: "Hence in order that there may be room for faith, it is necessary that everything which is believed should be hidden. It cannot, however, be more deeply hidden than under an object, perception, or experience which is contrary to it. Thus when God makes alive he does it by killing, when he justifies he does it by making men guilty, when he exalts to heaven he does it by bringing down to hell."[33]

A New Anthropology

One thing is always clear when we deal with Luther: he has a distinctive outlook on anthropology, the questioning of what it means to be human. For Luther, human life is a result of suffering the unconditional and absolute working of God upon us in all things. Luther is a "God-intoxicated" man. He cannot conceive of life in a secular way, as if there were some kind of "naked public square" either in society or even within oneself. While temporal matters are to be distinguished from eternal ones, they are no less *God's* affairs. This is an earth and cosmos that God claims as His own. For Luther, God is active and at work, "masked" in anything and everything, always addressing us. Of course, God is not everywhere active for our welfare. Much of what we experience in life is not God's mercy but His wrath or His hiddenness. But in Luther's mind, no human can experience life apart from God, whether that person honors God or not. Similar to H. R. Niebuhr's ethical aphorism that "God is acting in all actions upon you. So respond in all actions upon you as to respond to his action,"[34] Luther would reevaluate this directive as: "God is acting in all actions upon you. So trust that God is remaking you to be a person of faith in this way." It is not that Luther has no place for ethics—far from it.[35] But in his mind, our actions—our works—are on behalf of our neighbors and the world. After all, God does not need our works. Our neighbors do.

Most belief systems, whether religious or secular, affirm the dictum to "develop your potential." We can see such an affirmation in the various religious traditions of Augustinianism, the "negative theology" of mysticism, Thomism, much of Calvinism, Anabaptism, mainline (liberal) Protestantism, Hinduism, and Buddhism. Even secular approaches such as capitalism, Marxism, and humanism (even Nietzschean *Übermensch* nihilism) all affirm that we need to develop our potential! "Be all you can be!" is not far from *facere quod in se est*. Luther parts company with them here: our potential is not to be developed for ourselves, for some benefit that we might receive now, in the future, or in eternity. Instead, if our potential is to be developed at all, it should be for the sake of our neighbors, serving them as "little Christs," not for our own merit before God or whatever we consider ultimate.

In contrast to all these theologies and philosophical systems that require our active participation, in Luther's theology of the cross, God renders us passive. We suffer the sovereign workings of God in all our affairs. And in contrast to a "purpose-driven" approach to faith matters, much of God's work is painful. This is because there is so much that God must tear down before He can build up. Few have expressed this better than the Kierkegaard translator, the late Edna Hong:

> Our God has chosen to become involved in the divine failure—humanity. Our Savior chose to share with us the pain, punishments, and penalties of being imperfect humans. And God's Secret Agent of Reform chooses to help us imperfect creatures respond to the terrible call to be new creatures in Christ. For it is a terrible call, and it is a

long, long, painful journey. For there is so much to tear down before the Holy Spirit can build up. There are so many fake props to knock down. And the end of the painful road is not perfection, but perfect humility. Not morbidity and self-loathing, but a humble and contrite heart.[36]

Luther called this God's "alien work." This is God's work of rending our self-righteous defenses so that God can do His "proper work" (*opus proprium*) of nurturing us in faith. This is the truth of thesis 18: we must utterly despair of our own abilities. Said colloquially, we must let go of being our own "higher power" for ourselves and instead trust in the true God who proves His goodness in raising Jesus from the dead and raising us in Jesus as well. Some might wish to flee to God in order to avoid pain. But the only God we will ever encounter is the one who leads us into pain. God pains us, indeed kills us as old beings, due to the fact that it is very painful to let go of ourselves as controlling people, those who wish to be their own gods for themselves.[37] The end result of God's work is to lead us through pain and make us new creatures, truly free.

Deciphering the Era

It is commonly thought that our age is no longer driven by a sense of guilt consciousness. We are far more apt to dismiss guilt as an objective reality—a violation of God's commands—and speak subjectively instead of guilt "feelings," as if our guilt could be therapeutically worked through or denied outright. And if that is the case, perhaps Luther's (and the classical Reformers') concern about guilt is no longer relevant. It has long been said that our society wrestles not with guilt but with meaninglessness; that is, contemporary people are haunted no longer by guilt but by anomie. We do lots of things, but we lack an ultimate purpose that gives meaning to all the things we do. Of course, we might respond, "Who is responsible for this?" and ignore the fact that we ourselves are complicit in this culture of anomie. In light of this, Alan Jones, an Episcopal dean in San Francisco, several years ago noted that we live in an age when everything is permitted and nothing is forgiven.[38] But simply because we are not alarmed by our guilt hardly means that we are innocent. People are not less sinful than they were years ago. We simply have more tricks to let ourselves off the hook and not feel so guilty.

In that light, one might listen carefully to the preaching of late. At one time, preachers condemned sin outright from their pulpits. The pulse now seems to be that if you accept Jesus as your Lord and Savior, everything will be just fine. This type of preaching might be popular, but is it true to Christian discipleship? Is it true to Jesus, who told us that we too have a cross awaiting us (Mark 8:34–35)? Does it not render religion into the very trivial thing for which the classical atheists, such as Ludwig Feuerbach, Karl Marx, and Sigmund Freud, ridiculed religion—that faith is a kind of sugar pill? At some level, perhaps, the atheists have some insight into some forms of so-called Christianity.

In days of yore, Lent and the confessional service were taken with great seriousness. During Lent, but often before receiving the sacrament at any time of year, people actually were asked to examine themselves, in thought, word, and deed, along with their confessor in light of the Ten Commandments. This was due not to some kind of self-loathing but instead to the desire to be really honest about oneself before God. What we Christians no longer seem to be doing has been taken up by people seeking recovery from addictions. There, one needs to do a "fourth step" in which one does a "searching moral inventory" of one's life. This process becomes the basis for a "fifth step" in which one confesses this moral inventory to oneself, another, and one's "higher power." Even to this day, this process is a standard procedural step in programs of recovery. What we Christians seem to have forgotten is what people in recovery know.

Even so, one might quickly object to Luther's line of thinking. After all, who tries to do good works to earn salvation? This objection might have a point. Perhaps quite untrue to Luther, we hardly see God as a judge anymore. However, our failure to acknowledge God as judge or our denial of it will not abate His judgment. Indeed, we will be judged for failing to acknowledge Him as the ultimate judge (Matt. 25). In spite of this, with our secularistic outlook, neither does this mean that we are relaxing more. It is fair to say, at least for Americans, that our workaholism is killing us. Even those of us who ignore the need for a gracious God can hardly find a gracious workplace. Our own lack of civility in the workplace comes around to bite us. Evidence indicates that the chief thing that American workers complain about is not poor salaries and benefits but their fellow workers.

And few of us escape what a therapist might call an "inner critic," often an inner abuser, for whom none of our works measure up. On top of that, no therapy or drug seems to be able to silence this inner critic or abuser. In a world hell-bent on glory, we need a word of grace. As Luther reminds us, "The law says, 'do this,' and it is never done. Grace says, 'believe in this,' and everything is already done" (thesis 26).

Abandoning the biblical God, the one who judges the quick and the dead, will not free us from theology, at least, a theology of glory—for that theology is the perennial theology of a fallen race. Even those of us for whom God as working in all things is absent still face critique from coworkers, fellow students, parents, our "inner critics," and a whole host of things that trigger such self-critique. Ultimately, whether we believe it or not, it is God who will critique us. Our (Gnostic[39]) centering of ultimate matters in ourselves and relegating matters with God as penultimate will be found wanting. As Luther says in thesis 11, "Arrogance cannot be avoided or true hope be present unless the judgment of condemnation is feared in every work." Hence our unbelief and our workaholism might be nothing other than a defense—against God, our ultimate and truthful judge and critic. Few thinkers have understood such self-defense as well as the late anthropologist Ernest Becker, who in his book *Denial of Death* claimed that we humans use symbols in order to gain a sense of an ultimate worth in view of the pervasive death that erodes such confidence.

> But man is not just a blind glob of idling protoplasm, but a crea-
> ture with a name who lives in a world of symbols and dreams and
> not merely matter. His sense of self-worth is constituted symboli-
> cally, his cherished narcissism feeds on symbols, on an abstract idea
> of his own worth, an idea composed of sounds, words, and images,
> in the air, in the mind, or paper. And this means that man's natural
> yearning for organismic activity, the pleasures of incorporation and
> expansion, can be fed limitlessly in the domain of symbols and so

into immortality. The single organism can expand into dimensions of worlds and times without moving a physical limb; it can take eternity into itself even as it graspingly dies.[40]

In Becker's mind, such quests to symbolically secure self-worth fail us. The cross is unavoidable and inevitable, no matter who one is or whether one seeks to honor the Creator or not. For Luther, the cross is a particular event—the death of Jesus of Nazareth. But it has bearing upon all people in all times. Its point is that self-justification—the very reason we put Jesus on the cross—will do us in. And ultimately, it is God who is doing every sinner in, rendering them all quiet and passive so that He might do His work in them. There is no better response to the charge of quietism leveled at practitioners of the theology of the cross than that eventually we'll all be quite quiet, six feet under. Hence for Luther: *Crux sola est nostra theologia* (The cross alone is our theology.).

To Make All Things New

In her book *Bright Valley of Love*, Edna Hong describes the dark days of Hitler and how they bore upon the epileptic colony of Bethel, sponsored by the German church and led by Pastor Fritz von Bodelschwingh. Hitler's goal, of course, was to liquidate all epileptics. At Bethel, hope was given to a cripple, Gunther, who lived with his epileptic friends. One Advent, Pastor Fritz, following up on Gunther's inquiry, asked the children why Christmas was so great. Gunther's friends struggled for a response, but it was specifically Lena who provided the answer:

> Lena, who had covered her face with her hands and laid it on the table in perfect imitation of her Uncle Pastor, beat and cudgeled her brains. Why, oh why did God send his Son at Christmas? And finally in that dim brain box a great light burst. Lena climbed from her chair to the table. "Because," she shouted triumphantly, "Because everything has a crack!"
>
> Pastor Fritz strode to Lena's side and gathered her into his arms. From that lofty perch she could kiss the top of his head ecstatically. Pastor Fritz knelt beside Gunther's chair. Their eyes met. By

the same path that pain had sped from one to the other, a radiant trust returned.

"It is true, Gunther, that there is a crack in everything. God sees the crack better than we do, and the crack is ever so much worse than we think it is. That is why God sent his Son from the heavenly home to our earthly home. Not to patch up the crack, but to make everything new. That is why Christmas is so great, Gunther."[41]

To make everything new! This is what God is about in raising the dead. As noted above, resurrection is the other side of the cross. A theology of resurrection is the complement to the theology of the cross. And it is something that only God can do. But that means that God refuses to work with zombies. You really do need to die to playing god for yourself. And it is that death from which God raises you. Because God has raised Jesus from the dead, God makes good on His promise. And this promise is given to you in the very words of absolution: your sins are forgiven.

In faith we are united with Christ and His goodness; we receive His gifts. But we share in Christ's goodness only because He was willing to become the "greatest thief, murderer, adulterer, robber, desecrator, blasphemer, etc., there has ever been anywhere in the world,"[42] bearing our sin and that attack that is heard in His cry of dereliction: "My God, my God, why have you forsaken me?" (Matt. 27:46) While our theorizing about the atonement is appropriate in order to keep us in the true faith, we need to keep in mind that the atonement cannot be reduced to a theory. Ultimately, the atonement is God's action to save us in Jesus' cross and resurrection. It is a scriptural truth. But just for that very reason, this truth must be delivered in the word of promise—the gospel—in public preaching.

Categorical Gift

For Luther, our earthly and worldly reality is not to be seen as a mere portal to the eternal that is born out of our desire to rest in God and to live comfortably to God. The "wise" (wisdom of the world) see in beautiful things an opportunity to ascend to beauty itself. As noble as that sounds, it does not free us from ourselves. Our wills remain in control. Hence Luther notes in thesis 14, "Free will, after the fall, exists in name only, and as long as it does what it is able to do, it commits a mortal sin." Again, God's attitude about beauty is so very different from ours. He "does not find, but creates, that which is pleasing to it" (thesis 28). God deems us sinners as beautiful because He sees us as His creatures—and as redeemed.

In light of what has been said, it seems that with your defenses or guard up, you never see the world as it actually is. You only see it through the broken lens of self-protection at every corner. God's proper work permits us to see the way things really are, permits us to experience the world as a creation, as a sure and pure gift (and not as the starting point for heavenly ascent) or as a project whose perfection is our task. In contrast to the German philosopher Immanuel Kant's affirmation of a "categorical imperative," in which we must do those things that should be a universal law for everyone (and thus thereby fulfill our deepest human potential), German theologian Oswald Bayer proposes that God's grace is simply and nothing other than a "categorical gift."[43] What more can God give you than the forgiveness that He has already given you in Jesus Christ—and with that forgiveness, life and salvation? Unlike the theology of glory, grace is not a supplement for human willpower, something by which we can perfect nature, be elevated to the eternal, or achieve a utopia of peace and justice. Rather, grace liberates nature. It sets it free from being "curved in on itself." And set free, we are free for others and this good earth, in their needs and their calls to us.

In light of a theology of the cross, we can name sin for what it actually is. It is not merely misdeeds. At a deeper level, sin is a kind of addiction to self (seeking one's own in all things). In that regard, we can see why Luther contends that "desire" can be extinguished.[44] Why? You have already been given the gift. What more could you be given? You have received forgiveness of sins, and where there is forgiveness of sins, there is new life—openness to creation as a gift and not as a resource for our self-development. How? Forgiveness opens you up by making your defenses go down. Where your defenses are down, you can live outside your skin in others and their needs. As Rowan Williams noted, "To know forgiveness in the midst of hell because of the cross of Christ is the true criterion of the Christian faith."[45] Or one might say, in God's eyes you are "validated." As accepted by God, as God's own, we are free.

How Free?

Gerhard O. Forde once told the following story:

> A pastor friend related an interesting reaction from a teenager to *Free to Be*, a little book on Luther's Catechism by James Nestingen and myself. He said he didn't like the book because it seemed to tell him he could do anything he wanted to do! Now what is one supposed to say to that? The most immediate reaction, I suppose, would be to jump in on the defensive and thunder, "No! No! No!—of course not, you can't do whatever you want to do!"

Forde responds,

> But think for a moment. Perhaps then the whole battle would be lost. One must sail into the storm. Should one not rather say, "Son, you are right. You got the message. The Holy Spirit is starting to get to you." For now, you see, the question is: "what do you want to do? Who are you now that God has spoken his word to you?" But is that not dangerous? Of course it is! But God has taken a great risk to get what he wants. We can only follow him in that. Is it not "cheap grace"? No! It's not cheap, it's free! "Cheap grace," you see, is not improved by making it expensive, a "bargain basement" special. It's free.[46]

Such freedom is dizzying. We are all afraid that such freedom is no guarantee that we will not abuse our freedom. But St. Paul's point is well taken: how can we who have died to sin still live in it? We should not run from gospel freedom. After all, if the Son sets you free, you will be free indeed![47] Our freedom in Christ may terrify us, but for the anxious conscience, nothing can be sweeter. Jesus has come not for the righteous but for the sinful, and if you are at all aware of your sin and its consequences, you simply cannot get enough grace, enough gospel. When it comes—through a preacher's mouth—you jump for joy and want more.

Conclusion

As we are free, as we are open to this creation, as God's creations, in faith we can serve. We are offered a path indifferent to that of either antinomianism (the view that the old Adam and Eve did not need the law) or legalism (we are bound by the law). Instead, we are confident that a good tree issues good fruit, naturally and spontaneously. At its core, even our sanctification, ultimately, is not our doing, not a program, but the work of the Holy Spirit. In sanctification it is God who gets more of us and not so much we who get more of God. As we are being conformed more and more to the image of Christ, we are less and less concerned about our spiritual progress and more concerned about matters at hand: how can I honor God and serve my neighbor in word and deed? That is the meaning of growth in grace: focusing less on oneself and more on God—and all of this due to God's own doing! This is our pilgrimage, our *itinerarium*. And the more sway that Christ has over me, and the less sway that the old Adam has over me, is there not more power, even more growth, in Christ-likeness, even if such growth defies calculation and measurement?

Our life is that of the cross and the resurrection. No one can escape the pain that life brings, especially if we seek to do what is right in the world. Yet such events are not beyond God's work. God works through the crushing events of life precisely to raise the dead, to call sinners as His own, to remove them as the centers of their own universes and replace them with Himself as center. God provides us a new path upon which to walk, good works to serve our neighbors, and a grateful heart from which to praise Him. For this, we can be most grateful.

CHAPTER 3

Theses on the Captivated
and Liberated Will

1. The most fundamental challenge for presenting the gospel in the current North American context is that the gospel presupposes a bound will, while most North Americans presuppose a free will. More than anything, Americans value choice. With respect to God, however, they habitually make a category mistake. They think you can accept or reject God just as you might accept or reject a product.

   Of course, the type of product that God is perceived as in today's world is a therapeutic one. God's job for most Americans is to help us feel better about ourselves. If that is correct, it is impossible to see how God as usually understood by Americans of either liberal or conservative persuasion is the same as the biblical God.

   A will captivated? Not really neutral but bound to be ridden by either Christ or the devil? Given our addictions and habits designed to squelch worry, I don't think this assessment of the human is as farfetched as it first sounds. We become addicted to our own anger, desire to fix things, pride, and so on. Perhaps the most telling question we can ask of ourselves is: What captivates me? On top of this, God Himself wants to catch us in our own trap. The self is a prison that can only be unlocked from the outside. We are all trapped in our own sin and need a deliverer, Christ Himself, to free us. The law simply becomes another means that entraps us, and it can't get the job done.

2. The issue of free will is not about whether people make choices or not. The problem is that the choices that people make are made by wills captivated to the self. The sinful human is unable to trust God and, for that reason, feels more secure in trusting the self.

    The question is really whether I can trust my life with God. I know what it means to trust myself. But to let go and entrust myself into God's hands? That is a great unknown. When the pain of trusting oneself outweighs trusting God, then I really have no choice but to trust in God.

3. Our transgression against God and our neighbor certainly can be seen in our various thoughts, words, and deeds. Yet it goes much deeper—to the very core of our condition. We are held captive by our own wills. When God says we must not eat of the Tree of the Knowledge of Good and Evil, we suspect God may not be good and may be holding something back that we need. So we create our own future and manage life itself. Thus we are unable to create or will faith in God or goodness on our part.

    When I trust in God, I no longer live inside myself but outside myself, in God and in my neighbors. If I don't trust in God, I will inevitably concoct some kind of idol by which I imagine or picture my "higher power" (which isn't the true higher power).

4. The question of the bound will has nothing whatever to do with choices before the world (*coram mundo*) but only concerns choices before God (*coram deo*). The teaching that the will is free, neutral, or uncaptivated endorses the view that the human as a subject can stand over the gospel, that it can interpret God's word as a mere text, and that it can decide either for or against Jesus Christ as the promise of new, eternal life.

    God and the world are in an asymmetrical relationship. My relationship with God is vertical, and my relationship with myself and the world is horizontal. The staircase between

God and me only goes down. And the bridge between the world and me goes out into service.

5. Sinners in their captivity have already made a decision for Christ: it is to put Him on the cross!

    Hence it no longer makes sense to pray a sinner's prayer to decide for Jesus. It only makes sense to repent and give God the glory that is His due.

6. If God is all-powerful and all-good, then the will, *coram deo*, is not free. It is rather captivated by its own perception of its own good and, thus, bound to reject and crucify Jesus Christ. We are thus curved in on ourselves, and to be saved means to be delivered from a twisted shape. If Jesus Christ is to be Lord, the sinful person must die and the new person in Christ must be raised.

    God promises to raise the dead but only the dead. We are not zombies. We really die—on our last day, we are made completely passive before God. This is God's alien work, and it is premised on God's proper work, new life.

7. Our religious identities (or lack thereof) indicate the idols to which our wills are bound. Evangelical Protestants, no less than Roman Catholics or secularists, assume that we deal with a God whom we can choose. This is most manifest in current evangelistic tactics: if I accept Jesus as my personal Lord and Savior, then Jesus will help me fulfill my potential—psychologically, economically, and socially. To accept Jesus on my terms is, in truth, to reject Jesus Christ as Lord and make myself into an idol.

    We have to admit that much religion and "spirituality" is diseased. Health is when I walk by faith, free of self and its choices. It is to pray with Christ in Gethsemane: "Yet not my will, O God, but yours."

8. While touting radical difference from mainline Protestantism, evangelical Protestantism strikingly parallels mainline Protestantism. In a way, both liberal and conservative modes of American religion are the same tune but played in strikingly different ways. Both evangelicals and mainliners accentuate the subjective dimension of religion. Both seek a therapeutic Jesus, who can heal my

psychological pain, in order to issue a socially transformative Christ. For the political right, this Christ liberates an agenda that supports stability for the traditional family but license for the economy (even when that economy is indifferent to the traditional family's well-being). For the political left, this Christ liberates an agenda that promotes diversity in family structures but seeks to tame an economy run amok.

9. As responsible citizens, we might find ourselves persuaded by proposals for social renewal presented by political ideologues. However, we must be clear that counter to all secular visions of politics on either side of the aisle, politics cannot save. Politics are for the ordering of community, matters of the first use of the law.

   Conservative Christians tend to be premillennialists, believing Christ will rapture His saints before the Great Tribulation but will reign on earth for one thousand years. Mainline Protestants are no less millennialists, but they tend to be postmillennialists, holding that through preaching and spreading peace and justice, the ideal kingdom will arrive on earth, and Christ will reign through such goodness. Both parties seek the evidence of some visible change in the world and, thus, turn Paul's words to the Corinthians upside down. They walk by sight, not by faith.

10. It is not clear that the Christian faith should fit itself into a political agenda. Instead that political agenda must be tested, step by step, with the Christian faith. When it is accepted that politics cannot save, then there is no reason ever to translate the faith into the requirements of any political ideology.

    Christians as Christians deal not with penultimate matters, such as politics, but with ultimate matters, such as salvation. Of course, Christians as new creatures and citizens in the agora and public square should seek a politics and an economy that serve people.

11. Both evangelicals and mainliners accept the "Christ transforming culture" perspective (H. Richard Niebuhr). Evangelical-Lutherans should reject this core fundamental

assumption of both the left and the right. The role of the Christian is not to Christianize culture but to be salt and leaven and to serve as a little Christ within one's vocation.

The truth is: There is not nor will there ever be an unambiguously "Christian" culture, and that's OK.

12. The self is not primarily a consumer of religious goods but, even in spiritual matters, is bound to will what one wills. Only law and gospel, properly distinguished, can free sinners from such self-centeredness. This is why sharing Jesus Christ, not primarily as an example but as a promise that saves and delivers directly in preaching, is the most important outreach that the church can offer to sinners.

It's not as if Jesus as a moral example isn't important. Of course it is. But it is law and, in one way or another, it will do us in. Even so, Jesus remains our example. Through faith we are so unified with Christ—one with Christ—that Christ is one with our own egos and does good works, things that actually help people, through us. We are quite unaware of how Christ works in us and should remain so unaware if we are to be true to faith. Ultimately, Christ in us is not a matter of measurement, observation, or control; nor can it be.

13. Free choice, accepted by scholasticism, humanism, Roman Catholicism, evangelicalism, and mainline Protestantism, assumes the continuous subjectivity of the self. That view is incompatible with Evangelical-Lutheran teaching in which the accusing law and/or the hidden God mortifies and kills such subjectivity in order that the new person in Christ might walk by faith. In the Evangelical-Lutheran perspective, the chief heresy of our time is Pelagianism, the view that the sinner can save himself apart from grace, or semi-Pelagianism, the view that the sinner, with a jumpstart from grace, can grow more godlike. The answer to such heresy is that we are justified by grace alone through faith alone. The Christian walks by faith not by sight, whether that sight be psychological wholeness, a "Christian family," material prosperity, or moral rectitude. It is faith, and faith alone, which both sets limits to the law and fulfills the law.

So am I so free that I can do whatever I want? No, the question is, now that you've died and been raised in Christ, how do you want to live?

14. The gospel is not a repair job on the old being or God's acceptance of us "just as we are" but a summoning of the dead to life. In Christ, we have new life, a new Lord, and a new kingdom. It is because God loves the sinner that the sinner is reckoned by God as lovely. To have a Lord means that at the core of one's being, one will be provided for and protected.

    Yes, this means it is OK to relax. The Sabbath really is our best way to honor God!

15. Sanctification, then, is not the goal but the source of good works. God is so for us in Jesus Christ that He becomes one with us—akin to fire being one with heated iron. Only preaching delivers these goods. Only this truth can extinguish that desire in which we think we can use God to control our fate.

    Don't I have to grow in grace? But once you start trying to measure such things, you've already lost your "first love." You can really stay in your "first love" but only by knowing that you are loved first.

16. The Christian seeks not the moral reform of the world but rather to confront the secular realm with the truths of the first commandment—challenging any and every idolatry by which secular government and society would justify their behavior.

    We should be wary of any utopianism. Things like selves and worlds are simply not perfectible. So let's let go of that. Instead, we'll do what we can to help.

17. In the Holy Scriptures, God interprets sinners— simultaneously condemning them to hell and granting new, resurrected life. In whatever form God's word comes (spoken, written, in bread and wine, or in the Word made flesh), we are fitted into God's agenda, not vice versa.

    God is a poet who creates the verses of our lives intertwined with the world. God is also an art critic who evaluates

His own work. His evaluation of us is that we are justified for Jesus' sake.

18. The freed will, paradoxically, is captivated by God, not the self, and now has a new object and driving force. It fears, loves, and trusts in God above all things. And in that light, it lives outside of itself in God and one's neighbor, seeking the latter's well-being.

     When I am no longer in myself but in God (through faith), I am really free. And such freedom allows me to care for others (through love) and thus serve them.

19. The doctrine of justification depends on the doctrine of election. God chooses, and the one whom God elects is Jesus Christ. God's eternal election of the believer in Christ is made real in the actual proclamation of Christ as forgiveness and promise. The doctrine of justification by grace alone through faith alone as a God-centered (not human-centered) theological perspective creates a new heart and right spirit within the sinner so that the sinner in faith gives God the glory and praise that is His due.

     The Christian life isn't about what I do but about what I undergo. It's not about the accumulation of merit and development of virtue. Instead, we move from virtue to grace, from progress to mercy, and from self-improvement to resurrection.

CHAPTER 4

A Contemporary View of Faith
and Reason in Luther

In many respects, the relationship between faith and reason is *the* agenda in contemporary theology, as it has been for the better part of the last century and longer. Why? It would seem to be due to the widespread success of "secular reason," for which the academy and the wider public believe that they need no recourse to theology for understanding the world since reason alone is sufficient for understanding it, and matters of faith are relegated to private feelings. Is Luther complicit in this marginalization of theology as truth claims in the modern world? Does his thinking contribute to contemporary secularization? For some, it would seem so.[1] On the other hand, for others, Luther is the epitome of irrationalism. Given the oft-cited sound bites that reason is the "devil's whore" or that faith needs to "slaughter reason," it is not surprising that someone like Richard Dawkins would appeal to Luther as paradigmatic of religious authoritarianism and irrationalism, an exemplary villain in the "Religious Fanatics Hall of Shame."[2] But is this characterization of Luther justified, or is it a caricature, a way of policing faith through ridicule, keeping it out of the public domain?[3]

Regardless of where Luther stands with respect to irrationalism, we must admit that increasingly there is a very real and entrenched irrationalism in the academy.[4] That is, the contemporary practice of theology, seen for example in venues such as the American Academy of Religion, all too often reflect not classical approaches to faith but instead the autobiographical peculiarities of various theologians

themselves.[5] A theology that claims truth has been eclipsed by the
free-floating stream of consciousness of theologians themselves. In
support, Luther's delight in paradoxical approaches to faith is used
to legitimate theological relativism—arguing that such paradox
leads to "ambiguity," an open-ended, nondiscursive, purely emotive
approach to theology, sidestepping objective truth. We must ask
whether Luther's view of paradox has been adequately understood.

Given the apparently contradictory claims that Luther makes
about reason—that "in comparison with other things of this life,"
it is "the best and something divine"[6] but also that it is the devil's
"whore"[7]—Theodor Dieter helpfully notes that we cannot speak of
a *single* understanding of reason in Luther—or only with great reservation.[8] Nor for Dieter can we assume that by *ratio*, Luther means
what we mean by reason today. Summarizing his research, Dieter
notes that for Luther, reason has several facets: (1) it is a "faculty";
(2) it speaks of doctrines manifest in philosophy and applied to
theology; (3) it is expressed in the daily lives of people—especially in
relation to their faith; (4) it is often a power contradicting God; and
finally, (5) Luther's praxis is "more rational than many of his explicit
expressions about *ratio* would lead us to believe."[9]

Given the tendency of some to present Luther as a thoroughly
medieval thinker and others to present him as a protomodern thinker,
with accompanying positive or negative evaluations of either medieval or modern perspectives,[10] the topic of faith and reason in Luther
is one for which we might have benefitted had he written a specific
treatise. However, Luther has no comprehensive statement on the
relation between faith and reason, so we can ground our judgment
only on close readings of specific texts usually dedicated to various
theological topics other than that of reason per se. Dieter notes that
Luther's often paraphrased and categorized comments on reason are
insufficient. What must be done is to examine his comments on reason in their specific contexts.

Acknowledging Dieter's inductive approach to Luther's views
and thus recognizing that an accurate presentation must be tied to
specific texts, a brief overview of the terrain on faith and reason in
Luther as it is typically presented is nevertheless helpful. Dennis
Janz offers a useful summary: for Luther, reason (1) is God's greatest gift, (2) is competent to arbitrate matters in civil society, (3) can

overreach its bounds (in which case, it is a "whore"), and (4) as "enlightened" can discern revealed truth.[11] In the most general terms, Luther sees reason as pertaining to *visible* matters such as ethics, while theology per se deals with *invisible* matters such as belief in Christ.[12] Of course, when he is not a commentator on Scripture, Luther is mostly an occasional writer, often a polemicist. The attempt to systematize Luther is fraught with danger, especially the temptation to accentuate some aspects of his thinking at the expense of others. Overall, an inductive approach that interprets pivotal texts in Luther's corpus is best. My own examination here can only supplement Dieter's exhaustive analysis[13] and perhaps indicate some facets for further exploration.

The charges of fideism and irrationalism against Luther are inaccurate. Nor should Luther be caricatured as an ancestor in the genealogy of secular reason or nihilism. Luther believed that reason is useful not only for ethics[14] but also with assessing various theological truth claims, provided that such claims are themselves grounded in the grammar of faith, as testified to in the Holy Scriptures.[15] Provided that logic follows the distinctive grammar of faith, it, too, has a role in theology to help establish and defend doctrinal truth via disputation and argument as public inquiry into theological truth. Even so, the most important principle is not that "the articles of faith" are not "subject to the judgment of human reason" or that "the forgiveness of sins and the mystery of the incarnation and eternal life" are "to be deduced by logic."[16] Instead, the "cardinal point" is "that God is not subject to reason and syllogisms,"[17] and "therefore in articles of faith one must have recourse to another dialectic and philosophy, which is called the word of God and faith."[18] In this regard, both contemporary secularist views and Luther are in a similar boat: ultimate matters transcend our ability to access them since we are finite, limited beings. More honestly than secular views do, however, Luther admits that such matters are faith matters. As Janz notes, if fideism were true for Luther, then there would be no prospect for a theological enterprise. Instead, all one could do would be simply to reiterate the articles of faith—instead of discerning the fidelity of their presentation.[19] In contrast to the modern tendency to ground religious truth claims in feeling—such as Schleiermacher's "feeling of absolute dependence"—and thus allow Christian piety to situate the content of Christian faith and contribute to the theological irrationalism mentioned prior, Luther contended that we need to honor the *objectum fidei* and thus distinguish the faith that believes from the faith that is believed.[20] For Luther, there is such a thing as "right reason,"[21] which would comport with faith.[22] Likewise, the medieval sense of philosophy as a "handmaid"[23] is not lost on Luther.

Appropriation of Philosophy

As is widely known, Luther can be very critical of philosophy—particularly Aristotle's views of souls as mortal and the world as eternal—just as he has negative comments about reason.[24] Yet a balanced approach to Luther's view of philosophy, like that of reason, will acknowledge Luther's positive appropriation of philosophical methodology. More than anything, for Luther, theology's positive appropriation of philosophy honors and employs the tools of Aristotelian logic—as schooled by the grammar of faith. Luther highly valued the public exercise of such logic in disputations because it was through disputation that Luther achieved major insights at both Heidelberg (1518) and Leipzig (1519). After becoming Dean of the Theological Faculty in Wittenberg, in 1533, Luther restored the practice of regular disputation. Nevertheless, Luther acknowledges an intrinsic conflict between philosophy and theology, especially due to philosophy's inability to acknowledge the incarnation and justification by grace alone through faith alone. In this regard, Luther is indebted to nominalism, which was less hopeful than realism in establishing common turf between philosophy and theology. However, we need to keep in mind that both nominalism and realism saw reason as useless for providing a foundation for dogma. In both nominalism and realism, revelation is indispensable for getting at truth.[25] For Luther, this required that reason, like philosophy, needs to be limited to its proper sphere. Nevertheless, for Luther, nominalists failed to follow their own rule: they blatantly *mixed* theology and philosophy rather than following the grammar of faith alone to which Scripture testifies.[26] Likewise, prereformation theology pictured nature and grace as on a continuum, whether it be that of the greater reality of universals with respect to particulars (realism) or a *pactum* or covenant between

God and His creation (nominalism). In either case, the continuum is based on our contributions to win God's favor. The Reformer rejects this continuum since it contributes to or enables self-righteousness implied by the *facere quod in se est* doctrine.

For Luther, there is no attempt to correlate the answers of faith to the questions of philosophy, as Augustine in a sense does within the Neoplatonic tradition or Aquinas does in a looser sense with Aristotelianism. For Luther, the first encounter between philosophy and theology is conflict.[27] That does not mean that there is no positive appropriation of philosophy by theology. Rather, the limits of truth accessible to unaided reason must first be clearly established; there is a tendency for philosophy to overstep its bounds. Here, Luther is on a continuum with both Augustine and Aquinas, since for both these theologians, faith, not metaphysics, situates ultimate truth. Nevertheless, unlike Luther, both Augustine and Aquinas are more optimistic that philosophy can make positive contributions to the substance of faith and not merely the logical presentation of the grammar of faith, which Luther maintains. Said stronger, Augustine and Aquinas, appealing to different schools of philosophy, not only seek a compatibility but even verge toward a kind of commensurability, where possible, between philosophy and theology. So for Augustine, philosophy as he knew it, Neoplatonism, was a fitting preparation for disposing the mind to Christian faith.[28] After all, faith and understanding both seek beatitude, but philosophy alone cannot reach it because it does not know Christ. Nevertheless, philosophy can be affirmed because it asks the right questions: it wants to know God and the soul and thus moves us beyond the sensible and temporal to the intelligible and eternal. Hence Augustine's reading of Cicero's philosophical *Hortensius* was a marker in his movement toward conversion.[29]

Aristotle's works had been incorporated into the medieval university curriculum after they were rediscovered during the crusades. Some scholars, such as Sigar of Brabant, approached Aristotle's corpus with an uncritical endorsement. Discovering some connections between Aristotle and Christian faith, Aquinas nevertheless opposed Aristotle's rejection of personal immortality and his affirmation of a single intellect, common to all, whether active or passive. Similarly, indebted to Aristotle's logic, Luther also repeatedly raises objections to Aristotle's affirmation of the mortality of the soul and the immortality of the world. In addition, for Luther, there is no intrinsic eudaimonistic quest for self-fulfillment of one's nature as perfected by grace, either through greater advances in mimetic participation in truth, beauty, and goodness or via an arbitrarily granted *pactum*. If we receive our final good, the fulfillment of our nature, purely gratuitously, then such a quest is tantamount to seeking oneself in all things.

Luther's High Praise for Reason

When it flourishes in its proper sphere, Luther has high praise for reason. He claims that humans were created with reason.[30] Indeed, reason is itself closely associated with the *imago dei*: "In Adam there was an enlightened reason, a true knowledge of God, and a most sincere desire to love God and his neighbor, so that Adam embraced Eve and at once acknowledged her to be his own flesh. Added to these were other lesser but exceedingly important gifts . . . namely, a perfect knowledge of the nature of the animals, the herbs, the fruits, the trees, and the remaining creatures."[31] And in the "Disputation on Man" (1536), Luther offers a kind of paean to reason, noting that, thankfully, reason survives the fall and, with respect to temporal matters is itself, as noted earlier, a "kind of god."[32] Hence, reason is to be trusted in temporal though not eternal matters.[33] Unaided by God, creatures are only left to guess with respect to eternal matters (our final end is not clear to the natural man), and with respect to eternal matters, we want certainty.

Hence, the proper sphere of reason is worldly human affairs, where reason proves to be a necessary and sufficient tool for ordering life. Luther's is a pragmatic approach to reason, not a speculative one. For the Reformer, humanity needs no other light than reason when dealing with human or mundane affairs. Luther notes that "God does not teach in Scripture how to build houses and to make clothes, marry, make war and similar things. For these the natural light [of reason] is sufficient."[34] For Luther, reason thus is closely aligned with the law: "Human reason has the law as its object."[35] God's ongoing creativity even through the machinations of sinful humans is exercised in human reason. Hence the same person who is "drawn in wickedness and is a slave of the devil has a will, reason, free choice, and power to build a house, to carry on a governmental office, to steer a ship. And to do other tasks that have been made subject to man according to Gen. 1:28; these have not been taken away from man. Procreation, government, and the home have not been abolished."[36] And "in the worldly kingdom men must act on the basis of reason—wherein the laws have their origin—for God has subjected temporal rule and all physical life to reason."[37] In short, for Luther, "to some extent reason is able to perform [civil righteousness]."[38]

Natural Theology

Influenced by Augustinian and other forms of medieval apophaticism, Luther acknowledged God's incomprehensibility.[39] But this does not mean that we know nothing of God. Luther maintains that there is a twofold knowledge of God, a general and a particular: "All men have the general knowledge, namely, that God is, that He has created heaven and earth, that He is just, that He punishes the wicked, etc. But what God thinks of us, what He wants to give and to do to deliver us from sin and death and to save us—which is the particular and the true knowledge of God—this men do not know"[40] (and can only be known in the gospel promise).

Given a general knowledge of God, Luther does not rule out natural theology. For instance, one can find allusions to the cosmological and teleological "proofs" for God's existence, though these are never offered as proofs, strictly speaking. Better said, they are generalizations about God, accessible to all thoughtful people whether they are consciously aware of them or not. For instance, Luther writes, "Human reason and wisdom by itself can come this far, that it concludes, although weakly, that there must be a single, eternal divine Being, which has created, preserves, and governs all things. When reason considers such beautiful, exquisite creatures both in heaven and earth, governed in such a wonderful, orderly and sure way, it must deny the possibility that the origin and preservation of these things are accidental or spontaneous."[41] Similarly, Luther notes,

But even as I rate Aristotle above Cicero in native ability, so I have to realize that Cicero discussed these very matters with far greater discernment. . . . He shifts the discussion to a consideration of the creature, about which it is possible for reason to make certain judgments. He observes the harmony of the motions of the celestial bodies; he observes the unvarying changes of the seasons and of the fixed forms of the products of this earth; and he observes that man was created both to have an understanding of these things and to derive benefit from them. Therefore he is disposed to assert both that God is the eternal Mind by whose providence all these things are controlled in this way, and that the soul of man is immortal.[42]

More often, however, as we see in his description of the terrified sailors who flee to God in his "Commentary on Jonah" (1526), Luther perceives the general revelation of God less on the basis of inference from design or the ultimate *telos* of human life and more through an anamnesis in which all people *a priori* remember that there is a God.[43] This more Platonic, less Aristotelian, remembrance of the truth of God may be one reason that in the philosophical section of the Heidelberg Disputation (1518), the early Luther favors Plato over Aristotle.[44]

For Luther, the existence of God is never in doubt, but God's disposition toward humankind is: "That there is a God, by whom all things were made, that you know from his works . . . but God Himself, who he is, what sort of divine Being he is, and how he is disposed toward you—this you can never discover nor experience from the outside."[45] True knowledge of God must acknowledge awareness that God cares for His world. This divine love is foreign to the philosophers: "Philosophers argue and ask speculative questions about God and arrive at some kind of knowledge, just as Plato looks at and acknowledges the government of God. But everything is merely objective; it is not yet that knowledge which Joseph has, that God cares, that He hears the afflicted and helps them. Plato cannot determine this; he remains in his metaphysical thinking, as a cow looks at a new door."[46] If one is to have true knowledge of God, one cannot escape the forensic, *pro me* dimension if such knowledge is in fact true: "You have the true knowledge of God when you believe and know that God and Christ are your God and your Christ. This the devil and the false Christians cannot believe. Thus this knowledge is nothing else than the true Christian faith; for when you know God and Christ in this way, you will rely on Him with all your heart and trust in Him in good fortune and misfortune, in life and death."[47] To call Luther's view of the knowledge of God "existentialist" would be anachronistic, but it is true to say that Luther's perspective is highly experiential without permitting experience to be a source or norm for his theology. Of course, our experience with God is often quite painful for, as he says, "it is by living—no, not living, but by dying and giving ourselves up to hell that we become theologians, not by understanding, reading, and speculating."[48] Reason quickly becomes defective in matters most important to Luther: How are we saved; how are we justified before God; is God willing to help?[49] Thus we have no guidance in the most important matters.[50]

When Faith Loses Its Virginity

Conflict between faith and reason arises when Luther articulates the nature of saving faith. It would be a truism to say that Luther's entire career focuses on the nature of saving or justifying faith.[51] An example of this conflict is found in Luther's "Lectures on Galatians" (1535):

> Here let reason be far away, that enemy of faith, which, in the temptations of sin and death, relies not on the righteousness of faith or Christian righteousness, of which it is completely ignorant, but on its own righteousness or, at most, on the righteousness of the Law. As soon as reason and the Law are joined, faith immediately loses its virginity. For nothing is more hostile to faith than the Law and reason; nor can these two enemies be overcome without great effort and work, and you must overcome them if you are to be saved.[52]

Sinners attempt to import what is so effective in problem-solving in daily life—reason—into eternal matters, where reason not only cannot solve the problem resulting from our conviction that our works can contribute to our salvation but actually contributes to and magnifies this problem. Indeed, moral philosophy requires a good will (*bonam voluntatem*) and right reason (*rectam rationem*)—but these cannot achieve remission of sins and everlasting life.[53] For that we need an active and generous Christ. And we *coram deo* (before God) are rendered quite receptive and passive. Nevertheless, the tendency of sinners' reason is to side with self-righteousness. This trust in works

> is the height of wisdom, righteousness, and religion about which reason is able to judge; it is common to all the heathen, the papists, the Jews, the Mohammedans, and the sectarians. They cannot rise higher than that Pharisee in Luke (18:11–12). They do not know the righteousness of faith or Christian righteousness. . . . If I do this or that, I have a God who is favorably disposed toward me; if I do not, I have a God who is wrathful. There is no middle ground between human working and the knowledge of Christ; if this knowledge is obscured, it does not matter whether you become a monk or a heathen afterwards.[54]

No resources intrinsic to sinners, including reason (for all its nobility), are able to rescue them from the law's accusations, and in fact, they feed self-righteousness, which can never square with honoring the deity of God. Luther concludes that a saving faith is fundamentally a work of God by means of which we take hold of[55] or "apprehend" Christ,[56] in which knower and known are unified through sharing a common form, Christ Himself, and in that way, acquire saving knowledge.[57] Reason thinks that when the law says, "Do it," that means you *can* do it, as opposed to showing us our inability to fulfill the law and thus killing us. Hence for Luther, the role of the law is counterintuitive: we would assume that "ought implies can," but the truth is precisely the opposite for sinners.

Similarly, Luther's appeal to the language of mysticism, admonishing us to "ascend into darkness, where neither the law nor reason shines, but only the dimness of faith (1 Cor. 13:12), which assures us that we are saved by Christ alone, without any Law," seems to rule out any path of self-righteousness, affirming that *coram deo* we walk by faith not sight.[58] No wonder that elsewhere, Luther looks to the ear and not the eye as the proper organ by which we relate to God.[59] We are to trust the word and rule out self-righteousness even when our reason would affirm it. Faith itself is trust in Christ alone as our "formal righteousness" and not in our works of love intended to shape this faith: "Yet the Christ of whom faith takes hold is sitting in this darkness as God sat in the midst of darkness on Sinai and in the temple. Therefore our 'formal righteousness' is not a love that informs faith; but it is faith itself a cloud in our hearts, that is, trust in a thing we do not see, in Christ, who is present especially when He cannot be seen."[60] Not surprisingly, Luther maintains that it is faith that consummates the deity, not, of course, in God Himself but in us. As uniting us with Christ, it is faith then that gives "right knowledge" of God.[61]

Faith and Understanding in the *Bondage of the Will*

Luther's conviction that faith alone is both necessary and sufficient for our justification before God and our fulfillment as creatures whose good is oriented toward God is likewise accentuated in the *Bondage of the Will* (1525), written to counter Erasmus's affirmation of free will *coram deo*. Yet this bears on the relation between faith and reason. The logical implications of Luther's affirmation of faith in Christ as necessary and sufficient for justification undermines Augustine's old quest of "faith seeking understanding," where understanding is a higher means of unity with God than faith.

A central claim of Luther's treatise is that each thing happens necessarily if God's action is necessary or there is a necessity of consequence (even if it has no necessity in its essential nature); all things take place by necessity.[62] However, that leaves nothing for sinners who want to contribute something to their justification. Again, such truth functions as law, confronting sinners with the truth of their own nothingness, bringing them to a despair of the self since salvation properly understood is utterly beyond their powers. Such sinners, reduced to nothingness, can only but wait for God to work in them.[63] Similar to what we learned in the "Lectures on Galatians" (1535), it is not the case that ought implies can, even though that makes sense to reason. Instead, the law exposes our impotence *coram deo*.[64] If Christ is necessary for our justification before God, then there can be no free will. "Reason" would hook into God's commands as implying

choice and thus anthropological agency of the sinner on the sinner's own behalf, but Scripture simply opposes this as false.[65] For
the Reformer, an imperative does not entail anything about capacity
but only requirement. Hence grace is given not to those who try to
do their best but only to those who despair of themselves.[66] As is
well known, Luther distinguishes God's alien work of mortifying
us as sinners seeking our own in all things (including piety) from
that of His proper work, vivifying us, quickening us through faith in
Christ. Faith's object, Christ, is heard through the proclamation of a
preacher but not seen.

Paradoxically, God kills in order to make alive. However, in
contrast to Augustine's contention of faith seeking understanding,
this paradox befuddles and subverts our understanding: "If I could
by any means understand how this same God who makes such a
show of wrath and unrighteousness can yet be merciful and just there
would be no room for faith. But as it is the impossibility of understanding makes room for the exercise of faith when these things
are preached and published; just as when God kills, faith in life is
exercised in death."[67] Far from faith functioning as a launching pad
for understanding that could transcend and surpass faith in greater
mimetic participation in God, faith alone is necessary and sufficient:
it gives us everything we need.

Like the "Lectures on Galatians" (1535), we encounter the language of mysticism in the *Bondage of the Will*. But this language is not
there to entice or encourage us in a ladder of mystical ascent into the
divine, but instead its inherent apophaticism functions to take away
any basis for self-righteousness *coram deo*. God as *inaccessible* light
is just that: inaccessible. That is why we need to cling to the word and
occupy ourselves with "God Incarnate, that is, with Jesus crucified,
in whom as Paul says . . . are all the treasures of wisdom and knowledge (though hidden); for by Him man has abundant instruction
both in what he should and in what he should not know."[68] Indeed,
because God "has kept Himself free over all things" (less nominalism
and more apophaticism), this allows him to be "God preached" and
work to the "end that sin and death may be taken away, and we may
be saved."[69]

Paradox and the Role of Reason

For Luther, we learn in the "Heidelberg Disputation" (1518) that the reality of God is given to humanity paradoxically, under the sign of its opposite.[70] As indicated in theses 19 and 22, it is a threat to all analogical reasoning with respect to God and, thus, to theological reasoning as it is usually done.[71] As Vítor Westhelle notes, the scholastics believed that reason provides an infrastructure for faith. They taught that faith fulfills reason and brings it to perfection by means of analogy.[72] By contrast, Luther provides an ironic deconstruction of analogy in theology and thereby frees theology from the dominant modes of rationality of his time, which were influenced primarily by Aristotle. For Luther, Scripture, not Aristotle, provides the norm for theological reasoning, and analogy no longer is to rule in theology. However, as Knut Alfsvåg has demonstrated, Luther's appropriation of Scripture is mediated through Neoplatonic apophaticism. The young Luther was conversant with both Plato's *Parmenides*[73] and the writings of Dionysius the Areopagite.[74] As Alfsvåg notes, for Luther, Dionysian apophaticism presents reality far better than Aristotelian metaphysics. Nevertheless, Dionysian apophaticism is spiritually inadequate in that it is too theoretical. It ignores the terror that results for sinners who are not in a proper relationship with God.

Commenting on Luther's evaluation of Aristotle's inadequacies, Alfsvåg notes that Aristotle "remains satisfied with a positive investigation of the sensible; the dialectics of negativity established by the present of the infinite is simply not there." By "dialectics of negativity," Alfsvåg refers to Luther's "discussion of oneness in Plato's *Parmenides* [in the philosophical theses of the Heidelberg Disputation], where [Plato] . . . first deprives oneness of everything until it is reduced to nothing, and then gives everything back until there is nothing left in which oneness is not. There is thus nothing that does not exist through participation in oneness, which in this way at the same time is outside of and in everything."[75] Summarizing Luther's appropriation of Dionysius and the "dialectics of negativity," Alfsvåg writes,

> Luther never rejected the dialectics of negativity as a fundamental aspect of Christian theology. On the contrary, this was the breeding

ground from which the more well-known dichotomies in Lutheran thinking, like law and gospel, or reason and revelation, developed. Admittedly, the mature Luther missed an emphasis of the terrifying experience of being confronted by the wrath of God in the Dionysian exploration of negativity. But this is an emphasis that may (Luther would certainly say should) be added to the basic Neoplatonic thought structure without breaking its fundamental philosophical suppositions.[76]

Luther permits the use of analogy in philosophy and politics, insofar as they are limited to temporal, earthly matters, but reason should not be granted permission to dictate God's word.[77] Luther's theology is marked less by analogy and more by paradox. This does not mean that analogy is absent in Luther's theology. Luther repeatedly uses analogies to clarify the two natures united in the person of Christ (like the fire and iron unified as heated iron[78]) and the new life we have in Christ (the happy exchange of property between husband and wife or the shared *forma* between the knower and the object of knowledge[79]). But such similarity-in-difference is situated within paradox. Paradox accentuates not similarity-in-difference between related things but actual opposition. Such paradox undermines a continuum between nature and grace as we might see in realism or the conventional, yet reasonable, agreement between the divine offer and the required human response in the *pactum* theology of nominalism.

One certainly reasons both outside theology as well as within it. But reasoning within theology is accountable to the incarnation and God's paradoxical work of redeeming sinners, claiming sinners as righteous. Reason is accountable to the gospel narrative in which God chooses "what is low and despised in the world, things that are not" (1 Cor. 1:28). Indeed, as we saw in the "Lectures on Galatians" (1535), faith obtains knowledge, even if it is starkly different from knowledge that would accrue from the law: "But Christ is grasped, not by the Law or by works but by a reason or an intellect that has been illumined by faith. And this grasping of Christ through faith is truly the 'speculative life', about which the sophists chatter a great deal without knowing what they are saying."[80] But faith is not circumscribed *a priori* by the categories of what the Aristotelian tradition defines as rational. Indeed, the gospel transcends such circumscription.

As Janz notes, analogy builds into its structure both similarity and dissimilarity between the related matters (*relata*).[81] Christians, however, disagree on the nature of proposed analogous talk about God. Should we affirm Thomas Aquinas's "analogy of being," which adheres to the dissimilarity between God as uncreated and the world as created, in spite of God's imprint built into everything He has made? Such an approach to analogy can be contrasted with the contemporary theologian Eberhard Jüngel, for whom, due to the incarnation, the gospel as analogous talk establishes a "still greater similarity" in the midst of such great dissimilarity between God and the world.[82]

Presenting this contrast moves us from historical theology to contemporary theology, but it can help us understand better the contrast between paradoxical and analogical reasoning. Jüngel raises the question about the nature of analogy as a strategy to undermine the Roman Catholic scholar Erich Przywara's view of analogy, which developed on the basis of the Fourth Lateran Council (1215): "Between the Creator and the creature so great a likeness cannot be noted without the necessity of noting a greater dissimilarity between them."[83] For Przywara, the relation between God and the world reflects a greater dissimilarity within so great a likeness between the Creator and the creature. For Jüngel, such a view is incompatible with the incarnation, God's "identifying" with the man Jesus. He proposes instead an "analogy of advent," in which God, as an "event," comes within language, incorporating parables such as the waiting father (Luke 15), which indicate the nature of God's love. God's mystery is not in the claim that God is unthinkable to the human but rather in the triune narrative of God's generosity to humanity.

Both views of analogy, either that of "being" (Aquinas, Przywara) or that of "advent" (Jüngel), are undermined by Luther's teaching.[84] For one thing, if the incarnation is true, we would have to say that there is truly *univocal* talk about God: that God is a specific man, Jesus of Nazareth, is no analogy but univocally true. More to the question, while Janz is right to emphasize that analogy includes an element of dissimilarity, accentuated more in the apophaticism of Przywara's Roman Catholic tradition and accentuated less in Jüngel's

Barthian tradition of an "analogy of advent," paradox is based less on dissimilarity between two *relata* and more on the opposition between two propositional truths (which semantically refers to realities in Luther's way of thinking). That is, in analogous thinking, similarity parallels dissimilarity, and vice versa, regardless of which of the two we emphasize in the polarity. However, opposition, with which we deal in paradoxes, pits sameness against its opposite. The pairings aligned with the theology of the cross, and Luther's theology as a whole, such as "strength in weakness," "granting life through death," and "giving grace through judgment," present not merely dissimilarities but actual oppositions. Such oppositions, encountered in the gospel's claim of sinners, confound reason's ability to develop analogies, at least with any overall speculative scheme between faith and reason (as might be seen in a thinker like Hegel), and put reason on a different track as an instrument accountable to what God has actually done.[85] Later, in his "Lectures on Galatians" (1535), Luther noted that law and gospel are not only distinct but "separated as more than mutually contradictory."[86]

Now, the concept of "sameness" is a different matter from that of "dissimilarity." Sameness and its opposite incorporate conflict, even incompatibility, which the polarity of similarity and dissimilarity does not. The polarity of similarity and dissimilarity may transcend commensurability as one-to-one correspondences that can be compared and contrasted. But it carries a more neutral tone than that of sameness and difference.[87] In the latter case, we are dealing with matters that are incompatible. In the case of the theology of the cross, it is the incompatibility between life and death, whose opposition thwarts any attempt at systematic synthesis, especially that of Hegel's. In a sense, seen abstractly, the same is the opposite of its opposite, while the opposite of the dissimilar is harder to establish since the similar includes an element of difference with respect to that to which it is compared, and vice versa. Here, there is more than mere incommensurability but instead an incompatibility built into the structure of the relationship itself. Only if God recreates new life out of death can some thread of a relationship be maintained. As Luther later put it in the *Bondage of the Will*, such opposition between God's proper work and alien work is so that faith will remain faith: "Hence in order that there may be room for faith, it is necessary that everything which is believed should be hidden. It cannot, however, be more deeply hidden than under an object, perception, or experience which is contrary to it. Thus when God makes alive he does it by killing, when he justifies he does it by making men guilty, when he exalts to heaven he does it by bringing down to hell."[88]

Paradox and Discursive Truth

Rightly seen, we should not assume that Luther's paradoxes lend themselves to ambiguity. At least, that was not the perception of post-Luther confessionalism. That paradox lends itself to irrationalism seems more a Kierkegaardian theme than a Lutheran one. Some paradoxes, such as "nothing is so small but God is still smaller, nothing so large but God is still larger, nothing is so short but God is still shorter, nothing is so long but God is still longer, nothing is so broad but God is still broader, nothing so narrow but God is still narrower, and so on. He is an inexpressible being, above and beyond all that can be described or imagined"[89] are due to Luther's apophatic approach to God. Others, such as the relation between law and gospel or, better said, the relation between God's alien and proper works, in which the alien work is for the sake of the proper work, are not truly (i.e., irresolvable) paradoxes because the opposition is resolved when one comes to faith—God's alien work is subordinated to God's proper work. Third, Christological paradoxes seem to be due to the intersection of philosophy's opposition between the finite and infinite and theology's assertion of unity between the two natures in the person of Christ. Finally, there does indeed seem to be a genuine paradox expressed when Luther asserts that we are responsible for our behavior even though we have no free will *coram deo*. Paradoxes can be discussed discursively, but they also limit the prospects of speculative inquiry. Hence as Luther puts it, philosophy is not to infringe or encroach on theology, which is far more likely to happen than theology encroaching on philosophy.

Secular Reason

That Luther categorizes reason along with law with matters that pertain to the temporal as opposed to the eternal means that his view of reason is established through a distinctive theological lens, that of the proper distinction between law and gospel. The medieval view of the Christian pilgrim, or *viator*, was defined by a ladder of ascent into the divine life. As the nominalists put it, if we do our very best (*facere quod in se est*), God will reward us by conferring that very grace that enables our finite nature ultimately to be elevated to eternal life and us to be healed of sin. For Luther, this ladder is a one-way street—from God to us and never us to God. Freed from the self-centeredness in which such works-righteousness binds us, Luther is confident that we will spontaneously exercise good works on behalf of the neighbor. In Luther's view, the temporal world is not primarily an analogy of God, but neither is it a secular, godless, depthless space. Instead, it is a mask of God (*larva dei*), a means whereby God continues to speak to us, in creation—a speaking to the creature through the creature, as Hamann so pointedly put it[90]—as part of God's ongoing providence, promise, or command. Nothing in the world is present as a stepping stone for salvation. Instead, this world is means whereby God provides for us and a space in which we are free to live out our vocations on behalf of the neighbor's well-being and to the glory of God.

The Enlightenment, in particular, began the quest for the public square to be secular. It relegated Christian faith to mythology and sought instrumental reason—particularly the quest for efficiency—as the basis for truth. Efficiency, however, leads not to truth but to more advanced techniques to control the world. Ironically, as Peter Gay noted decades ago, the secular sphere is no less mythological or religious than medieval perspectives, but modernity's religion is a retrieval of paganism,[91] either in a Gnostic variety, where nothing is quite as sacred as the self, or in an Epicurean variety, where within moderation all can seek the greatest happiness for the greatest number.[92] Most recently, secular reason fails to establish a basis for a sound moral discourse, as Steven Smith in *The Disenchantment of Secular Discourse* points out.[93] Secular reason proves to be successful in matters of quantification. However, apart from smuggling into public discourse notions of a purposive cosmos or final causes with a providential design, banished by secular reason, we have no recourse by which to affirm the freedoms we so cherish. By "smuggling" Smith means:

> Our modern secular vocabulary purports to render inadmissible notions such as those that animated premodern moral discourse—notions about a purposive cosmos, or a teleological nature stocked with Aristotelian "final causes," or a providential design. But if our deepest convictions rely on such notions, and if these convictions lose their sense and substance when divorced from such notions, then perhaps we have little choice except to smuggle such notions into the conversation—to introduce them incognito under some sort of secular disguise.[94]

Hence, we introduce notions of freedom and equality, sufficiently general to escape the taint of partisan or religious affiliation, and claim that our argument follows from them. As Stanley Fish notes, "But Smith points out (following Peter Westen and others), freedom and equality—and we might add justice, fairness and impartiality—are empty abstractions. Nothing follows from them until we have answered questions like 'fairness in relation to what standard?' or 'equality with respect to what measures?'—for only then will they have content enough to guide deliberation."[95]

If there is a pagan theological core to secular reasoning, then theology concedes too much by not challenging it. Unable to prove it false beyond a shadow of a doubt, theologians still need to name it for what it is. The underlying mythology situating secular reason is no more scientific than that of the Christian mythos. Indeed, we should ask what it was about Christianity that enabled the germination and eventual growth of scientific reasoning among Europeans and not other groups.[96]

Additionally, how the human mind is able to map matter or match the nature of material reality with mathematics and various scientific methods, such as can be found in physics and chemistry, is itself a mystery. It is insufficient to claim that the mind's ability to do such intellectual cartography of mapping reality, insofar as we can conceive of it through models and via publicly accountable methods, is due solely to the survival value of such skills. The reduction of the success of mind matching reality in physics and chemistry to the luck or chance of a materialistic understanding of human evolution staggers the imagination. In other words, why or how the universe should be sufficiently "anthropic" for us to understand it, at least to some degree, is a mystery. Hence mystery is to be found not merely at the core of theological reflection, in such topics, for example, as the nature of the Trinity or the atonement, but it is also the access or gateway to all truly scientific reflection. In that light, the more we know, the more we don't know. No matter how someone answers the question "Why something; why not rather nothing?," it can only put us in the realm of faith, not knowledge, even if such faith fails to correspond to biblical faith.

Conclusion

Luther's approach to reason is helpful and fosters sound reasoning because he steers a course that is neither rationalistic nor irrational. He honors the truth that the human ultimately is bounded by mystery and that only narrative and not reason per se, with its attempt at its own self-sufficiency, can construct a seamless metaphysical garment. Reason is necessary and sufficient in dealing with this-worldly matters. However, it does not have the resources by which to grasp the whole of reality. At its core, the whole of reality ever is upheld in mystery. Nor can reason establish parameters for how the gospel grants God's grace to sinners. There is a kind of inner logic to salvation. God's alien work exists for His proper work, for example. But a transparency between our limited, let alone sinful, human understanding and that of ultimate reality is nothing other than a dream. Substantive matters of philosophy are ever ad hoc, and with respect to faith, even logic must follow the grammar of faith. Nevertheless, reason is well suited to engage the public good and the flourishing of human life—especially when it is acknowledged as a good creation and not the basis for an alleged liberation from religion.

Likewise, theologians must seek to ground their work not in the eccentricity of their own experience but in the objectivity of the word. Only then will theology be able to command attention from wider publics and actually contribute to the well-being of the church and the world. Here, Luther is our master guide.

CHAPTER 5

Toward a More Robust
Lutheran Theology

Response to Dennis Bielfeldt

Dennis Bielfeldt raises the question of how theological discourse is true. For Bielfeldt the real crisis in the ELCA (Evangelical Lutheran Church in America) is one of truth. We do not seem to have a standard or criteria by which to test or evaluate theological positions and, with that vacuum, those positions that win are the ones that garner the most popular support. Of course, our church constitution assures us that the ELCA grounds its doctrinal stance on the Holy Scriptures as the word of God and the Lutheran Confessions as faithful and true witnesses to Scripture. De jure we are loyal to the Scriptures and the Confessions. De facto, however, we promote a pluralism of theological methods and teachings in ELCA-related institutions. In a sense, we are no longer a synod—meaning "same path"—but a polyodoi—meaning "many paths." Bielfeldt urges us back to a concern for truth in his quest to ground theological discourse in an epistemology of critical realism. My response will not disagree with the overall content or thrust of Bielfeldt's work but hopefully will nuance it in light of my own reflections about the nature of theology and the mission of the gospel.

First, I think that we need to be clear that theology, following Luther, is not primarily about developing propositions about God, as is widely believed, but instead about evaluating discourse in light of the truth that the human is sinful and that God is justifying.

If theology is to regain the sense that it deals with truth, then we will have to challenge the centuries-long tendency to reduce truth to measurement or mapping. One of the great achievements of the European and North American Enlightenments has been to seek to map all reality. We see this evidenced in the cartographies of continents and galaxies, the periodic chart of elements, the proposed evolutionary history of life, the human genome, and the attempt to monitor and alter tastes and trends in economic and public life. Much good has sprung from the technologies resulting from this quest for greater control over the forces of nature and even human behavior. There may also be significant drawbacks, as many of us today worry about global warming, overpopulation, the pollution of drinking water, and other environmental concerns. These remarkable technological achievements have been accomplished in tandem with a view of truth that links truth to exact propositions confirmed empirically, through the senses.

The goal of philosophers has been to establish comprehensive systems to explain reality or, more humbly, analyses of the nature of language on the basis of "clear and distinct" ideas. Following Aristotle, reason is the monarch that is to rule as we seek to understand our experience. The goal of modern philosophy, historically, has been to get our thinking to conform as much as possible to mathematics. The motive for this is that mathematics appears actually to help thinking progress. Through mathematics, the mind is able to map matter. We see this confirmed in how scientific experiments result in projects that actually work. Research in atomic physics lends itself to the production of nuclear reactors or nuclear arms. These are tangible payoffs that confirm the empirical method and confirm our intuition that we are able to map reality as such.

Thoughtful philosophers acknowledge that the scientific method must presuppose a metaphysics. When I ask students, "Can you touch, taste, hear, smell, or see a number? Or an electron?" they look puzzled. I'm urging them to think about the status of the reality of things of which we have no direct sense awareness. How are they real? My students do not want to give up the view that numbers or electrons are real, but they are challenged when they try to explain how these things are real.

Quite frankly, the fundamentalism to which Bielfeldt refers ironically accepts a view that truth is a result of exact mapping through measurement, the same view of truth adopted by many modern people. In that light, fundamentalism is not especially a conservative viewpoint. How so? Medieval views of truth tended to be less literal than modern views. Ancient and medieval views of truth acknowledged the limits to literal approaches to reality. Mathematics was employed not only for exact measurement but because numbers were also seen as highly symbolic. Just think of biblical numbers: twelve, seven, three, and forty. Quickly we are in touch with the symbolism—and acknowledge that there are multiple layers of symbolism in them. Such symbolism is often lost on my students, who are less informed by a literary culture and more by technological and entertainment cultures. Fundamentalists adopt highly literalistic approaches to Scripture, to the extent that they often cannot discern poetry, metaphor, and figure in Scripture. They are hypermodern with respect to literalness as a criterion for truth.

Metaphysical questions result when we ask, "Why should every effect have a cause?" or even more basic, "Does every effect have a cause?" Surely, as David Hume acknowledged, we cannot prove beyond a shadow of a doubt that every effect has a cause. As Hume tells us, this is a "customary association" that we make. It is not something that we can scientifically prove. What's the point here? The truth about truth is that it perhaps should not be limited to mapping, exactitude, or even "clear and distinct ideas." Even the scientific method calls for a metaphysics, but metaphysics is limited in its ability to deliver clear and distinct ideas to the degree that it reaches greater generalizations about reality and experience.

Both modern ways of viewing truth, and Bielfeldt, prefer propositional ways of looking at truth. Such views tend toward seeing truth as a correspondence between language and reality or an attempt at coherence, trying to bring a unified conceptual scheme to experience and our reflections on experience. Luther's Reformation discovery does not easily or quickly mesh with these views. The reason for this is, first, because the gospel is primarily a performative word. The form of the gospel is not language that describes reality as such or expresses inner feelings or directs behavior but instead language that does something. For instance, sins are forgiven in the words of absolution; a blessing is bestowed in the benediction.

Second, this is because paradox is an inescapable center to how Luther operates. Quickly we can think of such paradoxes. Whoever would live must die. A specific man, Jesus Christ, is God. Only the sinner is justified. And the list could go easily on. At its core, this fondness for paradox is grounded in a view of God, quite radical by any standard or measure, in which God puts to death not only our sins but also our righteousness. Faith means, for Luther, to agree with God's promise against the evidence of the accusing law or the threat of God's indifference as divine hiddenness.

Yes, this is realism indeed! The reality of God is crushing us through the drive of the law such as we hear in the mandate that you must fulfill your potential. Or, it is crushing us in the terror that we as insecure creatures face with the prospect of chaos or the void. In fact, this is the strongest case for realism—human passivity *coram deo*. All people are suffering divine things. We are ultimately recipients with respect to God. Even the call for human authenticity, apart from any objective criteria by which to test that self-actualization, as Jean-Paul Sartre urged us, simply means that we are "damned to be free." Damned if you do; damned if you don't. Either way, Luther's take on Sartre's perspective is that the theologian is forged through such damnation. And for him, unlike Sartre, there is a clear criterion by which we are measured—God's law. Counter to Sartre's existential *autopoiesis* (self-making), we must claim that the freedom to think or do is dependent on this prior gift of God's creating us.

The truth of reality at its core as being paradoxical also implies that the quest for a total system, a grand unified theory of reality, is not likely wise. Experience is itself much too big for theory. Theories become refined as we seek greater conformity to experience. Think of how our picturing of the atom has changed over the last century. It changed from being a "raisin-pudding model" to a "planetary-orbit model," while now we find it hard to picture, given quantum theory. What will our view be like another century from now or a millennium from now? The quest of reason to be a monarch—to be almost like Sauron's ring ("one ring to rule them all, one ring to find them, one ring to bring them all, and in the darkness bind them")—is thwarted by the fact that God's disquieting hiddenness and revelation, the accusing law and the promising gospel, and providential order are not harmonizable into an overall system this side of the eschaton.

For Bielfeldt, there is a tendency to see truth in terms of true propositions that either designate what is the case as correspondence or picture how all experiences can cohere. Following J. L. Austin's view of language, we can say that he sees theology as tied to constative propositions, language seeking to describe states of affairs.

There is a place for this approach. It is aligned with the scholastic approach to theology, which confirms theology as an academic discipline whose primary method is *disputatio*. However, with Oswald Bayer, we must ever keep in mind that theology primarily begins and ends with the worship service. That is, it is a reflection between yesterday's proclamation and gifts and today's. More fundamental to the task of theology per se is the need to analyze the performative character of the language of proclamation and worship, particularly an analysis of how law and gospel are used in language. The point is: the liturgical, monastic approach to theology is to be done in tandem with the academic, scientific approach to theology. Both need to be intertwined if our theology is to be faithful to Luther's and the Confessors'.

Bielfeldt's affirmation of realism is driven as a response to the deep-set psychologizing trends that we see adopted in theology so much since Friedrich D. E. Schleiermacher. Schleiermacher was concerned not that theological propositions conformed to reality but that they corresponded to the deepest religious sentiments of the Christian. Schleiermacher's attempt to make theology conform to the viewpoints of the bourgeoisie "cultured despisers" of religion actually makes theology evaporate into anthropology as Bielfeldt points out—the human writ large, as Barth put it.

Schleiermacher's perspective adopts a view of the human in which the core of the human is, as Gilbert Ryle describes it, a Cartesian "ghost in the machine." The self as such is thinking and nonextended in space, and the body is nonthinking and extended in space. The self as thinking is prior to language, culture, and history—exactly those factors to which Bielfeldt appeals when he tells us that our perception of reality is historically conditioned. Hence for Schleiermacher, we deal not with a word that transforms the feelings, the emotions, and the imagination—but all such is a result of a prelinguistic substratum. If I read Bielfeldt right, though, it is language, not feelings, all the way down with respect to human reality and experience until we reach a metaphysical foundation.

Such romanticism is experienced in today's seminary education. When I was a senior at Luther Seminary twenty years ago, we were expected to develop our own theology, which we then submitted to the seminary faculty who evaluated it on behalf of The American Lutheran Church to establish our fitness for ministry. We were actually urged to be expressive, explore our creativity. We were not urged to be orthodox and confess the faith of the church established in Scripture, the ecumenical creeds, and the Evangelical-Lutheran Confessions. Hundreds of candidates for ministry were concocting their own theologies. One can imagine: Barth, Tillich, Bultmann, and me! The result is a plurality of confessions within an allegedly confessional church. How can we have loyalty to the cause in the ELCA when we do not share a common faith? Indeed, we find ourselves fighting each other over securing a particular political agenda. Here it is not knowledge that gives power, as Francis Bacon would tell us, but power that gives knowledge.

My response to Bielfeldt is that the constative and performative are or should be more intertwined. As Oswald Bayer notes, academic tools are regulative for theology, but liturgical spirituality is constitutive for theology. The former makes theology scientific, while the latter guarantees that it is theology, tied to the worship service. The proposition "God creates the world," as Bielfeldt notes, calls for assessing its truth in terms of its correspondence to reality. Hence Bielfeldt is so concerned about divine causality. However, his concerns need to be nuanced. Is it possible to understand the days of Genesis chapter 1 apart from their liturgical and confessional import? But as much as such questions of a constative nature arise, the sentence also carries liturgical freight. That God creates the world may be a threat: if God creates, then I'm ultimately not in charge, and I'm also beholden to God for my existence. As God addresses me in creation—masked in it—I am comforted in His rainbow of promise, which He will provide. Talk of creation is propositional and commends itself to the academy. It is also—and primarily—creedal and fosters the life of faith and the community of worship.

Bielfeldt is adamantly opposed to the subjectivistic trend in theology. However, that trend is to be distinguished from a cultural-linguistic approach to ecumenism. Subjectivism tends to make theology into a product of the imagination. A cultural-linguistic approach to theology tends to say that the imagination is a result of linguistically, culturally, and historically conveyed signs and symbols, which are not granted sense by a community but, conversely, give sense to a community. The apparent similarity is that neither seems to endorse realism. We should be careful in evaluating this perspective, however. Lindbeck does not rule out realism on principle. Rather, he is skeptical of our ability to get there. The "critical" in his critical realism is the reservation that in our quests for knowing, we bring something to our perceptions. Such are often distortions.

Again, my suggestion of a case for realism is that following Luther, we suffer divine things. That is, God is ever working upon us as He is mediated in creation, Scripture, and the sacraments. Through such means, God accuses, comforts, threatens, and provides. This God gives us freedom in His very promise of life. Our realistic position is embodied in a narrative—for that is exactly how the promise of the gospel is conveyed. If you are asked, "How do you know that God claims you as a sinner?" you must answer, "Look at what Jesus did for me (and the entire world—objective justification)." And this can only be said because God raised Jesus from the dead.

The faith is both story-based and accountable to the best academic research available. We need to honor both poles in our theologizing. This has many repercussions as Word Alone anticipates supporting a Lutheran House of Studies. Theological education has tended, in this country and Europe, to dichotomize head and heart, separating the liturgical-spiritual moment of theology from the academic moment. All too many seminary professors are too beholden to the American Academy of Religion or the Society of Biblical Literature—the "guilds," if you will. The tendency in theological education, affecting both seminaries and church-related college religion departments, has been to be too enamored of the secular modes of thinking that translate faith into knowing, as we see in the philosopher Hegel and his followers (Biedermann, Pannenberg, Robert Jenson), doing, as we see in Kant and Marx and their followers (Ritschl, Moltmann, liberationism, feminist theologians), or feeling, as we see in Schleiermacher and his disciples (existentialism and all "hyphen" theologies).

When our ancestors established seminaries and colleges on this continent, it was not that they were unfamiliar with these ways of doing theology. They knew them firsthand in Europe. Rather, they intentionally avoided these approaches as counterproductive to the mission of the gospel. The institutions they established were far more akin to the European mission schools than the universities. Theologically, they tended toward orthodoxy, for the most part. While much can be said against a wooden and stale proof-texting approach to theology and mission, theological leaders in our seminaries and colleges back in the late 1950s through the 1970s intentionally felt that the wave of the future for religion would be away from the proof-texting that they had received in their education by a previous generation. That presentation of faith came across as dead for them and unable to address the needs of an increasingly secular world. But that led to the situation that Bielfeldt criticizes today. These leaders, whether knowingly or not, adopted those very secular, accommodating theological methods of knowing, doing, and feeling that our ancestors knew were not serving Europeans at all well. That move entailed an increasing secularization of theological seminaries and college religion departments. Theology became less tied to real parishes and more attuned to the secular university—an audience that is not sympathetic with the gospel. If a wooden orthodoxy was no longer viable, the solution was even worse. The promise of the gospel was transformed into ethical agendas, psychological explorations, or grand unified systems. The interconnection between Scripture, worship, doctrine, and pastoral conversation was lost. Word Alone stands now in a position to reclaim a more holistic approach to ministry and faith. Ought not this topic serve as our theme for next fall?

More than anything, the theological task is fundamentally a pastoral task of distinguishing law and gospel. Apologetic tasks, which we see heightened in Bielfeldt's work, are legitimate and necessary. However, they are subordinate to this primary theological task. The task of theology as pastoral is grounded in the narrative of the Holy Scriptures (the "historical *a priori*," as Oswald Bayer calls it), in the wider ecumenical, catholic heritage of the church as a discussion and sometimes disagreement about the interpretation of the Scriptures, and with an eye to evangelical outreach and social mission. Luther taught us that all are theologians since all are Christians. Some are very good theologians and others not so good. But we are all condemned to be theologians in one way or another, and it is *only* through *being damned* that one is made into the best kind of theologian, a theologian of the cross.

Bielfeldt is right to highlight critical realism as an alternative to Schleiermacherian subjectivism, which reduces theology to anthropology. He is right to affirm theological propositions as conforming to states of affairs in so far as we, as sinners and creatures, all suffer divine things. Theological language, however, analyzes not only constative forms of discourse but, even more important, performative discourse, words that convey God's reality impinging upon us primarily as either command or promise. And there is no point for theology at all, whatsoever, unless it serves the gospel. The gospel alone is the only mandate for the existence of the church.

CHAPTER 6

A Lutheran Case for Apologetics

Increasingly, there is a resurgence in evangelism. This passion is not unique to our time. We forget that throughout most of our history in the United States, Lutherans were growing in number. Until very recently, Lutherans increased their membership decade by decade. Sometimes that was due to the fact that in bygone days, Lutherans had big families, but growth in the past was due to more than that. Lutherans were marked by a passion for sharing the gospel. The prevailing model for starting congregations was not hierarchical, top-down, and bureaucratic. Instead, it was congregation-centered. Congregations freely granted time to their pastors, who helped start congregations in neighboring communities wherever there was a call for help. A congregational "to-do list" included starting daughter congregations. Helping to give birth to other congregations was embedded in a congregation's DNA. We cannot underestimate the power within congregations to establish much good in the world—proclaiming the saving word and administering the means of grace but also mentoring children and youth by providing a healthy community and a safe haven for those beset by trials, as well as ministering to the underprivileged.

Peter's Directive and New Contexts

A major difference between today's missionary context and that of yesteryear is the fact that our country is no longer a "Christian nation," as many had billed America. That's not to say that Americans are not religious or spiritual. A majority of Americans claim to believe in

God. But today, evangelists encounter more criticisms of the faith than in the past. Chances are you are quite familiar with these criticisms. Here's a list that I bet you've heard before: (1) Christians are hypocrites; (2) Christianity is a crutch; (3) the Bible and science are incompatible; (4) a loving God would never send anyone to hell; (5) evil is incompatible with an all-powerful, all-loving God; (6) I'm not so bad, so how can you say I'm a sinner?; and (7) there are many paths to God, and you need to choose the path that's right for you.

Disciples of Jesus cannot turn a blind eye to these objections. Even if you have not raised these concerns yourself, you may find your own children or grandchildren challenging you with them. We are caught off guard when we do not know our faith well. To truly be conversant in the faith is not only to know the Scriptures and the catechisms inside and out but also to be aware of criticisms of the faith and have thoughtful responses to them. Some people raising these criticisms are insincere. They use them as a defense mechanism in order to minimize the impact of God's claim on their lives. But others are sincere. God comes across as hidden to them—not just that God cannot be seen but that His ways are foreign to them. Like the God-fearers on the fringes of the synagogues Paul preached to, those folks are great prospects for receiving the gospel. They already have a sense of their need. But the degree to which you cannot respond to these folks' sincere objections is the degree to which they will never hear the gospel from you. So Paul calls us to "do your best to present yourself to God as one approved, a worker who has no need to be ashamed, rightly handling the word of truth" (2 Tim. 2:15). Even stronger is Peter's charge: "But in your hearts regard Christ the Lord as holy, always being prepared to make a defense to anyone who asks you for a reason for the hope that is in you; yet do it with gentleness and respect, having a good conscience" (1 Pet. 3:15–16).

The faith of yesteryear could assume a public where people were at least nominal Christians. But in today's world, Christians work beside Hindus, Muslims, and unaffiliated secular men and women. Christians need resources to be able to defend their faith. That's where apologetics comes in. Apologetics means defending your faith. Apologetics does not mean defending God. God does not need your defense. He can take care of Himself—thank you very much! Instead, apologetics calls us to think about faith—in light of its critics.

The Christian faith receives unfair slights, smears, and inaccurate publicity. Should that be surprising? The old Adam and Eve always want to remain in charge of their lives, captains of their own fates. They do not think they need a God. Or, at best, they conceive of some kind of "higher power" that meets their own felt needs. A God who claims sinners totally as His own is a threat to those sinners' autonomy. No wonder Paul said that "the word of the cross is folly to those who are perishing, but to us who are being saved it is the power of God."

Even stronger, Paul elaborates:

> Has not God made foolish the wisdom of the world? For since, in the wisdom of God, the world did not know God through wisdom, it pleased God through the folly of what we preach to save those who believe. For Jews demand signs and Greeks seek wisdom, but we preach Christ crucified a stumbling block to Jews and folly to Gentiles, but to those who are called, both Jews and Greeks, Christ the power of God and the wisdom of God. For the foolishness of God is wiser than men, and the weakness of God is stronger than men. (1 Cor. 1:18, 21–25)

Argumentation alone will never win someone to Christ. Instead, to be won to Christ, we must encounter the Holy Spirit who calls us through the gospel, enlightens us with His gifts, sanctifies, and keeps us in the true faith. But argumentation can help undermine those barriers that the old Adam and Eve erect to protect themselves. It can set straight the slights, smears, and bad PR of secularism. While apologetics cannot confirm the truth of Christian faith beyond a shadow of a doubt—for in this life, we walk by faith not by sight (2 Cor. 5:7)—it can reinforce our conviction that the Christian faith offers a deeply satisfying approach to life (John 10:10) that other religions and secularism cannot give. The Scriptures unlock the meaning of the entire history of the cosmos and humanity as the story of God's self-giving, sacrificial love, given most clearly in the death and resurrection of Jesus. Our lives have meaning when we see ourselves within that story. Outside that history, it is not clear what our lives would mean. As Luther put it, God created us just so He could redeem us. This is the clue to the mystery of the world. We have a reason to live because, though sinners, we are beloved of God and we are called to share that love with others.

So the faith is something that we can genuinely commend to our children and grandchildren as well as our neighbors. But we cannot do that if we do not seek to mature in the faith ourselves through the study of the word and its bearing on this world. The faith integrates all aspects of humanity: our heads as well as our hearts and hands. Our hearts are guided to trust in God alone and our hands to reach out as Christ's to serve our neighbor. But Christ's renewing work also includes our heads as we learn to take every thought captive to Christ (2 Cor. 10:5). Apart from apologetics, we are apt to disassociate our hearts and hands from our heads. After all, thinking is really hard work. But disassociation is not Christ's way. He wants to be Lord over the whole person. That new man or woman in Christ sees God's "foolishness" as far wiser than any secular philosophy and God's "weakness" as far stronger than any economic system or worldly power.

One more point: I suspect many of you have felt betrayed by the theology that has paraded itself in the church for the last several decades. One reason for your sense of betrayal is that the church failed to take apologetics seriously. Instead of challenging secular agendas by attempting to see the world through the lens of faith, many theologians adapted or accommodated to this secular agenda and sought some little corner within it where they could still practice some kind of "faith." Rather than challenging critics, these folks internalized secularism and its criticisms so that their faith was watered down and even neutered of its power. But good apologetics leads us in just the opposite direction. While faith in this life can never be proved beyond a shadow of a doubt, it can be defended. Had the church done this, her faith stance would have been clearer, her teachings would have been more solid, and her passion for outreach would have been more vibrant.

My deepest hunch is that the church leadership of a previous generation believed that the wave of the future was to adapt as much as possible to secular perspectives. So pastoral care became like therapy, leadership became like the strategies of CEOs, theology became like secular philosophy, and Bible study became like either antiquarian studies or the self-help section of the local bookstore.

We forfeited the very power of God that remakes the world, all so that we might carve for ourselves a little niche in the wider secular public—a venue that itself has no respect for the church and that has many voices working at cross-purposes with the church. Making ourselves akin to another agency of this world, we lose our sense of mission and power. We stagnate. Confessional Lutherans have moved beyond this. In light of apologetics, pastoral care is restored to caring for souls, leadership is resituated as outreach, theology is reseen as the grammar of faith, and Bible study is returned to an encounter with the living God. This is because our defense of the faith means that no more will we attempt to find our niche in a secular world. The secular world does not want us. Instead, we will challenge the most fundamental assumptions of secularism and put them to the test.

The Nature of Secularism

What does it mean to be secular? To be secular means (1) to see life from within the immediate physical and temporal world without reference to God; (2) to establish one's own value system apart from any reference to God, who is only an "external authority"; and (3) to understand that there are no absolutes in life—that all truth is situational. Seeing life as its own end, people seek to find meaning by racking up experiences. Now, we Christians deny all this. But can we prove it wrong? We could if we could find some "bird's-eye view" or independent vantage point from which to argue. That is what the philosophers over the last several centuries have tried to do. But let's be honest: these philosophers have not been successful. But do we Christians have an independent vantage point? Again, let's be honest: no. We offer no truth that anyone outside of Christ could accept. Remember, Paul writes, "For no one can lay a foundation other than that which is laid, which is Jesus Christ" (1 Cor. 3:11). Jesus Christ is our foundation. He is the way, the truth, and the life (John 14:6). Truth relies on doctrines for its expression, but most important, truth is a person, Jesus. He is the measure and fulcrum of truth. Yet no one can come to Him or see this unless called by the Holy Spirit. So we must accept the fact that, for all the things we share in common with non-Christians, our most fundamental view about truth is not shared. How will that shape our apologetics? Very simply, apologetics deals not so much with *arguing people to the faith* as much as *arguing with them from the faith*. In arguing from the faith, we invite nonbelievers to consider what life would be like if they were believers. How would you see the world with Jesus as your Lord? What difference would it make for your life if the Bible were true?

Faith in Jesus is not shared by all, but there are some things that believers and nonbelievers do share. All people are on the same page when wrestling with life's tough questions, such as: What happens when we die? Does life have a meaning? Is there a God? We all do not share faith in Jesus, but everyone lives by some kind of faith. Again, this is because no one can prove beyond a shadow of a doubt the truth of what one thinks and feels about such questions. So all people are in a sense people of faith—the question is: In what do we, or should we, put our trust?

The Secular Mind: Running from God's Mercy

Close to five hundred years ago, Martin Luther called for a reformation of the church. He was not the only one to make that call, but no other reformer was as clear as he that what reformation should be about is God's grace offered in Jesus Christ. Late-medieval men and women knew Jesus as a role model for living and as a judge at the end of time, but they did not see Jesus as their redeemer—or at least as clearly as Scripture reveals it. Luther challenged all that and went so far as to base all saving truth on the authority of Scripture. What that means is that Scripture is the prism through which we are to understand God and the world.

Now, the old Adam and Eve do not like grace because it forces them to admit that they need Jesus. Like the first sinners, early modern people were apt to think that any talk of grace undermined their autonomy and agency. So they thought that the answer was to look to reason and not the Bible. Not long after Luther's reform, people sought another basis for truth than that of Scripture. Scripture seemed inadequate to convey truth in comparison with something like reason. Philosophers like René Descartes appealed to reason as the basis for truth, and later philosophers like John Locke appealed to experience. The upshot was that, insofar as it was honored, the Bible was evaluated in light of reason or experience and discarded as the context or prism through which everything else was understood (including reason and experience).

This was the beginning of the secular outlook. These early modern thinkers did not try to get rid of "God," but they reinterpreted God in generic terms as nature's God and the like. Over time, Europeans and some Americans began to feel that if humanity were truly to be set free from the old constraints of the nobility who lorded over peasants and censured free thinking, then that power to which the nobility appealed for their "divine rights," "God," had to be ditched. Their logic was simple: if God has all power, then we have no power. So for us to claim our own power, we must deny God. Some concluded that all "God" ever was is an illusion invented by the powers-that-be to secure their entitlement. The idea of "God" was devised as a ploy or ruse to keep people in line because they would fear God's judgment. Or "God" is merely some kind of crutch to help people cope with the changing shifts of fortune. Humanity becomes more mature to the degree that religion diminishes and is displaced by scientific reasoning. Now, this telling overly simplifies the history of secularism, but there is enough truth in it for our purposes.

Again, most Americans are not atheists. But most Americans see faith as a private matter not bearing on public life. We are inconsistent because we support a "civil religion" with paid military chaplains, chaplains for Congress, "In God We Trust" written on our money, Christmas as a national holiday, and so on. Even so, we undermine the view that faith gives truth. We tend to associate truth with math and science—"verifiable" matters—and religion with subjective feelings. But what really becomes of truth if we unmoor it from God? Can truth survive? In a sense, it does not. Why? Because in the secular perspective, we are *always* skeptical about reality. With such skepticism, all truth ever amounts to is describing what works but not what's real. Thus what used to be truth is reduced to opinion.

Now Christians need to challenge that assumption, if for no other reason than to be true to what science actually does. It's false that religion and science are incompatible. Think: science describes how gravity works, but it is unable to say *why* it should work. We can use mathematics to describe how gravity works, but we are clueless as to *why* mathematics should be successful in describing gravity. Faith alone answers the question of why. It is astonishing how math can be used to measure or map the cosmos in all its dimensions. The mind is quite adept at doing this. But again, why the mind should be so successful in mapping matter is a mystery! That's where faith is all so true to reality and experience. A truly mindful perspective honors this mystery. Such mystery does not stupefy us but instead allows us to enjoy the wonder—even magic—of it all.

Additionally, we need to remind our secular friends that it was Christians who discovered that if you want to understand the world, use math to do it. The master behind all this was a fourteenth-century monk and Oxford scholar, Thomas Bradwardine. Far from being opposed to religion, science as we understand it is one of Christianity's great gifts to the world. But science on its own can only describe physical processes; it has no ability to offer an explanation for them. Because it cannot, a secularistic outlook that attributes truth only to science offers at best only a description of how things work in the world. It dodges the question of *why* things should work the way they do. Such a secular perspective is inherently unsatisfying—at least when compared to the Christian faith, which honors that the mystery behind physical laws is none other than God Himself. God is the mystery of the world who makes sure that we can trust math to decipher physical laws. In so acknowledging God, we do not merely support a pragmatic approach to the world—that is, we do not limit our thinking to "what works"—but instead claim to know something about reality. That truth is summarized by the Psalmist: the heavens declare the glory of God and the earth shows forth His handiwork (Ps. 19:1).

But secularism is not just unsatisfying when it comes to truth; it also fails to establish a basis for sound moral discourse. As noted, it proves to be successful in matters of quantification. But unless it smuggles notions of a purpose-filled world or notions of a providential design into public discourse, then modern people have no recourse by which to affirm the freedoms they so cherish. Modern people treasure things like freedom, equality, justice, fairness, and impartiality. But apart from some vision of goodness as such, those words are just fancy abstractions. Critic Stanley Fish notes that "nothing follows from them until we have answered questions like 'fairness in relation to what standard?' or 'equality with respect to what measures?'—for only then will they have content enough to guide deliberation."[1]

We Christians must ask which is more likely: (1) that goodness is a ruse and all that ethics amounts to is "what works" or (2) that such matters accord with nature as God has designed it. True, we cannot prove the latter stance, but unless you are biased against God, it is a more satisfying approach to ethics than the former. At the very least, it is not inconsistent, unlike the former. When my students tell me that ethics are merely expressions of cultural norms and not beholden to universal truths, I catch them off guard. I ask, "If I grade you down just because I do not like you, has anything wrong happened?" These students who were all relativists very quickly become ethical absolutists: "Of course it is wrong to grade someone down just because you do not like them." When I push, asking, "Why?" they explain, "It isn't fair!" I push them even further: fairness is based on a God-given dignity that belongs to all who share in God's own image.

A secular outlook is unsatisfying with respect to not only truth and goodness but also beauty. Whether found in nature, music, or art, beauty is one of God's greatest gifts to us, offering solace, security, excitement, and joy.[2] It is a glimpse into God's intentions for this world. Atheists would have us believe that to be human is simply to be a combination digestive tract and reproductive system that walks. But how totally foreign is that thought to creatures who not only can enjoy beauty but also make beautiful music, art, dance, sport, and theater. If you believe that beauty gives a glimpse into reality, then it's hard to simply believe it is an accident of purposeless evolution. No, instead, it is an imprint of God on nature and expressed, too, in human making and doing. It takes a lot of faith to believe that life is as meaningless as the atheist makes it out to be.

Truth, goodness, and beauty: secularism has a hard time explaining these important matters. But Christians regard truth, goodness, and beauty as names for God, identifying who God is. For that reason, Christians, too, are skeptics. We are skeptical of secularistic skepticism. Belief in God as the Alpha and Omega is a more credible (even if not provable) outlook on life than the thought that everything is due to chance. After all, where did chance come from? For Christians, reason and experience do not float around untethered. They need a context. That's where the Scriptures come in. The Scriptures give insight into how God works with humanity and what humanity owes God and others. Far from constraining human freedom, the gospel liberates people by recognizing that in Christ, we are both lords and servants and that it is wrong to play one over the other. The Scriptures are profoundly satisfying—or as the Psalmist put it: taste and see how gracious the Lord is (Ps. 34:8).

Paul: Master Apologist

Now, here's where apologetics can be handy. Sometimes you cannot prove something beyond a shadow of a doubt, but you can show that the opposing position is empty. That might be the only kind of "proof" that can be afforded in such matters. If your opponent's viewpoints are shown to be inconsistent or unsatisfying, even though you have not proved your position, it is still the one left standing. So if Christian faith accords with reality as best as we can understand it, then something like atheism is ruled out. Indeed, as I hope to show in what follows, being an atheist takes more faith than being a believer because you must explain away so many things that appear to be obviously true.

But I need to mention a caveat: as defenders of the faith, we need humility. Just as in our overall evangelistic program, we are simply beggars showing other beggars where to find bread, so in apologetics we are not to beat people over the head with evidence for the faith. Instead, we are to raise hard questions: Is your secularism really consistent with reality as you believe it to be? Likewise, we need to challenge unfair stereotypes of Christianity that say we are intolerant, close-minded, and unscientific.

The fact that there is no other foundation than that of Jesus Christ does not mean that we are doomed to take a radically relativist stance, where people think, You have your truth and I have my truth. Such an attempt to dismiss truth is bound to fail. Why?

You contradict yourself when you suggest that the truth about the one truth is that there is no truth. So let's be honest. Knowledge, accurate information, and reason and logic are still what our brains use to function, but they must function in tandem with experience, wisdom, intuition, values, and faith. Even the scientific method must assume a much wider context than science itself. Again, apologetics calls us to think about the faith. The more we exercise our faith—the more we read the world in light of the Scriptures—the more we deal with unavoidable questions about what reality really is. Christians offer a real service to the world by keeping these questions alive. So the best apologists are ones who really know the Lord and then think about life in light of this knowledge.

We have a model for doing apologetics. It's Paul. Acts 17:16–34 outlines this model. Let's turn to this passage and examine it closely. Note that Paul was evangelizing in Athens, a city known as the center of philosophy. Over four hundred years before Paul, it had been the home to Socrates, Plato, and Aristotle:

"Now while Paul was waiting for them at Athens, his spirit was provoked within him as he saw that the city was full of idols. So he reasoned in the synagogue with the Jews and the devout persons, and in the marketplace very day with those who happened to be there" (Acts 17:17).

Notice the verb *reasoned*. Paul did not just give his testimony. He engaged these people's minds. We need to ask, What would it take for me to do that? When faith is being challenged, we should never be like ostriches and stick our heads in holes to hide from the world. Far too many of us rely on our feelings alone. What we need to do is engage the world with the Scriptures. It is the Scriptures that bring heart, hands, and head together. God has called us to love Him with our heart, soul, reason, and strength. Our sin is that we give short shrift to that third trait—reason—and do not use our heads. Let's love God as God asks of us and start using our brains in our faith walk.

Some of the Epicurean and Stoic philosophers also conversed with him. And some said, "What does this babbler wish to say?" others said, "He seems to be a preacher of foreign divinities"—because he was preaching Jesus and the resurrection. And they took hold of him

and brought him to the Areopagus, saying, "May we know what this
new teaching is that you are presenting? For you bring some strange
things to our ears. We wish to know therefore what these things
mean." Now all the Athenians and the foreigners who lived there
would spend their time in nothing except telling or hearing something new. (Acts 18:18–21)

Who were the Epicureans and the Stoics? Epicureans taught that
the purpose of life is to seek pleasure in moderation. Do what you
want, but do nothing to excess. They also taught that there are no
gods nor an afterlife. Since there are no gods nor an afterlife, you need
not fear death. There will be no judgment. While Paul encountered
this group two thousand years ago, it does not sound much different
from the secularism I spoke of earlier. "Nothing new under the sun,"
as the author of Ecclesiastes (1:9) said. We deal today with exactly
the same mind-set that Paul dealt with. As was said by Christians
in the 1970s, the "new morality" is nothing but the old immorality in
a new guise.

The Stoics taught that the soul is a divine spark and that it is
on a continuum with "god." The purpose of philosophy is to offer
self-help. Their attitude was: Since you cannot change the world—it
is far too bureaucratic—you can change yourself by changing your
attitudes about life. Again, there is nothing new under the sun.[3] This
sounds a whole lot like the self-help section at Barnes and Noble. In
fact, it is exactly what would have been called "new age" twenty or so
years ago and even today. Where it is similar to Epicureanism is that
both schools teach that you are responsible at least for yourself—even
though Epicureans see the self as having a lowercase s because we are
no different from other animals, while Stoics see it as having a capital S since our deepest cores are, by nature, one with "god." To the
degree that contemporary secularism pushes to affirm that you are
the author of your own life—a kind of "god" for yourself—it comes
across a whole lot like how many people think today.

Look how Paul got their attention! He earned their belittlement
when they called him a babbler. Yet they wanted to hear more! Paul
does not run from the name of Jesus but puts it right in front of them.
With the resurrection, Paul indicates that we are indeed accountable.
The Epicureans and Stoics are right to affirm human accountability.

But they undermine its seriousness because, as Paul points out, we are accountable before God. The resurrection will begin with Christ's coming to judge the "quick and the dead." Then eternal life will begin. More to the point, these philosophers are not totally insincere. We need to learn from that. Yes, Christianity receives some unfair smearing. But not all nonbelievers are insincere. Some are genuinely open to the Christian faith. How's our witness? Do we reinforce non-Christian stereotypes or do we in fact offer a wholesome and grappling witness—like Paul's? Would today's Epicureans and Stoics want to grab you to learn more about the faith?

> So Paul, standing in the midst of the Areopagus, said: "Men of Athens, I perceive that in every way you are very religious. For as I passed along, and observed the objects of your worship, I found also an altar with this inscription, 'To the unknown god.' What therefore you worship as unknown, this I proclaim to you. The God who made the world and everything in it, being Lord of heaven and earth, does not live in temples made by man, nor is he served by human hands, as though he needed anything, since he himself gives to all mankind life and breath and everything. And he made from one man every nation of mankind to love on all the face of the earth, having determined allotted periods and the boundaries of their dwelling place that they should seek god, in the hope that they might feel their way toward him and find him. Yet he is actually not far from each one of us, for 'In him we live and move and have our being,' as even some of your own poets have said, 'for we are indeed his offspring.'" (Acts 18:22–28)

The Areopagus was the highest legislative and judicial council of Athens. In a sense, it is like Harvard University and Washington, DC, combined. Here's Paul jumping right in. You and I would at least gulp or even try to run away—but not Paul. What gave him courage? Of course, Christ Himself did. But let's face it: Paul had done his homework too. He did not rely on having been raised in a godly home. Instead, he appropriated that faith for himself. He made it his own. He knew the Scriptures. But read the notes in your ESV (English Standard Version) in the bottom margin. Paul quotes Greek poets and philosophers: Epimenides of Crete and Aratus. Actually, his overall argument is not so foreign from how early Greek philosophers challenged the traditional Greek gods. For those philosophers, God could not be identified with Zeus, Hera, Poseidon, or Hermes because those gods were unethical—cheating on each other and lying—as well as just too plain human. Paul proclaims that the true God cannot be put into a box—like "temples made by man"—let alone be served by "human hands." The true God cannot be manipulated by us—a scary thought! And yet, this God is unavoidable: in Him we live, move, and have our beings. Again, there's another scary thought, because in light of God's judgment, we are accountable to Him. Paul will not let us off the hook. But see how different he is from a street preacher. He simply states the truth of our accountability; he does not shout, "Turn or burn." What we also can see here is that Paul appeals to the idea that all people have some inkling for God, whether big or small. In our culture, we would call that a "higher power." Again, Paul's point is that whatever we consider "higher" falls short of God. As the Creator of the galaxies, God is always greater. But God is also smaller: God sustains the energy that keeps all the gravity at the core of every atom in place (compare Col. 1:17). In either case, outside of Jesus Christ, God is a threat to sinners.

> Being then God's offspring we ought not to think that the divine being is like gold or silver or stone, an image formed by the art and imagination of man. The times of ignorance God overlooked, but now he commands all people everywhere to repent, because he has fixed a day on which he will judge the world in righteousness by a man whom he has appointed; and of this he has given assurance to all by raising him from the dead. (Acts 17:29–31)

In light of the proper distinction between law and gospel, one of the most important concerns of Lutherans, Paul is preaching law—calling people to accountability before God. But gospel is implicit: those who repent and believe in that "Man" appointed as judge will find mercy. Paul's word to the Epicureans and Stoics is just as pertinent to today's secularists. Our secularists today want to erase God from public discourse. But they cannot erase some sense of accountability:

if not to God, at least to their own senses of integrity. But that is really the gist of it: I'm no sinner because there is no God whose goodness would be the evaluator that condemns me as a sinner. The secularist is trying to justify himself or herself not by faith but (ironically) by unbelief! Erase God and there's no judgment. With no judgment, there's no way I could be deemed a sinner.

But secularists are not so easily let off the hook. Let me explain. The great payoff of not believing in God would be "freedom." Freedom here means that you can invent yourself. Life is one big buffet line of options, and you can take a heap of this or a spoonful of that to make yourself what you want to be. But if we are honest, we have to admit that we do not just make ourselves for ourselves alone. When you make the decisions by which you invent yourself, you are saying that *anyone* could—or perhaps even *should*—live just like you. So you not only invent yourself but, in a sense, invent the world. People who do not want to be atheists but who operate with this outlook end up saying about God, "I determine who God is." If my guilt before God is just too big for me to handle, I do not confess it and get it off my chest through the words of absolution. Instead, I try to reimage a god for myself who is of my "own understanding." And likely this is a god who says, "Boys will be boys" or something like that. We just cannot handle a God who steps right into our own guilt and bears it in His body for us—as Jesus did. If we were to accept that, we would have to admit that we need Jesus. But to do that, we'd have to give up being captains of our own fates. Unfortunately, we never know what it really is to be free—free of having to invent ourselves and be responsible solely for ourselves. Instead, we only have a fake freedom of self-invention.

But let's go back to our atheist. If atheists are really honest about it, they have to admit that they carry the weight of the world on their shoulders. Since they are inventing what is right and wrong, they are a whole lot like Atlas—carrying the entire world—at least insofar as they invent it. That's why the French atheist Jean-Paul Sartre called this responsibility "condemned to be free." Freedom for him means you invent what's right and wrong. Condemned here means that you and everything you deal with are held to this standard you invent. It is an unrelenting standard. There is no absolution for it. There is only the oppressive word of self-evaluation—and evaluation of whatever else that fails to live up to it. So secularist freedom, a "freedom without God," just does not come across as all that positive or good or even free. For atheists, that might be all they have, but a world independent of God's judgment and grace seems to be a world terribly diminished. Back to Paul: "Now when they heard of the resurrection of the dead, some mocked. But others said, 'We will hear you again about this.' So Paul went out from their midst. But some men joined him and believed, among whom also were Dionysius the Areopagite and a woman named Damaris and others with them (Acts 17:32–34)."

What's clear here is that if you are going to be an apologist, you'll need to develop a thick skin. Evangelistic work is not for the weak. It is guaranteed that if you witness, you'll be rejected. Now, many do not like to be rejected. We all like to be accepted. But if you intend to witness to Jesus, you can expect some to reject the message. Rejection is a normal reaction to Jesus. Indeed, it is the *modus operandi* of the old Adam and Eve. It's what put Jesus on the cross. So you already know something about it. But more important is the fact that God's word yielded fruit. Dionysius and Damaris responded to the word. Again, the point is (1) God is calling you to be a witness, (2) God provides a model in Paul, and (3) that model includes an example of defending the faith. The upshot is: get those skills that Paul had to help you defend the faith.

A Lutheran Difference?

Can Lutheranism contribute to apologetics? I think so. Many evangelicals like to marshal as much evidence as possible to support the faith. I do not think that tactic should be avoided. But the Lutheran stance is more apt to unmask secular perspectives as inconsistent or deceptive. Luther was insistent that all people have a "god." This is because the core of being human is your "heart," and the nature of the heart is to trust in something. Genuine faith trusts in God alone and expects nothing but good from Him. But idolatry happens when one's heart looks not to God but instead to some created thing for one's security and good. Instead, one should look to God alone. Luther saw idolatry expressed in the cult of the saints, when people prayed to saints and not God for help. However, even when eschewing God, secularism is its own kind of faith—it has faith in human progress as its alternative to faith in Jesus. We need to drop a Dr. Phil on this perspective: you have a "god"—how is that working for you? Naturally, some are hardened and will not hear of the gospel. But as you read in Acts 17 previously, some will respond. We are too hesitant to ask.

Another way Lutherans can contribute to apologetics is through the theology of the cross. The theology of the cross suspects that people want to be able to bring some quality of their own before God and so earn His favor. That, of course, is the theology of glory. By contrast, the theology of the cross acknowledges that God is at work especially when sinners "utterly despair" of themselves. In no longer looking to one's own resources to secure status before God or whatever "higher power" sinners can muster, we can then actually start to trust in God's love given to us in Jesus. Lutherans believe that God is doing this work of killing off rebellious men and women precisely in order to end rebellion and so open these rebels to receive God's mercy and grace. The theology of the cross recognizes that when people are in a cul-de-sac of their own making, when their own resources fail them, and when they are trapped with "no exit"— and so their defenses go down—then they are receptive to God's mercy. People are not argued into the kingdom. They are open to God's grace when life done on their own terms and in their own ways no longer works.

Finally, Lutherans recognize that God is often hidden, not seen, and not apparent and that His mercy is not always clear. That's why we regularly need preachers to bring us Jesus and His goods of forgiveness, life, and salvation. Jacob wrestled with the hidden God when he wrestled with an unknown opponent in the night. His descendants wrestled with the hidden God when they were in slavery in Egypt and in exile in Babylon. Jesus wrestled with the hidden God when He asked why He was forsaken. Those who struggle with pain and evil in their lives often wrestle with God's hiddenness and wonder when His mercy and healing will appear. Such pain calls for lamentation and even complaint, as we see in the Psalter. Again, we cannot figure out why suffering happens to people who surely do not seem to deserve it. The only thing we can do is uphold them with God's promise that He will surely deliver His people who suffer. Many people critical of faith are in fact struggling with God as hidden, and we need to be pastorally sensitive to them.

Conclusion

In closing, how could we briefly respond to those seven objections to the faith at the beginning of this address? Let's take a moment to look at each. First, *Christians are hypocrites.* True. They are; in fact, everyone is a hypocrite to one degree or another. Thankfully, you have a Savior who gathers in honest hypocrites like you. Second, *Christianity is a crutch.* But be honest: all people need assistance. At times, life can be unbearable due to fear, guilt, and misfortune. You can be thankful you have a God who keeps His word to sustain you. Third, *the Bible and science are incompatible.* No. Just the opposite—science was birthed in Christian culture and the Bible can provide a context in which the scientific method makes sense. Fourth, *a loving God would never send anyone to hell.* In this life, God's love reaches out to deliver every sinner who trusts in Christ. Those who refuse it must deal with the consequences. So here's the word for you: in your baptism, God has claimed you and promised you a place in His many mansions. Fifth, *evil is incompatible with an all-powerful, all-loving God.* Christians concede that why innocent people suffer and why wicked people prosper in this life is beyond our comprehension. This is a matter that we must hand over into God's care with the conviction that God will manifest His justice and healing in eternity. You are not left to your own devices in facing brokenness and evil, but God has you and these matters well in hand. Sixth, *I'm not a sinner; I'm not so bad.* If you think you need to earn God's approval—better get at it. Let's see how long it takes before you crave God's mercy. If you know you are a sinner, you are exactly at the place where God gives you mercy. Finally, *there are many paths to God, and you need to choose the path that's right for you.* Whether now or later, you will realize that you are not the captain of your fate and that your choices in ultimate matters mean very little. Even worse, it was your rejection of Jesus that put Him on the cross. What counts is that God has chosen you in Jesus

Christ so you can enjoy the privilege of living as His child; so repent of your sin, turn to God, and trust in Christ.

God inspires pastors and others to reach out and plant new missions. God, who has imparted this desire, will support us and bring this mission to fruition. As we reach out, apologetics can be our friend. It can help us mature in our faith-walk and help us make the gospel clearer to people. It can help you challenge misunderstandings of the faith and, in so doing, permit faith to germinate in lives far beyond your church doors. May God give us not only the zeal to grow but also the wisdom to share the faith with integrity, maturity, wisdom, and conviction.

Ethics

CHAPTER 7

The Thomistic Turn in Evangelical Catholic Ethics

Although Robert Bellah and his colleagues' book *Habits of the Heart: Individualism and Commitment in American Life* appeared almost two decades ago, it continues to be as relevant today as when it first appeared. For instance, the attitudes of one of the most unforgettable people interviewed in the book, Sheila Larson, continue to typify the privacy, individualism, and diversity of current American religious outlooks. Sheila described her religion as "Sheilaism," "her own little voice," which tells her to love herself and be gentle with herself. As Sheila expressed it, "You know, I guess, take care of each other. I think He would want us to take care of each other."[1] Sheila's religious ethics seem to substantiate Alasdair MacIntyre's supposition that current American culture is embedded with "emotivism," the position that all moral judgments are nothing but the expressions of personal preference.[2] Even if people seek to appeal to an ethical system, such as deontology with its affirmation of human rights or utilitarianism with its standard of seeking the greatest good for the greatest number, as providing universal import, we still act as if emotivism were true.[3]

Sheilaism and the emotivism of which it is a species are a result of the "fact/value" split that limits reason to an instrumental function and ethics to subjectivism. The "fact/value" split guarantees that God does not interfere with how humans arrange their lives for their own personal happiness.[4] Indeed, modern—or more specifically, Kantian[5]—autonomy, in which persons seek rationally to accord their behaviors to a universal and necessary standard tested by practical reason, has now evolved into *autopoiesis*,[6] whereby one arbitrarily creates one's own values for oneself. However, a problematic dichotomy is assumed about reason here: rationality is configured via either antique Neoplatonic "participation" or modern "instrumentality." Lutherans, by contrast, will wish to maintain that when reason is not a whore, she is a servant. Nevertheless, if one were to evaluate Sheila Larson's *autopoiesis* in light of ancient heresies, it is clear that she is both antinomian and Gnostic. How is she antinomian? She is finally accountable only to herself for creatively generating her own values. "God" exists only to validate the correctness of her *autopoiesis* to herself. How is she Gnostic?[7] For Sheila, God and self are so closely linked that they are hard to separate. One surmises that Sheila would affirm that her innermost self is divine.

What is the church to make of such contemporary antinomianism and Gnosticism? The purpose of this essay is to examine critically one alternative paradigm, the "Thomistic Turn," in light of another, "Radical Lutheranism." Both propose an answer for how Lutherans ought to respond to contemporary antinomianism and Gnosticism. The Thomistic Turn posits that a responsible postmodern approach to antinomianism and Gnosticism requires, similar to the medievals, a reappropriation of God as the human *telos*, the highest and constitutive good by which we order our lives. Hence our freedom is not to be found in the contemporary *autopoiesis* of developing a personal value system but in the directing of our lives toward our highest good by means of achieving greater degrees of mimetic participation in God. Radical Lutheranism,[8] by contrast, posits that the only answer to the problem of antinomianism and Gnosticism is the reception of God's eschatological work in time, the creation of a new being whose identity is one with the story of Christ's and for whom the law is fulfilled by faith in Christ—the only way the law can be fulfilled—and not human potential. Christ as the *telos* (goal) and *finis* (cessation or suspension [abrogation]) of the law for the new person establishes the appropriate use and limit of law within the context of service. This paper will present the inner logic of both positions by means of examining their evaluations of human agency, moral order, the constitutive good, the role of Christ in the Christian life, and an appropriate Christian response to modernity.

The two positions will be tested with regard to confessional fidelity as well as systematic coherence with the truth claims implied by the gospel. To anticipate my conclusion: while the Thomistic Turn can raise the question of the need for Christians to articulate a common good for the earthly realm, Radical Lutheranism accords better both with the theological anthropology implied by the confessional tradition, which asserts a fundamental passivity of the human before God, and with a view of God who can be honored *only* by faith. The gospel limits the law to the concerns of this present age. The law is finally fulfilled by means of faith in Christ and not human potential. Radical Lutheranism is able to deliver the effective word that recreates a new being, while the Thomistic Turn does not secure the new life it promises.

The Thomistic Turn on the Relation between Freedom and Order

What is the Thomistic Turn?[9] In a word, it is the attempt to link freedom and order by means of a *telos*, God as the highest good, particularly as expressed in the Thomistic tradition. If Christians are to avoid the pervasive antinomianism and Gnosticism prevalent in our culture, then they must seek to order their lives on the basis of the Ten Commandments and unique practices of the catholic tradition as an embodiment or outgrowth of our participation in God as our *telos*, via grace. In this paper, the Thomistic Turn will be represented by the works of David Yeago[10] and Reinhard Hütter.[11] These men's theologies are marked by important differences.[12] Nevertheless, due to their commitment to seeing the Christian life primarily as participation in God by means of their appeals to Thomas Aquinas's (ca. 1225–74) thinking, they share many features in common with regard to ethics. Very likely, they would describe themselves as "Evangelical Catholics." Undoubtedly, there is more than one "Evangelical Catholic" position. Some Evangelical Catholics might have serious misgivings about the Thomistic Turn. However, one detects in Yeago's and Hütter's ethical thinkings the legacy of F. J. Stahl (1802–61), who argued that visible unity with the Roman Catholic Church is desirable for Protestantism in order for it to protect itself from the insinuations of modernity.[13] The Thomistic Turn could be summarized in Hütter's own words: we are to let all our desires be ordered by and fulfilled in the communion with God that begins by grasping Christ in faith. That is: "Instead of being governed by the unsatiability of our desires seeing fulfillment in finite goods, we become free to desire our ultimate good."[14]

Of course, there is more than one Thomas Aquinas, given his many interpreters post-Trent and by neo-Thomists. Hence we need to be specific: Whose Thomas? Which teleology?[15] These questions can be answered rather simply. If we examine the writings of Yeago and Hütter, it is clear that the Thomas appropriated by the Thomistic Turn is codified in the papal encyclical *Veritatis Splendor.* The encyclical appeals to Thomas's thinking with its insistence that genuine freedom is not an arbitrary exercise of specific individual wills but the choice to participate in the highest good by means of conforming our lives to that good by means of developing virtue and Christian practices.[16] When freedom and order are untethered from the *telos* of the highest good, "freedom" degenerates into arbitrary choice (perhaps for the sake of self-fulfillment, dominance, or pleasure) while order is seen to be likewise arbitrary as heteronomous, "repressive," or "oppressive." For some thinkers, such as the Anglo-Catholic John Milbank, such unyoking of freedom and order historically was begun in nominalism, codified in Protestantism, and perfected in Kantianism. Its ultimate outcome is nihilism or despair, since the *telos* of an objective highest good alone can provide a meaningful context for human action.[17] Both Yeago and Hütter respond to this purported devolution by disassociating Luther from Protestantism. Luther did not rediscover the gospel. It was never lost in the patristic and medieval churches. Rather, Luther shares an "Aristotelian realism" with Thomas: the human's *final cause* is God. Sin wounds our ability to reach this goal. Grace aids us in a pilgrimage toward becoming *comprehensors*, beholders of the beatific vision. The Reformation was a mistake due to political machinations. Modern Protestants fail to hear Luther's Aristotelian-Thomistic realism because neo-Kantianism has biased Luther-interpretation against it.[18] Thomistic Turners might agree with Ernst Troeltsch's (1865–1923) assessment with respect to the Ritschlians that Luther was thoroughly medieval and that Karl Holl (1866–1926) was wrong to "modernize" Luther, though they would, contra Troeltsch, affirm medieval ethics as an antidote to modern culture viruses.[19]

The key metaphor for the Christian life here is "participation."[20] One should develop one's potential as one grows toward God, the basis for one's happiness and eternal success. The church militant can aid this process by helping people focus on distinctive, countercultural practices,[21] such as fasting, devotions, and catechesis (Yeago), as well as holding forth the commandments as limits to the modern, "self-creating" self (Hütter). In this way, the church would have a "public effect"[22] on the extraecclesial world and not merely serve as a club that individuals use for personal reasons. One might wonder, however, whether from modernity's perspective, this move would simply transform the church into a selective club with tighter rules and higher admission standards.

More specifically, though, how is the Thomistic Turn faithful to Thomas? It emphasizes the following Thomistic themes: (1) Christian progress is a movement from vice to virtue; (2) love as the shape of faith is to be configured by caritas (*fides caritate formata*),[23] not *cupiditas*; (3) natural law orders nature to the eternal; (4) grace perfects nature and thus helps one in the journey as a viator; and (5) justification is primarily seen as inner renewal that can initiate and motivate love and only secondarily as forensic or imputative.[24] In essence, the Thomistic Turn parallels *Veritatis Splendor*'s view of teleology as the means to combine freedom and law in order to avoid contemporary antinomianism and Gnosticism. There are differences, of course, between *Veritatis Splendor* and the Thomistic Turn. The encyclical follows Ambrose's logic about the relation between Christ and the law. For Ambrose (339–97), the fullness of the law is in Christ (*plentitudo legis in Christo est*). Hence Christ Himself is the "new law" in person. Such claims generate a genuine Protestant reaction in Hütter, who affirms (1) that the law always accuses the sinner (similar to the *lex semper accusat* of the *Apology of the Augsburg Confession*), (2) that the designation *new law* as a term is to be understood analogously and not univocally when applied to Jesus Himself and, following Luther, (3) that Christ is not only an example (*exemplum*) but also a gift (*donum*).[25] Furthermore, for the Thomistic Turn, justification is not the result of a process, an evaluation of the moral agent, as it was for Thomas, but the initial inclusion into the household of faith. It follows, then, that sanctification is the growth in holiness within the moral subject.

For Yeago, Luther held that freedom and law should be combined, since Luther affirmed fundamental Aristotelian-Thomistic convictions. Yeago seeks to find a "Catholic Luther."[26] He notes that for Luther, God's mercy overcomes a moral order alienated from grace. Furthermore, grace sets the human heart "in order," permitting it to develop toward its true end. Indeed, Luther affirmed with Aristotle (384–22 BC) and Thomas that the human is defined by means of its "final causality" and not merely its "formal," as Mathias Flacius Illyricus (1520–75) maintained. This final causality was the original righteousness of Adam's nature. For Yeago's "Catholic Luther," the natural world on its own is not capable of reaching its intended *telos*. Only God's grace can heal the wound incurred by sin and elevate humans as pilgrims to achieve their true end. For Yeago, Luther is similar to the modern French Catholic thinker Henri de Lubac (1896–1991). Both affirmed that grace is not purely extrinsic (as forensic justification seemingly maintains) but participatory. Appealing to Luther's *Lectures on Genesis*, Yeago also discerns a positive appropriation of the law in the divine prohibition forbidding Adam and Eve to eat from the "Tree of the Knowledge of Good and Evil." Seemingly in opposition to many Lutheran views, the prohibition was neither to attain righteousness nor to accuse of sin but to give concrete, historical form to the divine life of the human deified by grace.[27] The law under sin is an external, prohibitive code. It loses its connection with grace. It is also abused as a means of self-justification. However, the "spiritually understood" law, though still an accuser, is a "paradise" for the believer. Nevertheless, Yeago's claim that Luther had an Aristotelian teleology needs to be carefully examined. Perhaps not too much should be made of Luther's discussion of original righteousness as a "divine drunkenness," because it could be read as an indirect accusation about human inability *post lapsum* to love God from the heart or grow toward God. Elsewhere in the *Lectures on Genesis*, Luther saw Aristotle's attempt to indicate the goal of human nature as purely hypothetical.[28] And in the "Disputation on Man" (1536), Luther charges that Aristotle does not truly know the final cause of humanity.[29]

In Yeago's thinking, if we are to correct the anomie and nihilism that pervade contemporary Western cultures, we need to move from talk of values to that of virtue.[30] Modernity—particularly in its Kantian guise—has alienated freedom, now understood as autonomy, from law. With a countermodern move, Yeago affirms that freedom and law need to be recombined by means of a *telos*, God as the highest good. This would enable humans to fulfill their potential and grow in grace toward deification,[31] thus giving them substantive and not merely formal or procedural good. Communities should then be able to flourish as embodiments of divine life as configured by social practices that form and transform human life. For the Thomistic Turn, the goal is to de-Kantianize Protestantism and re-Aristotelianize it. This move is deemed necessary because Kant's "rational" autonomy has been transmuted into Max Weber's (1864–1920) individualistic view of freedom as entailing a plurality of subjective, irrational ends.[32] As alleged nominalists, denying the participation of things in higher degrees of reality, Protestant thinkers easily adapted to Kantianism. The result of this move was to privatize faith as merely an existential experience within the self. Protestants mistakenly configure the gospel as a private, nonextended, momentary, experiential, existential flash or "dimensionless moment of encounter" with God that helps one cope with the world but not change it.[33] Privately, one experiences justification by faith alone.[34] Publicly, one lives an "autonomous" life and supports a state that endorses this view of *autopoiesis*. Hence for Yeago, Protestantism is inherently antinomian.

Seeking to avoid this problem, Hütter claims that we must (1) retrieve God's commandments as the shape of Christian life and virtue, (2) affirm the role of desire as the homing device that motivates and energizes us in our behaviors and allows us to be self-evaluative in light of our highest good, and (3) contend for natural law as the answer to legal positivism and relativism. The commandments can shape human life within specific communities by helping humans alter their perceptions of the world and desires, which allows them to become truly free by means of being drawn into God's own life. For the Thomistic Turn, the doctrine of justification is affirmed as the floor,[35] though not the hub, of all other doctrines. If all other doctrines were to be configured in terms of the doctrine of justification by faith alone, we would commit the "Protestant fallacy." This fallacy, which misunderstands justification by faith as primarily imputative and not unitive with God, leads to "Protestantism Lite," which prioritizes the accusing nature of the law at the expense of its ordering function. It offers freedom from law, not sin.

 For the Thomistic Turn, true freedom entails the ability to exercise one's potential to participate in the good. Virtue is enhanced by means of communal practices that help one be ordered to higher levels of participation in one's final *telos*. It is in clear opposition to a Kantian view of order that deems such a *telos* as heteronomous. In the Kantian scheme, one exercises one's freedom when one conforms one's will to a universal law that would be true for all rational agents. This deontological approach, rejecting reason as participating in a good construed teleologically, was not able to prevent reason from being understood as *solely* instrumental, typified in mathematics and the empirical sciences but not in ethics. Hence Max Weber's subjectivism with regard to human ends simply expresses the evacuation of reason from ethics when reason is reduced to an instrumental use alone.[36]

This analysis of Kantianism is relevant for understanding the current antinomian and Gnostic stances with which the Thomistic Turn charges Protestantism. Hütter especially claims that neo-Protestantism inscribed its own agenda into Kant's.[37] First, Kant is taken to claim that the externally encountered law is heteronomous. As such, it fails to help one develop habits that would promote virtue instead of vice, enabling one to order oneself toward better participation in God. Second, the gospel is described only in its external, imputative effect and not its internal transformation as motivating one to love God and thus helping lead one toward deification. Specifically, any *shape* to the new life in Christ is rejected. Hence the Protestantism Lite "gospel" only offers an ethics of motivation, not one that shapes our public lives. Indeed, it allows the "first" or civil use of the law to be eclipsed by the "need" to affirm people at any cost. Freedom, then, is defined apart from any gestalt, embodiment, or practice. Faith becomes a kind of gnosis. The Christian life permits doing anything you want as long as you help others. Hence this charge: To be radically Protestant is to be radically modern.[38] How? With neo-Protestantism, the original theocentric position of Christianity is now accommodated to an anthropocentric one. However, with the charges of heresy already on the table, one wonders how Yeago and Hütter can avoid a theology of merit. It is true that the Thomistic Turn, unlike Thomas himself, does not refer to merit. For Thomas, charity is the principle source of merit and, by means of divine grace, we can accrue the merit needed for deification. If Yeago and Hütter concede that there are degrees of participation within God, then how can the issue of merit be avoided? Would they see merit as compatible with the view of justification by "faith alone" that seemingly they are also attempting to maintain?[39]

Hütter lists the following sources that have permitted the Thomistic Turn to relate freedom and order by means of a *telos*, similar to the papal encyclical. He notes that (1) Karl Barth's (1886–1968) attempt to unify ethics and dogmatics by means of theological explications of the commandments, (2) the rediscovery of Aristotle and Thomas by Protestant and secular thinkers in recent decades as an alternative to modern ethics, and (3) the recontextualizing of the moral agent by liberationists and environmentalists have all contributed to his countermodern move.[40] Also, with regard to sources, Yeago notices that Lutheranism has been divided on the issue of using the law as a way to embody churchly practices. Hence Protestant heroes who counterculturally gave the church practices that embody catholic identity include Wilhelm Löhe (1808–72), Charles Porterfield Krauth (1823–83), Arthur Carl Piepkorn (1907–73), and Robert Jenson. However, others such as Immanuel Kant (1724–1804), Albrecht Ritschl (1822–89), Karl Holl, Paul Tillich (1883–1965), Rudolf Bultmann (1884–1976), Gerhard Ebeling, and Gerhard O. Forde have tended to interpret the gospel as centered in preaching that nurtures the inward life unconcerned with its public effect, an existential redemption that finally changes nothing in the world. Nevertheless, is the Thomistic Turn right in thinking that all these latter thinkers construe righteousness as solely imputative and/or indifferent to social structures? Ebeling, for instance, emphasized that participation is a fundamental category for understanding justification. Indeed, "*coram* relationships"—how someone exists in the sight of someone else—are central, he thinks, to understanding Luther's view of justification.[41] Furthermore, Ebeling noted that for Luther, forms and orders within creation help make earthly righteousness possible.[42] The Thomistic Turn looks to Risto Saarinen's view that the interpretation of Luther in German theology has been undertaken in a thoroughly neo-Kantian framework. Karl Holl's emphasis on Luther's faith as a "religion of conscience" certainly implied a view configured by such "internalization." Holl also framed justification in Kantian terms as an "analytical judgment" that encompasses God's analysis of the whole process and its successful completion because God knows one will become just, rather than a judgment that "synthesizes" what it declares.[43] However, the degree to which Luther-interpreters unearthed his eschatological approach to the gospel is the degree to which (post-) Kantian form/content and fact/value schemas have evaporated in their work.

Radical Lutheranism on the Relation between Freedom and Order

The crux of the disagreement between the Thomistic Turn and Radical Lutheranism on the relation between freedom and order is the role of justification by faith alone in theology. As noted, for the Thomistic Turn, justification by faith alone is a floor upon which all other doctrines can be built. However, their structures might be guided by a different plan than that of justification. For Radical Lutheranism, justification by faith is not the floor but the hub that centers and frames all other doctrines. Similar to the centrality that the Thomistic Turn gives "participation," justification in its forensic, imputative form has a central, all-encompassing focus. However, and this is crucial to the debate, if justification by faith alone is the hub for all Christian teachings and life, then the Christian life cannot be construed as one's progress toward one's own *telos* (even if it is alleged to be one's highest good) but conversely as the kingdom of God's progress toward us.[44] If that is the case, then virtue as the attempt to claim for oneself progress before God is as problematic, indeed, "sinful," as vice. Hence in direct opposition to the Neoplatonic and Augustinian traditions upon which the Thomistic Turn relies, there is no analogy or ontological continuum between humanity and the divine whatsoever whereby humanity can be initiated into a journey that would end in deification. Indeed, human quests for deification can be unmasked as power struggles with God over the issue of our inability to accept creatureliness. It is not our vice but God's judgment of us that makes us sinners. From the perspective of Radical Lutheranism, the Thomistic Turn, which assumes that a "positive synthesis"[45] between the law as an ordering mechanism and freedom as our self-ordering toward our highest good, is itself indicative of the human inability to accept God's gift of mercy. The human wants to claim ownership on the basis of one's efforts toward what is not properly one's own. Indeed, the human is bound to do this because of insecurity—the confrontation with one's own limitations (such as death) and the desire to secure oneself or achieve validity, recognition, even immortality—in the face of one's own finitude. The Thomistic Turn is a reaction against modernity via a postmodern turn to premodern ethics. Radical Lutheranism finds both the premodern quest for deification *before* God as well as the modern quest for a secular form of self-deification *apart from* God problematic. Hence Luther opposed not only the medieval thinking of Thomas on works but also the incipient protomodern thinking of the humanist Erasmus, who like Thomas wanted to reserve some agency or recognition for the human will before the divine.[46] For Luther, there is no free will *coram deo*, though there is choice *coram hominibus*. Since both medieval and modern perspectives wish to affirm human free will either *coram deo* (medieval) or autopoietically as a "god" (the modern "sacred self"), both are relativized with respect to each other vis-à-vis Luther's radical critique.

Radical Lutheranism's key metaphor for justification by faith is "death and resurrection." By this is meant that God's desire is to create new beings out of the death of sin and evil that humans inflict on themselves. For Luther, the real, actual death that can be experienced is that of baptism as unifying us with Christ's death and resurrection, not the death that we suffer at the end of our lives.[47] Hence discontinuity is more telling of our relation to God than continuity. Thomistic teleology then is undermined because human agency is not based on self-development *coram deo*. In opposition to the medieval perspective that one should develop oneself in and toward God and the modern perspective that one should develop oneself as an agent that promotes the right or the good, Radical Lutheranism responds that self-development in either mode is not

what the Christian life is about. Instead, it would affirm that the
old, self-centered being, whether as pious or "secularistic," has died
with Christ and likewise daily should be put to death so that a new
being can live in and from Christ as a servant. Agency, then, is not
centered in or on the self and is *not definitive of the self.* In radical antithesis to both antique and modern construals of the role of
human agency in ethics, Luther maintained that it is not good works
that make a person good, but a good person naturally does good
works.[48] One's being is defined not on the basis of what one does
or does not do (one's works) but from God's evaluation of the sinner in Christ Jesus. Human activity is grounded fundamentally in
passivity, the "categorical gift," as Oswald Bayer put it, in opposition
to the Kantian "categorical imperative."[49] God's forensic judgment
rendered temporally and publicly through His ambassadors, the
preachers, to sinners is one of neither "not guilty" nor "more or less
guilty" but rather "guilty but forgiven *for Christ's sake*"[50] and for the
sake of nothing else. How then might Radical Lutheranism interpret Sheila's behavior? Sheila's fundamental problem is not primarily
her disembodied existence from the church or the commandments.
Rather, her fundamental problem, the root of her individualism, is
her attempt to play her own "god" for herself, which Luther would
name as her *ambitio divinitatis*—her own self-affirmation as the
ultimate judge of the value of her life as based on her works.[51] Her
antinomianism is exposed as an "autonomianism"—where the self is
both a law and a "god" unto itself. Thereby, the nakedness of her sin
is all the more exposed.

The Thomistic Turn, of course, is worried that Radical
Lutheranism leads inescapably to contemporary libertinism or per-
missivism. However, Radical Lutheranism claims that it does just the
opposite. It proposes a view of the gospel that genuinely establishes
the law, apart from the human quest for self-improvement before
God or even as a "god." Against the Thomistic Turn, it charges that
if there is no end (*finis*) to the law, then humans inevitably will seek
to relativize it.[52] Indeed, modern atheism as the attempt to erase
away God as the legislator and judge of the world could be seen as a
way for some to relativize the law and attempt to bring it to its cessation.[53] For Radical Lutheranism, the law is fulfilled, ironically, by
faith alone and not action. Indeed, faith does what the law cannot

do and was never meant to do. It secures God's honor by means of a "solemn exchange."[54] Faith gives glory to God and thus honors the first commandment on its own terms by agreeing with God that His decision to justify the sinner *for Christ's sake* is just and appropriate. Faith also embraces a "happy exchange" that trades human sinfulness for Christ's righteousness. Sin is not properly understood as vice or misdeeds but rather one's being "turned in upon oneself." No amount of human effort can possibly allow one to get outside oneself. Only God's word entering the human from *without* can create faith *within* the human heart and permit the possibility of living spontaneously in loving service to the neighbor.

Freedom for Luther means to be freed *from* such incurvation and free spontaneously *for* service in and to the world and God. Radical Lutheranism posits that antinomianism is, finally, an impossibility.[55] The attempt to erase, discredit, or change laws will not secure the end of the law. To attempt to rid ourselves of the law apart from Christ will only guarantee that the law will come at us in another way.[56] Only Christ can end law, because Christ is the eschatological power that secures the new being in the world. With respect to Christ, the law is a "disciplinarian" (Gal. 3:24). When faith is gone, the self will arrogate to itself mastery of the law, often attempting to water it down in order to fool itself that it is doable. Hence neither the Aristotelian-Thomistic view of participation as progress toward our highest good nor Kantian autonomy now manifested as *autopoiesis* properly defines the human. Neither position has room for faith. Neither can decenter the subject. Faith, in Eberhard Jüngel's insightful definition, means allowing oneself to be given something, to become a receiver.[57] One is most fully human not in reaching one's alleged highest good but when one lets go of one's *ambitio divinitatis* (ambition to be God) and allows God to be for and to serve one. The old being is not able to produce what it needs. It needs a new self. God alone, however, can re-create a new being. Such re-creation is not to be understood in an existential sense as a way in which the self relates to the self, a new way of potentiating the self, as Bultmann saw it.[58] Rather, one's new self-in-Christ entails the end of one's autonomy altogether, for autonomy is simply a species of incurvation and not genuine freedom. The new being is construed not via self-relationship but through self-dispossession in the life of

God and the neighbor. How then is the Christian different from the non-Christian? What is the "public effect" of the gospel here? Luther maintained that in a vocation, one as a Christian simply lives not for oneself but for the neighbor[59] and that he or she has the Holy Spirit as a comfort in trial and affliction.[60] For the Thomistic Turn, this may not seem like much. However, the person curved outward with a "faith active in love" is fundamentally free *for* the well-being of the earth and its communities.

In Radical Lutheranism, the theological use of the law—God's accusation against our self-deifying ways—is ever present and central.[61] However, it is not the only function of the law. The law also has a civil use that entails God's *providential* ordering of the world for the world's well-being. The civil use of the law highlights God's care for the earth by means of social order. In this sense, it is a statement of what created life should naturally be.

> The gospel is the end of the law because and in the same way that the world to come is the end of this world. It is the end in the sense of goal or aim. The law ends because in the gospel its goal is reached. But this does not mean doing away with law by erasing or destroying it. Just as hope in the world to come, the true end, and goal of existence, does not compete with or destroy this world, so also the gospel does not compete with or destroy the law. Hope in the world to come creates the faith and patience to live in this world; it gives this world back to us by relieving us of the burden of our restless quests. Freedom from the world makes us free for it. Just so faith in the gospel does not despise the law or destroy it, rather it places the law for the first time on a solid basis. Because its goal is given, it is no longer our enemy. Because we need not fear it, we can begin to see its proper use.[62]

Faith then does not abrogate law for the old being. Rather, it puts law in its proper place for the new. It helps us see that the Sabbath was made for humanity and not humanity for the Sabbath, as the religiously self-justifying human has been prone to do. When Christ is the end (*finis*) of the law, then it cannot be misused. It is misused when we apply the law as a way to order our lives to the eternal (Thomistic Turn) or accord an ultimate significance or worth to ourselves apart from the biblical God (the modern). Rather, the law ought to be applied solely to this world alone, to curb *libido dominandi* (the lust for power) and thus provide space and time for all God's creatures *as creatures*. One message of the law for us is to serve our neighbors and not use them. Hence for Radical Lutheranism, theological anthropology ought to recognize that human nature cannot be fully expressed apart from honoring certain boundaries. The law helps set these. Its coercive use serves as a "backup plan," a way of preserving creation until the kingdom comes in its fullness. In the face of contemporary anomie, Radical Lutherans claim a public responsibility to raise questions about the common good. Indeed, it is appropriate to move from "values clarification" to talk of civic (not theological) virtues in public life.[63]

Hence the human is primarily a receiver before God. If that is the case, then rejecting Thomistic teleology is one aspect of helping rehumanize humanity. The gospel allows the human to be understood as a creature, a receiver, by affirming an ontological discontinuity between the human and the Creator, ruling out a path for the human as a viator to climb to God. Modern autonomy is likewise a form of *ambitio divinitatis* that feeds Promethean self-centeredness and self-aggrandizement. For Luther, good works accord with God's *providential* ordering in both the world and the church.[64] Both commandments and church practices can foster such providential ordering, which is to be rigorously distinguished from the Platonic-Augustinian-Thomistic envisioning of order as a path that takes humanity from beyond nature into supernature. In Radical Lutheranism, grace restores humans to nature; it does not elevate them beyond it. Sin is unnatural; grace liberates nature to be nature.

How then does Radical Lutheranism construe the relation between form and freedom? It certainly rejects how the modern way construes it. In the modern perspective, when order is increased, then freedom-as-autonomy decreases. For modernity, the self is sovereign. Radical Lutheranism also rejects the ancient and medieval perspectives. In the antique perspective, form orders freedom-as-self-development toward the *telos* of the highest good. Rather, for Radical Lutheranism, faith and faith alone brings form and freedom together. Christ (who is one with God's providential work), as the *form* of faith,[65] and freedom (the naturalness of the new being to do good) are one.[66] Christ, the form of faith, *is* freedom who

works in the baptized to do good for the neighbor in need. What
faith (not Platonic[67] or Neoplatonic philosophy) joins together, let
not modern autonomy put asunder! No amount of self-actualization
fulfills the law or honors God. Only when the self is displaced in faith
and Christ is centered in one's life through the daily reaffirmation
of baptism is God glorified and the law fulfilled. In the Christian
decentered self, the self is constituted by another, Christ, and constitutes one *for* others, the neighbor and the earth. Indeed, for Luther,
the believer's story becomes one with Christ's story, a "narrative
identity"[68] shared between the believer and Christ, since the believer
is "one cake" with Christ.[69]

It should be clear not only how un-Thomistic the Radical
Lutheran position is but also, counter to the charges of the Thomistic
Turn, how un-Kantian it is. The believer is not liberated from nature,
akin to the Kantian "transcendental ego" that is, by definition, with
respect to nature independent of it but for nature and even as nature.
Indeed, the turn to eschatology reframes ethics. The affirmation of
autonomy as an important goal of ethics is subverted by the eschatological death of the incurvated self. Furthermore, the sense that
one's identity is constituted by language in terms of story—Christ's
story as a re-enframing of one's own story as well as a proclamation
as a preformative, imputative word that likewise re-enframes one's
identity—subverts the Kantian supposition that "self" is logically
prior to or independent of language. The imputative word then cannot be psychologized. Preaching appears as a wholly "public" event
ex post facto one's conversion. Prior to conversion and even after
conversion, it is always "foolishness" (1 Cor. 1:18) to the old Adam or
Eve. Hence the imputative word is far better understood as a divine
cosmic word that embattles the external, very real forces of evil[70]
that would work *incognito* in and through the self-deceived, self-
legitimating human will and/or the "will of the people." As an embat-
tled life, the believer fighting forces both *within* (self-dispossessing
spirit against incurvated flesh) and *without* (self-giving spirit against
self-deifying world) invariably lives a cross-formed existence, wholly
unlike the continuum posited between the Neoplatonic-Aristotelian-
Thomistic *telos* and ourselves. The Christian life is best understood
in this regard not first of all or primarily as an ordering of our lives
to the commandments or church practices, a continuum from vice to

virtue, but instead as trusting God despite the appearances of divine indifference or threat that can be encountered in the world.

Two Positions Contrasted

Before proceeding to an assessment of the Thomistic Turn from a Lutheran perspective, it will be helpful briefly to summarize the differences with regard to ethics and modernity reflected in the two positions. For the Thomistic Turn, ethics should be construed teleologically, while for Radical Lutheranism, the Christian life should be understood on the basis of an eschatological word proleptically[71] pronounced in time that recreates a new being in Christ. The Thomistic Turn configures ethics eudaimonistically, while Radical Lutheranism posits an "extinguishing" of desire (concupiscence)[72] within the human, since desire is completely reconfigured through the lens of a gift. The first views the self as able to transcend itself via an infusion of divine grace, which helps order the self to a supernatural life and frees it from its tendency to be curved toward earthly things. The second views the self as hopelessly incurvated upon itself and needing a new being. The first affirms an "ascent" toward God by means of imitatively participating in greater divine harmonies until the highest good is reached. The second affirms a "descent" or incarnation[73] of the new being away from *ambitio divinitatis* toward the neighbor, one who is "a person like me."[74] The first emphasizes, along with realism, that things participate in God. The second emphasizes, not especially nominalistically,[75] that things are gifts from God. The first claims that freedom and law are held together by means of a *telos*. The second claims that the gospel alone limits the law, which can be fulfilled by faith alone and not human potential. The first assumes that the law can apply not only to this world but also to a journey to the world to come. The second claims that the gospel permits the law to be a this-worldly matter alone. The first prioritizes a transformative over a forensic approach to justification and bases the latter on the former. The second prioritizes a forensic (the imputative word) over an effective (the happy exchange) approach. The first believes that the church has a public effect by means of its practices or following the commandments. The second identifies the public effect of the gospel in helping people serve in their vocations for each other's well-being.

Since both positions are responding to issues raised by modernity with respect to the gospel, it is important to outline differences between them here too. The Thomistic Turn responds to antinomianism with the view that freedom and law should be combined by means of a *telos* so that modern individualism can be challenged. Radical Lutheranism suggests that antinomianism is, in essence, a charade. Humans are always in the process of being shaped, and such shapes are not meant for self-justification. Here, a Lutheran antiautopoietic stance is inherently anti-Gnostic: the self is created and not a divine creator. With respect then to individualism, the first is apt to affirm that one ought to find oneself within the *totus Christus*,[76] Christ as head and members of the body, diachronically extended within and as an institution of the Spirit. The second is apt to affirm that the church, by contrast, is a "creature of the word" and that it is the word that structures one's identity in the church. If the church is a *voluntary* society, it is not (in contrast to John Locke[77]) because one has chosen to join it but because God has chosen one to participate in it. In response to the pluralism of commitments that inevitably develops in the contemporary church construed in Weberian terms as having an irreducible plurality of values as defined by the conditions of individualism, the first seeks to reclaim a church authority and discipline, which it calls "catholic," while the second affirms that the church always depends on the proclamation of the radical gospel to those entangled in the law as their ordering *telos*. With regard to modern autonomy that puts God on the margins of society and tries to create a "secular" public space, the first responds that the church should be a counterculture defined, to use H. Richard Niebuhr's familiar categories, both as a (Catholic) "Christ above culture" and as a (sectarian) "Christ against culture." The second is apt to endorse the law as offering a "hermeneutics of suspicion" that decodes much of modern "secularism" as itself religious, bound to appeal to ultimate standards and religious symbolism to legitimate its authority, yet deceiving itself since the creature can never serve as its own creator.[78] The church can serve counterculturally to our current "culture of narcissism," but its focus should primarily be external, driven by mission. Hence for the first, the fundamental anthropological problem is defying one's true *telos*, while for the second it is *ambitio divinitatis*. Undoubtedly, Luther himself would fault modern individualism as hopelessly "Epicurean" (the sixteenth-century way, shall we say, of designating *autopoiesis*).

The Two Positions with Respect to Luther's Ethics

This evaluation of Luther's ethics will position four aspects of Luther's thinking relative to the two views that are both attempting to be faithful to his thought: (1) the *simul* doctrine, (2) teleology, (3) agency, and (4) service. Luther's view of justification by faith entails a *simul iustus et peccator* as *total* states of sin and righteousness, not the transition of one to the other. With this in mind, one can regard sanctification not as a goal but as the source of works. Indeed, the union with Christ expressed by means of the "happy exchange" is not progressive but total. With the metaphor of death and resurrection, the Christian life is best understood not as a *transitus* from vice to virtue but as one from virtue to grace. Indeed, since it is Christ who sets limits to the law for the sake of service to the neighbor, Luther can infer that the *telos* of the law entails, in a sense, its "suspension" for the believer. The law is relativized; it is not eternal. Luther indeed said that with the light of the gospel, one can have a love and delight in the commandments,[79] as would be expected given that Christ is the *finis* of the law. However, for the sake of the neighbor's well-being, Luther even advocated that the Christian might wish to develop "new decalogues"[80]—indicating the spontaneity of the new life in Christ. As "Christ to our neighbor,"[81] we share in and serve as God's providential outworking in creation, God's instruments or "channels"[82] in the world. As established by faith, the law now limited to this-worldly matters by the gospel can be seen as the gift of God, indeed, the best of all in the world.[83] Yet the law is understood not as the crux of our unique identity with respect to a non-Christian world but as a form of service to others.

Second, human teleology *coram deo* is eliminated in Luther's thinking. It is dismissed because God has already come to us. God as the "highest good" is not wholly foreign to Luther's thinking.[84] Yet we have been given our highest good in faith. Again, if this line of reasoning is correct, then the process of self-fulfillment is jeop-ardized. For Luther, the Christian is indeed a viator.[85] However, since we have received our *telos*, our highest good, in the imputative word, we are not especially going anywhere for ourselves. We need not journey up or out or beyond. Instead, each day is a new beginning, a rejourneying to the waters of baptism. Hence Luther maintained that "to achieve is always to begin again."[86] It is Christ who is the form of faith, not charity, as Thomas teaches. Luther's focus for the question of the essence of the human is not on our self-definition via our deeds but on God's working on and in us. For Luther, justi-fication by faith is itself the definition of the human.[87] With respect to human nature, our being as defined by God has ontological priority over our doing. Thus Luther contended that "we are the simple material for the future life"[88] upon which God is crafting us. Human freedom, then, is to accord with God's providential work-ing within nature. God preserves order for human well-being within creation by means of various stations or vocations, the *status ecclesi-asticus*, the *status oeconomicus*, and the *status politicus*, which like-wise serve as God's "masks" within creation.[89] The ethos of faith, if we can speak in such a way, is to humanize us. Humans find (and not establish) their good not as a result of a process of self-development but instead by means of living outside themselves in and for the neighbor.

Luther's antiteleological focus makes all ethical talk suspicious, at least to some degree. Ethics, as an expression of the old being, all too often is how people attempt to justify their behavior. Indeed, in the modern world, ethical systems such as Marxism, consumeristic capitalism, and various socialisms are often construed soteriologi-cally, as ways by which a utopia can be promulgated.[90] The "free-doms" that these systems attempt to establish are often purchased by much human blood. In this light, "freedom" is an overused word in the modern world, open to much misinterpretation. Even Eberhard Jüngel overstated or perhaps misstated the relation between the Reformation and modern autonomy, in contradiction to his many other writings on theological anthropology, when he suggested that there is a road between the Christian freedom proclaimed in Reformation Wittenberg and modern freedom proclaimed in revo-lutionary Paris.[91] As Gustaf Wingren pointed out, the quest for nirvana, an authentic existence, or a classless society are contemporary attempts to achieve life's meaning, when in fact this is already given in and by the gospel.[92] Luther's thinking relativizes both medieval and modern views. The medieval is allegedly theocentric and the modern anthropocentric, but both affirm and assume that one's identity is established by means of self-actualization, either toward God or toward developing human potential for its own sake. For Luther, the medieval view is not especially theocentric if it is unable to honor God for His own sake. It is, in Augustinian terms, not genuinely enjoying God but merely using God. Luther recognized that Augustine's (354–430) theological method is not capable of achieving Augustine's intended goal. To enjoy (*frui*) God, all talk of merit must cease. Hence our alleged "highest good" might simply be an idol of our own projection. Also, the modern view does not prove to be as godless as it might initially appear. Modernity is permeated with ultimate goods and secular gods, which are likewise idols.

Third, in Luther's thinking—and this is in sharp contrast with most of Western thought either ancient or modern—humans are primarily to be understood not as agents but as receivers. God's action to claim humans in His word becomes definitive of human reality. If humans' real problem is incurvation, then no amount of human agency, even religiously motivated agency, can liberate the human. However, the human self as such is not properly to be understood as a self-realizing agent—even in action we are utterly passive, that upon which another acts.[93] Hence for Luther, the bond between good works and self-realization is severed. This creates the reversal between the relation of being and doing, as noted earlier. Hence Christ *does all* in us and our works are to be understood as "fruit."[94] It is God who perfects faith in us, not ourselves. Or, stronger than this, faith *does all* (*fac totus*).[95] Luther can also speak of human cooperation (*cooperatio*) with God. However, we cooperate in the sense that a servant can use his limbs to fulfill his master's wishes.[96] Receptivity, not Platonic or Neoplatonic teleological agency, is the key that unlocks human nature. Hence theology, for Luther, is, unlike Whitehead's view of philosophy—*not* a series of footnotes to Plato.

Finally, with regard to service, Paul Althaus (1888–1966) was on target to infer that for Luther, faith lives in works just as works are done in faith.[97] Indeed, Luther's apocalypticism permitted him to discern that God's kingdom was not in human hands but that service in the this-worldly kingdom was. Hence his response that he would plant a tree if he knew Christ was returning tomorrow indicates the power of the gospel to help incurvated humans accept their responsibility with regard to the rest of creation. Christ is the Good Samaritan who has bound our wounds. From this perspective, Luther affirmed the Golden Rule[98] and charity as virtues[99] (as formed by faith [Christ]). In Christ we can understand that our neighbors (in contrast to the later Hobbesian view) are not "wolves" but people very similar to ourselves.[100] Furthermore, far from a quietistic and passive spirit, Christians might be called to challenge the political "powers that be." Christian service operates in social structures framed by "natural law," which is not a mimesis of "eternal law" but instead cultural forms or social structures by which human life is providentially shaped. In our current context, which frames duties toward the neighbor in terms of rights, Carl Braaten in the early 1980s appropriately inferred that justice is the form that love takes in society. To love neighbors includes the will to be concerned with their basic rights.[101] In light of the concerns raised here with regard to Luther's ethics, it would seem at every point that Luther harmonizes better with Radical Lutheranism and not the Thomistic Turn. Luther directs us to receptivity and (not "participatory" activity), a faith that unleashes love (and not love as the form of faith), an incarnational descent for service (and not a deifying ascent that perfects us), and a teleology in which God reaches us (and not in which we reach God).

Preaching as the Primary Public Mission of the Church

At a fundamental level, might the question about the gospel's "public effect" imply an "ethicization" of the church; that is, an attempt to justify the church to the world before the bar of ethics? In contrast, the church, for Radical Lutheranism, is first of all accountable to God. Her accountability before Him ought to be based on fidelity to the gospel, which has been entrusted to her by the risen Lord and for which she has been empowered by the Holy Spirit. However, the Thomistic Turn's tendency to "ethicize" the church deeply reflects a modern outlook on the validity of the church's ministry. Modern theology has sought its relevance by making itself into a sophisticated theory that encyclopedically encompasses all knowledge (Hegel) or focusing on religious feelings as the clue to religion's validity (Schleiermacher) or offering practices that can help the world become an idyllic, tolerant "kingdom of ends" (Kant).[102] Thomistic Turners are, in this respect, perhaps more modern and Kantian than they would like to admit. Their focus is often toward justifying faith before the world on the basis of distinctive, life-enhancing practices. For modernity, salvation has been recast into secular terms as political and utopian, often a Keynesian "postmillennialism" or a Marxist "premillennialism."[103] Modern "salvation" is not above the world, as it is for medieval thinkers. Nor is it in the divinely ordained world to come, as it is for Luther. Instead, in a wholly secularized though no less Pelagian fashion, it is an outgrowth of human *poiesis* that ought to achieve the material abundance that will eventually eradicate the poverty that allegedly leads to human evil. Or, it will be achieved by means of a tolerance that embraces all libertine forms of behavior (provided "no harm" to others is incurred), a view that affirms the "sacred" nature of the individual exercising his or her choice. While the Thomistic Turn rejects the godless utopias of modernity, it is entwined with modernity's obsession with the value of human potential. It rejects the goals, but does it, with its drive for a "public effect" for the gospel, reject the means of modernity, especially since it—minimizing human passivity and receptivity—construes the public largely, if not solely, as a realm of activity geared toward an agent's self-improvement, albeit by means of a *telos*-fulfilling *poiesis*?

One must wonder: how much stock does the Thomistic Turn invest in proclamation, if the alleged public/private split can only be overcome by means of an ethicization of the church? Is not the preacher God's *public* ambassador, a crucial voice of God's in the world? Practices are important and should not be neglected. However, this concern is not due to the fact that practices help us participate in the divine as we share in God's *reditus*. Rather, it is because practices are forms of tradition that help to order human life within God's providential care. Reappropriation of Aristotle, such as the quest for a common good, may be helpful for ethical matters in this world, but he has no voice in matters of the world-to-come.

The word of proclamation, the primary public mission of the church, makes it clear that if there is a "growth" or progress to the Christian life, it would be that we are to become *more* human—living more and more by faith as we daily face challenges. Under the conditions of *ambitio divinitatis*, we are "less human." Sin makes us become out of touch with our nature. Our nature is to be creaturely. Faith in God helps us to accept and foster our creatureliness, including through service to the neighbor. Justification by faith counters Athanasius's (ca. 296–373) claim that God became human so that we might become divine. Rather, we should say that God became human so that we might become more human, specifically by means of trusting in God's deity as appropriate for God and our humanity as appropriate for ourselves. If we wish to overcome antinomianism, then we cannot evade the deadly effects of the law. The only way to affirm the law is to allow the gospel to limit it to the affairs of this life. If we wish to overcome Gnosticism, then we must allow the autonomous "sacred self" to die daily in remembrance of baptismal waters so that a new self, formed in and by Christ, can rise in joyful love of God and eager service to the neighbor.

CHAPTER 8

The Mystical-Political Luther
and Public Theology

Cynthia Moe-Lobeda, similar to her mentor Larry Rasmussen,[1] has attempted to claim Luther for the liberal Protestant agenda.[2] Her claims need to be challenged because, as the ELCA (Evangelical Lutheran Church in America) continues to move more toward liberal Protestantism, theologies similar to hers are taken too seriously and to the exclusion of a more faithful reading of Luther. For the sake of developing a "public theology" that fosters a specific political agenda, she seeks a resource for moral regeneration from Luther's doctrine of justification by faith alone. The chief article, in her view, should be seen as enhancing a moral-spiritual power that can enable us to free people from global capitalism's violation of self-governance. Her move, however, violates the fundamental law-gospel distinction that is at the core of the doctrine of justification—thus the reason for this paper.

Moe-Lobeda evaluates theology not in terms of its ability to help deliver the gospel but in terms of its ability to foster a worldwide political community that promotes human rights and a sustainable economy.[3] Her goals are noble. However, her perception easily falls prey to Jean-François Lyotard's postmodern critique of the "metanarrative of emancipation" as a form for legitimating academic inquiry in modern society.[4] The metanarrative of emancipation tells us that the most fundamental story of humanity should be one of progressive liberation. Hence the academic vocation for theologians is to help individuals further their autonomous self-governance. For

Moe-Lobeda, the villain that thwarts this freedom is globalization,[5] or global capitalism. Globalization, at this point in history, is inevitable. For Moe-Lobeda, it is unambiguously negative. It is not clear that she is right. While globalization, like all human enterprises, has a mixed ethical track record, Jeffrey D. Sachs indicates examples where globalization is actually helping to raise the living standard of many people worldwide.[6]

Moe-Lobeda notes that global capitalism reconfigures all life, threatening "life systems, cultural integrity and diversity, and the poor for the sake of exorbitant consumption and accumulation of wealth."[7] Likewise, such conspicuous consumption disables moral agency: we acquiesce to global economic arrangements that make us exploit others and the earth. For Moe-Lobeda, democracy—people's self-governance—is subordinated to unaccountable economic power, ideologies of domination, and the commodification of life.

Moe-Lobeda seeks a "public" theology "open and accessible to all"[8] so that it might promote social well-being, prioritizing the needs of the most vulnerable, and support ecological sustainability. From her perspective, theological systems that pit personal, private, or existential matters against social, public, or ethically transformative concerns are quietistic and should be rejected: "We tend to claim the comfort of justification by faith alone, while eschewing its ethical implications. We may cling fervently with good reason to justification, while not acknowledging its consequences for how all aspects of life are lived. Lutheranism in the North Atlantic world has leaned toward disconnecting salvation from its impact on public life."[9] The doctrine of justification must now be so configured that its social, economic, and ecological emancipatory implications are utilized. (Is the doctrine of justification in fact moldable to our desires?) To be public, a theology, for Moe-Lobeda as for Marx, ought to change the world and not merely interpret the world.

In order to draw out the emancipatory implications of justification by faith alone, she appeals to Tuomo Mannermaa's approach to effective justification, the role of Christ in the believer's life.[10] For Mannermaa, forensic justification, the forgiveness of sins for Jesus' sake, is based on and grounded in effective justification, which in his view is Christ's union with the believer, a mystical presence. Moe-Lobeda sees this mystically present Christ as motivating us to political action, toward a mystical-political ethos. In her view, morality is the primary way in which our humanity is expressed. In other words, we are at heart agents, not receivers. Christ's *inhabitatio* should motivate and direct believers' ethical engagement with others. Believers' actions, then, ought to accord with the metanarrative of emancipation, especially from the violence of global capitalism.

The context of the phrase "in faith itself Christ is present" (*in ipse fide Christus adest*) in the "Lectures on Galatians" (1535), so important for Mannermaa's interpretation of Luther's view of justification by faith, is the question of comfort for the conscience terrorized by the law.[11] When laid low by the law, Luther urges that we "take hold" of Christ in faith.[12] Luther contends that God is so *for us* (imputation) that He becomes *one with us* (impartation) in the marriage of Christ to the conscience. Moe-Lobeda fails to understand the context of Mannermaa's thinking, which was done for the sake of ecumenical rapprochement with Orthodox Christians and in opposition to the liberal (Kantian-based) Protestant heritage, which figures so prominently for her. A result of her reading of Mannermaa, though, is to reject the ethical viability of the traditional Lutheran "two kingdoms" teaching: that God rules the political arena through the law with His "left hand" and the human conscience through the gospel with His "right hand." In her view, this teaching aids and abets ethical passivity and is no longer serviceable for conscientious Lutherans.[13]

For the *Formula of Concord*, Luther's affirmation of the indwelling Christ, what Lutheran orthodoxy would call the *unio mystica*,[14] is consequent to the imputation of Christ's righteousness.[15] If one contends that it is God's acknowledgment of Christ as already present in the believer's heart that effectuates justification as imputation, we end up with a view similar to the *intuitu fidei* approach to justification as it was understood by its nineteenth-century North American defenders.[16]

Moe-Lobeda worries that a forensic approach to justification is intertwined with current privatizations of faith, neutralizing the prophetic critique of unjust social structures implicit in biblical faith.[17] We need to keep in mind, however, that construing faith as interlocked with the conscience, as with Luther, was never intended to disassociate faith from public life. Indeed, Luther's view of faith ever led him to challenge publicly those abuses that arose from the enmeshment between church and state in medieval society, in which bishops sought to be princes and princes sought to be bishops. Similar to Luther, the original purpose of freedom of religion, for thinkers like James Madison (1751–1836), was not intended to make religion a private matter. Rather, it was to limit the state's suppression of the freedom of conscience, particularly for religious minorities like Quakers.[18]

Many factors have contributed to the privatization of religion in the modern world: (1) the rise of capitalism, which believes that the "hidden hand" of the market will itself providentially order self-interest, the most fundamental human drive, for the well-being of all, apart from governing our lives by a teleology that specifically seeks a common good (ultimately grounded in God);[19] (2) the growth of research universities, which have construed science as objective and public while seeing life's meaning as subjective and private;[20] (3) the supposition that the self at its core is self-creating (*autopoietic*) and that one ought to be as free as one wishes, provided no harm is done to others; and (4) the perception that when religion is construed as private, then there will be greater religious tolerance in a time of increasing pluralism. In spite of this, culture remains permeated with religious symbolism, even in "secular" Europe. Privatization simply means that Christianity's claims on public life are eclipsed supposedly for the sake of tolerating a diversity of religious perspectives. The upshot is that the public agendas of what had been Christendom are curtailed. In the metanarrative of emancipation, particularly as it has molded Moe-Lobeda, the academy does not generate knowledge for its own sake, advocated by those (like Stephen Hawking) seeking a grand unified theory of reality, but for the emancipation of the self from artificial, constrictive structures of dominance so that all people can exercise the self-governance to which they are entitled as rational, self-interested agents. To the degree that this perspective survives, the Enlightenment religion is in place.

In light of modernity's ubiquitous assumptions in politics and economics, we can appreciate Moe-Lobeda's helpful exposé of the following fundamental capitalistic beliefs as inherently emplotted or mythic: (1) economic growth benefits all; (2) freedom is market freedom; (3) we are at heart economic, consuming, and dominating;

and (4) corporate-driven globalization is inevitable.[21] Economics is not a pure science. It is, as Lyotard would remind us, plotted within its own story of emancipation, which includes the following features: the ideal world of self-governance and continuing scientific and technological progress is impeded by crime; crime is due to poverty; and poverty will be relieved, indeed, overcome, through either the laissez-faire trickling down of wealth (political right) or transfer payments from the rich to the poor (political left).[22] However, Moe-Lobeda fails to similarly demythologize the metanarrative of emancipation, which seems to have a nonnegotiable status for her. The result of her uncritical stance toward the metanarrative of emancipation entails that she never tests whether autonomy as such accords with the doctrine of justification.

That theology is in fact and will continue to be public, in spite of many current suppositions to the contrary, is borne out in actual theologies, whether they lean toward either the political right or left. For those on the political left (such as Moe-Lobeda), theology should be public by challenging unjust economic structures and honoring private decisions of individuals. For those on the political right, theology should be public by having a hands-off policy with respect to the economy and by promoting the nuclear family.[23] Neither position is fair to those who see a libertine economy as a challenge to strong family structures. Theology, whether we like it or not, will continue to be public as long as people appeal to some higher power or idol by which to justify their behaviors, particularly with respect to the legitimation of war, the limitation of individual rights, or the threat of capital punishment. An implication of the doctrine of justification *sola fide* is to evaluate the truth of such public or civil theologies in light of law and gospel.[24]

Again, we face a perennial problem: who sets the agenda for the church? It would seem that the answer for many Christians continues to be the world—from the utopian perspectives of either the political right or left. In truth, the risen Jesus Christ has given His church a mandate that is both necessary *and sufficient* for the church's mission (Matt. 28:18–20).

A New, Unstable Ethical Synthesis

The doctrine of justification is the teaching by which not only *the church* stands or falls but also *the entire world*, since it is the world (and not only the church) that is objectively acquitted in the saving work of Jesus Christ.[25] The doctrine of justification is, however, reconfigured within Moe-Lobeda's perspective. All intellectual and moral endeavors should help promote emancipation, akin to the ideals of the French Revolution (liberty, equality, fraternity), for all humans in tandem with ecologically sustainable practices. Since (in her own mind) she represents a minority voice objecting to globalization, advocating a "Christ against culture" approach, to use H. Richard Niebuhr's helpful typology, it is hoped that eventually such protest will issue in a "Christ transforming culture,"[26] a kind of politically left third use of the law.[27]

As noted, the quest to frame theological ethics within the metanarrative of emancipation is a long-standing strategy by which to accommodate Christian theology with modern culture, and it can be seen in various Kantian-inspired theologies. The desire to accommodate Lutheran ethics to these specific agendas has resulted in various ethical positions, many of them at the core of contemporary theological education in mainline Protestant seminaries. Moe-Lobeda's approach is unique in that while it is largely deontological, in which the dignity of agents is to be honored above all, she applies the indwelling Christ as the moral power and motivation to help us accomplish these lofty goals. Christ becomes Moses, and the beams of the cross become the tables of the Decalogue.

Clearly a major problem with all ethical reasoning is that knowing the good does not necessarily entail doing the good. Although acknowledging radical evil, Kantians are apt to think that ought implies can. But as Moe-Lobeda points out, the global economic system trumps the goodness of moral discernment and intention. Moral humans are enmeshed in an immoral society that is at cross-purposes with moral intentionality.

Moe-Lobeda thinks that if we are to subvert the demonic hold of globalization, then we need to combine a virtually medieval mystical view of *gratia infusa*, which had been integral to the Augustinian and Thomistic viator ethos, in which one as a pilgrim is ever developing the potential to imitate Christ in faith, hope, and love, with the modern deontological concern for the rights of the underprivileged for their own self-governance. Such mysticism lends itself not only to emancipatory politics but also to pantheist metaphysics.[28] Luther's acknowledgment of God's threatening or comforting proximity—God as masked in all things—is garnered again for ethics: the creation itself as the habitation of God bears deontological weight. Hence we must treat everything in creation comparably to how we would honor God. Here the creation as God's address loses its significance as interwoven signs of communication—as providential sustenance and order, pointed accusation, terrifying hiddenness, or promissory comfort—rendering us receptive to God's good gifts. Instead, it, too, feeds our role as ever-active agents on the playing field of responsibility. Our agenda, as the arms and legs of Christ, is to heal the world (not a small task!). Union with Christ empowers us to be ethical. And to be ethical is to take a stand against "globalization." Mysticism is the fuel of Christian political life; emancipatory politics is the social manifestation that such mysticism must take.

The traditional two kingdoms doctrine inhibits this emancipatory transformation. Its attributing God's governance as either through political and social orders or through the gospel works hand in glove with a world that wants to render the former as public and the latter as private. For Moe-Lobeda, in contradistinction to seeing the gospel solely as a word of promise, rather than as directives for living, we must relocate and base ethics in the cross, resurrection, and living presence of Christ. (The cross becomes an ethical theology of glory!) Hence the law-gospel distinction, so treasured in Lutheran preaching, pastoral care, and worldview, is undermined here. God has not two words—one of requirement and one of promise—but one. Similar to Barth, surprisingly, for Moe-Lobeda, the law is the form of the gospel and the gospel is the content of the law.[29] For Moe-Lobeda, the confessional Lutheran approach of distinguishing law and gospel lends itself to political quietism, and the moral exigencies of our time should not tolerate such passivity.

Moe-Lobeda's synthesis of *gratia infusa* with the indwelling Christ as the moral-spiritual fuel for emancipatory social and economic transformation is inherently unstable. Luther employed the concept of union with Christ as language taken from the "bridal mysticism" of medieval monasticism.[30] He framed it, however, largely in nonteleological terms. This is because the verdict of the Last Judgment is not awaited by the Christian. It is spoken in the words of absolution. But when Moe-Lobeda attempts to appropriate Luther's view of the indwelling Christ, as mediated by Mannermaa, the language of bridal mysticism is returned back to the medieval teleology that Luther and the Confessors rejected. In this teleology, grace is infused so that we might be led to our ultimate goal, the beatific vision of God as the true, beautiful, and good.

By the same token, Moe-Lobeda tries to meld her inherently teleological approach to union with Christ with a deontological view of ethics, which is concerned not for the development of our potentiality toward deification but for honoring our recipients and ourselves as ends in themselves. In contrast to the medieval view, the self here is not subordinated to the ultimate good of the beatific vision, which would by definition be heteronomous. In contrast to such eudaimonism, the dignity of one's ability to govern oneself by means of the categorical imperative, seeking a "universal law of nature," is a good in and of itself.

Moe-Lobeda's view of infused grace, the *inhabitatio dei*, is not readily isolated from the teleological framework in which it was formed and that forms it: that the Christian life is a movement from the earthly to the heavenly, the temporal to the eternal, the sinful to the virtuous. That ethical perspective runs counter to the very different viewpoint of the deontology at the core of her work, which advocates an ethics of claims, rights, entitlements, and redress for the powerless so that the fundamental equality between all peoples and their rights to self-governance are honored.

However, that concern is only an indicator of wider concerns. It is never clear, for Moe-Lobeda, with what ethical system we are dealing: utilitarian, deontological, or responsibility ethics. Reading between the lines, we are tempted to think that she affirms the "no harm" principle of rule utilitarianism in private life, a rigorous deontology with respect to issues of minorities and a responsibility ethic with respect to the environment. Here, too, her ethical thinking becomes unstable. It is not clear if there is an inherent dignity to the individual (which presumably she affirms) or if all behavior is to be evaluated in terms of producing overall happiness or the least amount of pain.

Moe-Lobeda surprisingly fails to tap a rich resource for countering globalization run amok: does global capitalism help foster the social health of families or rather undermine them? It would seem that global capitalism is just as pleased to see families split up if that should create more (short-term) wealth, and thus it can be quite indifferent to the well-being of families. However, the emotional stability of families is an indicator of the well-being of children.[31] Strong economies will seek strong families.

Many Lutheran theologians have noted that the two kingdoms doctrine protects us from making politics salvific and making salvation political. If we do the latter, we take the penultimate—the good order and social health of the political realm—and give it an ultimate status. Such a move does violence to the eschatological dimension to the gospel, since the kingdom of God is at hand and not in hand (Mark 1:14–15). Faith will not be transformed into sight (2 Cor. 5:7). The Christian task is not to heal the world but to bear witness to that power that is the balm of healing for the world (Rom. 1:16–17). If current economic theories are couched in false doctrine, our calling must be to challenge them.

Moe-Lobeda is right to expose violence inflicted upon the peoples of the world and the environment that results from greed. In that regard, it is not only the death that God finds in the violence that we inflict on others but also the death that God works, in that through such a rejection of God, God's world, and our neighbors, God sentences us to death.[32] And in Luther's view, it is not only our evil that God kills but also our goodness.[33] We are wholly receptive *coram deo*. As such, we can be wholly active *coram mundo*. As citizens, we ought indeed to seek to bring as much sanity and wholeness as we can to a world bent on self-destruction. All the while, however, we need to acknowledge that this is God's world, to do with as He pleases, and not ours.

Try as much as we will, we cannot step outside of the history through which God crafts our identities intertwined with all other creatures, with a plan for action to thoroughly diagnose and solve the world's ills. There is no devisable blueprint that will garner a just or perfect world order. Instead, we can work for and anticipate "traces" of justice and be grateful for them when they happen.[34] Additionally, we as church leaders need to strengthen the church, through whose ministry the well-being of creation is restored and that will survive numerous empires within the vicissitudes of historical fortune.

In a sense, Moe-Lobeda's ethics is a kind of theodicy, a defense of God for the cultured despisers of religion. Clearly life is unfair (as it has always been since the fall). Is God also unfair? In light of that core anxiety, one response is that we must aim to make the world as fair as possible in order thereby to make God credible or real. Expressed differently, she offers what Gerhard Forde called a "negative theology of glory," in which the one good work we think we can offer God is our compassion for or solidarity with victims.[35]

In history, we quickly encounter God's backside—the *deus absconditus*. And that God will never be made credible. In view of what Luther called the light of nature, we will never understand why the good suffer and the evil prosper. That is why we look to the light of grace, in which God graciously forgives sins. By that light, we will never understand why God saves so few and damns so many. For that reason, we look to the light of glory, when we shall see God face to face and know God even as we are known by Him.[36]

At heart, Moe-Lobeda reframes the doctrine of forensic justification into a mystical-political view because she wants to secure an anthropology that accentuates the human potential for an ideal social world community, a vision clearly articulated by the Kantian legacy of a "kingdom of ends."[37] For her, the human is by definition *homo semper agens*, not from the first or primarily a receiver. The great anthropological insight of the Reformation is that the human is most fundamentally ascertained not with the question "What should I do?" but instead "What have I received; what is given to me?"[38]

Luther on Economics

Luther, of course, was no economist. The discipline as such did not exist in the Renaissance. However, Luther is too quickly dismissed as hopelessly naïve when it comes to economics. We need to keep in mind that Luther stood at a unique point in Western economic history, the crossroads between feudalism and modern capitalism.

Moe-Lobeda is helpful to point out that Luther's views of economics do not fit hand in glove with global capitalism.[39] However, Luther is not so naïve as to think that, as the new being contends with the old, dreams of a utopia on earth, either communist or capitalist, are possible. Economic transactions remain penultimate, not ultimate, matters. Although dead in Christ, the old being still daily rears its head, thwarting perfect social relations. Nor does the gospel, as a word of promise, offer directives for establishing a perfect social order. It rather restores us to creation as God intends it.

For Luther, property is a gift of God to be used not for self-gain but for the well-being of the neighbor.[40] We have no absolute right to property, to do with it as we wish. We are stewards of creation; God is the owner. For oneself alone, one is not entitled to anything. Our relation to material goods is to be deciphered through their ability to help us further the well-being of our neighbor. Note well how different Luther's views are from modern ethics. Unlike Jeremy Bentham (1748–1832) or John Stuart Mill (1806–73), he offers no utilitarian calculation of overall pleasure and pain for all sentient beings. Nor does he, with Kant (1724–1804), advocate honoring the autonomy of one's self and one's recipient. However, he is just as different from medieval perspectives: the poor are not willed by God so that through charity to them, the rich could be saved or achieve a higher status in the afterlife.[41] As Carter Lindberg has helpfully noted, this medieval assumption is completely discredited by the Reformation view of law and gospel. Saved by grace alone, no such quest for atonement is effective. Hence the existence of poverty can no longer be legitimated in that way. In economic transactions, instead, we must honor our neighbor's well-being, as we are all simultaneously lords and servants within the network of all created life. Self-interest as the sole economic motivator is a description of the desires of human nature as distorted by sin.

Most importantly, for Luther, no economic system can save. All too often, capitalistic views of economics are crafted within the framework of a mythical postmillennialism in which the trickling down of wealth, along with education, will eventually eradicate the poverty that lends itself to social discord, sin, and violence. Similarly, communist views of economics are scripted within a mythical premillennialism. The outcome of the conflict between the proletariat and the bourgeois will be a classless society in which all wealth will be shared, eradicating likewise the poverty that lends itself to sin.[42] With Luther we must concur: the gospel alone saves; no economics will ever be able to create heaven on earth. Life has always been hard work for humans and will continue to be so in the future, regardless of the economic system. At its best, economics provides a venue through which the Christian lives his or her calling, in service to neighbors and creation.

Following Luther, we should question the view that any one economic system is somehow more compatible with Christianity. Decades ago, J. Michael Reu and Paul Buehring were quite right to contend that Christianity does not favor any particular economic system but opposes moral wrongs that may develop under any economic system.[43] As noted earlier, we are never sufficiently outside our economic histories, like a mechanic is outside an automobile, such that we can fix or perfect them. No economic system can save us from sin; in fact, any economic system can provide a viable and often safe haven for sin to flourish. This will always be the case until Christ returns in judgment and glory. Christianity has survived feudalistic, capitalistic, and socialistic economies, with all their benefits, opportunities, and evils. The fact, however, that our ultimate loyalty should be to Christ and the Christian faith in no way implies indifference on our part to economic matters. We seek an economics that serves people, in opposition to all economic systems that seek people to serve them.

With respect to the globalization that Moe-Lobeda seeks to counter, Luther foresaw its dangers. Carter Lindberg contends that Luther was concerned not merely about an individual's use of money but also about the structural social damage inherent in the idolatry of the "laws" of the market. Ideas of an impersonal market and autonomous laws of economics were abhorrent to Luther because he saw them as both idolatrous and socially destructive. He saw the entire community endangered by the financial owner of a few great economic centers. The rising world economy was already beginning to suck up urban and local economies and threatening to create an as yet unheard of opposition between rich and poor.[44]

For Luther, the three major abuses of capitalism are (1) the lawless fixing of prices, (2) the loaning of money at unfair rates of interest, and (3) the giving of security on a loan for someone else, which would place yourself and your family in jeopardy.[45] Luther agreed that wealth, as in the case of Abraham, does not affect one's relationship with God.[46] However, one must recognize that one is "a transitory figure on the stage of life" and that one's goods do not belong to one personally. Hence Luther could be quite free (even flippant) with respect to finances. One "must loan money to those in need without charging interest, give freely without thought of his own advantage, aid in a systematic method of taking care of the poor in the community."[47]

For Luther, our relation with our neighbor is constitutive of our own life. Employing the metaphor of "play," it is not the case, at least ontologically, that we play alongside one another as opposed to playing with one another. Rather, we are constituted relationally. If we assert an isolationism for ourselves, we are out of touch with our beings, which are beings-in-relationship—with God primarily, with others, and all created things. It is through worship as God's service to us (*Gottesdienst*) that we are enlivened to serve and help others. As Lindberg notes, "For Luther, in the Eucharist, the union between the believer and Christ renders union between believer and neighbor. Those unions engender community ontologically oriented around addressing people's needs—including material needs."[48]

While Moe-Lobeda inaccurately configures the relation between forensic and effective justification, she does bring to the fore some aspects of Luther's views of economics, so free from the self-justifying, obsessive goals of current economics to establish security and status through wealth. However, counter to Moe-Lobeda, who sees economics as salvific, Luther actually provides what a "secular" approach to economics ought to be, since economic transactions have no status whatsoever with respect to salvation, whether that salvation be construed as the beatific vision (medieval) or an economic/educational heaven on earth (modern). That truth relativizes both medieval and modern views with respect to each other. In contrast to the assumption that whatever you work, you own, Luther contends that all things are gifts—including our own abilities to labor. Only when all life is lived in fear, love, and trust in God can life be free of the tyranny of the idolatry that worships and serves the creature rather than the Creator (Rom. 1:25). As Wilhelm

Mauer notes, "Economic planning must be determined by trust in God; otherwise the taking of surety, for example, arrogantly replaces divine governance."[49]

Two Kingdoms Revisited

As is well known, Luther contended that the Christian lives in two realms: a secular, temporal, or civil realm and a spiritual one.[50] The former, for Luther, is not to be disparaged. Luther wrote, "Worldly government is a glorious ordinance and splendid gift of God, who has instituted and established it and will have it maintained as something men cannot do without. If there were no worldly government, one man could not stand before another; each would necessarily devour the other, as irrational beasts devour one another."[51] Through the spiritual kingdom, God provides saving grace. Through the secular kingdom, God provides a space for human life to flourish.

Given the extensive literature that the doctrine of the two kingdoms has generated in light of the German church conflict in the 1930s and recent social and environmental concerns that have called for thoughtful Christian deliberation,[52] one hesitates to discuss it. However, examining the two kingdoms is unavoidable, since Moe-Lobeda contends that the two kingdoms doctrine garners ethical quietism. It is hard for Lutheranism to divest itself of the old canard that it (Lutheranism) "is the Protestant way of despairing of the world and of claiming victory for the religious ideal without engaging the world in combat."[53] The charge of Lutheran quietism has been led especially by Reinhold Niebuhr (1892–1971) and Ernst Troeltsch (1865–1923).[54] In their view, justification by faith comforts the anxious conscience but leaves the world in the hands of the devil.

There are marked similarities between Troeltsch's and Moe-Lobeda's critiques of the two kingdoms. Troeltsch sees a fivefold indifference to the world in Luther's theology.[55] Culturally, Luther remained within the medieval socioreligious synthesis of the *Corpus Christianum*, demanding a uniformity of beliefs from all those living within a Lutheran territory. Biblically, Luther made the Sermon on the Mount, emphasizing revolutionary discipleship, subservient to the Decalogue, with its upholding of conventional social order, as the basis for social ethics. Ethically, Luther's two kingdoms view sanctions a double-standard morality for Christians: private morality should be governed by the "absolute" natural law of love, while public morality should be guided merely by the "relative" natural law of justice. Politically, Luther limited the power of Christian faith and love to the realm of inner, personal experience and disposition, thereby leaving society at large free to act as an autonomous law unto itself. This proved to be historically disastrous when combined with Luther's refusal to sanction the personal right of Christians to engage in political revolution. Finally, the Lutheran church has made no real effort in social transformation at all. All matters of legislation and social welfare are left to the state.

These critiques are hardly novel. They reproduce *Schwärmer* objections already raised in Luther's own lifetime. They are not plausible. With respect to the first criticism, it is hard to imagine the role of freedom of conscience in the modern world apart from Luther and his numerous heroic stands. Second, interpreting the Sermon on the Mount as a code for Christian discipleship already assumes that the law is the form of the gospel, and vice versa. Third, Luther is in fact quite sensitive that we all do not share the same callings. Some are called to radical discipleship, and others are called to rear families. (Luther himself, it seems, was called to do both.) Luther's genius is not that he offers a new blueprint for social reform but that all blueprints are questionable. His realism acknowledges the plurality of ways and means through which God is creating and providentially upholding the world. Fourth, "inner" and "outer" for Luther are to be configured not as private versus public but instead as the conscience seen as either free or bound with respect to its public vocation. When the conscience is free with respect to securing the self from attack, the public person is then free for the well-being of others and not merely to use others in a kind of "higher hedonism."[56] More to the point, when the gospel is at stake, we are called to resist government authorities. Finally, what constitutes social transformation is bound to be configured in terms of either capitalist or socialist assumptions. While democracy was most immediately given birth to in colonial North America during the Calvinist-inspired Enlightenment, it is hard to image this development apart from Luther's Reformation, in which, for the sake of the gospel, Luther was willing to challenge any ecclesial or political authority.[57] This by no means affirms a direct trajectory between the Reformation and the Enlightenment. It is only to assert that the freedom of conscience for which Luther fought eventually took root.

It is simply not true that the two kingdoms view lends itself to social passivity. And it is a teaching that guarantees that the gospel be heard not as a directive or a description or a desire but as a promise. Indeed, the two kingdoms theory was, at its origin, quite radical. As John Witte reminds us, it rejected traditional hierarchical theories of being, authority, and society. Note well, Luther did not reject a chain of being in the world. However, the network of interrelationships is horizontal, not hierarchical, as it had been construed in Neoplatonic thinking and the Middle Ages: "Before God, all persons and all institutions in the earthly kingdom were by nature equal."[58] For Luther, as Heinrich Bornkamm noted, the medieval perspective hopelessly confused the Augustinian acknowledgment of two cities, the earthly and the heavenly. This resulted in a twofold perversion of government power: the bishops wanted to rule outwardly, and the princes wanted to exercise a spiritual rule.[59] For medieval people, church and state were inseparably intertwined with detrimental consequences to the conscience. While the church did indeed serve as a political counterpoint to the state, it did so through politics similar to that of the state and thus failed to provide a genuine alternative to the state. Most importantly, the two kingdoms doctrine honors the distinction between law and gospel, which in fact challenges the attempt to divorce the realms of sacred and secular from each other. All life is sacred for Luther, even as the church's mission is decisively a worldly affair. The church's mandate is to proclaim the gospel. If it is made into an agent in God's kingdom of the left, the gospel is changed into law and the law into gospel, thus promoting a "dangerous monism."[60]

Monism is "dangerous," as the rioting peasants found out in 1525, when the eschatological promise is made into a temporal reality, the peace of God turned into submission to theocratic rule, the result of which "can only be tyranny, disillusionment and, ultimately, death. In unadorned Lutheran terms, this world cannot be ruled by the gospel. It must be ruled by the political use of God's law through the exercise of human power and reason. And the end of law is not salvation, but justice."[61] John R. Stumme summed it up well: "The doctrine of the two kingdoms is necessary to safeguard the eschatological and soteriological reality made present for us in the gift of faith in the gospel of Jesus Christ. Just as one makes the distinction between law and gospel in order that the gospel will be heard as gospel, so also one underlines the duality of the two kingdoms so that the kingdom of Christ will be that kingdom where Christ alone reigns."[62] In a word, government exists because the old sinner, while crucified, remains to some degree or another in all. With spirited optimism, Luther claimed that if all were Christians, there would be no need of secular government.[63] But obviously all are not Christians.

True, Luther feared social chaos. Who doesn't? However, he feared legal coercion even more, since he was a specific victim of that crime. Against the peasants, Luther felt that to compel reform undermined preaching and transformed the gospel into law: "Ministry in the kingdom of Christ, then, is always focused on proclamation, not coercion."[64] It is noteworthy that in principle, Luther supported many of the peasants' demands. However: "When they resorted to violence, when they set out to kill the lord and ransack their estates, they rebelled against a divinely established order which existed 'since the beginning of the world,' and thus Luther opposed their tactics."[65]

Following the mantra "for the healing of the world," Moe-Lobeda tends to soterioligize politics and politicize soteriology, giving people a false hope of an ideal community and depriving them of the absolution that could open them to moral activism on behalf not of self-growth but of the neighbor's needs.

Public Church, Public Theology

In our day, it is hard to separate the criteria for something to be public from Enlightenment standards for truth. The Enlightenment seeks standards of truth that garner universality and are independent of authorities and specific cultures or traditions. It has always favored "clear and distinct" ideas, always appealing to mathematics not as symbolic thinking but as measurement.[66] Indeed, the modern world has been one of continuous cartography: mapping hemispheres, genomes, consumer tastes, the brain, and whatnot.[67] Knowledge is power (*Ipsa Scientia Potestas Est*).[68] The metanarrative of emancipation, in which Moe-Lobeda does theology, is one such Enlightenment view.

However, there is a sense, of late, where power is knowledge.[69] That is, those in authority set the criteria for truth and justice. Whether or not this is a truthful approach to life, it seems to be increasingly an accurate perception of how the world actually operates. We can learn as much from Jean-François Lyotard, who from his postmodern perspective sees modernity as an escape from narrative for a metanarrative by which to legitimate social power. With his and others' critiques of modernity, it would seem that modernity is going out not with a bang but with a whimper. Most specifically, Lyotard analyzes two modern forms of legitimation within the academy, which he believes are no longer plausible. First is the quest for a grand unified theory of everything, which honors knowledge for its own sake. The paradigmatic work here is Hegel's *System der Logik*. The second, which we see operative in Moe-Lobeda, is the narrative of emancipation: "The principle of the movement animating the people is not the self-legitimation of knowledge, but the self-grounding of freedom or, if preferred, its self-management . . . its epic is the story of emancipation from everything that prevents it from governing itself. It is assumed that the laws it makes for itself are just, not because they conform to some outside nature, but because the legislators are, constitutionally, the very citizens who are subject to the laws."[70] With respect to the academy, this view implies that "knowledge has no final legitimacy outside of serving the goals envisioned by the practical subject, the autonomous collectivity."[71]

Of course, the freedom of conscience that Luther sought at Worms was echoed, albeit imperfectly, in both the quest of American democracy, asserting the right to self-governance, and the goal of the French Revolution, seeking independence from all traditional political and ecclesiastical hierarchies. However, Luther's primary concern, even in his opposition to the papacy, was not to liberate Europe from oppressive forms of religious control. It was, rather, to challenge the church and the world with the idea that the gospel is found as a promise for Jesus' sake. All Luther's reform hinged upon that truth. It was certainly not to create a *saeculum*, a public arena of human creativity independent of God's evaluation. Just the opposite. For Luther, the public arena is the arena of God's creative activity. Not only the gospel but also the law cannot do its work when law and gospel are conflated, as happens when the two kingdoms distinction is not honored.

Helpfully, Reinhard Hütter notes that "the ironic result . . . of a 'political theology' that attempts to 'politicize' the church can only and unavoidably deepen the church's irrelevance and undermine the church's public (political) nature by submitting and reconditioning the church according to the *saeculum*'s understanding of itself as the ultimate and normative public."[72] Similarly, George Lindbeck notes that liberals start with experience, with an account of the present, and then adjust their vision of the kingdom of God accordingly, while postliberals are in principle committed to doing the reverse.[73] The former, he claims, make it easier to accommodate to either the political left or the political right. In an increasingly postmodern milieu, the need or desire for such accommodation seems less plausible. The church offers the world the most when it offers the world something that the world cannot generate of itself: the promise. The world indeed offers gospels aplenty, all false. The gospel that God raises the dead—indeed *only* the dead—and that God's fidelity to this promise is validated in the resurrection of Jesus Christ is nothing that the world can generate of itself.

In the Middle Ages, the public space was defined through a Christian Neoplatonic teleology in which all goods were to be ordered toward the *telos* of the true, beautiful, and good. In the modern world, the public space has been defined in terms of perceived self-interest and/or survival. As the world becomes smaller, more global, it is increasingly difficult to determine the nature of the public space. We experience it as an agora of ideologies and insecurities, a menu of conflicting options. Into such an environment, we are called to share both law and promise. Not the least of which must be the church's mission to question all mythological legitimations of social order and freedom—innovation.

One option is to see the church itself as a polis by analogy. Such separatism, advocated by Hauerwasians and "radically orthodox," is attractive—we could escape from the violence and silliness of the world once and for all. This has ever been the monastic and

Schwärmer ideal. It is very hard to maintain the paradox of *in* the world and not *of* the world when it appears that the barbarians are not merely at the walls but within the city itself.[74] More to the point, the church in and of itself is hidden, not visible to the world.[75]

Despite the church's de jure hiddenness, as an assembly of people, it is sustained through the word. This word, as both law and promise, opens a horizon of communication—particularly as interpretation of Scripture—not only diachronically across the ages, as the church has reflected on Scripture, but also synchronically, as we listen and speak to others within the household of faith. The church does have a public voice. How is that public voice to be understood? Here the work of Hannah Arendt (1906–75) may help us. Arendt notes that a public is not constituted by an undefined, essentially open space for the very reason that a general openness in all directions destroys the public.[76] For Arendt, the public is a human sphere of coactivity constituted and defined by its surrounding borders and by the standards determining it. The public has a specific *telos* and laws as preconditions for its character. More specifically, it is defined by four features: (1) a specific *telos*; (2) mutually binding principles expressed in distinct practices, laws, and doctrines; (3) a movable locale; and (4) the phenomenon of freedom. The church, by these standards, constitutes a public. First, her *telos* is sharing the promise with those with whom she is in fellowship and with those outside her membership. Second, she is bound to teachings grounded in Holy Scripture and witnessed to in the confessions, through which she prays and on which she reflects across the generations and cultures. Third, she is nomadic in the sense that she is directed by the Holy Spirit: she is led to move into unsafe turf in the world for the sake of fulfilling Jesus' mandate. And finally, as a community of communication,[77] she shares in a gospel-generated freedom, since her members are liberated from the fear that leads to incurvation, the blight that stymies all genuine communication.

Does the church move forward into wider publics—in spite of the rejection of the metanarratives of emancipation or knowledge for its own sake? The church moves within a world of many publics and even social oppression and chaos; we do not need a perfect world before the goods of forgiveness of sins, life, and salvation can be delivered. If delivering these goods were at the forefront of our work, synod assemblies would be marked less by the quest for social activism and more by developing strategies for evangelization. (What empirical evidence is there that resolutions from synod assemblies actually alter the moral fabric of society?)

Conclusion

As humans, we need to work for a world not mired by those evils specific to global capitalization. As Christians, we would want a world that honors others' dignity and freedom—as grounded not in a metanarrative of emancipation but simply in our creedal affirmation of God as the Creator. Moe-Lobeda's rejection of globalization is often naïve and uncritical. The results of globalization in reality are neither 100 percent good nor 100 percent bad but mixed, as is all of life since the fall. It is not likely we can step outside of history to fix history. But neither should we assume that we are the fated puppets of our own machinations for power and control.

The church brings no greater mission to this milieu than that of confession: Jesus Christ is Lord. As Lutherans, we must affirm that the "chief article and foundation of the gospel is that before you take Christ as an example, you recognize and accept Him as a gift, as a present that God has given you and that is your own."[78] And we must also ensure that "the essential task of Christian doctrine" (*summa totus Christianae doctrinae*) remains wrestling with the proper distinction between law and gospel.[79] While Moe-Lobeda helpfully brings a major concern of our age to our attention, she fails to bring the best of the Lutheran tradition to bear upon the world.

CHAPTER 9

Discipleship in Lutheran Perspective

Discipleship has once again become an important topic for Lutherans. In worship Lutherans sing of the desire to follow Jesus: "Let Us Ever Walk with Jesus" or, more recently, "I Want to Walk as a Child of the Light," to cite just two hymn titles that bear the theme. In assemblies and publications of all kinds, Lutherans are taught techniques for effective discipleship. Congregations devote staff to help their members connect faith with daily life. Current approaches to discipleship tend to run along one or the other of two tracks. One type copies the neorevivalist tactics of North American evangelicals. It anchors discipleship in a unique experience of God in worship and serves then as the basis for specific practices that move "nominal" members of the church into more disciplined lives of faith. The other, far more prevalent, approach mimics the mainline Protestant "social gospel." It conceives discipleship in terms of progressive social agendas, sees "moral deliberation" as the dominant purpose of congregational life, and views the public witness of the church primarily in terms of social and political action. This essay critiques both approaches and proposes in their place an understanding of discipleship grounded in the classical Lutheran distinction between law and gospel. Accordingly, discipleship is pictured as a matter of death and new life.

God uses the law to reduce sinners to nothingness and the gospel to create new beings in Christ. In this light, discipleship is more properly viewed as something God does to believers, rather than something that believers do for God or for the world. The law/gospel approach to Christian life resists reducing discipleship to acquired techniques. Instead, it views discipleship in terms of Christians faithfully living out their vocations as baptized children of God. Through the preaching of God's law/gospel word, believers are created and formed to live by trusting God's promise to be God and by loving the neighbor in service of creation's well-being.

Critique of the Recent Approaches to Discipleship

Both contemporary types of discipleship are apologetic in the technical theological sense of the term. The first responds to modern secularization by accommodating the secular conviction that faith does not interfere with public life but is properly located in the privacy of experience. Practices are fostered in order to help sustain such "God experiences" deep within the pious. The fundamental attitude with respect to religion in the modern world has been to make it a private, interior matter, and the first type concedes to this tendency. The second seeks to justify the legitimacy of faith through its ability to effectuate ethical change in the world, particularly on behalf of the powerless and voiceless. An important aspect of modernity—challenged in light of world wars, genocide, and abuse of the environment—is social progress, the quest to establish an ideal community in which class divisions will have disappeared. Both socialists and (perhaps surprisingly) many capitalists have sought such an ideal community—albeit through different, competing economic strategies.[1]

In contrast to the prevailing approaches to discipleship, the Lutheran tradition is more ambitious, more radical. It speaks to the heart of personal and public sin. The aim is not to reform immoral humanity or immoral society but to announce the death of sinners. Sinners, along with the old order, are passing away. The Christian gospel declares God's promise to bring forth a new creation in Christ. The Lutheran tradition continues to approach discipleship in the tradition of Isaiah and Jeremiah's confidence in the power of the word of God alone to make disciples (see Isa. 55, Jer. 18 and 31, and Rom. 9:20ff.). The church can make the most difference in the world when it tends to the word. It tends to the word in catechesis and proclamation. The church is most authentic when it makes truth claims that deal with ultimate matters in distinction from penultimate matters. Its critique of society is always to unmask idolatry in the public realm for the sake of a truthful relationship with God. In addition, it moves Christians and others to speak up on behalf of the oppressed in the wider public. As a "creature of the gospel," the church is sustained by God's grace. Its mission is to administer, freely, this grace to sinners who are in no position to reciprocate with merit. The church offers a genuine alternative community to a politics prone to idolatry and an economics prone to greed. Its uniqueness is found not primarily as an alternative ethical community. Rather, it is a community established through the word, a recipient of grace given in the proclaimed gospel and administered in the sacraments. Its life is grounded in God's truth and generosity; its mission consists of sharing this truth and generosity with others.[2] Christians continue to be *in* the world (as God's good creation), yet not *of* the world (in rebellion against God). Offering no excuse for "quietism," they trust that ultimately God will rectify injustices in His left-hand rule. Discipleship happens best when peoples' horizons are situated and discerned through the variegated and manifold lens of Scripture and guided by properly distinguishing law from gospel. In this essay, I will first examine Luther's view of discipleship, then critique the two schools of discipleship mentioned previously, and close with a brief elaboration on the alternative suggested here.

Luther's View of Discipleship

Some historians contend that for Luther, discipleship was a superfluous notion. In their view, the concept of discipleship adds nothing to ethical reflection that is not already present in Luther's view of the two kingdoms. According to the two kingdoms outlook, God is working in the political community, God's "left hand," to maintain social order and stability, in which humans can grow and thrive. This kingdom is distinctively a realm of law and justice, an aspect of God's ongoing creativity. The purpose of authorities, among other things, is to curb violence so that life can flourish. It is to be distinguished from God's "right hand," in which God offers the means of grace, forgiveness of sins, and new life.[3] For these historians, then, discipleship, conceived as a student's mimetic following of Jesus as a teacher and role model, offers nothing that cannot already be discerned from the ethical reflection available in God's left hand. Discipleship in this view distorts the nature of Christian ethics and establishes a hierarchical self-righteousness.

Additionally, if discipleship implies self-improvement, moving from sinfulness to righteousness, it is incompatible with Luther's central affirmation that we are ever simultaneously righteous and sinful. Discipleship that conceives the Christian life as continuous growth via learning through trial and error is an inappropriate category to apply to Luther's theology.[4] There is no progress to speak of in the Christian life but instead, as Gilbert Meilaender, critiquing Werner Elert, expressed it decades ago, only a continuous oscillation between the accusing law and the comforting gospel.[5]

There is no question that these critiques of discipleship touch on important aspects of Luther's approach to the Christian life. Since the initial impetus for Luther's approach to reformation was his critique of Gabriel Biel's view that God gives His grace only to those who do their very best, all approaches that see the Christian life as one of progressive, or upward, growth must undergo critique. Luther rejected both medieval Roman Catholic approaches to spirituality and renewal movements initiated by reformation groups. Specifically, Luther's critique was leveled against traditional medieval Catholicism, which advocated a two-tiered approach to faith comprising (1) those who led a distinctive, and superior, "religious life" by following the "evangelical counsels" that included poverty, chastity, and obedience and (2) those ordinary Christians who simply lived their callings in the world.[6] Later, Luther's appraisal was directed against the Anabaptists, who envisioned discipleship as offering an alternative ethical community wholly defined by nonviolence. The upshot of Luther's critique was, as is often noted, an affirmation of ordinary life. Imitation of Christ is expressed not by living a unique, "holy" life, antithetical to the world, but by one living as a "little Christ" right *within* the world, in the specific vocation that God gives.[7]

Carter Lindberg points out Luther's objection to the two-tiered approach to Christian living. Luther observed that it was inherently self-righteous to claim that some Christians, through their self-sacrificial behaviors, are superior to others.[8] Lindberg explains that Luther's breakthrough was based on "the discovery that God's righteousness is a gift, not a demand" and that this "displaces the principle of likeness by that of unlikeness as the basis for fellowship with God. The sinner does not ascend to God; rather, God descends to the sinner." Luther's use of biblical "bride-bridegroom" imagery contrasts sharply with the way that other medieval thinkers saw it. For them, the bride needed purification. For Luther, as brides of Christ, believers are "poor, wicked harlot[s]." Luther reinforces this metaphor with that of "testament" as a monergistic, unilateral giving action of God, a promise: "There is nothing which the sinner can bring to God in order to attain forgiveness—except his or her sin! It is only the ungodly, only the sinner, who is acceptable to God. Paradoxically, to acknowledge sin is to justify God and thereby oneself. 'Real sin,' not likeness to God, is the presupposition for justification."[9] Justification by faith alone allows God to be in charge of the sinner's salvation—allows God to be God, while simultaneously allowing the human to be human. We are one and the same, sinner and saint. It follows that discipleship does not involve growth in holiness as traditional Catholicism with its evangelical counsels or as the Anabaptist and spiritual movements have taught.

Luther clearly was skeptical of the human ability to contribute to our growth in the Christian life. He saw that the nature of the old Adam and Eve is always to exploit programs designed to improve the lot of nominal Christians. The old Adam and Eve appropriate such techniques in service of do-it-yourself righteousness. Luther approaches the question of discipleship more soberly and more realistically. In the tradition of Augustine, he sees that self-righteousness constitutes the core of our sin. This does not mean that Luther lacks a positive outlook on discipleship. His positive teaching about discipleship can best be seen in his reinterpretation of Augustine's view that Christ is both *sacramentum* and *exemplum*.[10] But Christ as example is only understood from Luther's dictum: "It is not the imitation that makes sons; it is sonship that makes imitators." As he states in his 1519 "Commentary on Galatians" (Gal. 3:14),

> This faith, I say, was promised in the blessing. Here again, therefore, he [Paul] touches briefly and obscurely on the fact that the Gentiles will be children of Abraham, not because they will imitate him, but because they have received the promise; and that they will imitate him because they will be his children as a result of God's promise and its fulfillment, not as a result of the deeds and the imitating of the Gentiles. It is not the imitation that makes sons; it is sonship that makes imitators.[11]

Christ as a sacrament means that He is a sheer gift. But as a sheer gift, He is also the end of our self-righteousness, and thus we as sinners die with Him in His death. But we also share with Him in His resurrection and walk in the newness of life. It is because we are adopted children of God that we can imitate Christ, not vice versa. Christ as our example, understood in this way, precludes self-righteousness. Christ is not our example in the inherently self-righteous, two-tiered approach to Christian life seen in the evangelical counsels or its reinstatement among the so-called radical reformers. Instead, Christ is our example as we live lives of service to others in the various offices that we hold in relation to others.

Helpfully, Oswald Bayer notes that in Luther's view of ethics, the "table of household duties" is balanced with the concept of "imitative discipleship." The household duties ground ethics in the stuff of lived experience, while imitative discipleship provides the criteria by which to evaluate how we proceed in such duties.[12] If imitative discipleship alone were to reign in the Christian life, untethered from the daily obligations of household duties, Christian faith would tilt toward perfectionistic or utopian leanings. By contrast, if the household duties alone were taken into account apart from imitative discipleship, there would be no distinctively Christian standard by which to evaluate problem solving in life. While, for Luther, we follow the example of Christ, that does not make us Christian. What makes us Christian is nothing other than God's favor granted to sinners. It is God's external word that renews the inner person. And this word is distinguished not by its ability to empower us to do good works but instead in that it grants the freedom to do them—when and where they are needed.

And this word proclaimed in preaching or the sacrament grants us a new identity and a shared life not only with Christ but with those in need. Commenting on the fellowship deriving from the Lord's Supper, Luther indicates that

> Christ with all saints, by his love, takes upon himself our form [Phil. 2:7], fights with us against sin, death, and all evil. This enkindles in us such love that we take on his form, rely upon his righteousness, life, and blessedness. And through the interchange of his blessings and our misfortunes, we become one loaf, one bread, one body, one drink, and have all things in common. . . . Again through this same love, we are to be changed and to make the infirmities of all other Christians our own; we are to take upon ourselves their form and their necessity, and all the good that is within our power we are to make theirs, that they may profit from it. That is real fellowship, and that is the true significance of this sacrament.[13]

Bernhard Lohse notes that Christ as *sacramentum* and *exemplum* was not a holdover from Luther's early pre-Reformation theology but instead a theme by which he understood the Christian ethos throughout his life: "What is important here is that discipleship consists precisely in 'offering oneself to the cross,' not in supplementing the sacramental appropriation of salvation through one's own works. At this important point, Luther not only had adopted central ideas from Augustine, but very early had given them precision in his own way."[14] We offer ourselves to the cross not in that our suffering saves us. Rather, Luther has a realistic conception of life and alerts us to the reality of conflict and suffering. It is guaranteed that following Christ in the world will garner opposition from the world. To be true to God will provoke opposition from the adversary, who is operative in *both* the world and the church (and not just the world). Just as one dimension of Christ's suffering was that of being a faithful witness, which led to his martyrdom, so, too, our witness may very well make us martyrs.[15]

Hence for Luther, Christians in the world encounter suffering and the cross and are called sometimes to martyrological witness precisely because they are disciples of their Lord. Indeed, a distinguishing mark of the church (one of seven)[16] is the "holy possession of the cross," in which believers "endure every misfortunate and persecution . . . by inward sadness, timidity, fear, outward poverty, contempt, illness, and weakness, in order to become like their head, Christ. And the only reason they must suffer is that they steadfastly adhere to Christ and God's Word, enduring this for the sake of Christ."[17] Indeed, if there is any analogy that exists between the Christian and Christ, it is established not by growth in holiness but instead by suffering—we are being conformed to the image of the Crucified.[18] Properly speaking, it is not we but God who makes us Christ's disciples.

In spite of his criticism of growth, when it is evaluated on the basis of likeness between our achievements and the achievements of Christ, Luther claims that we make "some progress" in the Christian life.[19] That is, the Christian life is no perpetually reoccurring oscillation between law and gospel, accusation and liberation. Not oscillation but simultaneity—*simul iustus et peccator*—characterizes Christians, even when they flee from God as wrath to God as mercy. Nevertheless, it is precisely God's word defining this *simul* that opens another dimension—the horizon of living *outside* oneself, first of all in honoring God, the source of goodness, and second, in serving the neighbor. As new beings, we are not trapped in the oscillation because the gospel's goal is to effectuate trust in God's promise, which allows us to live outside ourselves in God and the neighbor. Or, as Gerhard Forde put it, "There is a kind of growth and progress, it is to be hoped, but it is growth in grace—a growth in coming to be captivated more and more, if we can so speak, by the totality, the unconditionality, of the grace of God. It is a matter of getting used to the fact that if we are to be saved it will have to be by grace *alone*."[20] In other words, if I thought I needed grace yesterday, I need it even more today. But even with this conviction that we do make some progress, a growth in grace, there is no empirical gauge by which to measure the impact of this growth on our behavior. Perhaps we can notice over the decades that we have grown to some degree in being more patient. The degree to which we are where God wants us ultimately to be is solely in God's hands, however, and not in our estimation. Luther's insight is always that old beings are prone to self-righteousness, especially in religious and moral matters. Luther will have nothing to do with that. We walk by faith—all of our life is in God's care—and not by sight—namely, our ability to measure and master our progress.

Lutherans should not give up on the language of discipleship, first of all, because that discourse is so closely bound to the identity-formulating narratives of the Christian New Testament.[21] True, the gospels are primarily about Jesus—"passion narratives with extended introductions."[22] But that does not displace the fact that the gospels provide an identity for Jesus' followers. No slacker with regard to the proper distinction between law and gospel, Werner Elert beautifully illustrated this truth:

> Jesus could direct the attention of all who wished to practice them [traits of Christian discipleship] to himself because he was master of these virtues. He could say, "Learn from me." He who learns from him is his *mathetes*, whether this means "pupil" or "disciple." If a pupil has a good teacher he can learn from him what gentleness is or means; the disciple learns from his master how to practice it. To preach the cross is no simple task and, humanly speaking, Paul did it "masterfully." But in order to bear the cross we do not look to Paul but to Jesus, "the author and finisher of our faith."[23]

Discipleship answers not the question "How am I saved?" but instead "What is my life about?" Ponder the words of Luther's Morning Blessing: "I ask you [God] that you would also protect me today from sin and all evil, so that my life and actions may please you completely. For into your hands I commend myself: my body, my soul, and all that is mine."[24] This pithy expression within the context of prayer summarizes Luther's view of Christian motivation. For Luther, the fact that we no longer need to justify ourselves before God liberates our nature: it means that we want to honor and love God for His own sake and thus please Him in all we say and do.

Luther opened a whole new way to approach the Christian life when he claimed that before God, we live a wholly passive life. While grace is not given to empower good works in the world per se, we can be confident that such grace-filled living will issue in good works—an active life.[25] Luther is indeed an "activist"—not primarily as a politician but as an academic, writing with the intent of changing the world. (There was no separation of church and state in the sixteenth century.) The fact that he did not side with the peasants during their rebellion (1525) indicated his firm commitment to the need for social order.[26] For Luther, no social health can be obtained when everything is marked by social chaos. Indeed, Christ frees us to receive once again the gifts of creation (including order) as gifts—not as threats or idols (to worship or appease or abuse). Nevertheless, from early to late in his career, Luther was concerned for the well-being of the poor.[27] Luther's "activism" is highly realistic and tinged not one whit by idealism or utopianism. In it we bear the identity of coworkers with God.[28]

Discipleship versus Fixing the Church

Having summarized salient features of Luther's view of discipleship, we are now in a position to examine contemporary attempts at embodying it. First, we will examine the model of discipleship situated by a "God-experience" and then the view that enfolds discipleship within various social agendas. Many appeal to "discipleship" as the cure that can revitalize congregations. In adopting "evangelical style, Lutheran substance," they have bought into the revivalism of the North American evangelical establishment. In this mode of doing church, the church needs a jumpstart for a renewal of conservative American social values. The church delivers an experience that Americans want and for which they are willing to give of their time and talents through regular attendance at worship.

In this paradigm for renewal, if specific marks of discipleship are encouraged, then one can expect greater commitment to the church—moving the church from an oasis of members to a strip mall of discipleship. What are these marks? One author notes that there are six crucial characteristics of discipleship: (1) prayer, (2) worship, (3) Bible-reading, (4) service, (5) cultivating spiritual friends, and (6) giving or stewardship.[29] These characteristics distinguish discipleship from mere church membership. For this particular author, membership is about getting; discipleship is about giving. Membership is about dues; discipleship is about stewardship.

Membership is about favoring a select group; discipleship is about changing lives.[30]

In contradistinction, the Lutheran tradition contends, as the baptismal service proclaims, that church membership entails discipleship. If the church takes the sacrament of baptism seriously, then there should be no difference between membership and discipleship. To be a member is to be a disciple, and vice versa. Promises made in baptism and promises made at confirmation are substantially the same as the requirements listed for discipleship previously. However, the critique on the part of the "disciple-centered" advocates that the church is now competing with other civic and social organizations merits attention.[31] They may have a point. But if they do, it is a damning critique of our mission and ministry. At what point did we stop seeing ourselves as a body that deals with *ultimate* matters—God's *wonder* and *mystery*—and start viewing ourselves as *penultimate*, one civic organization or club among others? No doubt, the church as an institution in this world has a civic dimension to it—but is that or should that be the only reality that we encounter in the church? Even more to the point, have theologians contributed to the loss of the church's identity and focus on ultimate matters?

If our congregations have become clubs—perhaps something akin to the Masons, who also promote good ethics, fellowship, and a "spiritual" dimension to life—it would only betray that we no longer believe the proclamation of the baptismal liturgy or the Lord's Supper. Apparently, we speak words that claim salvific efficacy—dealing with ultimate (not penultimate) matters, but we do not believe them. Employing the language of salvation without actually believing it is most sad and troublesome. It would betray that we have become the hollowed-out shell of a church.

Adherents of the "discipleship model" of congregational reform and church renewal are greatly concerned about the church's losses. All mainline Protestant churches are losing members, and no churches, including evangelicals, are growing at a rate that would match the overall population growth of our country. The urgency of these reformers and the attempt to establish discipleship as an alternative to membership is understandable. Still, questions remain: Is discipleship something different from membership? Does the technique approach to discipleship work? Can the rhetoric of discipleship fix the church?

The rhetoric of discipleship may seem fresh and new. But historians will tell you that the church has heard it before. Current approaches to discipleship are similar to Spener's proposals for reform in *Pia Desideria* (1675). The new pietism links itself to the old by its focus on *experience*.[32] The contemporary practices of discipleship aim to sustain the private "Jesus" experience. This formula for revival is similar to the program of revival advocated by the nineteenth-century American revivalist Charles Finney. It is not miraculous.[33] What Finney did not say explicitly is that you can manipulate a revival with the right instruments and tools (like the mourner's bench). Today's ways are primarily through praise bands, big-screen video presentations, and flashy showmanship. Post-1950s Lutherans eschewed the legalistic pietism of its past. Today's pietism likewise eschews such legalism that had been centered around policing card playing, dancing, and drinking and offers instead a highly therapeutic, upbeat, can-do approach to faith. Given Luther's marks of the church, what is strikingly different between Luther and the new pietism is that the new pietism is a "crossless" Christianity. It is exactly the criticism that Bonhoeffer leveled toward American Christianity (seen for example in Harry Emerson Fosdick's upbeat, low-stakes moralism at the Riverside Church).[34] Bonhoeffer's digs against cheap grace should primarily be seen as targeted not against Luther (certainly Bonhoeffer himself did not see it that way) but instead against his own safety-seeking Confessing Church as well as the heritage of Schleiermacher and Protestant Liberalism in general, for which religion is adapted to the needs of the "cultured dispersers"—and rendered completely harmless and voiceless in the process. For Luther, there is no forgiveness without repentance, no grace without the cross. Possibly, from the perspective of the new pietism's therapeutic moralism, the cross does not sell.

The "discipleship model" of congregational renewal is pietist because it builds into its diagnostics an inherently two-tiered hierarchy between those who are the disciples versus those who are mere members, rather than seeing all in the church as disciples (even if some seem to take their discipleship more seriously than others). Can such self-righteousness serve the church? Is "discipleship" here really discipleship, or is it more akin to the values of the scribes and Pharisees (even though clearly it does not intend to be that). Likewise, pietism takes leave of an external word and seeks refuge in a specific inner, psychological *experience*—for many Americans, accepting Jesus as one's Savior or, as presented here, a more generic "God" experience. Historically, confessional Lutherans have distanced themselves from this approach because when experience is singled out as the source of truth, we end up on shaky ground. Experience is fickle. It comes and goes; often it deceives. Against the spirituality of inner experience, Lutherans have historically appealed to the external word as the source of truth.

There is no question that the church needs renewal. The question is whether or not the church can trust the *word* to renew the church. The church may have lost confidence in the word. That lack of confidence says more us than about the word, of course. About such an experience, the word of God is not silent. God's word promises to kill and make alive. As law, the word of God judges our lack of confidence but only so that as gospel, it might enliven our trust in the saving power of Jesus. Remember how it was for the disciples of Jesus in that frightening storm at sea. In panic they had awakened Jesus: "Lord, save us. We are perishing?" To which the law of God asked, "Why are you afraid, you of little faith?" (Matt. 8:18ff.) The law of judgment was not, however, Jesus' last word to them. He went on to save them from the raging storm, to their utter amazement (Matt. 8:26–27).

Discipleship versus Fixing the World

The other route of "discipleship" current today seeks to fix not the church but the world. Frederick Schmidt calls this the "issue-driven church."[35] These church leaders do not place themselves within this new pietist camp. It is not as if they are insulated from pietism, but theirs is a pietism of a higher order. More than a private "God experience," it seeks to make the world peaceful and just. Accordingly, the church is an instrument by which to create a genuine moral community on earth. If the new pietism centers faith not in the word and sacrament but in experience, then this more sophisticated moralism centers faith in moral transformation, the promise of an ideal community. Discipleship here is best seen as doing ethics within a community of moral deliberation.[36] Or as Kant said, "The true (visible) church is that which exhibits the (moral) kingdom of God on earth so far as it can be brought to pass by men."[37]

Who doesn't want a world of peace and justice? But how do we get there? Conservatives and liberals both have a formula to accomplish this. As different as the formulas may be politically, they share a common orientation. Both conservatives and liberals spring from the *common* heritage in Enlightenment thinking. It affirms individual autonomy, in opposition to unfair and artificial hierarchical class structures, and a capitalist economy (which likewise is perceived as a better alternative to feudalistic economics). Historically, the Republican vision of the ideal world is invested in a laissez-faire, hands-off approach to the free market, confident that wealth will trickle down to the lower classes. As well, the Republican vision champions the traditional family as a safe environment for child rearing. In contrast, Democrats tend to affirm government regulation of the economy, with transfer payments for the least well-off, along with affirming a hands-off approach to family life as a private matter.[38] In either case, under the administrations of *both* leading parties, the rich become richer and the poor poorer.[39] That phenomenon is not likely to further peace and justice, in either this country or the world. The political right and left should be seen less as genuine alternatives and more as extremes of the same thing—both autonomy and capitalism are nonnegotiable in each view. We should honor the truth that God's promise of the kingdom to come demythologizes political programs, left and right. They do not usher in the kingdom. Political visions deserve to be debated on the ordinary basis of what serves the common good of the temporal order most justly and peaceably.

The current movement to view congregations as centers of moral deliberation—presumably not in opposition to congregations as centers of the word and sacrament—needs to be examined critically from a theological perspective. More specifically, it needs to be examined from the perspective of the classical Lutheran insight regarding God's two kingdoms. For all the criticism that the doctrine leads to quietism, its concern has been to liberate Christians from a postmillennial fantasy for the genuine care for *actual* (not hypothetical, idealized) flesh-and-blood victims. Further, it seeks to instruct the Christian community that the creation is most effectively cared for through worldly means. On its face, moral deliberation sounds like a good thing. But under closer scrutiny, several problematic concerns arise.

First, counter to many convictions, moral deliberation is not something for which Christians, or anyone else, need to strive. It is a given, a fact of life. All human communities deliberate morally—hospitals, businesses, universities, and the government have codes of ethics and often committees set aside to ponder the ethics of specific decisions and goals. Likewise, congregations have always had to deliberate over the stewardship of financial and other resources. Moral deliberation is an "is" that does not need to become an "ought"—unless, that is, we in the church foolishly believe that we can somehow deliberate better than people in the world. Perhaps we believe that we can bring God into the picture and that other communities fail to do this. But if that is our rationale, then I suspect just the opposite holds true. It is not that our moral deliberation in the church makes the world more spiritual but, instead, the church simply becomes more secular.[40] Our nod to the authority of Scripture while doing moral deliberation is undermined by the many different criteria and agendas for ethical assessment brought to the table in moral deliberation. We simply import into the congregation the maelstrom of ethical opinions that is so distinctive of our pluralistic society. Thereby, the Bible is a resource and not the authority when we do moral deliberation. If that is the case, we become more relativistic in our approach to ethics. Relativism may seem to encourage greater tolerance, seemingly an attractive alternative to the moral absolutism of previous generations, but it is more likely that such relativism ironically enervates change agency in the world: at best, we agree to disagree. But that does not result in greater solidarity with victims. Deliberation is relatively easy; rubbing shoulders with people in need is not.

Second, the value of the products of moral deliberation, such as social statements adopted by churchwide assemblies, needs assessment. In higher education, we are constantly asked to assess the effectiveness of our work. We claim to teach—but do our students actually learn? Where's the documentation? It is time to assess: do our social statements do what they are intended to do? Mainline Protestants tend to provide social statements on various ethical matters. However, it is worth bearing in mind that the *active membership* of the Evangelical Lutheran Church in America (ELCA) is a tiny fraction of the total USA population. Rather than centering the witness of the church on what other agencies ought to do, the witness of the church is more profitably spent on what the church *alone* can do. Instead of the church duplicating measures that properly belong to God's left-hand rule in the world, the church per se should primarily focus on *ultimate* matters—God's wonder and mystery—and not on penultimate matters. Such a witness would certainly include publicly critiquing any politician or government that claims ultimate authority over peoples' lives. That is idolatry, and the church, true to its mission, will publicly declare the truth of it.

As believers, we may trust that God is working in the world through the political process and through temporal institutions to establish His righteousness in the world. Not only Christians but all people are capable of ethical insights—and moral deliberation and action. As active in love, faith works *within* worldly venues on behalf of the powerless, never naïve to the fact that the world—for the most part—prefers the status quo. Our point here is not to argue against ethical reflection in congregations. We certainly are not making the case to privatize faith. The point is simply not to ethicize the gospel. Let God's law be law, and let God's promise be promise.

If the church is transformed into another advocacy group, then the message of the church is cheapened and the importance of advocacy is undermined. Churchly social advocates are under the illusion that the church has some kind of big say in the world. In today's world, "Lutheran" is as meaningful to our non-Lutheran neighbors as "Lollards" is to us—and this is increasingly true even in those old-guard Lutheran strongholds like Pennsylvania, Minnesota, and Missouri. If we truly care about the world, we are advised to let the church be the church; let it do what no agency in this world can do—bear witness to God's wonder and mystery, not least of which is the mystery of Christ's death and resurrection. There we need to trust that the word of God can and will change the world as God sees fit.

The church need not compete with or supplement the wisdom of the world in seeking to address temporal problems. God has never abandoned the world. It is not Christians alone who have the motive or the wit to improve the world. And even if the world cannot be fixed, God provides the world with capable people who help sustain His ongoing creativity. Certainly, Christians want to work with non-Christians in the world to address social issues. But we should keep in mind the standard of justice, and the quest for equal opportunity and freedom, is not the only way by which to approach such matters. Stewardship of resources might prove to be an equally good, if not better, persuasive and effective strategy. Ultimately, no economic theory affirms that poverty and hunger, for instance, provide efficient usage of resources. When lives are wasted, there is an economic incentive to address poverty and hunger, even when the most well-off are oblivious to such needs. It is not in the self-interest of the well-off to remain indifferent.

The church does its calling best not by imitating an advocacy agency, but instead by challenging all powers with the truth that no human power is ultimate and that all human power is dependent on the all-powerful, all-good God to whom all humans should be grateful and to whom they should render their worship. The church has no more important mission than to challenge such penultimate powers with what is ultimate—God Himself. So, akin to Bonhoeffer, we need to ask the state to be the state and not pretend to be its own self-serving cult.[41] Unfortunately, for many, the rhetoric of "moral deliberation" comes across as more an attempt to alter the fabric of the church along the lines of a partisan progressive social agenda rather than an attempt actually to help the world. In wider society, thoughtful people of goodwill are bound to disagree about both the means of and the ends for social justice and improvement—and such rifts are best handled in wider democratic society and not the church.

The More Promising Approach to Discipleship

Where do we go with respect to discipleship? How might we be true to Luther's view of discipleship? Given the challenges facing today's church—long in the making—the "solution" I propose will appear ridiculous: Can we trust the word? Will we tend to it and preach it—*let it have its way* with us? We have lost confidence in both tending to the word and preaching it. By tending to the word, we must seek to cultivate a renewed catechesis.

Most people leave the church due not to burnout but to indifference. If we are one more agency or club among many, we have no right to insist that people stick with it. The more promising approach is to tend to the word, allowing people to walk within the thick narratives of Scripture—to see themselves in the accomplishments and failures of Israel's history and the early church, to see themselves as Jesus' sometimes brash, sometimes cowardly disciples and to learn from Him. Imagine the vitality of a church membership engaged with the prophetic books of the Bible, believing that they speak to us and challenge us every bit as much as they spoke to Israel of old. Imagine a church membership that has learned to express joy and grief as we pray the Psalter and meditate on Wisdom literature. What if it were to get in our imaginations that Revelation's longing for Christ's return is our longing? Wouldn't the promise of it compel the leaders of the church to tend to the biblical story as though it were the story of disciples today? The Christian Scriptures make ultimate claims on believers. In that way, people will see penultimate matters in a new light: the life of the disciple is not about religious self-improvement but about the freedom of trusting God to be God and taking care of His creation. We are, after all, intertwined with all creatures and called to be stewards promoting the health and well-being of the earth.

When Scripture is at the forefront of our imagination, we have a compass by which to discern our discipleship to Christ, wherever we are called in the world. There is no "one size fits all" here. Instead, how we juggle our responsibilities and the accountability that we have before God and the world, measured in tandem with our abilities, can only be discerned by us. This is no license for relativism. God's commands stand. However, our assessment of how each individual is to live as a disciple of the crucified Lord, within the places where each lives, will be distinct, just as Peter's or Mary Magdalene's or Paul's ministries were different from one another. Each bears witness to Jesus, but each does so in his or her own way. Clergy need to be at the forefront of educating youth and adults, inviting them into the horizons and depths of Scripture.

However, we must also preach law and gospel so vitally that God's promise may clearly be heard by sinners who are, for all practical purposes, lost in hell. Our preaching is not simply to keep cantankerous people at bay or entertained. There is no technique by which to fix the church, any more than there is a technique to fix the world. In fact, it is not our job to redeem God's creation. As citizens, disciples of Jesus, like all other citizens, we are obligated to speak out against injustice as it is encountered in social structures. In living out the obligation of citizenship, disciples require wisdom, not technique.

And as disciples in the world, it is our calling to feed the hungry, clothe the naked, and care for the sick and imprisoned: "Truly I tell you, just as you did it to one of the least of these who are members of my family, you did it to me" (Matt. 25:40). It is appropriate for us, as citizens of this world, to call the powers of this world to accountability on behalf of those whose well-being is least well-off. But in so doing, along with Luther, we acknowledge and honor God's right- and left-hand ways of governance and do not confuse the two. We are motivated not by the goal of achieving a (post-) millennial utopia but by easing the pain of those who hurt and providing hope to those whose power is limited.[42] Ultimately, it is the forgiveness of their sins for which Jesus died and not, as Marcus Borg or Benjamin Franklin (who, in fewer words, long ago presented Borg's image of Jesus as a sage) would have us believe, an egalitarian political community, as desirable as that may be. As the church, the calling of disciples is to administer the office of the keys—to forgive and retain sins.

In so honoring this distinction, we actually fulfill Stanley Hauerwas's admonition to let the church be itself.[43] That is, the church continually witnesses to ultimate and not merely penultimate truths.[44] But we stand against Hauerwas at the point where he truncates his own conviction, seeing the church as a "political alternative."[45] The church is not a political alternative, as, say, Vatican City is with respect to Italy. Instead, it is in the world as a witness to the King of kings and Lord of lords, whose coming reign shall last forever.

We have lost confidence in the gospel; we have been so seduced by the world's promises, whether they are the promises of therapy or politics or the economy. If we tend to the word, there is a promise that the word itself will open us up from the inside out—just as it did at the time of the Reformation—and use us to change the world. To be wrapped up in the Scriptures and in their proclamation of good news may occasion the change that we seek. As Klaus Schwarzwäller puts it, we would move from kneeling (prayer) and sitting (study), as necessary as they both are, to enter the fray, fighting for the well-being of the world, cooperating with the Lord, who is ever creative, of the world.[46]

CHAPTER 10

Bioethics and Honoring Humanity

A Christian Perspective

If you could design your own "perfect child," what would he or she be like? Intelligent but also athletic? Socially cooperative and well mannered but with a competitive edge? What standard would you use to make such decisions? More to the point: How could you know that your standard would actually deliver your ideals? And in a highly competitive society, if you could give your children a genetic advantage—that is, improve their intelligence, appearance, and strength—but failed to do so, doesn't that mean that you are a poor parent? After all, if you didn't give your child a competitive edge, wouldn't you fail in your role as a parent? In the words of one advocate of genetic enhancement: "If we could make our baby smarter, more attractive, a better athlete or musician, or keep him or her from being overweight, why wouldn't we?"[1]

Such questions are not merely theoretical. Just think what can be done that would have been unimaginable only a few short years ago. As ELCA (Evangelical Lutheran Church in America) ethicist Paul Jersild notes, "Today, among many options, one can buy eggs and sperm over the Internet, select the sperm of famous people at sperm banks to 'upgrade' one's own progeny, freeze eggs for career-oriented women for later impregnation and implantation, arrange for surrogacy in which a woman who is not the biological mother gives birth to the baby, and sort sperm according to the X and Y chromosomes, allowing parents to select a boy or a girl."[2] How very different reproduction is today from the past! Today, the market offers us options so that we can be selective with certain traits in our children. In the past, having children included an element of luck. There was no guarantee that a baby would be healthy or even survive. Our technology today fosters greater control on our part. We contend with luck less and less.

With respect to the important question of what standard we should use to improve our progeny, Jersild notes, "The fertility industry is market driven, which means it attempt to come up with a salable product for every conceivable fertility-related need. Ethical questions about the consequences of the industry's policies and products are typically a secondary consideration at best."[3] Human reproduction has been made into a commodity. More and more, we can purchase enhancements to design our own offspring. Jersild observes, "In essence, we and our children increasingly will be reflections of our personal philosophies and values. Where today we sculpt our minds and bodies using exercise, drugs, and surgery, tomorrow we will also use the tools that biotechnology provides."[4] Most importantly, for Jersild, this would amount to a eugenics program, not dictated by the government (as was the case with Hitler) but driven "from the ground up" by the choices of parents who have the power to control the kind of offspring they desire.[5]

Much research in biotechnology is driven not by genetic enhancements but, as we would expect, to cure disease. Such diseases that biotechnology wants to tackle include Alzheimer's, Parkinson's, diabetes, and lower-body paralysis. No doubt, making progress with these diseases merits our attention. Many here have known people who have been afflicted with these diseases and the emotional and financial toll that they can take on individuals and families. The question for us, though, is: At what expense? Current researchers want to harvest stem cells from embryos to conquer these diseases. Defending the use of stem cells, Thomas Okarma says, "The potential for these cells is to allow permanent repair of failing organs by injecting healthy functional cells developed from them, an approach called regenerative medicine. The significance would be to broaden the definition of medical therapy from simply halting the progression of acute or chronic disease to include restoration of lost organ function."[6] Hence one goal of stem cell research is to develop a form of medical therapy that regenerates damaged or deteriorating tissue. These researchers want to find out whether or not inserting a colony of cells into a damaged heart tissue would regenerate the damaged tissue. They contend that regenerative medicine promises to go beyond stopping deterioration to provide the power of organ renewal. As ELCA ethicist Ted Peters notes, although it is by no means a sure thing, we could be finding ourselves on the eve of a magnificent revolution in medical science.[7]

It is indisputable that the attempt to cure these diseases is a praiseworthy goal. But should embryos be harvested to cure disease, or is that not a violation of human dignity? For Christians, we are made in God's image. This entails that we should treat our neighbor, at whatever stage of development, including that of the embryo, as a child of God and not as a product for our disposal.

However, for Christians, not only are the hoped-for medical benefits of stem cell harvesting problematic, but equally problematic (and, I would argue, flat out contrary to the respect and protection all human life deserves) is the quest for genetic enhancement, another possibility arising from stem cell research. It amounts to a kind of market-driven eugenics. Some proponents of this technology want us to farm embryos not only to cure disease but also to remake our progeny after the likeness of our ideals. Many of these researchers are willing to limit such harvesting to up until day fourteen of the embryo's life, the "blastocyst" stage. Since until about day fourteen, a blastocyst has the potential to split and form twins, these researchers believe that "the idea of personhood before this time is counterintuitive."[8]

At stake here is that this technology blurs the distinction between curing disease and genetic enhancement. As Jersild notes, "When we move from these extremes of curing devastating disease versus inducing dramatic enhancements to the much larger middle realm of disabilities, it becomes more difficult to make the distinction between therapy and enhancement."[9] Such research "fuels a drive for perfection, or in this case the removal of every possibility of disease."[10]

Just what are embryonic stem cells? "Found in embryos and the umbilical cord, stem cells help the body, when it is injured, to grow new cells. If the body is hurt and loses blood, stem cells are activated to make new blood. Stem cells are primordial cells that can develop into any kind of differentiated cellular tissue: bone, muscle, nerve, etc. In theory these primordial cells could be directed to form new bones, neural cells, cardiac tissue, and hence, to cure many diseases."[11] It was John Gearhart of Johns Hopkins University and James Thomson of the University of Wisconsin who in 1998 discovered how to create immortalized stem cell lines from human embryos. They learned how to continually produce stem cells, rather than tediously derive them from minute amounts of tissue from embryos or fetuses.[12] Gearhart and Thomson discovered how to make human embryos into tiny biological factories creating stem cells.

Now it is important to note that stem cell research does not need to be limited to what can be harvested from embryos. In 2001, scientists discovered stem cells not only in bone marrow but also throughout the human body. Scientists note that "brain stem cells can make almost all cell types in the brain, and that may be all we need if we want to treat Parkinson's disease or ALS. Embryonic stem cells might not be necessary in those cases."[13] This has an important impact on those of us who see stem cell research on embryos as akin to abortion. Such biotechnology does not have to be at the expense of embryonic life. However, the received wisdom of many researchers is that most adult organs contain few stem cells, not nearly enough to use medically, and adult stem cells are even harder to grow than embryonic stem cells. In other words, we require the use of embryonic stems cells if we are to be cost effective in "unlocking the secrets of self-renewal."[14]

How can any Christian defend stem cell research? An example is that of Ted Peters. Peters disagrees with Roman Catholics, evangelicals, and conservative Lutherans who wish to stop stem cell research because it requires the abortion of the embryo. The Roman Catholic encyclical *Donum Vitae* acknowledges blastocysts as unique, "ensouled" individuals—requiring our respect and just treatment. For Roman Catholics, the biotechnology of stem cell research is by definition wrong. It requires in-vitro fertilization, which, in Roman Catholic teaching, violates natural law. Hence, the storing of frozen ova risks the death of human persons. For Roman Catholics: "Discarding frozen ova is a form of abortion. So when scientists take advantage of discarded or spare embryos, they are complicit in the earlier illicit act of creating zygotes that might never be brought through a pregnancy to birth. Pressing such spare zygotes into medical service does not redeem the scientists from complicity in baby-killing."[15] For Peters, it is a category mistake to see blastocysts as human. He claims that even "if we understand opposition to abortion as the removal of a fetus from a pregnant woman's body, one could take a pro-life stand on abortion and still affirm that human embryonic stem cell research is morally licit."[16] For Peters, in-vitro fertilization of an egg—which has nothing to do with a woman's uterus—by definition cannot be seen as abortion, since no embryo has been removed from a mother's uterus.

No doubt, we respond that the place or locus of a fertilized egg—whether in the womb or out of it—is not relevant to establish human identity. At any rate, Peters upholds the perspective current in British law that forbids harvesting stem cells from an embryo after day fourteen. In England, a commission known as the Warnock Committee established the "fourteen-day rule," which "marks as an ethical threshold the adherence of the in vivo embryo to the mother's uterine wall and the appearance of the primitive streak. Prior to the fourteenth day, scientists should receive permission to carry on embryo research."[17] For Peters, prior to the fourteenth day, embryonic research can and should be conducted, since the overall good far outweighs any possible evil. Likewise, Peters reports with approval the standards devised in Singapore (which seeks to become the leading Asian center for biotechnology) by which to govern biotechnological research: "The creation of human embryos specifically for research can be justified only where (1) there is strong merit in, and potential medical benefit from, such research; (2) no acceptable alternative exists; and (3) on a highly selective, case-by-case basis, with specific approval from the proposed statutory body."[18]

In my judgment, Peters's standard of right and wrong is clearly utilitarian. For the utilitarian, there is no intrinsic dignity to the human whether adult or embryonic that intrinsically requires our respect. This clearly runs counter to the scriptural insistence that humans are made in God's image. For Peters, the basis for ethics instead is whether or not the greatest happiness for the greatest number—or at least the least amount of pain, for humans or any other sentient creatures—is achieved. The goal of ethics is not the respect of human dignity but the outcome of as much overall happiness as possible. If overall happiness is achieved through sacrificing some people, then sacrifice them. Of course, Peters doesn't see embryos as humans or even potential humans. For Peters, blastocysts are tissue. Nevertheless, in principle, I sense that it is a utilitarian perspective that governs Peters's thinking. It is due to Peters's utilitarianism that he is apt to downgrade the uniqueness of the human.

In that regard, we need to keep in mind that in the pagan world, prior to the rise of Christianity, people did not believe in such things as human dignity—at least, most people didn't believe in it. It was Christianity's countercultural contention that people are made in God's image and thus have dignity and should have freedom. Additionally, Christians affirmed that Jesus Christ was a substitute for all people and that the entire world was justified in God's eyes due to His sacrificial atonement. Humanity has dignity as made in God's image and as the unique recipient of God's love. These beliefs ran counter to the ancient Roman ideals and economy, which was based largely on a practice that inherently violates Christian truth—slavery. For the ancient Romans, slaves simply had no legal status whatsoever. They were property to be used as an owner saw fit. Christianity challenged such social inequity and injustice, and over time, in lands influenced by Christianity, slavery came to an end.

Likewise in Peters's judgment, there is no evidence that the blastocyst feels pain or that the blastocyst is even human. Against Paul Jersild's "gradualist" perspective on human development (which is itself counter to the conservative stance that one is human from conception, albeit in a different stage of development), Peters contends that the ex-vivo blastocyst is not an individual human person living as a fetus in a mother's womb and thus that no abortion is involved when it is harvested for stem cells.[19] Indeed, for Peters, the whole concern over embryos is misplaced. It is the victims of disease who should be our focus. In Peters's estimation, regenerative medicine could best be understood by analogy as the aid that the Good Samaritan offered to the suffering victim.[20] Developing Peters's logic, if we fail to help the hurt victim, then we follow the path of the Levite or the priest who in their neglect failed to follow God's will.

For me, Peters's most troubling justification for the use of stem cells, however, is his contention that our human essence is not in our origin but our destiny.[21] What does he mean by this? If we appeal to the human as made in the image of God, as I have done, then we are establishing human nature in its origin as coming from God and modeling God in how we use our intelligence and our will. We live out our divine image in how we use our brains and how we live. However, Peters thinks that new movements in theology—and even Scripture itself—would push us to focus not on the *imago dei* as the basis for human nature but instead on our destiny. We as baptized are destined to rise with Christ on the last day. While Peters himself probably thinks this last claim is highly mythological, he believes that this way of thinking implies that we won't be who we really are until human destiny is fulfilled. That is, it is the future that drives how we interpret what it means to be human. And if that is the case, our ethics needs to comply with an optimal outcome for humanity. Christians need to stop being so conservative and go with the flow that will achieve an ideal flourishing of human life, a community of peace and justice, toward which we are moving in the present.

Peters's utopianism—optimistic view of the future—is purely a faith matter. As I read Scripture, we can anticipate things to get worse before Christ returns. More problematic for Peters is the fact that the secular belief in biological evolution as is currently taught indicates that all evolution is based on the survival value of a living thing's genetics and that there is no goal to evolution as such. For secular evolutionists, the history of the world has not been geared to the development of human intelligence any more than the amoeba's. There is no goal to evolution whatsoever. Human evolution is merely an accident. But what is most problematic in Peters's thinking is: what is the standard of the future toward which we should move? I imagine Peters would tell us that it is "Christ"—Christ is the true omega. But what is the content of this "Christ outcome" that he proposes? It was, after all, Hitler who said that it is the Aryan future to which we must move. Jews can be slaughtered because their blood does not accord with the future—a *tausend Jahre Reich*—an idyllic community of peace and justice for all Aryans. What specifically is the future for which Peters hopes? How many embryos should we be willing to sacrifice in order to achieve it?

And even though Jersild's reflections are helpful, we simply must also contest his reasoning (as recorded by Peters): "Ethical reflection deals with how we relate with one another and with God.

Or, to apply this point of departure to the stem cell controversy, the relationship of a fetus to a mother counts ethically. This relationship is absent when dealing with a stem cell line created in the laboratory." For Jersild, "the dismantling and destruction of an embryo that takes place in stem cell research ought not to be labeled an abortion."[22]

While Jersild is wrong in his assumptions about abortion, he is helpful in showing us the consequences of adopting a biotechnology that wants to harvest embryos for their stem cells. He notes that this technology will simply fuel our competitiveness. The rich will have access to biotechnology while the poor will not. Over time, such inequities could result in social conflict. In Jersild's own words: "A society can live with an elitism that comes from success and achievement on the part of those who have the natural endowment to excel, but can society live with an elitism based on the ability to purchase that natural endowment? Should society be expected to live with that kind of injustice?"[23] And the answer for Jersild is that we curb our quest to play god on the basis of self-creation and creation of our progeny. Hence he claims, "Parental authority has limits; it does not allow for the kind of autonomy that seeks to 'design one's children.' That desire turns the child into a product that belongs to the parents, rather than a gift that calls for responsible stewardship."[24]

Ethicist Leon Kass, who served on President Bush's bioethics committee, echoes these appropriate concerns of Paul Jersild. He notes the corrosive moral effect of harvesting embryos: "Fewer people yet worried about the effects not on the embryos but on our embryo-using society of coming to look upon nascent human life as a natural resource to be mined, exploited, made into a commodity. The little embryos are merely destroyed, but we—their users—are at risk of corruption. We are desensitized and denatured by a coarsening of sensibility that comes to regard these practices as natural, ordinary and fully unproblematic. People who can hold nascent human life in their hands coolly and without awe have deadened something in their souls."[25] He senses that our current policies of research play on a misuse of freedom: "From liberty understood first as freedom of conscience and the negative right not to suffer under the rule of despots has come liberty understood as a positive right to self-expression, self-assertion and full self-re-creation. In a moral realm impoverished by an overgrowth of rights, liberty is indistinguishable from license and becomes perfectly compatible with licentiousness. The liberty of self-assertion is even said to include the right of assisted suicide, the self-contradictory freedom to choose no longer to be a choosing creature."[26] While the British philosopher John Locke, our forefather in political theory, claimed that each of us is a "property in his own person," Kass notes that Locke's claim was less a metaphysical statement of declaring self-ownership and more a political statement denying ownership by another (other, of course, than God). Hence properly understood, one's liberty entails that "my body and my life are my property only in the limited sense that they are not yours."[27] The quest for "designer babies . . . reached not by dictatorial fiat, but by the march of benevolent humanitarianism, and cheered on by an ambivalent citizenry that also dreads becoming merely the last of man's manmade things,"[28] ultimately seeks a pain-free existence. But pain and death are God's just judgment on a sinful humanity that insists on being its own god for itself—as is so very clear in the fall of Adam and Eve. As Kass notes, "Hidden in all this avoidance of evil is nothing less than the quasi-messianic goal of a painless, suffering-free and, finally, immortal existence"—what in Lutheran terms we would call a *theology of glory* as opposed to a *theology of the cross*. The theology of glory seeks to deify ourselves in some way or another, to keep us in control of ultimate things in our lives, whether through religion or biotechnology—as opposed to living by faith in Jesus Christ even in the face of painful things that take away our power.

In response to those ethicists, such as Mary Anne Warren, who believe that embryos and fetuses have no more right to life than a newborn guppy,[29] we must affirm with King David:

> For you created my inmost being; you knit me together in my mother's womb. I praise you because I am fearfully and wonderfully made; your works are wonderful, I know that full well. My frame was not hidden from you when I was made in the secret place. When I was woven together in the depths of the earth, your eyes saw my unformed body. All the days ordained for me were written in your book before one of them came to be. (Ps. 139: 13–16)

Fetus means "little one." And that is exactly how we should treat embryos and fetuses—with the same respect that we accord children outside the womb. Embryos are not for our experimentation or violation. If we do so—even for the sake of overcoming the diseases of those we know or even our descendants—we do exactly what C. S. Lewis said, "Man's power over nature turns out to be a power exercised by some men over other men with Nature as its instrument. . . . Each new power won by man is a power over man as well."[30] And such violence, for C. S. Lewis, leads to the "abolition of man." We become victims of our own technology.

Many people suffer in this life. Suffering is unavoidable for all. We should spur on the development of medicine as much as possible to help alleviate suffering. The church has always been at the forefront of building hospitals and universities. Nevertheless, we cannot accept harvesting the stem cells of others. Stephen Schwarz notes, "'At what point, or stage, in pregnancy does a human person begin to exist?' is a false question. That is, it rests on a false premise: that there is a point or stage during pregnancy (or at its end in birth) at which a human person begins to exist. There is not. The person is there all along."[31] The acorn is the oak tree, in its earliest phase, "and the zygote is the person in her earliest phase. In each case the early phase looks different from the later phases."[32]

In the movie *The Matrix*, artificial intelligences harvested humans as an energy source. We are repulsed by such a thing, even in fiction. Harvesting the stem cells of embryos is no less repulsive. It violates persons, and it opens a depersonalized future. As Christians, we should oppose it—peacefully and through appropriate legislation. To be human is to deal with imperfection, finitude, and loss. God gives us the strength to bear through these challenges and increases our dependence upon His almighty strength and love.

CHAPTER 11

Rethinking Social Justice

It is but a memory that at one time, the church reveled in the prospect of eternal life instead of reviling a host of alleged social injustices. In the *Service Book and Hymnal*, for instance, one could find occasional hymns urging equality and justice in society, but the content of the liturgy as such is, for those who repent and believe, centered on the promise of eternal life in Christ Jesus. In contrast, seldom does *Sundays and Seasons*, the weekly worship resource offered by the ELCA (Evangelical Lutheran Church in America), omit prayers advocating for justice. Indeed, often there are multiple petitions seeking justice for one or another oppressed community.

Likewise, ELCA Facebook pages shrilly demand justice for various minorities and promote social causes, most of which are defined by the political left. No doubt, the strident tone of late is due to the election of Donald Trump—who, more than any previous president, has lowered standards for civility in public discourse—as well as the perceived threat that the dominance of the GOP in national and state politics brings to the advance of progressive causes. To be sure, political conservatives were stridently vocal under Barack Obama's presidency. Now the complaints come primarily from political liberals. For half a century, "social justice" has been important to many in the ELCA and its predecessor bodies. Social-justice causes are the piety of our time. But should they be the heart of the church's mission?

More Kant Than Luther

For Lutherans, the value and validity of the Christian faith should not rely primarily on its utility in advancing political agendas. This is not because Lutherans are quietists. From the days of the Magdeburg Confession (1550) to the Norwegian Folk Church's resistance to Nazism, from Martin Luther King's address to American Lutheran Church Luther Leaguers in 1961 to Gudina Tumsa's protest of abuses in Ethiopia, Lutherans have a heritage of social engagement.

But this social engagement refuses to reduce the promise of the gospel to ethical directives. God's law is both necessary and sufficient to establish ethical directives. The current ways of advocating "social justice," so centered as they are on individual autonomy and social perfectibility, makes the ELCA more a disciple of Kant than Luther. Certainly the Bible advocates mercy for the poor and support for the outcast, but there is no direct translation of the Bible's social ethics into how a contemporary secular society should govern itself or help the least advantaged in its midst. No doubt, thoughtful and faithful Christians will seek to translate their faith into works of love that help the poor and disenfranchised and so impinge upon public life. But how to do this is less direct and simple than many mainline Protestants pretend.

We Don't Live in Biblical Times

There are at least seven obstacles that prevent the reduction of the gospel to politics. First, the political context of today's endeavors to achieve social equity is simply not the same as that of the biblical prophets. Ancient Israel assumed that religion and politics or church and state were one. In fact, for the Hebrews, cult and kingship often worked in tandem. Prophets of yore ever sought that both cult and culture would be loyal to the covenant and not be consumed by either idolatry or inequity.

But how does that concern, important as it is, translate into modern, pluralistic America, where it is not always clear whose justice and which rationality should prevail? One would need a more complex argument than a biblically grounded "preferential option for the poor" to do that. Many contemporary activists who are so vocal in rejecting biblicistic fundamentalism's apparent loyalty to American consumerism in fact simply proof text their own economic convictions from Scripture. Even more ironic, they often live a comfortable suburban lifestyle, fed by the very consumerism they abhor.

Contrary to the assumptions of many ELCA ethicists, there is little analogy between the theocracy that existed in ancient Israel, in which the role of a prophet as a spokesperson for God was an established institution within both the cult and the state, and our current democracy, which advances a separation between church and state. Obviously, ancient Israel had no such separation between divine matters and a secular, nonsectarian government. No doubt, there are modern-day prophets (such as Martin Luther King Jr.) who, even if they do not speak through inspiration as did ancient, biblical prophets, eloquently advocate for the oppressed in the face of racism and majority privilege. But thinkers such as King must assume the residue of a legacy of Christian history, culture, and presence in America in order to make their case. Such a Christian cultural legacy, however, is less and less privileged or viable today—certainly not in secular public universities and occasionally not even in the church.

The Problem with Ideology

Second, the alliance of the church with various secular ideologies undercuts the most basic tenets of the Christian doctrine of humanity. Christians can never affirm, following John Locke, that we are "self-owners," any more than they can affirm Karl Marx's materialism. Far from self-ownership, Christians belong to Jesus Christ, their Lord who has redeemed them and in whose life they are hidden. Undoubtedly, Christian ethicists, when it is possible, should seek common ground with non-Christians in the quest for a more equitable society. But Christians involved in that quest must be willing to critique secular ideologies, not merely translate the biblical message into contemporary ethical idioms.

One of the church's biggest mistakes historically was its usually uncritical alliance with the Roman Empire, beginning in the fourth century. Today's progressive Christians may not be tempted to make such a Faustian bargain with the government, but they are often eager to sign on with various secular ideologies—feminism, inclusivism, ecocentrism. Many of these movements have important things to teach us, but Christians cannot give up the responsibility of critiquing all such ideologies in the light of biblical teaching.

Who Would Have Thought It So Complicated?

Third, while it is true that there are many victims of "systemic distortions" in our society, it is also true that economic privilege and disenfranchisement are more complex than many assume. For example, some who are poor contribute to their poverty by not taking advantage of educational opportunities, literacy programs, and the like, which could help them raise themselves out of poverty. The old question asks, "Do you give someone a fish or teach them how to fish?" The correct answer is actually "Both." But many social justice advocates emphasize only the first, giving someone a fish. The Bible says that poverty is often due not only to systemic exploitation but also, on occasion, to sloth. Remember Proverbs 6:6—"Go to the ant, you sluggard." In other words, the Bible presents a more multifaceted, less simplistic perspective on poverty and victimization than those of many ELCA social justice advocates. It acknowledges that poverty is sometimes due to exploitation but other times due to a self-defeating mind-set.

There are certainly systemic racist underpinnings that create and sustain poverty. But at the same time, people's individual decisions also chain them to someone else's racist script. Deplorably, racism and poverty truncate the lives of many. But when we turn people into the objects of these horrible states, we rob them of their humanity and their own power to meet these challenges. Indeed, the powerless can equally become victimizers when they themselves gain power. The best way to alleviate poverty is to focus on rebuilding family units in impoverished communities, which helps keep people from sliding into poverty. In truth, there is more than one kind of poverty; spiritual poverty, for instance, is that with which the church, as the church, is particularly equipped to deal. Economic poverty, in contrast, is something that both Christians and non-Christians must seek to ameliorate in the world and through worldly means.

The Church Is Not a Whistle-Blower

Fourth, for ELCA social justice advocates, a major goal of the church is to alter the world and to do that from a certain political agenda. Thus the churchwide expression of the ELCA is a bureaucracy whose explicit vocation is to blow the whistle on many other economic and political bureaucracies. But that is inherently self-contradictory. After all, the churchwide expression of the ELCA is itself financially invested in global capitalism—and that to a much greater degree than any given congregation. It would be far less hypocritical for the church to fulfill its mandate to preach the gospel and rightfully administer the sacraments and only then encourage the laity to vote their faith-informed consciences, be engaged in grassroots initiatives for social mercy, and be involved in advocacy groups as they see fit. Pastoral leaders should trust the laity to make good decisions. Otherwise, we violate the theology of the "two kingdoms," which honors both the agency of the gospel to liberate sinners' consciences and the quest for a just society, in opposition to a stance that proclaims that there is but one overarching kingdom.

Utopia Means "Nowhere"

Fifth, ironically, mainline Protestant justice advocates, again very much like the Christian right they despise, seem to take scriptural passages that speak of a future utopia quite literally. They envision an ideal future, much like the fundamentalist view of the millennium (Rev. 20), where wolves dwell peacefully with lambs (Isa. 11:6). Historic Christianity has generally spiritualized such texts, seeing them as referring to heaven or the inner tranquility that believers can have with God through Christ. But for modern religious progressives, utopia is just on the horizon—if we would simply all conform to a progressive social agenda. This stance lacks a robust view of original sin, making our social justice advocates more disciples of Erasmus than Luther. What is more likely is that humans will muddle through the future just as they have muddled through the past. It is good to recall that the word *utopia* means "nowhere." It does not exist this side of the eschaton.

The Death of Evangelism

Sixth, social justice advocates so push a progressive agenda that those laypeople whose moral instincts do not coincide with theirs (or other ELCA leaders) either stop going to church altogether or start attending evangelical churches, where a resurgence of interest in evangelism is happening, as I mentioned in chapter 6. Progressive clergy are often unmotivated or unable to grow churches because this stance of progressivism undermines evangelism in favor of a political agenda. This political theology, in vogue in the ELCA and its predecessor groups for a half century, has contributed to declining membership in the ELCA, a drop from 5.4 million to 3.5 million and counting. Our seminary professors and other leaders should focus less on politics and instead train pastors as evangelists who do outreach to the unchurched and to those disengaged from the church, the "nones." After all, evangelism is something that the church is mandated by Christ to do, while advocacy can and should be done instead within political parties and advocacy groups.

Pitting People against One Another

Finally, the quest for justice pits people against one another and has a hard time unpitting them, since the injustices seem to remain entrenched or systemic. The system does not seem to change much for the better, even when various minorities are given power within it. The quest for justice as currently articulated is far less biblical than its advocates make it out to be. Instead, it is an outgrowth of autonomy where individuals are perceived as self-owners and have the right to develop their full potential however they configure it. Instead of buying into the alleged entitlements of the privileged self, a more biblical approach would honor the creatureliness of all humans, intertwined with that of all other creatures, along with a stewardship that seeks for ethical agents to offer their gifts for the sake of the well-being of the common good.

Consider the recent trend for ELCA assemblies to begin with some sort of ceremony lamenting the historical displacement of whatever native people formerly lived on the site where the assembly is being held. In some ways, it is a lovely gesture and certainly can be a consciousness-raising exercise. But how is it possible for Native Americans to receive justice from any of the nations of North or South America that are populated by immigrants of all different backgrounds and who are now imbedded in all their ancestral lands? No confession of sin can ever rectify the loss to Native Americans incurred by the European land grab of the Americas. Could financial compensation recompense them? It staggers the mind to think of the amount of wealth that would be required for this. Unfortunately, history is a stage with winners and losers, whether we like it or not. Even worse, there is often no way to rectify some social inequities.

But that should not set us back. Quite the contrary! In the face of such loss, we should instead seek to be good stewards of our current situation and so recover as much human potential and well-being for the creation as possible. The claims of justice often pit people against one another and all too often lead to ethical stalemates. But scriptural ethics are not limited to the quest for justice, which at best can be had only in snippets in this sin-drenched world.

Instead, inspired by the original human calling in Genesis to be good caretakers of God's garden, we can seek for the best steward-ship of the resources with which God has endowed in all humans and this planet. Focusing on the stewardship of human life in all its phases, along with sustainable practices enhancing the well-being of creation, may prove to be a better focus than that of justice, which all too often is framed through the lens of Enlightenment ideals far removed from the Bible. Indeed, we should no longer be tied to Enlightenment ideals of autonomy, which all too many current views of justice idealize. Instead, we should endeavor to unfold and express the "varieties of gifts" (1 Cor. 12:4) with which God has endowed people, all the while honoring the environment as the home that God has provided for us.

The Nature of the Gospel

Certainly, Christians should seek to uphold victims and care for the environment. What is in dispute is the nature of the Christian gospel and the church. Currently, social justice has become the gospel for many mainline Protestants. But that hardly offers truly good news,

especially to the poor. Marx was wrong to see the gospel as a nar-
cotic, the "opiate of the people." It is just the opposite. The gospel
empowers the poor and helps them move forward and remain hopeful in spite of social disadvantages. God has never abandoned the
poor but instead has often used them as His vessels to make this
world a better place.

After all, Mary—who received the promise from the angel
Gabriel and so was empowered for her role as the God-bearer—was
poor. So was her son Jesus Christ. We, too, need to reclaim the gospel as promise precisely for the downtrodden and for all, especially
in these troubled times. The church most makes a difference in the
world when it behaves as the church, providing an alternative to
the world, allowing people to live in but not of the world—and not
as the bureaucracy policing other bureaucracies.

In a word, the church offers the most when it deals with ultimate matters, matters of faith, and not the penultimate matters of
politics. In worldly affairs, the quest for good stewardship of human
life and creation can help move people forward toward establishing
a better, even more just, society. We need to remember that article 5
of the Augsburg Confession, on the office of preaching, comes before
article 6 on the new obedience and not try to flip-flop them. In addition, the Augsburg Confession offers no explicit program for how
article 6 is to be done. The church is most genuinely the church when
it proclaims judgment and grace, law and gospel, God's commands
and God's promises. Let's let that be our primary focus. Politics must
not be understood as a means of salvation but instead be honored
as a venue for service. In this way, the church will live and embrace
the fullness of response to God's word and not limit itself to one
humanly defined vision.

Church

CHAPTER 12

Should Lutherans Be Mainline Protestants?

If I were to pinpoint a core difference between the message of the church in which I was raised (The American Lutheran Church [TALC]) and the church today (the Evangelical Lutheran Church in America [ELCA]), I would say that the church in which I was raised focused on proclaiming the promise of eternal life in Jesus' name, in contrast to the righteousness of the law, while today's church centers on "social justice." By "eternal life," I understand that through Jesus Christ, and not through works of the law, one can have assurance of the forgiveness of sins, receive new life, and know that one's destiny beyond the grave is secure in the promise of heaven. From that word of assurance, one can live with courage in spite of the uncertainties of this life and contribute to this life with cheerfulness and confidence. I understand social justice to mean advocacy on behalf of minorities, the disadvantaged, and those oppressed, whether here or abroad. Naturally, Christians have always had a concern to help the disenfranchised and, in spite of criticisms, have a good track record in doing so. However, "mainline" churches, such as the ELCA, put a specific political spin on this that promotes the views of the political left and, in addition to standing up for "victims," seeks greater liberties in peoples' personal lives, such as their sexual relations. I need to be quite specific here because many theological and social conservatives share the desire to make the world better. But what "better" looks like differs on the basis of their different perspectives. Risking a generalization that borders on stereotype, the conservative mind-set tends to favor teaching people how to fish rather than giving people fish.

I have puzzled over these differences because the contrast between the church of my youth and that of today is striking. It is not as if the church of yore was socially indifferent. Many individuals in my congregation worked to help the down and out, the poor, and the oppressed. But the overall message of the church was focused on God's address to people as judgment and mercy, and outreach to the needy or oppressed was grounded in that truth. But the message heard in that same congregation today reshapes that message of judgment and mercy into a specific ethical formula. The church, seen as a denomination, is to collaborate with agencies to pressure the government into advocating for policies thought to alleviate the needs of the disenfranchised. This view of justice seeks to secure not only equal opportunities but even equal outcomes. Hence the ELCA has promoted quotas as a way to establish "justice" in the denomination. In public life, this translates into the church promoting such measures as higher taxes on the rich, higher levels of services provided to the poor, and a guaranteed minimum income. That may well be good, but for many reasons, I resist thinking that this should be the distinctive mission of the *church*. Is the church to be aligned with a certain political slant, or is there nothing of a distinctive faith stance—proclaiming the Name above all names—that is at the heart of the church's ministry?

When I was young, TALC was not fully a mainline Protestant church. It was on its way to becoming that, but it was not yet that *in toto*. What do I mean by a mainline Protestant church? Mainline Protestants, which includes such groups as the United Church of Christ, the Episcopal Church USA, the United Methodist Church, and the Christian Church (Disciples of Christ), have several features that characterize their identity.[1] It would not be possible here to itemize all such characteristics, and different mainline Protestant denominations accentuate some over others. But there are three I'd like to highlight. First, mainline Protestants look to the Bible as an important, even central, book of faith, but it is not to be trusted in its entirety. One must discern the husk from the kernel in it. Not only is the Bible filled with factual errors, but it may also have faulty religious concepts. For example, some feminists condemn the Bible as advocating "divine child abuse," since God the Father intentionally sent Jesus to His death as a sacrifice for the world's sin, in spite of the fact that the Eternal Son chose to bear the sin of the world. Likewise, some feminists are offended that God is designated as the "Father," since they feel that this indicates an authoritarian male bias. Second, mainline Protestants value tolerance and acceptance and so are apt to advocate Jesus and His ethic of love for the downtrodden as good but have issues with Jesus as an exclusive Savior. Mainline Protestants tend to see humans not as in a dire situation, oppressed by problems from which they cannot extricate themselves, like sin, a bound will, death, and the devil, but instead as capable of improving through science, technology, tolerance, and care. It's not that mainline Protestants never talk about sin, but sin is less about human rebellion against God and more about self-defeating practices that keep violence entrenched as a way of life. Third, in mainline Protestantism, the gospel is less about the promise per se—that God has committed in Christ to advocate on behalf of the sinner, even to recreate the sinner—but instead is about a liberating future of fairness, nonviolence, and unbridled self-expression, provided that no one is hurt. In the mainline perspective, the power of the gospel is to convert people to this enlightened ethics, and the agency of the Spirit in the church is to lead the world to this idyllic future.

The Fundamentalist/Modernist Debate

There is a long history to the rise of mainline Protestantism, which most recently can be traced in this country to the "fundamentalist/ modernist" controversies early in the twentieth century but also further back to the time of the Enlightenment and how European theologians reacted to the Enlightenment. Today's mainline Protestants are heirs of those voices early in the twentieth century who believed that Christianity must get in line with newer ways of thinking such as the historical-critical approach to Scripture, which looked at the Bible primarily as a human document. Historical criticism of the Bible challenged traditional views that Moses wrote the Pentateuch (first five books of the Bible) or that the entire book of Isaiah was to be attributed to one author or that Paul wrote the Pastoral Epistles.[2]

Likewise, liberal Protestants believed that miracles such as Christ's virgin birth or His substitutionary atonement should not be litmus tests for deciding who is in or out of the church, and similarly, Christians should adopt some version of the theory of evolution. Important for my concern, they also advanced a "social gospel"— that is, the notion that the gospel is about challenging capitalists who take advantage of workers through overwork and unfair compensation. Beginning in the nineteenth century, industrialization in America and Europe left many workers slaving in factories with little say about their wages and benefits and working at the mercy of their employers, who often were not fair. In the social gospel perspective, true Christians should advocate for these employees and help them improve their lot by challenging the injustice meted out by the employers. Many of the early leaders of liberal Protestantism were also pacifists, but the apparent justice of America's involvement in the Second World War would weaken the propriety of that stance. Fundamentalists, in contrast, ignored such social concerns and limited themselves to defending traditional Christian doctrines. In time, a view called *neo-orthodoxy* would develop in Europe, especially with the thinking of Karl Barth, which sought a compromise between the two views—particularly through the metaphor of the husk and the kernel. The Bible may have trappings bound to its time period, but even so, eternal truth can be found at its core.

The Big Three

For the most part, Lutherans stood outside this debate. I think that this was the case for a number of reasons, some apparent and some less so. The bulk of Lutherans in the early twentieth century lived on farms or in small towns. Modernist perspectives were more apt to find their home in the growing cities. But many Lutherans, particularly in the Upper Midwest, had been nurtured by mission agencies in Germany and Scandinavia, which had already in Europe been exposed to such "modernist" thinking in the philosophies of Immanuel Kant, G. W. F. Hegel, and Friedrich Schleiermacher and had quite intentionally rejected these stances. In fact, several theological faculties of European universities, such as in Oslo under the leadership of Gisle Johnson, discarded these modernist stances. So an earlier origin for the rise of mainline Protestantism can be found in the attempts of European philosophers and theologians to reinterpret faith in light of Enlightenment thinking. Enlightenment thinking advocated the autonomy of the individual self and the ability of science and technology to lead humanity to a brighter future. Authority, hierarchy, tradition, and the senses were often disdained by Enlightenment figures. Instead of seeing the gospel as promise, Kant saw it primarily as progressive ethics or "doing," Hegel saw it primarily as metaphysics or "thinking," and Schleiermacher saw it primarily as spirituality or "feeling."[3]

Kant believed that the truth of the Christian faith could be found not in its surface presentation of Jesus as a divine Savior, a mythological trapping, but instead as ethical truths. Jesus is a role model for the ideal ethical life. Now, for Kant, the core of ethical truth is not following rules hallowed by tradition and presided over by authorities. Instead, authentic ethics involves daring to think for oneself, growing up, becoming mature, and being independent of authorities, whether those of the state or the church or tradition.[4] If you do just what people have always done, you are not affirming your own voice, and so you cannot possibly be free. For Kant, thinking for yourself means that you must seek not just your own whims but instead universal truth, what would be ethically right for any rational creature. Kant designed a test to help people figure out such universal standards, the "categorical imperative."[5] The categorical imperative asks us to examine our motives and go only with that motive that everyone should follow. In Kant's perspective, the Christian faith can be valuable only insofar as it fosters such individual freedom or autonomy. We are not to follow the Ten Commandments, because that would be letting an Authority, God, determine our lives; instead, we must test our motives to see if everyone should follow them. You should only do what you can rationally determine to be right—universally so—for everyone.

Now while Kant believed we could know ethical truth, he was skeptical that we could ever step outside of our minds to know the world as such. All we ever know is how we perceive the world; we never know the world in itself. "God" as such is not a reality we could ever know, but instead, "God" is an idea that symbolizes how, eventually, all knowable things, at least how the mind conceives of things, will be cataloged, put in an encyclopedia, and thus understood. For Kant, to see the gospel as a promise shortchanges its ethical potential to create an ideal community where all rational creatures would honor each other's autonomy.

Hegel reacted to Kant's skepticism about humans' ability to know reality as such. He found it ironic that Kant could spend a lot of energy talking about knowing but end up being so skeptical about knowing reality as such (and not just how we experience it). But his take on the gospel as promise is no less problematic. For Hegel, the reason that reality as such is knowable is because we human knowers share much more with God than we realize. Hegel maintained that God is Spirit, which prima facie sounds pretty Christian, but then he goes on to claim that as Spirit, God is coming to know Himself more and more and that God does this in and through our human spirits. In other words, "God" is completely dependent upon humanity—especially the smartest humans of all, the philosophers, for God to fully be aware. So for Hegel, it is not only that humans can know God (Kant was wrong) but even stronger: God only knows Himself in and through humanity—especially philosophers like Hegel who are able to think such sublime and challenging thoughts. For Hegel, then, God is not some kind of totally other being than that of humanity but, in a sense, the entire evolutionary history of the cosmos, the divine curriculum vitae, finding its summit in human thinking. It is God thinking Himself into being through such human thinking. God is becoming more and more of Himself in and through us. Like Kant, the Christian faith is a mythical presentation of this truth. One must move beyond the mythological husk to get the worthwhile kernel. When Christians confess that God became human in Jesus Christ, that is really mythological talk for the real metaphysical truth that God's journeying beyond His own abstract spirituality by clothing Himself in concrete human history, particularly in Jesus' suffering and death, was all so that God might come out right-sided as the Spirit, which has truly integrated all history within itself.[6] Believe it or not, that is symbolized by the church. So for Hegel, to see the gospel as a promise is inadequate: the gospel needs to be presented as metaphysics, the quest for universal reality.

Finally, Schleiermacher looked for the truth of faith not in Kant's ethics of autonomous freedom nor in Hegel's metaphysics of "Spirit," which is able to differentiate itself into the physical cosmos and return to itself within human history, but instead in feeling—particularly when this is understood as the "feeling of absolute dependence."[7] That is, what Protestants call "the word" is really an expression of feeling. And the "feeling of absolute dependence" is the distinctive religious feeling that all people have, whether or not they are aware of it. It is their "God-consciousness." Christian faith is valuable only insofar as it gets people in touch with this specific feeling. The feeling of absolute dependence is the key that unlocks the truth of the Christian faith, the kernel underneath the husk. The church holds forth the image of Christ in its teaching, preaching, and worship, and that image helps people get in touch with their God-consciousnesses. Jesus Himself had perfect God-consciousness because He allowed the feeling of absolute dependence to shape all that He said, thought, and did, even to the point that His God-consciousness was a veritable incarnation of God in Him. Insofar as this God-consciousness is mediated through the message about Jesus Christ, we progress in our own paths toward becoming more and more like Jesus Christ. The promise then, for Schleiermacher, is transformed from a word coming from God into a feeling found in the depths of human self-consciousness. Becoming aware of this God-consciousness is the path to true human fulfillment or enlightenment.

These three perspectives, Kant's, Hegel's, and Schleiermacher's, were popular and well-known in Europe by the 1820s and 1830s. Those mission societies, agencies, and institutions that sent missionaries from Europe to this continent to gather people into Lutheran churches were aware of these perspectives but for the most part rejected them. They found them to be inadequate for mission and, in a word, untruthful. Our forebears were deeply influenced by renewal movements in the nineteenth century that emphasized conversion and new life, the essential truthfulness of the Scriptures and the Lutheran confessions, the viability of historic worship and the traditional liturgy, and outreach to the poor and marginalized. They did not seek a deeper truth in the kernel, in opposition to the husk. They were somewhat indifferent about university trends, or in some cases, such as the university in Christiania (Oslo), they got the upper hand over the more liberal theology. They were all influenced by romanticism, which gave no privilege to modern, "scientific" perspectives as somehow brooking "the truth," and instead believed that there was much value in the ancient and medieval traditions. The older perspective was aware that science requires a wider context than science itself in order to make sense.[8] In their view, the Bible provided that wider context.

If any credence were given to any of the prior "big three," Kant, Hegel, or Schleiermacher, it would have been Schleiermacher because he, too, was influenced by romanticism. But even so, our forebears had issues with Schleiermacher because of his tendency to favor feelings over Scripture. Our spiritual forebears were far more influenced by leaders such as Pastor Claus Harms in Kiel who, at the time of the three-hundredth anniversary of the Reformation, wrote his own ninety-five theses in opposition to the rationalist (modernist, liberal) theology that had gotten ahold of the church of his day. In a word, it is not as if our forebears had not been exposed to the more "enlightened" thinking. They had been, and they rejected it in favor of a more traditional approach to faith. They granted it no privileged position. Instead, they allowed the narrative of the Scriptures as a whole to configure what's viable for critical thinking and, for that matter, the modern world. The "big three" all highlight the ego, the self, as the source or focal point of truth. Our ancestors were aware that there is no self or ego apart from God's generous and creative mercy and grace upholding and sustaining it. They also understood that human justification before God would be on the basis of not our own doing, thinking, or feeling but instead faith alone in Christ.

William Streng: A Case Study

If my narrative is more or less correct, then how did a group like TALC become a mainline Protestant church? It is fair to say that as American universities became more "secular," critical of faith, and advocates of Enlightenment thinking—at the same time that the church became less rural and more urban and so more exposed to these Enlightenment ideals—many Lutheran leaders saw mainline

Protestantism as the wave of the future and wanted to get on board with it. Additionally, Lutherans, like most immigrants, wanted to become American—and becoming American in a religious sense meant adopting much of the language and thought modes of the dominant Calvinist paradigm, which highlights the goal of faith as transforming or Christianizing culture. Lutherans were able to fight this off as long as they had a leadership cadre that was well-educated in Lutheran thought modes, worship ways, and spiritual practices. When that education weakened, it was harder to identify the water in which we swam and in which we needed to offer our distinctives. In many respects, as Lutherans climbed the social ladder, so to speak, they wanted to be like their upper-rung peers.

As a case study, I appeal to the thinking of a professor of education at Wartburg Seminary, the late William Streng, and will specifically take up stances for which he was advocating in his book *In Search of Ultimates* (1969).[9] I need to be cautious here because students of William Streng repeatedly name him as a powerful mentor, a professor who truly cared for not just the academy but the parish. Repeatedly, they tell me that he was concerned with molding faithful and true pastors, and decades after their graduation from seminary, his students would single him out as the one professor who imparted wisdom about how to connect theology with the life of the parish. I have no wish to denigrate his work but simply intend to examine it in order to understand better how TALC became mainline. Likewise, the fact that I focus here on a representative of the American Lutheran Church of 1930 in no way is to be read that the Evangelical Lutheran Church of 1917 was no less complicit.[10] It merely indicates how numerous important trends can be found in one particular figure. Primarily, I will focus on three aspects of his work: (1) demythologizing the Bible, (2) situation ethics, and (3) his construal of pietism. Each of these features bears on how much of American Lutheranism became mainline. As we shall see, to demythologize the Bible ultimately undermines its unconditional authority. *Situation ethics*, a term that today sounds outdated, is an approach to ethics completely defined by care, doing no harm, and "justice." It maintains the inviolability of the individual and the individual's "right" to achieve his or her own good. It undermines the roles of tradition, authority, and sanctity, which are so important for most people alive and who have ever lived. Finally, Streng pits pietism against "servanthood," with the former presented as self-serving, narcissistic spiritual growth and the latter as productive, community-ordered service. Historically, pietism and "servanthood" were never pitted against one another, and the unintended consequence of Streng's move (which was, I think, widely shared at the time) was to undermine those very practices such as a rich prayer life, meditation on Scripture, and the like, which sustain a robust ministry.

Catching the Context

Since the book was published in 1969, it is worth our while to remember the major events in 1968–69. No doubt, the era felt revolutionary and explosive. Even as a ten-year-old child, I was struck by the endless reporting on the Vietnam War, the hippie movement, communes, greater sexual liberties, and the like. Specifically, events in 1968 included rioting in Chicago associated with the Democratic National Convention in August; the North Vietnamese launch of the Tet Offensive, a turning point in the Vietnam War (January–February); American soldiers massacring 347 civilians at My Lai (March 16); Czechoslovakia being invaded by the Russians and Warsaw Pact forces to crush a liberal regime; Martin Luther King Jr. being slain in Memphis (April 4); and Sen. Robert F. Kennedy being shot and critically wounded in a Los Angeles hotel after winning the California primary (June 5) and died on June 6.

The title of Streng's book, *In Search of Ultimates*, clues us into the fact that he is on board with the program of the "big three." His approach, designed to promote discussion in the parish, similar to the current ELCA trends advocating for parishes to be "communities of moral discernment," a values-clarification approach to ministry, wants to get his audience to distinguish the negotiable from the nonnegotiable, the real truth from perceived truth, the penultimate from the ultimate, and the husk from the kernel. Even after forty-five years, the book is remarkable in that any given chapter is devoted not to Streng's own narrative but instead to questions, challenges, and puzzles designed to provoke the reader to think outside the box. The not-so-subtle message here is that faith is not about doctrine but about open-ended inquiry liberated from any confining criteria for truth. What Streng fails to comprehend is that his antidoctrinal stance is in fact another type of doctrine widely held by mainline Protestants: that it is deeds and not creeds that count. Streng's allegedly open-ended inquiry just reveals his own captivity to modern thought modes. Obviously, these scenarios and questions would work best in small groups where several people could bounce ideas off one another. Occasionally, the questions lend themselves to a specific perspective, while others are genuinely open-ended. So for example, the first question in the entire book runs thus:

> A renowned Dutch Roman Catholic theologian maintains that one of the most heretical acts in which we can engage today is to recite the traditional, historic creeds. What is he trying to say? Do you agree? (p. 4)

Now of course, the unthinking reciting of creeds does not indicate the maturity of faith to which our catechetical instruction ideally wants to move people. But historically, the whole point of the creeds had been to preserve the church from heresy—to keep the message of the church about Jesus true so that people could hear the gospel of salvation in contradistinction to other purported "gospels." So what could this question be about? In a word, what Streng is suggesting is that the creeds have worn out their usefulness, because in today's world, we encounter newer perspectives from science and have a newer outlook on how to live (the individual has far more choices than what existed in the past), and so the creeds have become somewhat dated. What had been designed to protect Christians from heresy is now the new heresy because it keeps Christians trapped in the past. A living and vital Christianity will take the risk of opening the windows and letting in the fresh, new breezes. A Christianity that fails to do this will eventually die: "change or die," as Episcopal Bishop Spong has more recently put it.

The fourth question runs thus:

> How would you react to this statement: "The church should return to its basic purpose—leading unsaved souls to Christ. The individual

should be involved in social issues, but the church should stay clear of these issues." (p. 4)

Naturally, this gets to the heart of my most important concern: how did we move from centering our ministry on eternal life in Jesus' name to social justice? Of course, Streng leaves the matter open-ended. You can respond however you wish. But the fact that it would even be an option to downplay leading souls to Christ means that the farm has already been sold. Streng would never be asking the question if he was not already committed to the latter approach. The fact that he raises the question plants doubt about the former "option." Even more important, he conflates the church as "the assembly of all believers among whom the gospel is purely preached and the holy sacraments are administered according to the gospel"[11] with a this-worldly, or "left-hand," denominational institution, which now has run wild with social agendas. In truth, it is the denominational institution that is to support congregations, and not vice versa. The gospel, not anything else, defines the very being of the church.

Redefining Church

As noted, Streng fails at defining what he means by *church*. Some sixty-five years before Streng wrote this book, the old Iowa Synod from which Streng came was operated out of the parlor of Pastor Deindörfer's parsonage in Waverly, Iowa.[12] It was a one-room show. I take it by *church*, Streng is referring to the multifloored headquarters of TALC in Minneapolis, including its various departments and structures, educational institutions, and mediums for advocacy. In Deindörfer's time, the mission of the church was to start new congregations, train pastors and teachers, and support missionaries. The only way "the church" can advocate for social issues is when it is itself *another worldly agency* with a sufficient bureaucracy, staff paid to do such work. Throughout most of American Lutheran history, there have been no such denominational headquarters to do that. And indeed the growth of such denominational headquarters, most of which developed after the Second World War, with multimillion-dollar budgets, was due to the hard work of orthodox pastors, evangelists, teachers, and faithful laity who all believed that the church must grow precisely because they wanted to see heaven as full as possible. Within five years of Streng's publishing his book, TALC would begin to see its first decline in membership in its history. And this downward spiral remains unabated in the ELCA. Is it too outrageous to draw the conclusion that unless Christians invest in the spiritual life of their fellow humans, the church will not grow? Yet the current perspective on social advocacy in the ELCA assumes a top-heavy denominational headquarters with sufficient clout to match shoulders with secular governments, businesses, and agencies. Apart from that, Christians' motivation to advocate for social justice would simply have to be done within those preexisting structures in the world (or they would have to create such agencies, but quite independently of any church bureaucracy). It is to be noted, however, that in case after case, all mainline churches that focus on "social issues" are in decline. Ironically, those denominations that seek to adapt the most to "modern culture" decline—and some dramatically so. Between 1960 and today, the nation has doubled in population, but churches like the United Church of Christ (UCC) and the Episcopal Church are half the size they were in 1960. Likewise, we should note that our confession of faith serves to unite people from diverse backgrounds and political views. But a focus on social issues guarantees disagreement and infighting within a church because people naturally will not see eye to eye about what constitutes justice in any given case, let alone how to proceed toward obtaining justice even in those situations where people might agree. Possibly an unintended consequence, but Streng's direction is a guarantee to weaken the church.

Two Kinds of Righteousness

Most importantly, Streng's question fails to honor Luther's approach to social issues, which can be termed *two kinds of righteousness*, a passive righteousness before God and an active righteousness before our neighbors. Streng seems to put personal salvation and public justice on a par as two competing alternatives. But in fact, passive righteousness deals with our relationship with God, a vertical pole, if you will, and active righteousness deals with human interrelationships, a horizontal pole, if you will. The two poles need and should not be pitted against each other. But where our situation is different from that of Luther's is that unlike Luther, we live in a democracy. How justice is determined and is established is dependent upon the give-and-take between disagreeing and competing perspectives. When the church simply takes one side of this debate, sanctions it, and touts it as the genuine "Christian" approach, it is bound to alienate many. And so it has. Some issues, such as protecting the unborn and sanctioning sexual relations within traditional marriage, have biblical, catholic, and apostolic warrant and, prior to the sixties, were never thought to be open to negotiation. Historically, these matters are not open to debate. But for Streng, all such matters are now out on the table.

The fact that Christians take different stances on how to help the underprivileged is not the major reason for the membership decline in the ELCA. The major reason for this is that when the mission of the church is reduced to advocating for progressive politics, it loses its momentum for mission. If the gospel saves someone from eternal death and offers hope for and consolation in this life, there is a huge motive to share the gospel. To not share it is a truly uncaring act. But if the mission of the church is primarily, if not solely, to advocate for justice, then the church becomes one among many agencies, such as political parties, which can do such advocacy, and in fact, other agencies do even a better job. But no other agencies in the world are designated to share the gospel other than the church. On top of that, the political left (unlike the political right) has mixed feelings about religion. There is a percentage of the political left that does not favor left-leaning religion any more than it favors right-leaning religion. For this stance, all religion is deceptive and problematic because all religion undermines the centrality and sacrality of the individual.

Christian Discipleship as Philosophizing

Streng thus seeks a book that will help "serious and searching minds" (p. vii) not be alienated from the faith. He is sensitive to university-educated laity who have been exposed to (if not indoctrinated into) the newer approaches in ethics, which accentuate freedom

SHOULD LUTHERANS BE MAINLINE PROTESTANTS?   215

as the individual's ability to determine his or her own meaning. But for Streng to offer an approach to faith compatible with that view of freedom, which has been called *autopoiesis* (the self constructs its own meaning), then traditional Christianity must undergo scrutiny, testing, and sifting. Old fables, which no "modern man" can believe, must be challenged and let go of. In contrast to theology as he had learned it,[13] the Bible is not to be seen as a monolithic body of organized truths, objective knowledge about the facts of salvation, but instead, truth is the "eventful resonance of life with Life" (p. 3). Like Schleiermacher, for Streng, the truth of the Bible is valuable only as it resonates with experience. Education then is not instruction but discovery. The vocation of the contemporary, thoughtful Christian is to search things out for oneself (p. xi). But in so doing, one must discern what is essential in faith from what is accidental, what is of enduring value from mere tradition. And the punch line is that the coming struggle will be not (primarily) between liberals and conservatives but between those who affirm that the church must engage in social issues versus those who limit the church's mission to individuals finding their salvation (p. 4).

Christians should welcome scrutiny and testing: "Don't believe every spirit but test the spirits to see if they come from God" (1 John 4:1). Traditionally, Lutherans have emphasized strong catechesis of youth in order to give them a basis for future questions and understanding of their faith. Memorization was meant not to be mindless but to shape the thoughts and words so that one's confession of faith was truly one with the holy, catholic, and apostolic church.

Since each puzzle in the text is designed to get you to think outside the box, the metaphor that would best describe the Christian life for Streng is not primarily that of the disciple but instead that of the philosopher. Streng offers an approach to Christian education where he is much like Socrates, a gadfly provoking you to question or challenge everything you assumed was true. He does this through a kind of cross-examination (*enlenchus*) that gets you to break down your defenses and that then finally brings you to a state of perplexity (*aporia*). Once you admit that you thought you knew the truth but in fact you do not really know it, then you are able to begin to truly think and reflect. Then, like Kant, you are able to free yourself from oppressive tradition and finally grow up, mature, and become your own man or woman—no longer a child dependent upon catechisms you memorized or an authoritative preacher. In that way, Christianity can truly liberate you; you become a "philosopher" for yourself. That approach to Christianity is freed of its paternalistic (abusive) heritage.

What Streng cannot question or challenge is the "modern worldview" that so highlights justice for the individual. No doubt, as one of the photos in the book shows elderly white Catholic nuns demonstrating hand in hand with young black civil rights protesters, Streng understands his times and the importance that, in fact, "justice" is hardly obtainable in a Jim Crow America. Streng believes that Christians who fail to challenge traditionalism will simply keep that old Jim Crow America in place. On top of that, Streng believes it is the role of the institutional denomination to shake Christians out of complacency. Again, the church is defined not through its means to deliver the word and sacraments—proclaim Christ—but instead by its ability to alter the political turf. Everything rides on advancing earthly justice. Hence Streng says that if Christianity wants a rebirth, it must "start with the world" (p. 11). He quotes a young man who says that he had to turn away from established religion in order to grapple with philosophy and finally find one that would suit his own needs. Streng is greatly concerned that such people are not lost to the church. But his path is that the church must adapt to this young man's way of thinking. He has no sense to challenge this man—that in fact this man's true identity is to be found in God's evaluation of him and not his way of constructing his own philosophy of life.

Streng's Image of Jesus

The image of Jesus that arises in Streng's book is a man with whom the seeker above could identify. For Streng, Jesus is a heroic figure. Jesus dealt with ultimate, not peripheral, issues. He was not concerned with whether or not evolution is compatible with Genesis, but instead, He is a hip rebel. Jesus did not subject Himself blindly to the patriarchal authoritarianism of the religious elite of His day but instead challenged them (p. 13). Jesus is a kind of philosopher. So much so that He was a "college dropout." Jesus could have spent time in the university but was too busy helping others (p. 19). After all, it's not creeds but deeds that count. He would never be satisfied that people are born originals but die as copies (p. 22) and would fight against the fact that our culture more than any other treats the poor so poorly (p. 23). Jesus was truly concerned with people and addressed them in their actual situations and loved them to the bitter end (p. 29). Jesus, then, is a figure for the "man of today" who is concerned with not whether or not God is gracious but whether or not God actually exists. And God's existence is proved not in abstract reasoning but by how we live. If we are to take Jesus seriously, we have to admit that while the life of Jesus is important, it is the meaning of His life that is much more important. Streng's Jesus sounds much like Marcus Borg's—but long before Borg.

Likewise, the view of God that Streng advocates is one we'd be familiar with. Instead of opening worship with an abstruse, confusing triune name of "Father, Son, and Spirit," it may be much better to simply begin worship "in the name of God" (p. 30). A more generic God meets modern man's needs instead of the convoluted Trinitarian language.

Secularization: Yes! Secularism: No

For Streng, authority and tradition are always pitted against the individual and freedom. His is an uncritical Enlightenment perspective, one that his theological ancestors were aware of but that they soundly rejected. I puzzle over why this would be the case. Streng writes as if everything he is bringing up is somehow new. But it is not. It is exactly the stance that Thomas Jefferson or Benjamin Franklin would have taken with respect to the institutional church. So if these "new" concepts are not so new, and if in fact Streng's theological ancestors in the old Iowa Synod would have rejected them outright in the 1850s, why does this "modern" thinking have such a hold over him?

As I've mentioned, my deepest hunch is that the church with which Streng had been raised, the old Iowa Synod, was primarily rural and agrarian, composed not of members educated in a secular university that had exposed them to critics of faith like Friedrich Nietzsche but instead of literate but not secular farmers.

As the church became less rural and more urban, and as its members were exposed to an increasingly more secular education, along with the "revolutionary" spirit of the sixties (and even the fifties), theologians like Streng felt that the older orthodox theology was tied to such a rural, less secular mind-set. As the structures that had made the older theology credible were less in place, the church needed to get with the program shaping up in secular universities if it was to survive and if it were to be perceived as and actually be ethical. Not only that, but Streng's book indicates just how thoroughly he had imbibed the newer theology designed to accommodate this more urban, secular spirit. In other words, he himself believed what he was writing was the truth. Interestingly, he asks this question:

> Does this help? Secularization is a process or a liberating development in which we are freed from a closed religious or metaphysical world-view. It finds its roots in the biblical faith and is open to change and to involvement. Secularism is a closed system which keeps us in bondage to this world. (p. 66)

So Streng is opposed to "secularism" because it is just one more "ism," like fundamental*ism*. But "secularization," which opens our horizons beyond rigid, authoritarian, traditional, hierarchical, and patriarchal systems, is quite good, wholesome, and even necessary.

Streng's view of humanity is out of touch with reality. There is no thinking done apart from some sense of authority, tradition, and hierarchy. Scientists are accountable to a guild, which, counter to popular imagination, is prone to conservatism—that is, scientists do not like changing their minds unless mounting evidence forces them to. They have a guild, a hierarchy of PhDs who monitor how knowledge is assessed in their field. Scientific research builds on a tradition, whether it be a tradition of molecular theory or the extent of biological change within species. Streng buys into an Enlightenment perspective that is simply unwarranted based on how people actually behave. He is critical of the tradition he has received, but he has very little skill or ability to challenge that tradition. He believes that this is necessary to save Christianity, but in fact his defense of the faith sells out the faith in the same stroke. The tendency in his secularizing approach is to reduce matters to this-worldly consequence. Eternal life matters little since sin is a fixable problem. "Social issues" are of the utmost importance because genuine care only applies to this-worldly affairs. For Streng, we are being saved from oppressive tradition in order to establish our own agency in our own voice. He is convinced that since we want this for ourselves we will want to do that for others—especially those deemed oppressed.

Demythologizing the Bible

Of course, for Protestants the authority for matters of faith and life is the Bible. Here Streng urges we must *declutter*, separate the ultimate from the peripheral, drop its mythology so that we can encounter its ultimate concern. The point of indicating that the Bible is strewn with mythology is not to dismiss it but to decode it (p. 51). The Bible is good insofar as it witnesses to God's saving acts and the ramifications of those saving acts for an enlightened ethics. Quoting Harvey Cox, Streng asks,

> What is your reaction to this statement: "The poverty question comes up in many ways: Should the church remain largely as one of the 'helping agencies' and thereby continue its traditional social-service view of poverty? Should it cast its lot with non-governmental organizers, such as Saul Alinsky, investing money, staff, and prestige in building political power for the poor? These, not the Virgin Birth or the inerrancy of Scripture, are the issues church leaders discuss most ferociously today." (p. 63)

Doctrine is rather trivial, but eliminating poverty is consequential. That, of course, was the aim of Lyndon B. Johnson's Great Society. What is rather naïve here is that the "causes" of poverty are so numerous that some poverty simply cannot be eliminated. Some are poor because there is no work available. Others are poor because they do not save. Some are poor because they are sidelined. Others are poor because poverty is often where many start out in life, and they are unable to move beyond it. In fact, poverty, not affluence, has been the norm in human history. No doubt, Streng would agree with Karl

Marx that the point of philosophy is not to understand the world but
to change it. But in fact, the gospel unleashes an incredible power to
do just that since before God (*coram deo*) neither what we have nor
what we lack defines us. Instead, Jesus Christ does. Christians should
join hands with all humans to seek to eliminate poverty, insofar as
that could be done. *But to pit the faith against ethics is foolish.* And
it is not by any means conservatives who are doing that, but in fact,
here it is Streng. One wonders if it is less because he wishes to press
specific ethical aims and more because he so disdains tradition. In
fact, it is because there is a vertical dimension to faith that the poor
can claim dignity before anyone in the world. So if we are truly concerned about social ethics, we should not sell out doctrine or pit doctrinal truth against ethics. But we should not be so naïve as to think
that poverty is the sort of thing for which one answer suffices.

New Morality and Old Immorality

Streng's tendency uncritically to adopt the secularizing approaches
in higher education is evident most clearly in his discussion of the
"new morality." He brings up the response I heard as a youth that
the new morality is simply the old immorality but rejects it outright.
True to his antiauthoritarian, antihierarchical bent, he disdains codes
or commandments (such as we find in the Scriptures and the catechism) and replaces them with "love" (pp. 100–107). What the world
needs now is love, sweet love. He characterizes the new morality as
rejecting authority, pragmatic (what works), intensely personal, and
situation based. Again, "modern man" (now modern humanity) must
reinvent the wheel with respect to ethics. Otherwise, if we blindly
follow tradition and commands, we remain immature, childish, and
insensitive. His is an approach that would delight moral theorist
Lawrence Kolhberg: if we are to be ethical, we must move from conventional ways of thinking and become our own postconventional,
enlightened philosophers. Streng has no sense for a discipleship that
takes "every thought captive to Christ" and sifts the truthfulness of
ethical proposals based on the three thousand years of experience
informed by the Scriptures. Instead, that must all be decluttered.
He is quick to indicate that the new morality means that we are not

to do whatever we want but instead to do what is most loving. So he does have a standard for ethics. And if it were Augustine's "love God and do as you please," we might have something valuable. But instead it is all to reinforce the autonomy of the love-infused ethical agent. Surprisingly, the matter of same-sex relations arises in this context, a matter I would not have expected a professor from Roman Catholic–dominated Dubuque, Iowa, to have raised in 1969.

> The Playboy philosophy states that any act of love-making, especially sexually, is moral if it does not hurt anyone, whereas the Christian principle is that no sexual act, whether homo or auto or hetero, is moral unless it helps someone. Right? (p. 110)

For Streng, sexuality is to be seen in the context of self-expression, not child making or child-rearing. If it promotes love, then it is something for which one never needs to say sorry. Again:

> There are sharp statement in the Bible against homosexuals (such as in Genesis 19 and Romans 1). Were these people possibly incapable of normal sexual relations? (p. 114)

Streng asks us to sympathize with homosexuals in spite of biblical injunctions against such practices. The autonomy of the individual trumps traditional mores. The roots of the 2009 ELCA decisions go back many decades. For Streng, the loving thing to do is always to assist individuals in their own processes of self-enhancement in the face of traditional scruples or prohibitions.

After decades of seminary teaching, for some reason, it does not occur to Streng that while prohibitions and exhortations exist in scriptural ethics, it is not just reduced to these. Instead, scriptural ethics fosters as much a narrative identity for Christians who learn from the shortcomings and successes of patriarchs, prophets, and disciples. The question of ethics is not just one of commandments (as central as they are) but also whether we will claim the courage of Elijah, the wisdom of Solomon, the humbleness of Mary, and the "justice" indeed shown by the waiting father in opposition to the older brother in the Parable of the Prodigal Son. The Bible raises

the question of not only following specific injunctions but also matters of character: who do we want to be like? Its narratives direct and
empower us toward the godly life promised for us in our baptisms.
Streng's view of faith is far closer to Luther's opponents, Erasmus's or
Müntzer's. As Erasmus said, faith is basically a simple ethics of love
that fosters wholesome living. As Müntzer said, such faith should
make Christians challenge "the system." Both stances are simplistic,
idealistic, and utopian and undermine the primary source of faith,
the Scriptures, which in fact empower Christian imaginations to live
like Christ.

Bye-Bye, Pietism

Finally, Streng's use of the word *pietism* has powerful repercussions
(p. 91). Lutheranism in the old world and in the new has been influenced to one degree or another by pietism. Certainly, this was true
of Streng's spiritual heritage. The legacy of pietism was to encourage
Bible study, private and group devotion, support for local and global
missions, and assistance to the underprivileged, such as orphans and
the destitute. Pietism billed itself as a reaction against a church that
believed the truth but failed to cultivate a relationship with God.
Orthodox Lutherans had always had issues with pietism. For one
thing, many of the Orthodox themselves had a robust spirituality
not in spite of their doctrinal systems but in tandem with and even
supportive of and supported by those systems. The orthodox theologians' chief charge against pietism was that it was all too prone to
mislead one into trusting one's feelings about one's status with God
instead of the objective word coming from God—such as the word
of absolution. Streng repeatedly presents pietism in a negative light
as focused only on individuals and their own spiritual growth in
opposition to "servanthood," which is focused on improving society.
The first deals only with one's interior, personal relationship with
God, while the second deals with social engagement. Streng's disdain for pietism, which was widely accepted by TALC leaders who
themselves had been raised in this tradition, would lead to specific
consequences. No doubt, some objected to pietism because they had
felt that rigorous spiritual discipline had somehow been forced upon

them in their youth, while with Streng, others felt that such pietism undermined the social impact of Christianity. Ironically, all mainline Protestant groups grew out of revivalist traditions similar to pietism (with the possible exception of the Episcopal Church USA). This is certainly true of the Christian Church (Disciples of Christ), the United Methodists, the American Baptists, and most Presbyterians. In a sense, mainline Protestants are "enlightened" revivalists. They are pietists burned out on traditional spiritual disciplines, but similar to the pietists with their social consciences, they have moved less toward helping the actual poor in concrete actions and more toward advocating for the poor through various agencies—indeed making their entire denominations serve as such agencies.

The legacy of the attempt to pit pietism against servanthood results in undermining spiritual practices (unless, of course, they are Buddhist or Hindu types of yoga or meditation). But private meditating on Scripture, group or individual prayer, and the like are perceived as self-serving and futile. But that takes away from pastors and faithful laity those resources that historically strengthened the individual's sense of outreach and witness in the world. Foolishly, Streng appeals to Bonhoeffer here as the role model of servanthood. No doubt, Bonhoeffer was that. But had Streng been aware of the degree to which Bonhoeffer centered his illegal Confessing Church Seminary in Finkenwalde, Germany, on the daily, even hourly, routine of such spiritual practices, Streng would realize that Bonhoeffer would not be his ally.[14] Bonhoeffer knew that in challenging times, the answer for the church was not to undermine spiritual practices but to buttress them. Luther, of course, was no pietist, and a good case can be made that pietism lacks continuity with Luther's teaching. But he was a man for whom the spiritual practices of prayer, devotional Bible reading, and the like were central and nonnegotiable. Such practices need not feed self-righteousness but instead strengthen the new person in Christ. We now have a cohort of clergy and laity who are able to lead Buddhist meditations far better than they can lead in free prayer or who look to the *Bhagavad Gita* for spiritual wisdom instead of the Psalter. Again, all this undermines the distinctive mission of the church, the ability to specify why a non-Christian ought to consider the claims of faith.

Assessing Streng's Legacy

But this leads me to a question. Streng so focuses on where young sixties mavericks are coming from but never looks to a convert to the faith. What if Streng had studied not secular humanity but instead those for whom secularism is not working? Why would someone come and ask for catechesis and baptism? How might traditional faith be attractive for those wrapped up in the anomie that secularism produces? How might the onus on creating your own meaning in life be oppressive—given that you have to invent your own standard for what makes life worth living?

In a word, for Streng, the value of Christianity, if properly understood, is that it can advance your own autonomy. Of course, the one imperative that might limit that is the imperative to love. But what Streng seems completely unable to do is challenge the modern worldview. It is a given. At best, Christianity can only accommodate to it. If Christianity fails to do that, it will die. He has no sense that possibly, as George Lindbeck put it, it is the text, the Scriptures, that "absorbs the world," makes us understand the world.[15] That is, in the biblical perspective, it is the Scriptures that provide not only the compass for how to understand the world but also, only in and through the Scriptures, the way to see the world for what it is— a creation of God, a gift—and to understand that life at its core is not a task of self-determination for the sake of self-fulfillment but, rather, a gift to be cherished by means of fearing, loving, and trusting in God above all things. He has little sense that humans are sinners trapped with a bound will—that we are bound to will what we will and not what God wills. I'm reminded of what the late Eric Gritsch once told me about one of my teachers, Gerhard Forde. Forde's main approach in Luther research was to highlight that the old self dies in Christ's death and a new person is raised in Christ's resurrection: there is no continuous self apart from God's grace. Gritsch said that if you want to understand Forde, you need to understand his target—to whom he was really opposed. Naturally, I would have thought the answer to that would have been pietism or possibly Eling Hove (the Norwegian American equivalent of Franz Pieper of the LCMS [Lutheran Church–Missouri Synod]). But surprisingly, Gritsch, based on his talks with Forde over several decades, said

Thomas Jefferson. That certainly caught me by surprise. But instantly, I grasped what Gritsch meant. It's not that Forde was somehow anti-democratic, let alone anti-American, but instead that the view of the autonomous self forged in the fires of Enlightenment thinkers, like Jefferson's thinking (and Kant's, Hegel's, and Schleiermacher's), was simply incompatible with who Christians are in Christ—dead to their own self-wills and alive to God.

Streng writes in an era in which *Time* magazine (October 22, 1965) proclaimed God is dead and Americans were reeling over Vietnam and race relations. But what the church could offer Americans—the understanding of all such matters in light of law and gospel—he shies away from. He is convinced that advances in science mean that we must liberate ourselves from superstition—as if science must entail a naturalistic view of reality. It never dawns upon Streng to ask, How is it the case that modern science developed in a culture influenced by Christianity and its Scriptures, the Bible?[16] The deeper truth of the Christian faith is not so much to believe in Jesus as to love like Jesus, who was, after all, antiestablishment, communal, and honored people's autonomy, similar to Marcus Borg's view today. The obligation of the church is to foster and advocate for those structures that enhance individuals' autonomy, especially individuals who are racial and sexual minorities. Finally, we need to approach the Scriptures in a less anthropomorphic way. When Streng speaks of a search for ultimates, he uses thinly veiled Tillichian lingo. Liberal theologian Paul Tillich taught that we must distinguish humans' ultimate concern from their own sense of what's personally good and what is in fact, objectively, an ultimate good. The latter would be God, and people need to align their own subjective senses of goodness with what is objectively good. For Tillich, beyond the anthropomorphisms of biblical mythology is the "God beyond God," who is the true God and who is not entrapped by human anthropomorphizing and with whom, in mystical adoration, we can be one. But that faith stance undermines the deeds-not-creeds approach of Streng. There simply can be no faith stance that is creedless. All religions have at their heart or core a creed. If that creed is wrong, then behavior likewise will fail to be right. The creeds must be maintained, or the gospel that God became human all so that we might be in right relation to God, along with the ethical ramifications of that truth, will be lost.

Streng's accentuating of ethics instead of promise as at the core of Christian faith and life is all done within a partisan perspective. In a word, his perspective, following the thinking of another secular thinker, moral psychologist Jonathan Haidt, is WEIRD.[17] That is, Streng and those who follow him do not think like most people in the world who live or who have ever lived. Streng's thinking is Western, Educated, Industrialized, Rich, and Democratic. WEIRD people are the minority of the world's population. Their perspectives on ethics are reductionistic, limiting ethics to matters such as care (as opposed to harm), liberty (as opposed to oppression), and fairness (as opposed to cheating). Most humans have a fuller approach to ethics that also take into account loyalty (as opposed to betrayal), authority (as opposed to subversion), and sanctity (as opposed to degradation). The latter matters for most humans are not conventional matters. This means that loyalty, authority, and sanctity are not made-up conventions but part of the fabric of human DNA. Indeed, liberals sometimes go beyond equality of rights to pursue equality of outcomes—such as we see in the quota system in the ELCA—which are hard to establish in a capitalist system. American conservatives likewise maintain similar ethical goals but interpret them thus: don't tread on me (with your liberal nanny state and its high taxes), don't tread on my business (with your oppressive regulations), and don't tread on my nation (with your United Nations and your sovereignty-reducing international treaties). They tend to sacralize the word *liberty* and not the word *equality*. But in general, most people in the world, and this includes American conservatives, in addition to care and fairness also value loyalty, authority, and sanctity. For most humans, authority is not bad because it is seen less as a dictator taking advantage of fearful underlings and more as the relation between a parent and child, where that parent maintains responsibility for that child. In this reading, the more liberal approach advocated by Streng and mainline Protestants is too narrow. It appeals to only a small segment of humanity, those who are WEIRD, and ignores a wider spectrum of human interest designed to sustain moral community.

To highlight justice alone and to read it only through the lens of autonomy ignores the complexity of how people live. No doubt, there are oppressed people whom Christians as members of a society, not the church as an advocacy agency, need to support. But all too often, people quickly claim their statuses of being victims. Ironically, that very claim undermines their own abilities to improve their lots, makes them dependent on others, and holds them back. *Coram mundo*—justice is something that is to be worked through, established through intense debate, and a goal to be sought with the realization that in a sinful world, it is not fully obtainable. The promise of eternal justice is no flight from reality but instead the power that can sustain those who seek it. But the church even today has no stronger message than to afflict the comfortable, expose sin for what it is, and comfort the afflicted—give Jesus to every spiritual beggar who knows his or her need.

Conclusion

Should Lutherans be mainline Protestants? No. We need not seek a deeper truth within the Scriptures, the kernel in the husk, whether it is some view of ethics, metaphysics, or feeling. The words of Scripture themselves envelop our lives and bring sense to them. More important, the Scriptures convey a word that must be proclaimed and that by forgiving sinners, actually changes the world.

No doubt, in today's church, its institutions, outreach, and parishes, the kind of thinking displayed by Streng has long had the upper hand. It is not likely that things will change any time soon. The answer is not to become "evangelical" as opposed to mainline. As indicated, mainline traditions were birthed by nascent American evangelicals. The answer is to boldly confess our Lutheran heritage as an alternative both to evangelicalism and to mainline Protestantism.

There are some voices in the wilderness that remain and call this church to repentance, but they are few and far between. In my view, the biggest problem in mainline thinking is that it so idolizes the modern perspective on the self and its autonomy that it substitutes this in place of the honor that we as creatures are to bestow on God. When we focus so much attention on a utopian future, we fail to give God's law and gospel to people right now who desperately need it. Those words, more than any other, allow us to receive the world as gift, find security in our relationship with God, and draw us to love our neighbors as ourselves. May God's Spirit empower His preachers and all the faithful to honor this word and share it.

CHAPTER 13

A Confessional Response to North American Lutheran-Reformed Ecumenism

The *Formula of Agreement* between the Evangelical Lutheran Church of America (ELCA) and three mainline Reformed churches, the Presbyterian Church (USA), the Reformed Church of America, and the United Church of Christ—building on the *Leuenberg Agreement* in Europe and heralded as an ecumenical breakthrough—raises important questions for confessional Lutherans. This paper will primarily examine Lutheran-Reformed relationships in the North American context in light of the earlier work of *Leuenberg*.[1] There are similarities and differences between both Europe and the United States that contribute to the conciliatory stance between these confessional groups. Unlike the sixteenth-century Reformers, however, many contemporary Protestant ecumenists are indifferent to the question of salvation, at least as it was seen by the Reformers, ultimately, as a rescue from the wrath of God.[2] Since salvation from God's judgment on sin is no longer on our theological radar, the previous disagreements over doctrine have become mere formalities that are easily sidestepped.

Those North American Reformed bodies that view themselves as orthodox, such as the Christian Reformed Church or the Orthodox Presbyterian Church, and their counterparts among Lutherans, such as the Missouri Synod or the Wisconsin Synod, still frame the discussion in terms of the classical disagreements, largely guided by Christological issues, such as the *genus maiestaticum*[3] and

Christ's bodily presence in the Lord's Supper.[4] Disagreements over these loci remain important because they, like the Reformers, are inextricably attached to a Christology and soteriology that state that we are being saved not only from our own misdeeds but also from God's judgment.

At stake for Lutherans is the view that God does not save what He does not assume.[5] But it is this very claim that is jeopardized by the *extra-Calvinisticum*.[6] The Reformed affirm a reserve in the Godhead with respect to the incarnation. But if there is such a reserve, then how are we saved? No doubt, if all of Christ in both natures comes and assumes all human space and time, then our human agency is ruled out. There would be nothing left over or with which we could exercise our free will and thus claim the law as our own righteousness.[7] Our free will *coram deo* would be excluded. Now, it is not as if the Reformed teach free will *coram deo*. But free will always wants to stake a claim wherever it can. A consistent Lutheran Christology is thoroughly informed by grace and thus leaves no place for free will. Such a negation of our free will liberates us from its illusions, giving us real freedom from the self-deifying self, and allows us to be creatures living by faith. But if there is some reserve in the incarnation, as the Reformed maintain, then God is less a threat to our space, being, and self-definition.[8]

In contrast to the Reformed objection that Lutherans confuse the two natures of Christ, we must—for the sake of the clarity of the gospel—affirm that the incarnate God is thoroughly enfleshed, that there is no reserve in the Second Person of the Trinity as incarnate. The entire person of the Son is incarnate in the man Jesus. Thereby, the resurrected Christ is inextricably attached to a human soul and body, now omnipresent through Christ's exaltation. And it is this very body that on the cross bore sin and expiates God's wrath. It is given as a *testament* in the Supper for our forgiveness and new life.[9]

The Agenda of North American Protestant Ecumenism

The reason it would seem that mainline Lutherans and the Reformed can so quickly come to an agreement about their historic differences is that they no longer are governed by a belief that we need salvation from God's wrath. The real agenda behind many Lutheran and Reformed ecumenists is well expressed in *An Invitation to Action*, the summary of the 1981–83 North American dialogues: "Humankind seems bent upon bringing the end of the world upon itself and all creatures of God by nuclear holocaust. Our churches are already enlisted in a common mission: participation in God's preservation of the world, God's struggle for justice and peace, and evangelization."[10] What ties these ecumenical partners together, at least in North America, is the fact that "each of our churches independently has addressed issues common to our local communities, our nation, and the world, such as: nuclear armament, peace, justice for the poor of our country and the world, prison reform, sex, marriage, and the family, economic justice, the yokes of race and class, ecology, and the advocacy of all persons denied their right to achieve their potential."[11] Hence the classical differences are not nearly as important as other issues, such as saving the world from humanity itself or becoming all we can possibly be. In my judgment, mainline Protestants should be challenged on this very matter. The church has no more important outreach than that of proclamation—specifically of the promise, in contradistinction to the law, which saves from sin, death, the devil, and wrath.

This is not said to undermine the achievements in the *Arnoldshain Theses* (1957), which affirm that Christ's body and blood are imparted in the consecrated bread and wine, or the various agreements that led to *Leuenberg*.[12] But it is to note that the overall direction of Lutheran-Reformed ecumenical discussions has been to see the disagreements of the Reformers as anachronistic. We "cultured despisers" have moved beyond these issues. But on what basis have we moved beyond them? It would seem that we agree with Schleiermacher, who claimed, "There are in our Augsburg Confession certain imperfections, and because of them I did not really want us to accept and endorse it anew word for word, so to speak, as our own confession. Among these imperfections is the fact that one finds in it still far too much talk about the wrath of God."[13] Instead of whistling away God's wrath via academic fiat, we need to distinguish God as He comes in His promise from God outside His promise: "For Luther, distinguishing God in and outside the proclaimed word is what theology is for. This theology is the business of the church. This is the only theology that lives under a living God, and does not speculate about God according to human designs or desires. It is what makes humanity aware that God always comes to hearers as a person: as the Father who speaks, the Son who is spoken, and the Holy Spirit who hears by creating new beings through the church's message."[14]

Across the vast spectrum of confessional traditions, no two groups seem to be as close as Lutherans and the Reformed. For this very reason, the Lutheran identity has been forged as much with respect to argumentation with the Reformed as with Roman Catholicism. Historically, the debate has been heated precisely because of our similarities. If differences only prevailed between these two confessional traditions, there would be little to discuss. However, the reason to find doctrinal agreement or disagreement between the two traditions can only be sustained for the sake of the proclamation of the gospel promise and for no other reason (even as noble or good as progressive social agendas). The criteria for any ecumenical rapprochement can only be the adequacy of the confessional tradition accurately to proclaim the gospel promise in both word and sacrament.

The ELCA as "Ecumenical Catalyst"

Retired Presiding Bishop of the Evangelical Lutheran Church in America, H. George Anderson, has spoken of the ELCA as an "ecumenical catalyst," specifically noting that ecumenical proposals with mainline Reformed denominations in the United States "ask that we recognize in print what we probably all believe in our hearts—that we are not the only church body with the truth."[15] In so designating the ecumenical role of the ELCA, Anderson was only hearkening back to the ELCA constitution, adopted in 1988 by those Lutheran bodies that merged into the ELCA,[16] whose ecumenical agenda reads:

> (4.02) To participate in God's mission, this church shall:
> f. Manifest the unity given to the people of God by living together in the love of Christ and by joining

with other Christians in prayer and action to express and preserve the unity which the Spirit gives.

(4.03) To fulfill these purposes, this church shall: Foster Christian unity by participating in ecumenical activities, contributing its witness and work and cooperating with other churches which confess God the Father, Son, and Holy Spirit.[17]

In a little over a decade, the ELCA was close to fulfilling these ambitious ecumenical goals. As Edgar Trexler, former editor of *The Lutheran*, the official magazine of the ELCA, noted,

> Even though harsh language and organized resistance to ecumenical relationships stretched both the patience and unity of the young ELCA, the Evangelical Lutheran Church in America by 1999 completed a series of ecumenical actions that left it poised to enter the 21st century at the forefront of the world's ecumenical scene. No other church had adopted official ties with such a spectrum of Christendom—full communion with the Episcopal Church, with three churches of the Reformed tradition, and with the Moravian Church. As a member of the Lutheran World Federation, the ELCA was a participant in the signing of the Joint Declaration on the Doctrine of Justification with the Vatican, a document that brought agreement on the key doctrinal issue that divided the churches and produced the Protestant Reformation. Quite a track record for a new church's first 15 years.[18]

In this same ecumenical trajectory, most recently, the 2009 ELCA Churchwide Assembly declared full communion with the United Methodist Church.

With respect to the actual enactment of the *Formula of Agreement*, which places the ELCA in full communion with the leading mainline Reformed churches in the United States, Trexler notes, "On August 28, 1997, at 10:02 A.M., by a vote of 839–193 (81.3 percent) the ELCA Churchwide Assembly adopted the Lutheran-Reformed *A Formula of Agreement*, marking the first time confessional churches took official steps to mend the divisions between them since the 16th century."[19] Describing the celebration that followed this vote a year later, Trexler writes,

On October 4, 1998, more than a year after the favorable vote on the Formula, some 1,500 worshipers came together in Rockefeller Chapel, Chicago, for a service that Presiding Bishop H. George Anderson called "the celebration of a miracle milestone reached" that is "only the beginning of an unfolding relationship." Entering the gothic nave from four directions and pausing at a font to acknowledge the brokenness of their separation and their oneness in baptism, leaders of the three Reformed churches and the ELCA symbolized their churches' "full communion" by forming a single procession. Heads of each church distributed the Eucharist.[20]

It should be noted that full communion does not seek the organic union of a transconfessional church, like the United Church of Canada (originally a union of Methodists and Presbyterians) or the historic Union Church in Germany, which has confessionally different congregations within one church. Instead, altars, pulpits, and preachers can be exchanged indifferent to the historic doctrinal differences between these churches.

Disagreement over Ecumenical Direction

The struggle to which Trexler earlier alluded was not due primarily to organized resistance to any ecumenical endeavors in the ELCA on principal, as if a nonecumenical agenda were an option, but instead toward which ecumenical directions the ELCA should lean. One party composed primarily of former Lutheran Church in America theologians, such as George Lindbeck (Yale University), urged that ecumenical endeavors be directed toward Lutheran–Roman Catholic dialogue "in part from a conviction that Lutherans should operate in continuity with the Reformers at Augsburg in 1530. They sought reform within the Catholic Church as Christians who stood in accord with authoritative Catholic sources."[21] For this party, the affirmation of the *Joint Declaration on the Doctrine of Justification* by the August 1997 Churchwide Assembly of the ELCA with a vote of 958–25 is considered an impressive achievement.[22]

By contrast, other ELCA leaders, many of The American Lutheran Church background, see the Reformation not only as corrective but also as a constitutive event and therefore give priority to dialogues with other Protestants.[23] With respect to the *Leuenberg Agreement*, one advocate for ecumenical rapprochement with the Reformed, Walter Sundberg (Luther Seminary), challenged his opponent on the pro–Roman Catholic side, Robert Jenson: Where does *Leuenberg* err? Sundberg contended that a fair evaluation of *Leuenberg* would find no mistakes that would violate the *satis est* of Augustana VII.[24] It was Jenson's contention that the North American Lutheran context was not commensurable with the European. In his judgment, European Protestants respond to a cultural hegemony of Roman Catholicism, while North American Lutherans respond to a cultural hegemony of a Reformed ethos.[25]

Such disagreements over ecumenical direction lend themselves to disputes over matters of polity and worship. The former camp has tended to favor the adoption of the "historic episcopate," a prerequisite of the ELCA agreement with the Episcopal Church USA (ECUSA), and the desire that worship be done as much as possible in continuity with the Roman Catholic mass. The latter camp has tended to react negatively to the adoption of the "historic episcopate" and favors seeing worship as having its own Protestant shape. In some ELCA circles, opposition to the Accord of the ELCA with the ECUSA, which went into effect on January 1, 2001, was so great that even prior to its realization, in March 2000, pastors and laity established the Word Alone Network as a renewal movement, specifically in opposition to the "historic episcopate." In March 2001, the Word Alone Network oversaw the formation of a new ecclesiastical body for congregations breaking away from the ELCA, named Lutheran Congregations in Mission for Christ (LCMC).[26] The polity of LCMC is decidedly "postdenominational" and congregationalist, unlike the historic polities of most North American Lutherans, which had, over time, avoided both Episcopal and Congregationalist stances, adopting instead a Presbyterian-like form of governance.

Reflecting on such wide-ranging ecumenical rapprochement, with Roman Catholics and Episcopalians on the one hand and the Reformed on the other, former ELCA Ecumenical Officer William Rusch claimed that the Augsburg Confession itself allows the ELCA to enter into such extensive negotiations: "Article VII is freeing, for it permits confessional Lutheranism to seek fellowship without insisting on doctrinal or ecclesiastical uniformity, while at the same time striving to achieve common formulation and expression of theological consensus on the gospel."[27]

The Role of *Leuenberg*

The basis for "full communion" between the ELCA and the three mainline Reformed Churches is *A Formula of Agreement*. While familiarity with the *Leuenberg Agreement* is attested to in North American Lutheran-Reformed dialogues and is affirmed in *A Formula of Agreement*, it was never adopted, since dialogue participants sought an indigenous North American approach. *A Formula of Agreement* built upon earlier Lutheran-Reformed dialogues, such as *Marburg Revisited* (1962–66), but especially *A Common Calling: The Witness of Our Reformation Churches in North America Today*.[28] In light of the disagreements over ecumenical directions for the ELCA—whether to verge more toward Rome or more toward Geneva—predecessor church bodies of the ELCA developed different responses to ecumenical ventures with the Reformed. Trexler notes of TALC and the American Evangelical Lutheran Church (which left the Missouri Synod in the mid-1970s) that they

> virtually adopted full communion with the Presbyterian Church (U. S. A.) and the Reformed Church in American as churches "in which the gospel is proclaimed and the sacraments administered according to the ordinances of Christ," approving the sharing of pastors and occasional joint services of communion. The LCA, however, was not sure about the reformed commitment to the real presence of Christ's body and blood in the sacrament and never adopted Invitation to Action, choosing instead to adopt a less far-reaching statement of friendship and cooperation. When the ELCA was formed, the ALC and AELC relationship with the Reformed churches ended on December 31, 1987.[29]

Clearly, such divergent tracks were brought into the ELCA and contributed toward ecumenical infighting among ELCA theologians.

The ecumenical goal with the Reformed (and the Episcopalians as well) is not what in earlier days was called "pulpit and altar fellowship" but instead "full communion." What is meant by this? It means that due to a result of ecumenical cooperation, bilateral and multilateral dialogues, and preliminary eucharistic sharing and cooperation, ecumenical partner churches can then host the interchangeability of clergy and venture in joint efforts such as planting mission congregations, publications, and the like. It does not entail confessional agreement. In this way, full communion is exactly like the fellowship attained by the *Leuenberg Agreement*. As Johannes Friedrich, the Presiding Bishop of Bavaria and the new Presiding Bishop of the Vereinigte Evangelisch-Lutherische Kirche Deutschlands (VELKD), notes, "The Evangelical Church in Germany (EKD), according to our founding documents, is a church fellowship based on the model of the Leuenberg Agreement." Specifically, for our purposes, he says, "The Leuenberg Agreement, the foundational document for fellowship among churches of varying confessions, pronounces the way to productive ecumenism via Augsburg Confession 7: The binding confessions of the churches that have joined it are not negated. The Leuenberg Agreement does not presume to be a confession per se, but allows for various confessions to enter into fellowship as they grow in mutual recognition, which follows from a common understanding of the Gospel."[30]

Differences between the European and American Contexts

It is important to acknowledge that there are specific differences in the background of *Leuenberg* from that of North America. Of note is the church struggle in the 1930s, the reaction of the "confessing" Protestants to the pro-Nazi "German Christians," which was bound to provide cohesion between Lutherans and the Reformed against a common enemy. Likewise, *Leuenberg* itself spells out the greater affinity between Lutherans and the Reformed in Europe: "In the course of four hundred years of history, the Churches of the Reformation have been led to new and similar ways of thinking and living; by theological wrestling with the questions of modern times, by advances in biblical research, by the movements of church renewal, and by the rediscovery of the ecumenical horizon" as well as by acknowledging "historically-conditioned thought forms."[31] As noted, Robert Jenson argued that not only the *Kirchenkampf* but also joint opposition to Rome, whose cultural legacy is pervasive in Europe, tends to unite Lutherans and the Reformed.

Perhaps the most significant difference between the contexts of European and North American heirs of the classical Reformation is that of the spiritual and political edge that "evangelical" or "born-again" (decision theology) Protestantism brings to bear in North America.[32] Such "born-againism," an heir of revivalism, historically so important to American religious life, especially as it moved into the frontier, trumps matters of classical doctrinal dispute in favor of a born-again experience, in which one accepts Jesus as one's personal Savior and Lord, independently of the formalities of rituals and sacraments, and that establishes one on a path of upright living. Of course, such "trumping" of doctrine is only a ruse. Born-again religiosity is permeated by doctrinal stances and assumptions through and through. But a cardinal "doctrine" of "evangelicals" is that academic doctrinal debate is of little value. The assessment of truth for such born-againism is deeply pragmatic: Accepting Jesus as your Savior "works." Embedded within American evangelicalism is a deeply anti-intellectual attitude. Arguments over matters of traditional doctrine, such as the validity of infant baptism or baptism as regenerative, are passed over by means of a pragmatic criterion of truth—the liveliness of the born-again experience and the growth of their suburban churches are what impress. Some mainline congregations, including those from North American Lutheran synods of all stripes, are numerically successful by copying these very tactics of evangelicals.

North American Lutherans, especially after the waves of German and Scandinavian emigrants came to the United States after the 1840s, increasingly reacted negatively toward such revivalism. Not only did confessional renewal in Europe at Erlangen and Christiania (Oslo) lend Lutherans a vigorous polemic with revivalism, but homegrown Lutherans in the original heartland of North American Lutheranism, Pennsylvania, such as Charles Porterfield Krauth and his disciples, also sought to reclaim the Reformation heritage as "conservative" and distanced themselves from the Reformed.[33] The doctrine of justification by faith, and a wholesome appropriation of the sacraments as external means of grace, were affirmed not only in opposition to

Roman Catholicism but particularly against revivalism. The basis of faith is grounded not in a subjective experience of a new birth but in the objective promise as mediated through the word and sacrament. In opposition to revivalist-minded Lutherans, who sought to alter the wording of the Augsburg Confession and to make it more palatable to revivalistic and sometimes Enlightenment ears,[34] Krauth, with his colleagues in the General Council, led a charge to appropriate a confessional heritage for North American Lutherans in both theology and worship. The direction of this initiative, which lasted for well over a hundred years, did not lead American Lutheranism closer to Rome or Canterbury, but it surely distanced it from Geneva and Zurich, which had fewer resources to combat revivalism.

Krauth's directions for North American Lutheranism were furthered by the more recent European emigrants, especially those indebted to the work of Löhe (the Joint Synod of Ohio and the German Iowa Synod) or Walther (the Missouri Synod and the Wisconsin Synod), as well as Lutherans from Scandinavian, Slovak, and Finnish backgrounds. In other words, for almost a century, the majority of North American Lutherans distanced themselves theologically from the Reformed, who were viewed as all too similar to and without resources to counteract revivalism. Today, some ELCA members favor ecumenical partnering with the Reformed for the very reason that the Reformation is not only corrective but also constitutive—that is, centering the core of the church in the gospel—and others oppose it for the opposite reason. But surely our ecumenism should be based not on such teeter-tottering but instead on a fundamental agreement about the gospel. In the overall scheme of things, it would seem that what makes unity with the Reformed today not only palatable but desirable is that the ecclesiastical agenda has altered over the last several decades. ELCA leaders are far more apt to oppose "evangelicals" less on matters of salvation, as would have been done in the past, and more on matters of politics. Such moves reveal the most important agendas for the ELCA. Mainline Protestants have tended to adopt the program of the political left, which favors greater government intervention in the economy but a laissez-faire approach to matters of sexuality, privacy, and the family. "Evangelicals" go just the opposite route. They favor the political right and thus approve of a laissez-faire approach to the economy but greater regulation of sexuality, privacy, and the family. Some of us find ourselves in neither camp, since we favor neither an economy run amok nor families in fragmentation.

The Basis for a Common Calling

While many mainline Protestant denominations, such as the Episcopal Church USA, the United Church of Christ, the Presbyterian Church USA, and the United Methodist Church, have lost virtually half of their memberships over the last forty years—a period in which the population of the United States doubled—"evangelical," charismatic, and, increasingly, "nondenominational" (albeit Baptist-like) churches have grown, often taking in young families, the parents of which were confirmed in declining mainline Protestant churches. (However, the growth rate among "evangelicals" has not kept pace with overall US population growth.) Likewise, born-again religion actively sought (beginning after Roe v. Wade, the 1973 Supreme Court ruling that legalized abortion) to capture the Republican Party and use it for a specific "profamily" agenda, often working in tandem with the ideals of free-market capitalism. Regardless of how we might think about these issues (I tend to think that free-market capitalism is all too willing to sacrifice the integrity of the traditional family), it is clear that North American Protestants pick sides on a political divide: mainliners who favor a "peace and justice" agenda and a "mix and match" approach to the family versus "evangelicals" who favor laissez-faire capitalism and the traditional family. In this light, the contention of the editors of *A Common Calling* (1988–92) needs to be put in context: "To some observers it seems that the most important divisions within American religion today are not those that separate one denomination from another, but those that divide members within denominations along a conservative-liberal fissure. The civil rights movement, the protests against the Vietnam War, and the movement for women's rights have all contributed to the political tensions within American denominations."[35] This paragraph, written almost two decades ago, is no longer accurate. The truth of the matter is, more "liberal" perspectives have gotten the upper hand in all mainline Protestant denominations. The divide has for some time moved out of a liberal-conservative debate *within* mainline churches—where "conservatives," insofar as they survive in them, are given little voice—and more *between* mainliners and "evangelicals." Ironically, more conservative—pro-life—Roman Catholics side with evangelicals, while more liberal Roman Catholics side with mainliners. (It should be noted that Roman Catholics significantly outnumber Protestants in the United States.)

Sidelining the Classical Differences

Another similarity between *Leuenberg* and North American Lutheran-Reformed ecumenics is the perception that classical issues such as predestination, the mode of Christ's real presence,[36] the priority among uses of the law, and the ordering of ministry seem no longer crucial for the church's confession of faith. Those who try such an approach are seen as anachronistic. As the editors of *A Common Calling* note, "Whatever we may think of it, however, the reality of church life in the twentieth century has become increasingly oblivious to the sixteenth-century controversies between Reformed and Lutheran churches."[37] It is not as if they are unaware of the historical differences between Lutherans and the Reformed, which they nicely summarize. Lutherans historically have affirmed:

1. The corporeal presence of Christ in the elements of the Lord's Supper based on their firm conviction of an incarnational soteriology.
2. The objectivity of God's saving presence in the consecrated elements of the Lord's Supper.
3. The *manducatio impiorum* or *indignorum* of unbelievers or gross sinners coming to the Lord's Supper.
4. The *communicatio idiomatum*, the exchange of divine and human attributes in the one person of Jesus Christ. As the editors note, only a complete exchange of predicable properties seemed to allow for the full incarnational paradox of the presence of the divine and human person of Christ in the Supper. Historically, Lutherans feared a

Nestorian division of the one Christ into two, of whom only one, the divine person, is present in the Supper.

5. And the ubiquity (omnipresence) of Christ's human and divine natures. Again, Lutherans feared a local circumscription of the risen Lord that would curtail the divine omnipotence.

By contrast, the Reformed historically have emphasized:

1. The presence of the Lord at the Lord's Table by means of the Spirit. Calvinists feared the perversion of a spiritual reality into carnal eating and drinking and the assumption of human control over the divine promise.
2. The bread and wine as signs: believers partake of the flesh and blood of Jesus in the Spirit. Historically, Calvinists have feared approaching the sacrament as crude sacramental magic.
3. The Holy Spirit as the bridge between sign and thing (*res*). The bridging work of the Holy Spirit is seen in the "lifting up" of the hearts of the faithful (*sursum corda*) and the *epiclesis*. Historically, Calvinists feared an unwarranted reification of the gift in the community of faith and a loss of the Trinitarian understanding of gift and giver.
4. That a Lutheran Christology of deified human nature is no longer true human nature.
5. The local circumscription of Christ's body in heaven. For Calvinists, the ubiquity of Christ's human nature would jeopardize the reality of the historical incarnation and make the soteriological work of the Spirit redundant.[38]

The editors admit that with respect to these debates, "A common language for this witness which could do justice to all the insights, convictions, and concerns of our ancestors in the faith has not yet been found and may not be possible."[39] Similar to the spirit of *Leuenberg*, the editors note, "These theological differences are . . . crucial for the ongoing ecumenical relations between these traditions. We view them not as disagreements that need to be overcome but as diverse witnesses to the one gospel that we confess in common. Rather than being church-dividing, the varying theological emphases among, and even within, these communities provide complementary expressions of the church's faith in the triune God."[40] As an alternative to this perspective, lively, respectful discussion in which we dared to disagree with our fellow Christians and explained why we think doctrinal matters are important would garner more esteem. Non-Christians are not impressed with a fuzzy "let's get along" spirituality—they can get that at the "new age" section of the local bookstore or in a conversation at the local coffee shop.

Leuenberg at the Core

A Formula of Agreement makes ready use of *Leuenberg*. With respect to the historic "condemnations," the *FA* quotes *Leuenberg*: "The condemnations expressed in the confessional documents no longer apply to the contemporary doctrinal position of the assenting churches (LA, IV.32.b)." Likewise, with respect to the Lord's Supper, *FA* affirms *LA* III.I.18: "In the Lord's Supper the risen Jesus Christ imparts himself in his body and blood, given for all, through his word of promise with bread and wine. He thus gives himself unreservedly to all who receive the bread and wine; faith receives the Lord's Supper for salvation, unfaith for judgment."[41]

With respect to the mode of Christ's presence in the Lord's Supper, *FA* likewise looks to *Leuenberg*: "In the Lord's Supper the risen Jesus Christ imparts himself in his body and blood, given up for all, through his word of promise with bread and wine. He thereby grants us forgiveness of sins and sets us free for a new life of faith. He enables us to experience anew that we are members of his body. He strengthens us for service to all men" (*LA* II.2.15) and "When we celebrate the Lord's Supper we proclaim the death of Christ through which God has reconciled the world with himself. We proclaim the presence of the risen Lord in our midst. Rejoicing that the Lord has come to us we await his future coming in glory" (*LA* II.2.16). Clearly, the specific mode of Christ's presence is not acknowledged. As mentioned earlier, the ELCA has not adopted the *Leuenberg Agreement*. But perhaps this needs to be qualified. De jure the ELCA has not adopted *Leuenberg*, but de facto it has. In essence, the ELCA has used *Leuenberg* to shore up its agreement with the three mainline Reformed churches. The glue that brings Lutherans and the Reformed together in America today can sidestep traditional theological matters because they have a common opponent, born-again Americans and the political right with whom "evangelicals" are aligned, and they share a common view of salvation ultimately as social, political, and ecological "peace and justice."

One Basis for the Sidelining

Since it is clear that Lutherans and Reformed are not in doctrinal agreement, on what basis can fellowship as we see in *Leuenberg* or *A Formula of Agreement* be established? No one has responded more elegantly to this question than the late Warren Quanbeck in the first round of US Lutheran-Reformed discussion, *Marburg Revisited*:

> When the traditions are set alongside each other and examined in a sympathetic way, it can be seen that one does not necessarily have to choose one doctrinal tradition to the exclusion of all others. To be a loyal Lutheran does not mean that one can see no value in the dogmatic or liturgical tradition of the Eastern Orthodox churches, or that one must condemn the total doctrinal statement of the Roman Catholic or Calvinist traditions. The New Testament witnesses to a rich variety of theological motifs in interpreting the Lord's Supper: memorial, communion, thanksgiving, sacrifice, mystery, anticipation. No tradition in the church has done justice to them all; each tradition has sought to develop one or more of them. What is seen in the study of the Scriptures, and noted again in the development of the church's doctrine, becomes real and existential in ecumenical discussion.[42]

In light of this rhetoric, can it at all be surprising that while disagreement over the mode of the Lord's presence in His Supper (bodily [Lutheran] or via elevation by the Spirit [Calvinist]) persists, Lutherans and the Reformed can affirm that they substantially share a common faith?[43] With respect to Quanbeck, the question needs to be raised: Does a diversity of metaphors in the New Testament entail a diversity of doctrine? The one doctrine in Scripture can express itself through a variety of metaphors. Diversity of doctrine in the New Testament would have to be established on other grounds. Now, certainly, an appreciation of doctrinal differences among Christians is progress over mindless caricatures and mean-spirited judgments. But all in all, this tells us precious little about what we should believe, teach, and confess. The issue is further complicated by the fact that Lutherans and the Reformed do not see eye to eye with respect to what it means to be a confessional church.[44] Underneath doctrinal disagreements is the real concern of the teaching of the gospel: Is the gospel properly being distinguished from the law such that our "solipsistic self-preoccupation" comes to an end and that we are given a "sure foundation and thus a sure comfort in another—Christ"?[45]

Conclusion

That traditional disagreements between Lutherans and the Reformed are now considered anachronistic, at least by mainliners, is due to the fact that our attitudes about the gospel, specifically about from what the gospel saves us, have changed. The Reformers, both Lutheran and the Reformed, were so zealous over doctrinal differences because they believed they needed to be precise about the gospel, since after all, it is the gospel that saves people from God's wrath. But it would seem that we today no longer really believe in God's wrath, so prior theological disagreements with the Reformed are nonissues. Today, we are apt to say of death that it is something natural, not "guilt made visible," as Karl Rahner once put it.[46] Even born-again Christians are likely to tell you to accept Jesus as your Savior not because you will be saved from wrath but because Jesus will give you a "purpose-driven" life. But our assumptions beg the question: Do we in fact encounter God's wrath daily, and will we—outside of Christ—encounter it eternally? Do we not deal with God's judgment in, with, and under all other judgments, not because judgments of others or even oneself are true but because they are a result of a fallen world—and that ultimately it is God's judgment that is true and counts? We live, move, and have our beings within a world swamped in judgment, but, ultimately, behind all such judgments that we make or are made about us, we live in a fallen world that has the equivalent of a death sentence over our heads. Do we not need an external word (*verbum externum*) to save us? And do we not need a Savior whose divine nature is not only capable of the finite but capable of absorbing and even becoming our sin so that we might become His righteousness?

If that is the case, must not we Lutherans affirm precisely what we have confessed in the past? We must confess a robust view of the incarnation, the *infra-Lutheranum*, not only because of the *communicatio idiomatum* but because the Redeemer took on not only human life but, on the cross, sinful human life, indeed, was judged the "greatest sinner"[47] (*maximus peccator, peccator peccatorum*) in order to bear sin and its wages, death, away so that we can have eternal life now and forever.

The impulse for ecumenical dialogue is salutary but not at the expense of budgets that could be geared for evangelism, world mission, or, for that matter, social mercy. In that light, we need to distinguish an ecumenism "from above" from that of an ecumenism "from below." In the ecumenism "from above," churchwide budgets are used to legitimate bureaucratically preestablished harmony between various denominations, which are already "birds of a feather" with respect to their social and political agendas. (And a major agenda of these denominations, shared with their evangelical counterparts, is that classical doctrines are relatively unimportant.) Make no mistake: Many of the social agendas raised by mainline Protestants urging our support for the poor and the downtrodden merit our attention and action. But the quest for justice as such is not salvific but is instead a matter of social ethics. It entails fidelity to the Golden Rule. And its exercise is highly complicated, since we live in a global economy in which tracing accountability for decisions can be murky but from which no one gets away scot-free. On the exercise of justice, intelligent people of goodwill will disagree about how to rectify inequality of opportunity and establishing basic human rights. Even so, that is no excuse for Christians, in addition to all other citizens, to fail to work for basic human dignity and freedom, along with equality of opportunity, as a natural consequence of their vocations within democratic societies.

Contemporary ecumenism involves church bureaucrats initiating or sponsoring high-level committees that put together written agreements embodying some sort of doctrinal agreement (or doctrinal avoidance) so that clergy can be officially exchanged. North American ecumenism has tended to be focused on such upper-level church structures. It should be contrasted with the ecumenism "from below," which has been in place for some time in many parishes. This entails Christian cooperation among varying groups by operating food banks, clothing racks, homeless or domestic-abuse shelters, home rehabilitation projects, literacy and educational opportunities for underprivileged children and adults, opportunities to recover from alcohol and drug addictions, and other such venues. These activities extend social mercy to those in need. Likewise, open, genuine, and honest discussion and disagreement among thoughtful and informed Christians of goodwill can help us understand ourselves, our mission, and others better. However, until doctrinal agreement is established between different confessional groups, neither "full communion" among differing confessional traditions nor "open communion" at the altar should be our goal. Rather, the first step is to establish doctrinal agreement, and that for the sake of the purity of the gospel that alone saves.

Classical differences between Lutherans and the Reformed are anachronistic only to those already bewitched by Enlightenment "dogmas" of human progress and tolerance.[48] Not everything about these Enlightenment views (such as the quests for liberty, equality, and fraternity) is wrong. Surely, a democratic approach to governance is preferable to a feudal approach. Nevertheless, such views secularize Reformation teachings, reframing a conscience captive to the word of God as a conscience (gnostically) captive to the autonomous "self."[49] Hence Enlightenment doctrines need to be tested in light of law and gospel. And in that light, we flee from God as wrath to God as mercy. It is Jesus Christ, who stands by His promise, bears God's wrath, and gives us His very righteousness, whom we must uncompromisingly confess.

CHAPTER 14

Revival Time

With two "great awakenings" and numerous outbursts of religious renewal on smaller scales, Americans are addicted to revivals. There is no better way to fix America's immorality than through a revival. Unfortunately, of late, no matter how hard one tries to incite a revival, they just don't seem to take. Over the past four decades, the American population has doubled, but church commitment has plateaued, even declined. Yet the illusion that revival can cure our ills remains.

Even Lutherans want a revival. Lutherans are either "Ablaze" or "Book of Faith" people. Surely, these movements can light a flame that will shore up churches in decline. Both ventures come across like attempts to engineer revivals. Thereby, they are true to Charles Finney, the revivalist par excellence, for whom revival was "not a miracle." Revival is not a miracle because if you establish the proper conditions, it can be manipulated.

No doubt, revival has been successfully manipulated in various congregations. If manipulating through guilt—"turn or burn (in hell!)"—doesn't seem to coax as it once did, the flattery of enhanced self-esteem or secure parenting does. Americans don't believe that fellow Americans will end up in hell. If they are to accept Jesus as their Lord and Savior, it can only be because He will enhance their self-esteem, social prestige, or parenting skills. Why scare people with hell when you can supplement their self-help? Contemporary revival congregations have done away with the mourner's bench and the sawdust trail and have substituted slick multimedia presentations in upscale theater-style venues, complete with seats accommodating drinks and gimmicks such as driving motorcycles[1] into the "sanctuary." Gone are revival songbooks: praise ditties, sung by the "praise band," are projected onto the ubiquitous screen.

The long, hard struggle for "liturgical worship" against the inroads of pietism, rationalism, and revivalism is brought to naught by the pragmatic assessment of manipulative persuasion. A sermon that could have been scripted by Dr. Phil or Oprah Winfrey touches "felt needs" more than "traditional worship" could ever do.

It is not as if revival is totally foreign to North American Lutheranism. Certainly, the heritage of the General Synod was open to the mourner's bench, and it altered the sacramental theology of the Augsburg Confession in this light. The heirs of Hans Nielsen Hauge fostered a "Lutheran Evangelistic Movement," which at one time had some religious influence in the Upper Midwest. In my first parish, which had been established by the Haugeaner, I was told the week before "Baptism of Jesus Sunday" by a devout laywoman, "Pastor, you aren't going to preach on baptism are you? Everyone in this congregation is baptized but most are not saved!" (Of course, to this woman's consternation, I preached on baptism!) Even The American Lutheran Church (founded in 1960), for almost a decade after its origin, officially recognized the "Office of the Evangelist," institutionalizing this very Hauge spirit, until inroads from the Charismatic Movement brought it into disrepute.

What are the fruits of revivalism? The European context is markedly different than that of the American, given that it is far more secularistic. Secularism is no less religious than traditional Christianity, even though it fails to admit this. Secularism bills itself as a "scientific approach" to life. However, its ideal—seek pleasure in moderation, and you need not fear judgment after death since we are wholly composed of atoms that disperse upon death—is nothing other than Epicureanism revived. In this outlook, truly free, autonomous men and women are liberated from the oppressive ideologies and hierarchies of the church. Ironically, revivalistic pietism perhaps fed such secularism. Revivalism always undermined the institutional church as being dead; it held that the institutional church is composed of unconverted preachers, repetitious liturgy, and cold sacraments. God is really present at the prayer meeting, not the church, for the followers of Spener, Hauge, Beck, and Rosenius. Thereby, the church was undermined by those who purported to be her friends.

In a similar way, revivalistic congregations among the ELCA or the LCMS seldom take in the unchurched, as they so often claim. They usually take in the disgruntled from other congregations. Revival almost never reaches the unchurched. It isn't designed to do that. It is always designed, from its perspective, to turn a dead church around. This fact may seem at odds with revivalism's national presence in America. But it makes sense when we consider the fact that even though Americans don't have an official state church, America's Reformed heritage makes religion one with the culture. The earlier revivals really did reach a lot of Americans. And their memory may lead us to assume success even when the results don't add up.

Luther sought to reform a corrupt church. His reform centered on the gospel of Jesus Christ as sheer promise in contrast to the law as accusation. It was grounded in the objective word of truth, in contrast to both the *Schwärmer* of Rome (the pope as the interpreter of Scripture) and various "spiritualists" who wanted to ground human confidence in spiritual exercises. He knew that Adam and Eve were the original "enthusiasts" and that part of their original sin was grounded in such "god-within-ism." Revivalism tries to manipulate the will by making it want to will. As such, it shows that we only ever, as sinners, are bound to our wills and not to God. We are captivated by ourselves. Our piety is part of the problem: it keeps us in charge. And our consciences at their best will have nothing to do with this lie. Revivalistic pep rallies toy with God. And the God of Jacob will have nothing to do with us enthusiasts other than to engage us in a life-or-death struggle. In many senses, spirituality is a disease—God is here not to help me cope but to bring me to my demise, my end. Only in that way can a new person be reborn in faith, as trusting in the word of Scripture.

Blazing or Bible-thumping, denominational bandages will not be able to cure our membership slumps. C. F. W. Walther knew that the elect were in God's hands and that as God is God, the elect would be saved. Since that is the case, the most important part of our ministry is out of our hands. It's God's church, not ours. It's God's elect, not ours. And we can be quite *free* in letting God run His church as He pleases. Can we really trust the word that has been entrusted to us?

No amount of manipulation of others' consciences will save the church, and indeed, such will do the church in. True enough, we are to be urgent in season and out of season. But our urgency is not based on a neurotic need to inflate membership rolls but to share, as one beggar to another, where bread is to be found.

CHAPTER 15

Retrieving Confessional Identity— for the Public Good

For decades, noted evangelical historian Mark Noll has told Lutherans that their greatest contribution to the North American ethos and culture would be to claim their own unique identity, rather than fitting into either prevailing mainline Protestantism (what Richard John Neuhaus has called the "old-line" or "sideline") or born-again evangelicalism. In spite of that challenge, the ELCA (Evangelical Lutheran Church in America) continues its drift into mainline liberalism while some groups in the LCMS (Lutheran Church–Missouri Synod) mimic born-again Christianity. If Noll is right, one wonders why Lutherans would conform to directions in other denominations rather than contribute their own uniqueness to the North American context.

Past Confessional Identity

In the not-so-distant past, most Lutheran synods in North America understood themselves to be confessional—that is, they saw their identities primarily to be based on the proclamation of the gospel as promise. Their criteria for fidelity to this promise were to be found in the Scriptures and the Lutheran confessions. They differed from Christians who reconceived the gospel as a political agenda to attain utopia, an ethic to give voices to the voiceless, a psychological quest for feeling good about oneself, or a metaphysical description locating God in the actual map of reality.

Certainly, good psychological health, a concern to help the economically disadvantaged and socially marginalized, and a sense of how religion squares with science are important. But they need to be interpreted through the lens of law and gospel, not vice versa, if we are to be true to our confessional identity and to Scripture.

The Rise of Generic Lutheranism

The confessional identity of a bygone era was achieved through hard and diligent work. In colonial North America, Lutheranism was markedly similar to other Protestant groups, except its ethnicity was not Anglo-Saxon.

Several factors help explain such generic Lutheranism: (1) Halle pietism embodied in the Muhlenburg tradition, (2) so-called unionism between German-speaking Lutheran and Reformed groups, (3) rationalism as represented in Frederick Henry Quitman's New York Synod, and (4) revivalism adopted by S. S. Schmucker and others. All these things helped to characterize Lutheranism as simply another Protestant denomination, with interests and methods parallel to those of the dominant Anglo-Saxon churches.

Nineteenth-Century Renewal

Confessional renewal, in both Europe and North America, was to alter the fabric of Lutheran identity. The impetus for this movement was manifold, but some manifestations of it stand out: (1) Claus Harms' antirationalist polemic voiced at the three-hundredth anniversary of the Reformation (1817), (2) the liturgical and missionary endeavors of the Bavarian pastor Wilhelm Löhe, (3) a renewed appreciation for Luther and confessional theology in the Erlangen theological faculty, (4) the indefatigable labors of Charles Porterfield Krauth and others who helped establish the Mt. Airy Seminary and the General Council, (5) the spiritual and confessional awakening under Gisle Johnson in the theological faculty in Christiania (Oslo), and (6) the insistence on the bound will and the proper distinction between law and gospel in the polemical witness of C. F. W. Walther.

These factors all shaped a strong confessional identity among Lutherans in North America and helped recover Luther's insight that the gospel is distinctively a promise, not an ethical directive, a metaphysical description, or a psychological dynamic.

How Did It Change?

Well into the 1960s, most Lutheran synods continued to remain strong in confessional identity and, like most Christian denominations at that time, enjoyed growth commensurate with the growth of the general population. Why did those synods that eventually merged into the ELCA weaken this identity? How did pastoral care as unconditional positive regard or Christian ethics as an indiscriminate and naïve preferential option for the poor supplant the primary witness of the gospel as sheer promise?

While there were many factors, one major reason for such changes was a desire to fit in or accommodate to facets of American public life. Lutheran leaders in the 1950s and 1960s felt that the future of the church depended on freeing it from its isolationist theological and ethnic ghetto. Lutheranism needed to give up its parochial identity if it was to stand a chance in an increasingly college-educated American culture. Our leaders thus became convinced that the Lutheran churches needed to embrace the academic trends apparent in the Society for Biblical Literature and the American Academy of Religion.

Values Choice

Those trends are rooted in an apologetic for religion in the "public square," which allows for the unencumbered individual to choose one's own destiny and values. This humanistic approach affirms the human potential for self-exploration free of shame, the need for the underprivileged to attain self-development by the establishing of social equity, and a defense of the reality of God within a scientific/technological worldview. Slowly, Lutheran theological faculties and college religion departments began to mirror these ideals.

As it moved into the mainstream, Lutheranism tried to have it both ways. On the one hand, it embraced the humanistic endeavors of the academic camp (e.g., liberation theology, therapy, and "science and religion" discussions), but it also latched onto the ecumenical movement as a defense of Christianity against rising secularism. Slowly, theological faculties and college religion departments reflected these apologetic trends. The alternative path—challenging secularity from the perspective of confessional identity—was seldom taken.

This attempt to defend the faith resulted in a secularizing of the faith. Today's ELCA has become a church with a very weak confessional identity, far more like that of the General Synod of the 1820s than the more robust confessionalism contributed by the General Council and the United Synod of the South to the United Lutheran Church at its 1918 formation.

Political Salvation

The irony is that such accommodation actually marginalizes Lutheranism's impact on public life. Lutheranism's best witness would be to unmask the religious ideals embedded in a secular approach to politics. In the current humanistic approach, politics itself becomes salvific. Get the politics right, and you'll have heaven on earth.

Both mainline and evangelical Protestantism fall into this trap; both are indebted to the Enlightenment's bifurcation of private faith (subjective experience) and public life (political utopianism). For both the conservative and liberal wings of American religion—descendants of Charles Grandison Finney and William Ellery Channing, respectively—inner transformation is highly valued. Born-again Christians have an experience in which Jesus is accepted as Savior, granting psychological wholeness. Mainline Protestants likewise profess Christ as Savior but in a more sophisticated, nuanced, or symbolic way, in which Christ would help one be in touch with one's ultimate concern.

Similarly, with respect to public life, both brands of American Christianity are unabashedly millennialist. For born-again Christians, when "family values" are honored and government interference with the economy stops, then there will be heaven on earth. For mainline

Protestants, when society tolerates individual lifestyles and when wealth is transferred to those on the economic margins, then there will be heaven on earth.

Amillennial Lutherans

In contrast, confessional Lutherans are amillennialists, wise to the fact that we are saved not by inner transformation but by an external word. They also know that politics is remedial, addressing a fallen world; millennial utopianism is an illusion. Neither experience nor politics can save, and, in a sense, our salvation delivers us *from* both these things. Government at its best can only curb sin, not cure it. Prior to Christ's return, politics will remain forever messy.

Lutheranism can offer public life its best when it presents an alternative to both born-again and mainline religion. With social conservatives, Lutherans are apt to affirm the sanctity of life and traditional views of marriage. But with social liberals, they are apt to combat an unfair economic system in which the poor and weak need defense and remediation. A confessional Lutheran view thus defies current partisan politics.

What Lutherans Can Contribute

Indeed, Noll is right. Lutherans could contribute the most to public life by arguing that the public is not able to save itself, that government exists for the well-being of the neighbor, and that utopian enthusiasm is itself a disease. We should eschew the illusions of utopia, whether of the left or of the right. Instead, Lutherans acknowledge that God works in public life even when the public is unaware of it. We seek the well-being of the unborn, of children, and of all those who are poor and disadvantaged.

But even more important than a nonutopian social ethic, Lutherans could offer the American public the insight of the gospel as promise—not to be transformed into ethical directives, metaphysical descriptions, or psychological dynamics. The promise that Christ Himself forgives sinners would offer North America a lifesaving alternative to the usual religious fare in the contemporary milieu.

We Were Wrong

To do that, we'd have to admit that the weakening of confessional identity decades ago was wrong, leaving us unable to separate the content of the gospel from the cultural packages in which it is wrapped. We offer the most to the world when we embrace a robust confessional identity. And we offer an educated laity the best when we offer them the truth—the proper distinction between law and gospel, between God's left- and right-hand work—rather than the humanism into which we have channeled our energies.

Reclaiming a confessional identity within the ELCA is clearly an uphill battle, but it is worth it. As one young pastor put it, "I didn't realize there was a gospel other than the social gospel, but once I did, I've become far more passionate about ministry." It's time for the ELCA to reassess its situation and to consider change—change on the basis of honoring the distinction between law and gospel and proclaiming the gospel as promise.

CHAPTER 16

A Brotherly Office

For decades, alien agendas have sought to redefine the office of the ministry into that of the CEO, social worker, or therapist. Increasingly, entertainer can be added to that list. A church-growth expert recently told me that a pastor's height carries evangelistic freight: a tall pastor is more effective than a short one. Following this man's expertise, we now simply need to find ways to stretch seminarians some three to six inches!

At any rate, trends are in place among the ranks of the clergy to remake pastors into ones who can offer "unconditional positive regard" instead of serving as a *Seelsorger*, business managers instead of confessors, social engineers instead of those who comfort the afflicted and afflict the comfortable. In this maelstrom of social redefinition, pastors need to reclaim the task of defining themselves if they are to stay sane in their office. And in fact, the very notion of office (*Amt*)—found in *Augustana* V—is the best place to start; pastors primarily are servants of the word and sacraments. And the only ones who can help laity understand what pastors do are pastors themselves. They will need to teach congregations how they are to be treated and respected. And this will happen not through lecturing or directives from church councils or even church bodies but in simple day-to-day faithfulness in ministry.

When I was a young pastor, congregation members often wanted to address me as "Pastor Mark" or even "Mark," but as I mentioned to them, in the sick room or on the deathbed, "Mark" has very little to offer, but "Pastor Mattes" is beholden to offer comfort from God's word. And I'd leave the matter at that.

Other than preaching the gospel as sheer promise in distinction to the commands and accusations of the law, the single best way to honor the pastoral office with laity is to visit them in their homes. When one visits, one does not visit as a pal but visits as a confessor and as one who blesses. The office itself makes the opportunity for confession and blessing available. Pastors stand in a unique position to offer a blessing to children, youth, the elderly, and families. Through no other vocation can God offer such intimacy to those in need of both absolution (or correction) and blessing.

Not only do cultural trends tend to redefine the pastoral office in ways foreign to it, but pastors themselves all too quickly buy into such factors that cause them to alienate themselves from each other. Few professionals avoid competition. And that disease, in which we reduce our fellows to competitors, harms pastors' relationships to each other as members of a *shared* office. The late Ulrich Asendorf was wont to describe the preaching office as *ein Amt von Brüdern*, a brotherly office, which he brought to expression in closing his missives with "Dein Amtsbruder." Presumably, those holding this office would treat each other as family—not competitors! Above all, with each other we need to honor the eighth commandment.

The natural tendency to decipher who among our rank is facing congregational conflict or to boast of a raise or standard of living harms our working together. This is important. Who, finally, can console a downcast pastor better than another pastor? Who can mentor a younger pastor better than a mature pastor? Given the intensity and ambiguity of the experiences that pastors often face, as well as serving as an "ear of Christ" in the confessional office, no lay person can fully understand the complex dynamics and confidentiality that pastors need to honor. By building each other up, pastors indirectly help build up the entire church.

While serving as a pastor, I sometimes enjoyed the experience of being popular with laity. However, I always saw my work, as one holding the preaching office, as seeking to support even my successors in that office in the congregation. Of course, I had no idea whether my successors would be faithful. But my job was to uphold the office regardless of whom God would place as my successor.

Retired pastors do best to entrust the office into the care of another—which means that they will decline the request to participate in funerals, even if they view the deceased as their friend or if they know the deceased better than the present pastor in office. A retired pastor who truly trusts in God will entrust the congregation into the care of another and thus under all conditions stay out of its affairs.

Our culture does not like authorities. We like to equalize the playing field. At their best, congregation members know that the pastor carries confidences and that he is in a unique relationship with respect both to the congregation and to God. We need to uphold the office with as much integrity as we can muster—with respect to those we serve, those who share the office with us, and those who will succeed us. Retrieving the sense of a "brotherly" office can help strengthen the church in her outreach. This we must seek to do.

The well-being of a confessional identity for the church and the fostering of the church's mission hinge on the well-being of pastors. Pastors have an important and unique task in that they can uphold each other. This is done best when we take the office that we share seriously.

CHAPTER 17

How to Cultivate Biblical, Confessional, Resilient, and Evangelistic Pastors

Up until the last forty years, the overall trajectory of North American Lutheranism, and Western Christianity as well, was growth.[1] The motto of Henry Melchior Muhlenburg, patriarch of North American Lutheranism, was "The church must be planted."[2] Many congregations had already been founded when he was called to serve them. But he established a track record for growing these faith communities. Many assume that all Lutheran immigrants were eager to join Lutheran congregations, but that is a false impression. Synodical statistics for 1920 indicate that about 30 percent of Norwegians belonged to a synod with a Norwegian background.[3] Only 20 percent of Swedish immigrants joined the Augustana Synod. And a mere 10 percent of Danish immigrants held membership in one of the Danish synods. While a fraction of German immigrants joined Lutheran congregations, many more became unchurched, antichurched, or members of non-Lutheran denominations.

Lutheran missionaries to North American immigrants could effectively use ethnicity and language as natural draws. In an unfamiliar land, newcomers were attracted to the synods in geographical areas where their mother tongues were spoken. But to repeat: not all immigrants from historically Lutheran lands were eager to join Lutheran congregations, for whatever reasons. Those who did join did so because they were actively courted, evangelized, and welcomed into such fellowships. Pastors who wanted to build congregations reached out to them. Some immigrants rejected that welcome, but others embraced it wholeheartedly. Thereby congregations grew.

Nor should we assume that Lutheran churches grew because there were higher birth rates in the past. No doubt, there were higher birth rates, especially in rural communities with big farms and relatively stable families. Those baptized in infancy generally remained loyal to the church. But that was also because families, the community, and the church expected children and youth to be loyal. Nineteenth-century pastors did not encourage youth to experiment with various types of spirituality, "belief systems," or even other branches of Christianity to help them see what would be "right for them." Instead, they admonished those under their care to remain loyal because they regarded Lutheran insights as offering a distinctive approach to Christian faith and life, a reliable hope and consolation that other religious messages do not offer. They regarded it as offering the truth that would set young people free.

That is not to say that Lutheran pastors of an earlier era all assumed that there was no truth whatsoever in other Christian traditions. But they were adamant that truth with its greatest clarity was to be had in Lutheranism. Truth is something that any person of integrity will not want to betray—which raises the question: just how many of today's mainline clergy believe that they deal with *truth*? Undoubtedly, many clergy feel that they offer *a* truth—a perspective that may lead to better living and a better world—but not *the* truth. The latter would be perceived as too judgmental, narrow, and intolerant.

While it is no guarantee that churches that claim and affirm truth will grow, it is a guarantee that churches that fail to affirm that Christ is the way, the truth, and the life (John 14:6) will stagnate and die.[4]

Two Reasons for Historic Growth

With the advance of threshing equipment by the 1890s, birth rates dropped because it was no longer necessary for farm families to be so large. But Lutheran synods continued to grow, especially in the cities and eventually in the suburbs in the early 1950s. The Iowa

Synod, for instance, began in 1854 with about fifty souls. When it merged into the American Lutheran Church in 1930, it had grown to about 212,000 baptized members.[5] In honor of the seventy-fifth anniversary of that particular synod, G. J. Zeilinger wrote that "only occasionally were men sent out for the express purpose of doing home mission work. But *every pastor considered himself a missionary* and looked for missionary opportunities in the territory where God had placed him."[6]

For many Lutheran synods, such growth happened in spite of the fact that there was continuous migration out of rural areas, where most Lutheran congregations had been established, to the cities. There are two reasons for the church's continuing growth.

First, as mentioned, prior to the 1960s, Lutherans were convinced of the truth of their tradition. In the 1970s, when the editor of the Lutheran Church in America publication *The Lutheran* was asked if Lutheranism was the truth, he responded, "Yes," but then cautiously added, "But we aren't the only ones who have it."[7] The latter qualification was prudent in a religiously pluralistic North American environment. But what shouts louder and is more unique in our day is the editor's unhesitating answer that Lutherans do have the truth. In today's ELCA, we find greater reservations about affirming that Lutherans or even Christians have the truth. As one Upper Midwest pastor put it, "Christianity is about being nice. I am a pastor because I believe in being nice and a congregation is a good environment to promote niceness." For this pastor, the Christian faith is grounded not in doctrinal truth necessary for salvation but in charitable acts of kindness and that alone. Jesus was the nicest of men, we are to infer, and we Christians who need pious role models should be like Him. As a quip on a now-retired seminary professor's office door facetiously put it, "God's nice, we're nice, isn't that nice?" But if faith comes down to being nice, then why would we need the church when we have fine organizations and clubs like the Lions, Rotary, or Scouts? In fact, they probably do it better.

By contrast, if you believe your tradition is true or about the truth, you will have a zeal to commend it to others. Lutheranism's suspicion of self-righteousness lurking in all people should tip us off that "niceness" itself can be an expression of self-righteousness. But if the gospel is true, it isn't that God is opposed just to our sin. God is also opposed to anything we would use to accrue merit, including our best efforts—our niceness. If niceness could afford merit before God, then Jesus Christ would not be necessary. Or, as St. Paul put it, "I do not nullify the grace of God, for if justification were through the law, then Christ died for no purpose" (Gal. 2:21). What counts before God is not niceness but a "contrite heart" (Ps. 51:17).

We should keep in mind that the majority of our theological ancestors, such as Charles Porterfield Krauth, William Passavant, Henry Eyster Jacobs, Wilhelm Löhe, Mathias Loy, Hans Gerhard Stub, Ulrik V. Koren, and Conrad Emil Lindberg were well aware of the Enlightenment critiques of Christian faith and truth claims that led in many ways to the rise of mainline Christianity. They knew these charges—and rejected them. They could reject them because they could relativize them. They knew that reason was not to be reduced to rationality per se, as if rationality were perfectly objective and free from cultural or personal bias.[8] That view was simply Enlightenment dogma straining to eliminate mystery and miracle from the cosmos. Lutheran theologians challenged such assumptions and adhered to their historic truth claims, and that had a way of gripping the minds and imaginations of laypeople and future pastors.

To return to the reasons for growth: the second reason is that Lutherans of old had a percentage of pastors on their clergy rosters who were builders, not of buildings but of congregations. Obviously, not all pastors are builders by disposition. The word *pastor* means "shepherd," and shepherds care for the flock. For Lutherans, this care means truthfully preaching the word of God, administering the sacraments and the office of the keys, admonishing the erring, comforting the bereaved and distressed, teaching the Scriptures, and urging godly living. This is all certainly building up the body of Christ.

But throughout much of Lutheranism's history, there have also been a goodly number of shepherds who had the skills and obedient wills to increase membership and involvement in congregational life. Ask laypeople about a pastor in their congregation's history who was a standout, and a name will quickly arise of a pastor who was a builder. Some congregations were fortunate to have had two or three such pastors.

Builder-pastors exhibit distinctive character traits. They are unafraid of the unchurched and eager to engage them. They limit time in their offices and, like neighborhood police officers, they find various ways to get to know their beat. They see stressful situations as opportunities for both personal and congregational growth. And most importantly, they want to win people for Christ and ground them in a faith commitment.

In other words, builder-pastors have the gospel at the ready on their lips. They find ways to speak God's word to the unchurched, teach them the faith, and walk with them on the road to baptism and Christian fellowship. For builders, sharing the faith is not a shameful act of cultural insensitivity but a mandate from Christ. They refuse to let fear of rejection govern their witness, they quickly shake the dust from their sandals if rebuffed, and they proceed to find the next person to speak to. Builders are not only biblical and confessional but also resilient and evangelistic. The congregations in the ELCA today that are growing tend to have pastoral leadership that exhibits these traits.

Builders versus Caretakers

Far from being builders, many if not most contemporary mainline Protestant clergy would highlight their chief pastoral strength as caregiving, a variant on the theme of therapy. Some offer an "office-based" ministry that awaits members needing therapy to come for counseling or advice.[9] These pastors preach a message that centers on self-affirmation or advocates justice for oppressed peoples. The chief virtue in a sermon is not offending anyone, except maybe the designated oppressors. This approach is by and large endorsed by our educational systems, social service agencies, and even businesses, and it is certainly present in our seminaries.

Many of these goals are praiseworthy, noble, and should indeed be endorsed. But are mainline Protestants doing anything unique, something that no other vocation or profession could do in their place? Do they have a distinctive message—and is it something that only the church can offer? The truth is that such pastors tend to lack any gripping message in their preaching and teaching, don't know how to distinguish between law and gospel, lack zeal for communicating Jesus Christ as Lord, and so fail to hook youth or the unchurched into considering the value of the Christian faith. We may well ask whether they really regard God's word as a living word, a sharp two-edged sword, which creates what it declares (Heb. 4:12).

For some time now, seminary education has been focused on developing leaders. But if the kind of people attracted to seminary are inclined toward the therapeutic model of ministry, attempts to make leaders of them will fail. Such candidates are psychologically disinclined to take risks or take the heat for tough decisions. Instead they will prefer a safer, more comfortable environment where they can care for others and anticipate being cared for by others.

It's hard to imagine pastors like this serving as exorcists—a major component of the apostolic ministry, if the New Testament is anything to go by—when called upon to do so. And for all the talk of prophetic ministry, we rarely if ever encounter a real prophet naming evil at great risk to self and reputation, like Nathan naming the sin of King David to his face.

Worse still, a few understand the role of leader to be someone who orders others around. Thus students emerge with the idea that the pastor is a functional CEO who hands out directives. Perhaps such seminarians could be set straight if they would consider instead the military, where leadership is not about barking out commands but about setting the example of how to do something by being willing to do it oneself.

In contrast to the caretaking model, builders tend to have an outwardly focused vision, can work with a staff, prioritize outreach rather than office time, preach law and gospel, direct people to new lives in Christ, and preach sermons that are winsome, pointed, and evangelical. Their work evokes the interest of youth, "seekers," and the unchurched. Builders are not afraid of the unchurched but are instead excited about outreach. Nor are they averse to giving care, but they do so within the context of outreach and evangelism. They regard pastoral encounters as opportunities to deliver the gospel in the face of the law's alien, killing work.

Builders not only prioritize outreach; they also highlight education, and their congregations generally offer different levels of education. "What Lutherans believe" or "What the Scriptures teach" is the bedrock of their educational programs, for both the unchurched and those churched folks who want a review, along with Bible studies and other classes designed to help people to deepen their under-standing of the faith. They bring the gospel to those who have never heard it and to those who desperately need to hear it again.

Builders are rare on clergy rosters these days. And to be fair, there has never been a time when builders were the majority. We should not assume that pastors who are not builders are failing or poor at their jobs. Ultimately, the test of ministry is not increased numbers but faithfulness to ordination vows.

Over the last four decades, though, fewer and fewer builders have been attracted to the ministry. At the same time, there have been fewer social expectations to attend church, the family has frag-mented in numerous ways, and tremendous stress has been put on families through extended hours of work each week, not to mention academic, athletic, and musical expectations for children.

In times past, ordained ministry also would have been seen as a step toward upward social mobility. The Holy Spirit can use mul-tiple motives in ministry, including the drive to personal fulfillment as much as the desire to share the saving word. But a tipping point arose, where the number of builders entering the ministry became so scarce that it was guaranteed that the church would decline—and decline dramatically.

Unless a percentage of the clergy are builders, it simply is not possible for the church as a whole to grow. Builders have the charac-ter traits to serve small, medium, and large congregations, whatever problems they find there. Builders keep busy by visiting, teaching, and evangelizing. When historically large congregations call only nonbuilders to serve as their senior pastors, the vibrancy and health of those congregations are put in jeopardy.

Faith-Based Critique in a Pluralist Democracy

What accounts for the tapering off of the zeal for building that our ancestors in the faith had? No doubt, white flight from the cities to the suburbs, beginning in the 1950s, brought many central city congregations into decline. Likewise, the farm crisis of the early 1980s hurt many rural and small-town congregations. Reactions against the historic episcopate early in the late twentieth and early twenty-first centuries, along with the disputes about sexuality and scriptural authority in 2009, resulted in up to one thousand congregations leaving the ELCA.

But more than anything, what hurt the ELCA and its predecessor bodies was their eagerness to become more like mainline Protestants, embracing a more secular approach to faith. *Secular* here means that faith construed as a private matter, geared toward self-fulfillment, and unfettered from biblical, creedal, or confessional truth claims. A secular approach to faith is apt to see the assertion that salvation is found in Christ alone as intolerance. Secularism highlights not passion to reach the unchurched with the saving gospel but accommodation to various social agendas outside the centrality of Jesus Christ. It confuses the ultimate with the penultimate.

The fact that Christians believe that they have the truth does not automatically mean that they will harass those whom they believe not to have it. It is clear from Romans 1 that all humans know something of the truth, particularly God's law, or God would not be able to hold humankind accountable. Confessing truth, Christians also endeavor to speak the truth charitably, "in love" (Eph. 4:15), realizing that God the Holy Spirit is ultimately in charge of or able to judge anyone's salvation.

In contrast, secular approaches to faith tend to substitute a political theology that focuses on human liberation in place of salvation as deliverance from sin, death, and the devil by Jesus Christ alone. In the process, Christ's redemption of human beings is eclipsed by the need to advocate for the oppressed. This is not to deny that victims need advocacy! But it is no advantage to advocate for them at the expense of the gospel that will quicken and empower them.

To be clear: orthodox Christian faith need not and should not automatically translate into conservative politics, any more than it should automatically translate into liberal politics. The political right often highlights individuals as self-owners, in contrast to Paul's declaration: "You are not your own, for you were bought with a price" (1 Cor. 6:19–20). Orthodox confessors of the faith will defend the lives of the unborn and urge that sexual relations be within marriage, and they will also oppose blind, uncritical patriotism and unbridled greed in a free-market economy that tolerates or even creates extreme economic inequities.[10] Christ is Lord over all, thus no earthly or economic empire is Lord, even the American one.[11]

Instead of adopting a party platform wholesale, Christians need to test any given ethical or political matter—whether it is abortion, same-sex marriage, or economics—on a case-by-case basis, in the light of the Scriptures and the Confessions, striving to understand the complexities attendant on all such matters. Christians do not approach the world first of all from within a moral matrix of either the right or the left but instead inhabit the world as unfolded through the story of Scripture.[12] As George Lindbeck put it, "It is the text, so to speak, which absorbs the world, rather than the world the text."[13]

To be sure, in any given election year, Christians can offer good reasons to vote on either side of the aisle.[14] Often we vote for the lesser evil because the greater good is not to be had. But Christians desperately need the skills to step outside the moral matrix of either the political left or the political right instead of baptizing one ideology over the other. After all, political ideologies are all too often ways of salvation in disguise.[15]

The primary focus of the church should be on right-hand matters, the power of the gospel breaking into this world of sin and death to kindle new life, not left-hand matters of politics. This is *not* to devalue God's left hand or the humanitarian quest for justice. Quite the contrary, it is an active trust that God's people will seek to live ethically and serve their neighbors, especially the disadvantaged, as their lives are reshaped by the gospel.[16]

In this light, advocacy, when appropriate, is to be done within political venues and specific advocacy groups, not synodical or churchwide structures. It should arise organically as the Spirit brings faith when and where the Spirit wills and how the Spirit wills.

Nor does this stand validate the falsehood that the gospel is somehow a private matter in distinction to justice as a public matter. Rather, as Steve Paulson rightly notes, "In justification God is going public about God's real identity, and what is being done with creatures."[17] It is odd that leaders who would flinch at the thought of converting someone to Jesus have no trouble trying to convert someone to politically correct views on all sorts of cultural issues because, unlike the gospel, it does not require the death of the old sinner but only suggests a retrieval of one's better angels.

Unlike confessing the creed, the question of how to establish justice in any given situation in a democracy is open to debate, particularly over the means and what compromises might be required in a democracy.[18] Democracy has a hard time endorsing an all-or-nothing, let alone a winner-takes-all, strategy of either the extreme left or the extreme right. Rather, it is premised on a *dis*agreement regarding how to identify and rectify injustices. Churches, by contrast, seek to structure themselves around the common confession of ultimate matters of faith as specified in the Scripture, creeds, and confessions and commend laypeople to work for justice, as they see fit, in the wider public.

The Mainline's Leftward Drift

Many of our spiritual ancestors in the American church, such as J. Michael Reu, urged that Lutherans not move in the directions of "mainline Protestants."[19] But despite the outstanding theological efforts undertaken by a host of teachers, from George Forell to William Lazareth, whose work was grounded in the Scriptures and Confessions,[20] a new breed in synodical bureaucracies, colleges, and seminaries arose, starting in the 1950s, who felt that becoming like mainline Protestants and adopting their ecumenical and political agendas would be the wave of the future.[21]

We can't fault them for their good intentions, at least. How were they to know that the decisions they made would undermine the mission of the church? No doubt, many church leaders felt the need to acknowledge various social pressures arising from the quest for racial and sexual equality in a culture in transition, not to mention the assault on the environment and the plight of oppressed peoples throughout the world. It is right and good that they courageously sought to address such inequities along with the deep insecurity caused by the Cold War. We are indebted to their efforts.

But the same people were also driven by a desire to help Lutherans fit into the wider American agenda, no longer sitting at the margins of American culture. Both theological liberalism and the political left appeared to be the progressive, caring way to go, and so over many years, the predecessor church bodies of the ELCA moved in that direction. In this case, our leaders can be faulted for their failure to commend the Lutheran faith as offering something distinctive, even nonnegotiable, to the changing face of the North American religious landscape.

In practice, the tendency of the ELCA and its predecessor bodies was to adopt the ideologies of theological liberalism, focused on human liberation, and the political left, focused on greater personal liberties from the state, especially in sexual ethics, but tighter control of economics by the state. Mainline Protestants have sought to establish social justice by means of their churchwide bureaucracies guided by a left-of-center stance. In so doing, they have alienated members who do not share the same vision of justice, creating deep divisions and undermining loyalty.

Moreover, for many mainliners, a stigma has come to be attached to theological conservativism because of an assumption that theological conservatives must also and inevitably be political conservatives. While statistically that is often the case, the link is not guaranteed. Christians seeking to be ethically faithful will find themselves in a mix-and-match approach with respect to political ideologies. An orthodox approach to faith must challenge idols erected by either the political left or the political right. We are in, not of, this world (John 17:16).

The result on the ground is that when positions at the churchwide office in Chicago or in college theology departments and seminaries have become available, theological conservatives have been and continue to be overlooked, if not outright shunned. Those who won the jobs have tended to redirect the message of the church to this-worldly matters at the expense of the life to come; to adopt Bonhoeffer's terminology, they have pursued penultimate matters at the expense of ultimate matters, advocating for justice but not proclaiming the one way to eternal life. Pastors and laity on the conservative end of the theological spectrum have found no voice to represent them at the churchwide or synodical levels or in colleges and seminaries. Just as both major political parties have purified themselves of dissenting or moderate voices, so too has the church.[22] Theological conservatives are thus left with little obvious reason to remain loyal to the ELCA. When opportunities have arisen to leave, such as with the formation of the Lutheran Congregations in Mission for Christ or the North American Lutheran Church, many have done so.

The irony is that the theological-left desire to modify existing structures in order to eliminate systemic evils unintentionally undermines the motivation to invest in those systems.[23] For example, the ELCA designed its selection of leadership at the top based not on who had a track record of building or advancing the growth of the church but on quotas. The assumption was that putting minorities in leadership would attract a growing support base of the marginalized or underrepresented within local congregations. While, again, the intention was honorable, the practical result is that the ELCA has an insufficient number of leaders with a track record of advancing the life of the church by a successful practice of ministry.

And statistics show that this strategy has had no impact whatsoever on increasing the racial diversity of the ELCA. A *smaller* proportion of people for whom the quotas were instituted is active in the church today than when the ELCA was formed. In short, quotas do not increase denominational or congregational diversity. The only way to increase the percentage of minorities in the ELCA is through evangelism on the congregational, not churchwide, level, by evangelists who want to reach out not because a person fits in some desirable category but because the evangelists desire to share the gospel with anyone who will listen and respond.

The upshot of all this is that the job of the denominational headquarters should be to serve congregations and their mission, not to be a bureaucracy whose job is to blow the whistle on the injustices of other bureaucracies. Nor is public or legal justice to be seen as the only urgent matter of concern. Social investment to support stable families, the protection of the unborn and life at every stage, and the freedom to practice faith are also crucial matters for Christians in public life. All too often, the ELCA's calls for justice come across as partisan. Rather than paying lip service to welcome and inclusion, while in practice alienating large swaths of the population, the ELCA needs urgently to refocus its identity on the gospel that saves all people, regardless of their unique political or social identities, while educating and then trusting the laity to advocate for ethical causes as a result of their internalization of the faith in appropriate political and social outlets. In short, we need to ask more of our people—expecting them to know their faith deeply, share it, and act on it.

Theological Disengagement

Accompanying all these other problems is the catastrophic loss of interest in theology from top to bottom, from institutions to individual clergy.

Disengagement from theology can be discerned by the disappearance of historic journals and the decrease in subscriptions to at-one-time thriving journals such as *Dialog*. This cannot be explained merely by the notion that clergy read theological material online now. Some blame can fairly be apportioned to the irrelevance of much so-called theology to parish ministry, as in the arcane philosophical and linguistic debates in the American Academy of Religion or the Society of Biblical Literature.[24]

But this is a two-way street. Fewer candidates for ministry express an interest in theology, let alone a set of theological convictions advocated by a journal or other organization of theological concern. It's hard to imagine today a conference sponsored by three theological journals would have enough gravity to pull one thousand Lutherans in, as happened in the late '80s and early '90s at the behest of *Dialog*, *Lutheran Quarterly*, and *Lutheran Forum*.

Likewise, the secularism of the mainline churches that began in ELCA college religion departments, starting in the 1960s, did much to harm the passion for theology. Prior to the entrenchment of secular truisms like "Every religion is a path to salvation" or "Jesus was merely a great teacher, not a savior," Lutheran colleges served as pipelines to the seminaries. Up through the 1950s, a score of students graduating from Gettysburg College enrolled each and every year at Gettysburg Seminary. At Luther Seminary in the early 1980s, the majority of students came from the one ELCA Concordia in Moorhead, Minnesota, with St. Olaf in second place and the University of Minnesota in third. Another lost pipeline is that of campus ministries at non-Lutheran schools, which the ELCA has all but abandoned. Many of these campus ministries were strong feeders into parish ministry, not to mention they kept young people called to other vocations active in the congregational life of the church.

The educational mission of the church should be always catechetical—that is, to enculture its members more and more into the faith. It is the faith that gives congregational members joy and inspires them to share it. Speaking from a purely secular perspective, sociologists Roger Finke and Rodney Stark note, on the basis of their rational-choice theory of religion, "An individual's positive experience in a worship service increases to the degree that the church is full, members enthusiastically participate (everyone sings and recites prayers, for example), and others express their positive evaluations of what is going on. Thus as each individual member pays the cost of high levels of commitment, each benefits from the higher average level of participation thereby generated by the group. In similar fashion, people will value the otherworldly rewards of religion more highly to the extent that those around them do so."[25]

Biblical, Confessional, Resilient, and Evangelistic

If we are to raise up more candidates for ministry who can start congregations, grow congregations, and serve large congregations, we need more candidates who have the potential to build.[26] This is not just theoretical or ideal but urgent: over the next several years, a large number of ELCA clergy will retire, and so there will be a need for younger pastors. We need to scout them out and support them with prayer, mentoring, and scholarships. We need to ground them in a thorough knowledge of the Scriptures and the Confessions.[27]

One difficulty is that ministerial candidates no longer arrive immersed in the language of Scripture as they once did, though too many professors of the Bible still teach as though their main task was to disabuse their students of rigid fundamentalism. Seminarians need to learn to see not just matters "behind the text" (to use Paul Ricoeur's terms) such as authorship and redaction but also "in front of the text," how human life changes in light of the text, and "within the text"—the symbols and themes echoed throughout the Scriptures.[28] All too often, the frontloading of the historical-critical method has led to an unwarranted skepticism about the Bible that does not serve the church well. More helpful for our current situation is Brevard Childs' "canonical" approach to criticism, honoring the integrity of the Scriptures as we have received them.[29]

The pastoral candidates we need will be biblical, confessional, resilient, and evangelistic. They will be *biblical* in that they will love the Scriptures and seek to share them with others as one shares a good friend. They will interpret the world through the lens of Scripture, and not vice versa. They will find empowerment for ministry by praying the Psalter, facing disappointment by means of Ecclesiastes and Job, receiving spiritual quickening from Paul's letters, seeing their mission as belonging to the history of Israel and the church, and anchoring discipleship in the gospels.

They will be *confessional* in that they will honor the Lutheran Confessions as faithful expositions of the word of God. They will understand the doctrine of justification as the article by which the church stands or falls and will thus seek to comfort the afflicted and afflict the comfortable. They will honor the sacraments as means of grace and commend God-honoring liturgical worship. They will be leaders of faith and models of obedience as the Spirit works faith (Augsburg Confession V) and a new obedience (Augsburg Confession VI).

They will be *resilient*. In the face of stress and opposition, they will neither flee nor fight back with abuse but instead, as Paul teaches, they will bear all things, believe all things, hope all things, and endure all things (1 Cor. 13). They will know that God works through the bad as well as the good and so seek to find a blessing not only for themselves but also for the others with whom they are in conflict.

Finally, they will be *evangelistic*. They will have a passion to share the Name that is above every name, the Name at which every knee will bow and every tongue confess the lordship of Jesus Christ (Phil. 2). Christ's suffering and death have reconciled us to God, assuring them and enabling them to assure others that their lives have meaning, worth, and hope.

Two decades ago, Episcopal lay-theologian Thomas Reeves noted that "Christianity in modern America is, in large part, innocuous. It tends to be easy, upbeat, convenient, and compatible. It does not require self-sacrifice, discipline, humility, an otherworldly outlook, a zeal for souls, a fear as well as love of God. There is little guilt and no punishment, and the payoff in heaven is virtually certain."[30] A renewed vision of Lutheran faith will refuse to allow the secular mind-set to establish the agenda for the church. The gospel as we have received it from the apostles and mediated through the Reformers can still speak to people today if only we give voice to it. This is especially so in a world characterized by anomie or lack of purpose, where people demand to have their rights acknowledged but refuse to confess their own sins and amend their wrongdoings, where people insist on their own individualistic self-expressions but then ironically conform to other's expectations.

To spread this good news, we need to build up and support, financially and emotionally, a cadre of evangelists—not just caregivers but risk takers. For almost two decades, the ELCA has touted leadership as the guide to understand true ministry. But that is not enough. All builders are leaders, but not all leaders are builders. It is builders that the church needs today. We need to begin to challenge our bright and devout youth: Will you be a builder? We need to provide avenues for theological development and ways to inspire their imaginations for being a pastor in the next decades. We need to put them into positions of apprentice-building and give them a voice in the local church. And we need to promise them: you will have our support.

Sermons

Stranger Things from the Old Testament

CHAPTER 18

Balaam's Donkey

Numbers 22:21–39 (ESV)

21 So Balaam rose in the morning and saddled his donkey and went with the princes of Moab.

22 But God's anger was kindled because he went, and the angel of the LORD took his stand in the way as his adversary. Now he was riding on the donkey, and his two servants were with him. 23 And the donkey saw the angel of the LORD standing in the road, with a drawn sword in his hand. And the donkey turned aside out of the road and went into the field. And Balaam struck the donkey, to turn her into the road. 24 Then the angel of the LORD stood in a narrow path between the vineyards, with a wall on either side. 25 And when the donkey saw the angel of the LORD, she pushed against the wall and pressed Balaam's foot against the wall. So he struck her again. 26 Then the angel of the LORD went ahead and stood in a narrow place, where there was no way to turn either to the right or to the left. 27 When the donkey saw the angel of the LORD, she lay down under Balaam. And Balaam's anger was kindled, and he struck the donkey with his staff. 28 Then the LORD opened the mouth of the donkey, and she said to Balaam, "What have I done to you, that you have struck me these three times?" 29 And Balaam said to the donkey, "Because you have made a fool of me. I wish I had a sword in my hand, for then I would kill you." 30 And the donkey said to Balaam, "Am I not your donkey, on which you have ridden all your life long to this day? Is it my habit to treat you this way?" And he said, "No."

³¹ *Then the* L<small>ORD</small> *opened the eyes of Balaam, and he saw the angel of the* L<small>ORD</small> *standing in the way, with his drawn sword in his hand. And he bowed down and fell on his face.* ³² *And the angel of the* L<small>ORD</small> *said to him, "Why have you struck your donkey these three times? Behold, I have come out to oppose you because your way is perverse*[a] *before me.* ³³ *The donkey saw me and turned aside before me these three times. If she had not turned aside from me, surely just now I would have killed you and let her live." *³⁴ *Then Balaam said to the angel of the* L<small>ORD</small>, *"I have sinned, for I did not know that you stood in the road against me. Now therefore, if it is evil in your sight, I will turn back." *³⁵ *And the angel of the* L<small>ORD</small> *said to Balaam, "Go with the men, but speak only the word that I tell you." So Balaam went on with the princes of Balak.*

³⁶ *When Balak heard that Balaam had come, he went out to meet him at the city of Moab, on the border formed by the Arnon, at the extremity of the border.* ³⁷ *And Balak said to Balaam, "Did I not send to you to call you? Why did you not come to me? Am I not able to honor you?" *³⁸ *Balaam said to Balak, "Behold, I have come to you! Have I now any power of my own to speak anything? The word that God puts in my mouth, that must I speak." *³⁹ *Then Balaam went with Balak, and they came to Kiriath-huzoth.*

God is used to working with colorful figures. One of the most colorful in the Bible is Balaam. Hailing from Mesopotamia, Balaam was what we might call a shaman or a soothsayer. He was not a Hebrew. But he knew the God of the Hebrews, in addition to other purported deities he believed he could summon or charm. It would be well and good that Balaam knew the Hebrew God, but God did not approve of Balaam's methods: divination, witchcraft as a way of figuring out God's will. God doesn't like us resorting to witchcraft because when we do so, we use spiritual power in order to secure our own statuses, empower ourselves, even act as gods. We seek a security other than in Jesus Christ. Instead, what God wants for us is to be people of faith. That means that we can't always expect to be in control. We need to trust that God will work everything for good, even when it does not always seem so.

In contemporary terms, Balaam is akin to a television preacher, someone who is out to use faith matters to make big bucks. Now, like

Balaam, many television preachers are successful. They have wide followings—especially of people down on their luck and seeking prosperity. Like Balaam, they speak and whole worlds listen. There is power to their words, and on occasion, powerful politicians have sought advice from them.

Balak, king of Moab, was one such politician seeking help from Balaam. Israel was about to repossess the promised land, having traveled in the wilderness for forty years. Balak, and his people, the Moabites, were terrified of Israel, since Israel had become a mighty people, strong and powerful *and hungry*. Balak was alarmed that Israel would invade Moab and steal her crops and wealth. What to do? Balak wanted to enlist Balaam's help—to curse Israel! That would weaken Israel and make her unable to threaten Moab—sounds like a good plan. After all, Balaam was a mighty magician. Surely his hexes could do the trick. Except, what Balak didn't realize was that God Almighty was behind Israel. Any curse brought against Israel would simply boomerang back on the curser.

Perhaps you've heard of a teen begging to go to a weekend party: "Will adults be present?" asks the parent. "Of course!" promises the teen. "Will there be drinking? Drugs?" the parent follows up. The teen replies, "Of course not!" But you, the parent, are being fed lies: no adults will be at this party, and drinks galore will be present. No wonder God's wrath was turned against Balaam. Balaam knew that big money was wrapped up in his curses. He stood to profit big time if he cursed Israel on behalf of Moab. So just like the teen eager to run to an inappropriate party, so Balaam ran hog-wild to Balak in order to make mincemeat of Israel with his curses. Just like a television preacher salivating over just how much money he can make, Balaam pushed his donkey to get to Moab.

Now, Balaam's donkey wasn't like Shrek's. Balaam's donkey really couldn't talk, at least not naturally. But she was a wise donkey, and when she saw the angel with the flaming sword—just like the angel who guarded Eden after the fall or St. Michael the Archangel in the Book of Revelation—she knew that the angel was no one to mess with. She knew that his life was at stake. So three times she halted, even to the point of injuring Balaam, her master. Better that her master suffer some bruises than lose his life—and the donkey's own life as well!

That God freed the tongue of a donkey to speak is not nearly as awesome as opening Balaam's eyes to see the angel of the Lord. Much like ourselves at different times in life, Balaam was thick-headed. C. S. Lewis once pointed out just how differently angels were presented in the Bible compared to their representations in art. In art, angels all too often come across as harmless and nonthreatening, delicate creatures. But in Scripture, angels often have to say, "Fear not," because their appearances are so terrifying that those who see them are thoroughly startled. In the case of Balaam, the fright was increased because the angel was wielding a sword. Silly Balaam: he now saw that the donkey was only protecting her own life as well as her master's. More to the point, he saw that his own life was at stake! God will have nothing to do with the nonsense of seeking profit at His own peoples' expense. And finally, Balaam saw that his own dumb ass was a far better preacher than he would ever be. His donkey spoke the truth—indeed, spoke the truth in love, just as St. Paul, much later in the New Testament, asks of each one of us.

Preachers, even asses, are far more important than we make them out to be. True, God is everywhere. And if that is the case, why would you even need a preacher? Many people feel that they encounter God on the golf course. And no doubt they do. But nature, even at the country club, is seldom a clear indicator of what God's will is for each one of us. Nature is just as apt to take life as give it. It's not often that a golfer gets hit by lightning, but it has been known to happen. God might be everywhere present in nature, but it is not clear that He is there for our well-being. The hard truth is that God is not indebted to us. (But we are indebted to Him.)

This is why preachers are so important. Sure, they do preach judgment, which most of the time, we don't like to hear. And that judgment is a true word of God to sinners. God sets boundaries or limits to human behavior. God told Adam and Eve that on the day they eat of the Tree of the Knowledge of Good and Evil, they will die. Paul hit this truth home when he told us that the wages of sin is death. But Paul also hit it out of the park when he wrote that the free gift of God is eternal life through Jesus Christ our Lord. No matter how beautiful a sunset or a rainbow is, no matter how beautiful these mountains surrounding Birmingham are, no matter how gorgeous the lakes and streams near here are, nature provides no absolutely secure word that God is for us. But the job of preachers, those who preach both God's law and God's grace, is to impart words that both uproot sinners and plant saints—and those in one and the same individual. God is all about making you a new person—and that through trust in His love, revealed in Jesus Christ.

Preaching should never be about caving in to the powers that be, whether they are found in the politics on either side of the aisle. Instead, preaching is accountable to God's own word, which has the power to raise the dead, impart new life, forgive sins, and heal the brokenhearted. Preaching is accountable to God's love. Balaam and Balak are both right to understand that words do things. After all, when the justice of the peace says, "I now pronounce you man and wife," then you are married. When a preacher says, "You are forgiven," then you are forgiven. Words not only describe the world or provide directives for how we should live. But words also change the world. The gospel is such a word because it is a word of promise.

We are surrounded by well-intentioned Christians who tell us to accept Jesus as our Lord and Savior and that then we will be saved. But is this true? Is it our decision that puts us into heaven? Or is it not, instead, God's decision for us that does that? And if in fact we have ever decided about Jesus, is it not the decision that shouts "Crucify him! Crucify him!"? God's decision is the only one that counts when it comes to matters of salvation. And God specifically makes a decision about you. God takes you, me, and every other sinner who has put Jesus on the cross and says, "For my Son's sake, I forgive you." And we can count on the words of Jesus: if the Son sets you free, you will be free indeed.

As bad as Balaam was, he functioned as a mouthpiece for God. Later in the narrative, three times he was asked by Balak to curse Israel. But the only thing that could come out of his mouth was a blessing. Finally, during the fourth attempt to curse Israel, Balaam actually prophesied that a "star shall come out of Jacob and a scepter shall raise out of Israel." Christians have ever seen this to be a genuine prophecy of the coming of Jesus Christ, who is both our star and the scepter.

Surely, we hear in this passage the truth that God's people will ever be opposed. Sometimes that opposition is in your face and literally takes out millions of lives. Other times it is more subtle, implying that those of us who believe in Christ and confess Him as Lord just aren't very bright or are too old-fashioned or are less than adequate.

Jesus tells us to "be of good cheer" because He has overcome the world. Our identity does not come for these naysayers. It comes from Christ Himself. In Jesus Christ, God validates you and me as sons and daughters. Unlike the paranoid ancient Chinese king who built an army of terra-cotta warriors to defend him in the afterlife, we don't need such militia. We have instead the power of the word, which can bless and curse. But as Christians, loved by God, we need no longer curse our enemies. We are not, even for a minute, like Balak and Moab, even though they were descendants of righteous Lot. No. Instead, we are increasingly like our Master who prays, "Father, forgive them, for they know not what they do."

May God continue to empower us in word—so that we speak God's message honestly and not with guile as Balaam sought to do—and in deed so that we welcome our neighbors generously and not seek to oppress them as Balak sought to do with Israel.

CHAPTER 19

Fear and Love of God

2 Samuel 6:3–10[1]

They carried the ark of God on a new cart, and brought it out of the house of Abinadab, which was on the hill. Uzzah and Ahio, the sons of Abinadab, were driving the new cart with the ark of God, and Ahio went in front of the ark. David and all the house of Israel were dancing before the LORD with all their might, with songs and lyres and harps and tambourines and castanets and cymbals. When they came to the threshing floor of Nacon, Uzzah reached out his hand to the ark of God and took hold of it, for the oxen shook it. The anger of the LORD was kindled against Uzzah; and God struck him there because he reached out his hand to the ark; and he died there beside the ark of God. David was angry because the LORD had burst forth with an outburst upon Uzzah; so that the place is called Perez-Uzzah to this day. David was afraid of the LORD that day; he said, "How can the ark of the LORD come into my care?" So David was unwilling to take the ark of the LORD into his care in the city of David; instead David took it to the house of Obed-edom the Gittite.

Many Christians would see the Christian life as a movement "from fear to love." That's a therapeutic approach to faith, but I can understand why people think this way. Many people's lives are empty and meaningless because they are enveloped in various fears and anxieties. Surely, in the church we can affirm that the gospel comes to liberate us from fear because it offers us a God with whom we can entrust our lives. However, as I think about moving from fear to love, I couldn't help but be reminded of the Reformer, Martin Luther, and his explanations of the Ten Commandments in "The Small Catechism." Luther explains *every* commandment with the phrase: we should *fear* and love God. Now, this is no eccentric move on Luther's part. It is quite ecumenical, quite catholic: long before Luther, St. Bernard of Clairvaux emphasized that people of faith must fear and love God. He said you couldn't really "know yourself" unless you did.

Luther noted that we should fear and love God so that we honor God above all things and not merely use God for our own interests. And we shouldn't hurt our neighbors in any way but instead seek to help and support them. If so many today seek to move "from fear to love," then why does Luther tell us to *both* fear and love? Is this really what hurting people need to hear? What could the Reformer, or St. Bernard, for that matter, possibly mean? And how does he speak to us today?

When we hear Luther and Bernard telling us to fear God, perhaps we remember pastors and teachers who have told us that what this really means is that we should *respect* God rather than be terrified by God. In our contemporary setting, it is tempting for me to reinforce this reading of Luther and Bernard for you. If they really meant that we should actually be afraid of God rather than merely having a healthy respect for God, then perhaps some people might leave church feeling bad about themselves. The vast majority of us wouldn't want that. We've come to believe that a chief mission of the church is to help people feel good about themselves. We associate the "bad old days" with a view of religion as repressive—religion that shames people or makes them feel guilty. Indeed, some Christians thought that they had an inside track into God's ways; in their opinion, they could discern who, how, and why God was punishing someone. They were happy to tell people what they supposedly "knew." We can be grateful that these traits are lessening among Christians.

However, I was curious as to what Luther, specifically, really meant, despite what we might want him to mean. In reading his conclusion to the Ten Commandments, he makes his meaning quite clear: "God threatens to punish all who transgress these commandments. We should therefore fear his wrath and not disobey these commandments. On the other hand, he promises grace and every blessing to all who keep them. We should therefore love him, trust in him, and cheerfully do what he has commanded."[2] I doubt if St. Bernard would disagree. It doesn't sound to me that Luther actually means what we would call "respect" when he talks about fear. It seems he really means fear when he says fear, specifically, fear of punishment due to our sins. This must sound awfully strange to us. We have long come to think of God as one who has "unconditional positive regard" for us, a God who never threatens us because God is only capable of affirming us. After all, isn't it God's business to forgive, as the French scholar Voltaire taught us? We don't want people to feel bad about themselves in church. However, don't we inhibit the chances or opportunities for people to repent of their sins, if all we ever want to offer them is a God who is affirming and never angry? Isn't there a good chance that if I truly repent of my sin, I just might feel bad about myself? It seems that the kind of religion that we have invented is the one H. R. Niebuhr described as offering a "God without wrath" who "brought men without sin into a kingdom without judgment through the ministrations of a Christ without a cross." Even in our current cultural climate, in which we tend to think that no one should feel bad about themselves, shouldn't we at least feel bad about the wrong behaviors we have done? Shouldn't we fear God's anger at our sin? Wouldn't God care enough to stand up for the victims we have hurt or wronged?

In our reading, David learned to fear God. And it seems this was a good thing. For David to fear God was for him to understand the truth that if God is to be honored, He must be honored for His own sake and not just because of what He can do for us. Uzzah saw the ark slipping. He took this to mean that *God needed his help*. He assumed that if he didn't help God, the ark might fall. It might be soiled. It might be broken. This holy thing might touch the earth. The ark is properly God's—but from Uzzah's view, it's a symbol of his—or our—religion. We can't afford to have it broken or soiled. It represents our values and not just God's deity.

In his own view, Uzzah was doing God a favor. What Uzzah didn't understand is that God is Lord even over His own ark. He doesn't need our favors. Perhaps Uzzah was inclined to look at God as needing his help because he primarily looked at God as there to service him and provide for his perceived needs. If we look at the ark as a symbol of our own religion, that's exactly how we'd be troubled by the prospect of the ark falling. Aren't we a lot like Uzzah? We want our religion to help us feel good about ourselves. We are inclined to react negatively to a faith that accuses us of our wrongs. We want our religion to bring cohesiveness to our values, politics, ideals, families, and communities. Now, many of our values are good and wholesome. Nevertheless, they must be tested and evaluated in light of God's will. God provides the standard of justice and truth. We, after all, are apt to create idols that heighten our own sense of power and secure our own future. That's why we need to look to God. We want our religion to justify our politics, whether of the right or the left. We assume that Jesus would be on our side in the various debates that rock our era. We want our religion to provide for our needs of belonging and community; we want it to serve as a kind of social club for us. But will we sell out on our discipleship to Christ in order to provide for our own perceived needs?

Perhaps in our society today, we have too much fear about fear. Maybe fear isn't always a bad thing. My Aunt Marie told me very clearly when I was about six years old not to touch the hot burner on the stove. Of course, what did I do? You know the answer. Through this experience, I learned a healthy fear for heat and electricity. From one perspective, couldn't we even say that some kinds of fear are natural motivators that God gave us in order to help us survive various dangers in life? Nevertheless, Jesus tells us that many of the things we usually fear are things that are not worthy of our fear. He bids us instead to fear alone Him "who can destroy both body and soul in hell" (Matt. 10:28). Perhaps, many of the things we fear in this life are things we spend far too much effort and time fearing, and the One whom we should fear—because we are totally and wholly accountable to Him—we don't fear enough. Instead, we deface God by rendering Him harmless. Our temptation, like Uzzah's, is to use God for our own interests as if we are the center of it all. We lie to ourselves by trying to control what's not in our control and letting ourselves off the hook where we have real responsibilities. The ark is God's, not Uzzah's and not ours. If God wants the ark or even the church to fall, then so be it!

To have a healthy fear of God is to honor God for His own sake. When Moses encountered God on Sinai's heights, he was duly afraid.

When Isaiah encountered God in the temple, he was duly afraid. When Paul encountered the risen Jesus on the Damascus road, he, too, was duly afraid. If we never have similar experiences, do we really ever encounter the living God of Scripture? To fear God is to acknowledge that He is the Lord and not we ourselves! To encounter the living God is to recognize that we are creatures. It is to recognize that we have no bargaining chips with the powerful One. In things that really matter, He calls all the shots. However, if God is the Lord, then we are free from the attempt to rule over ourselves, be our own lords or ladies. Instead, as Psalm 100 tells us, we can be the "sheep of his pasture." Indeed, what's the context of the Ten Commandments, if not God's covenant with His people? God's covenant claims His people as His own. Hence Luther says that we should fear and love God. We should fear God because we are not God, and we shouldn't even try to be God. We have to accept God's decision to run the world His way—this Uzzah could not do. And because God claims us as His own, as the One who promises His very own life to us, eternal life, we can love God. From this perspective, we should not assume that even Uzzah's sin of disbelief could separate him from this covenanting God. God says no to our sin so that He can say yes to us as His creatures and, in so doing, make us His new creatures. If Luther is right, that God is indeed at times an angry God, angry at our sins, angry at the evil we inflict on others and the earth, and angry at the injustices and disrespect that we perpetuate and perpetrate; this is only because God is a caring God.

A parent who never gets angry with his or her children is probably a parent who doesn't truly love them. Because God is love and offers Himself to us in Jesus Christ, God cares enough to say no to our evil, indeed, to our attempts to mold religion or spirituality to fit our comfort zone. To fear God as well as to love God is to be in touch with who God actually is. And to be in touch with God permits us to be in touch with the truth about ourselves. To fear and love God allows us to fear earthly problems far less because God's power and care put all these problems in perspective. The only way any little ounce of love for God could ever arise in us is due solely to this word: for Jesus' sake, your sins are forgiven. And so, to make it very clear, I announce to you, in the name of Jesus and for His sake: I tell you who repent and believe; your sins are forgiven. You are free.

CHAPTER 20

Treasured Possession

Exodus 19:1–9

On the third new moon after the people of Israel had gone out of the land of Egypt, on that day they came into the wilderness of Sinai. ² *They set out from Rephidim and came into the wilderness of Sinai, and they encamped in the wilderness. There Israel encamped before the mountain,* ³ *while Moses went up to God. The LORD called to him out of the mountain, saying, "Thus you shall say to the house of Jacob, and tell the people of Israel:* ⁴ *'You yourselves have seen what I did to the Egyptians, and how I bore you on eagles' wings and brought you to myself.* ⁵ *Now therefore, if you will indeed obey my voice and keep my covenant, you shall be my treasured possession among all peoples, for all the earth is mine;* ⁶ *and you shall be to me a kingdom of priests and a holy nation.' These are the words that you shall speak to the people of Israel."*

⁷ *So Moses came and called the elders of the people and set before them all these words that the LORD had commanded him.* ⁸ *All the people answered together and said, "All that the LORD has spoken we will do." And Moses reported the words of the people to the LORD.* ⁹ *And the LORD said to Moses, "Behold, I am coming to you in a thick cloud, that the people may hear when I speak with you, and may also believe you forever."*

Last spring, my seventeen-year-old daughter urged me to watch *13 Reasons Why* on Netflix. Since as a college professor I always want insight into what makes young people tick, I watched it. It was not a joy to watch, but I kept with it to the end of the series. It is the story of a young woman who takes her life because she was constantly bullied by peers and let down by friends in her high school. I kept thinking that the series was filled with exaggerations. That is, some kids might have a tough go of it in some high schools, but overall, the series was fairly "over the top" or hyperbolic. Surely, high schools aren't nearly as bad as the series makes them out to be. It was clear to me that most kids aren't bullied, and if there is bullying, it isn't very serious. But when I asked my daughter just how accurate she felt the series was in portraying contemporary high school life, I was surprised to hear her say that she felt it was spot on. So I asked one of my college classes if they had seen this series and if they felt it was accurate. I was surprised just how many had seen it and that most felt it was pretty accurate. If these young people are right, then my instincts about bullying are wrong. There is a lot of bullying, and it can be quite vicious and cruel.

What really catches me off guard, though, is that these same college students who agree that bullying is quite a problem, and who are themselves just out of high school, don't seem either to be bullies or to have been bullied. Perhaps they cover themselves up pretty well. Many, if not most, of my students are of the "Sir, yes sir!" variety: they are polite, respectful, and kind, even if they are not as studious as I might wish they would be. Perhaps now that they are in a new environment, in college, they are starting over, charting a new path, one in which they no longer play the role of either bully or victim. I hope that is the case!

It strikes me that high school youth, like many adults, struggle with matters of "identity." My hunch tells me that to be human means that at times, anyone will struggle with questions about who they really are. But I also think that these anxieties are aggravated in our modern era. I remember on occasion having bad days at high school back in the '70s. I would go home, go to my bedroom, close the door, and "chill" or "veg out." Eventually, my peace of mind was restored. How different it is for many high schoolers today. I suspect that they go to bed with their phones, and this inhibits their ability to unwind or get "downtime." Instead, they are incessantly plagued by Snapchat,

Instagram, Twitter, and other annoyances that disturb their peace of mind. And unfortunately, they don't know when to quit.

How very different was our country a century ago. There were no cell phones then. And the majority of Americans still lived on the farm. They didn't have to struggle with identity as much as we do because there were not a lot of options or roles to choose from. There's no choosing about when to milk the cows or shovel in the barn or when to harvest or when to mend fences. These are all chores that simply must be done for people to survive. When one is working hard with fourteen-hour days, every day, and with physical labor, not much time can be spent on the question of who one really is, whether or not one is accepted, whether life has meaning, and the like. Those questions hardly matter. But at some point, the scales tipped: by the 1920s or so, more and more people moved to the big city, no longer worked such backbreaking jobs, and had time to explore their own identities. Professors have a word for the approach to life that has arisen from this. They call it the *ethics of authenticity*. What this means is that the purpose of life is for you to become more of who you are, provided no one is hurt in the process. But the quest for such self-discovery comes at a cost. That cost can be stated pretty simply: there is no clear standard, rubric, or metric by which to determine your authenticity, your real self. And those who aim to accumulate as much pleasure in life as they can, provided that they do no harm to others, often find themselves to be very unhappy. Think of the Kardashians!

I kept thinking about the young female protagonist in *13 Reasons Why*: what if she had a supportive church youth group in which to establish solid friendships? Would that have helped her? No doubt, church youth groups aren't perfect. But there is more hope in them for the well-being of youth than purely secular venues. Why? Because, though I understand this is not always the case, the ideal of Christlike behavior of love would be welcomed among church youth.

Identity remains an important matter not just for youth seeking to "find themselves" but for all of us. One of the most important things that happens in the Christian faith is that God establishes your identity. He did so in the days when most folks lived on the farm, and He still does so today. Sure, that goes against our culture, which says that the onus is on you to establish your own identity. But there is something really positive about God establishing your identity for you. You don't have to worry about a standard, measure, metric, or rubric by which to figure out if you have really pulled off authenticity. Instead, God breaks that all apart for you, just as He did for Israel. God says point-blank to you, "*You are my treasure.*" You are precious to God, just like jewels may well be precious to you.

The Hebrew word for "treasured possession" is *segula*. As I understand it, a Hebrew woman, not having pockets or aprons, let alone safes or safety deposit boxes, would chisel a hole through a coin or precious metal, and hang this treasured possession by a chain around her neck, keeping the treasure close to her heart. This is how God gives you an identity: you are a precious gem, close to the heart of God.

Remember the original context in which God gave this identity to His people: He had brought them "on eagles' wings" out of bondage, out of slavery, out of servitude to Pharaoh, and was in the process of bringing them to the promised land. Let's go back to *13 Reasons Why*: picking on someone over time can really affect a person's behavior. They lose confidence in their ability to succeed. They doubt their own instincts. They feel sorrowful a good portion of the time. And they often get used to it, so they don't know who they would be if they weren't bullied! Pharaoh and his minions were tyrants. To enslave people is worse than bullying them. But God is a promise-keeping God. God, who promised Abraham and Sarah's descendants land and to bless them, had no intention of allowing His people to be slaves forever. Pharaoh and his minions paid for their bullying as they drowned in the Red Sea. God rescued His people; they had always been a treasured possession, a *segula*, even when they were slaves.

God proved His truthfulness in deed, rescuing the people from slavery, and in word, validating them, granting them a new identity. They are no longer slaves; they are free. They are no longer objects of mistreatment but instead cherished and prized. God affirms His people not because they are perfect but because they are His people. This is why God is so adamant in pursuing prodigals. God's love defines His children, not their misdeeds or, for that matter, *even their good deeds!* This simply spells out our common Reformation heritage: not even our good works save us but instead faith alone in the power of Jesus' blood to cleanse us from sin saves us.

Driven by our quests for authenticity, for really becoming and affirming ourselves, we seek to validate ourselves by the stuff or the experiences we accumulate. Insecure to the core, we are jealous of what others have and often feel we are missing out. To top it all off, we suffer with what the French call *anomie*, a restless feeling of purposelessness. That leads us to ask, Is keeping up with the Joneses really worth it? How can we really know that all our efforts to validate ourselves really do the trick?

How different is our God! We seek to validate ourselves by how many experiences we check off the bucket list or how much stuff we accumulate. In contrast, God doesn't need any such things to make Him love us either more or less. The "Rock of Ages" teaches us: "Nothing in my hand I bring, simply to thy cross I cling."[1] God will have us on no other basis than that we humbly admit that everything we have is a gift. Every breath of air we take, every swallow we make, everything we see or do: it's all a gift. It is all grace. It is all mercy. When it hits home that it's all a gift, what other choice do we have other than to thank and praise, serve and obey our God?

When you read the Scriptures, it's tempting to think of the Holy Land as a big place. We imagine it panoramically, like a 1950s Hollywood big-screen epic, with Pharaoh's army pursuing Charlton Heston (as Moses) or David standing up against Goliath and all the Philistine hordes or Israel's defenders as guerrilla warriors (like Judas Maccabeus) fending off the mighty legions of Babylon, Greece, or Rome. Now, all these big armies did in fact envelop the Holy Land. But our imaginations about the Holy Land's geography are greatly exaggerated. It's a little place. It's only seventy miles from the Dead Sea to the Sea of Galilee. To put some perspective on that, it's eighty-four miles from Birmingham to Huntsville!

God gave Abraham land—but not a big imperial landscape, like Russia, China, or the USA. Back in the '70s, Israeli Prime Minister Golda Meir once teased how Moses could lead the children of Israel to the one place in the Middle East without oil. God loves His people not because they are mighty or full of wealth or prestige. If you have a child, you love that child not because of the awards, medals, or trophies accumulated, or even because of that child's looks, but instead because that child belongs to you. When you look into that child's eyes, you love him or her regardless of what anyone else in the world thinks of him or her.

In the same way, you, a sinner, are beloved by God. God loves you not because you are a sinner or because you are a saint (though, in fact, you are both at the same time) but because you belong to Him. You are God's cherished and priceless treasure. It is for this reason that God sent His Son. God is angry at sin. This is because God cares about His creation and creatures. Nothing can quell that wrath other than God Himself. The Son came to the world not so much because we owe God a debt that as sinners we cannot render. Instead, in Christ, God does not so much fix the crack within creation caused by sin and death but instead comes to make all things new.

In closing, during Lent I sometimes listen to J. S. Bach's "St. Matthew's Passion," an oratorio that presents the story of Christ's suffering and death based on the gospel of Matthew. It is potent and powerful music. But as stirring as it is, I am always left dissatisfied with it. Why? In this music, Bach gets us to Good Friday. But he doesn't get us to Easter. Now, no doubt, it wasn't his intention to get us to Easter. After all, this is music for Lent. But what is Lent without Easter? What is Jesus' suffering all about apart from the resurrection?

Dear friends, the Lord is risen! Jesus rose precisely so that the truth will hit home with you that you are God's treasured possession, God's *segula*. This you will be not only today and tomorrow but also forever.

CHAPTER 21

New, Clean Hearts

2 Samuel 12:1–15

12 ¹ *and the L*ORD *sent Nathan to David. He came to him, and said to
him, "There were two men in a certain city, the one rich and the other
poor.* ² *The rich man had very many flocks and herds;* ³ *but the poor
man had nothing but one little ewe lamb, which he had bought. He
brought it up, and it grew up with him and with his children; it used
to eat of his meager fare, and drink from his cup, and lie in his bosom,
and it was like a daughter to him.* ⁴ *Now there came a traveler to the
rich man, and he was loath to take one of his own flock or herd to pre-
pare for the wayfarer who had come to him, but he took the poor man's
lamb, and prepared that for the guest who had come to him."* ⁵ *Then
David's anger was greatly kindled against the man. He said to Nathan,
"As the L*ORD *lives, the man who has done this deserves to die;* ⁶ *he shall
restore the lamb fourfold, because he did this thing, and because he had
no pity."*

⁷ *Nathan said to David, "You are the man! Thus says the L*ORD*, the
God of Israel: I anointed you king over Israel, and I rescued you from
the hand of Saul;* ⁸ *I gave you your master's house, and your master's wives into your bosom, and gave you the house of Israel and of
Judah; and if that had been too little, I would have added as much
more.* ⁹ *Why have you despised the word of the L*ORD*, to do what is evil
in his sight? You have struck down Uriah the Hittite with the sword,
and have taken his wife to be your wife, and have killed him with the
sword of the Ammonites.* ¹⁰ *Now therefore the sword shall never depart*

from your house, for you have despised me, and have taken the wife of Uriah the Hittite to be your wife. ¹¹ *Thus says the LORD: I will raise up trouble against you from within your own house; and I will take your wives before your eyes, and give them to your neighbor, and he shall lie with your wives in the sight of this very sun.* ¹² *For you did it secretly; but I will do this thing before all Israel, and before the sun."* ¹³ *David said to Nathan, "I have sinned against the LORD." Nathan said to David, "Now the LORD has put away your sin; you shall not die.* ¹⁴ *Nevertheless, because by this deed you have utterly scorned the LORD,*[a] *the child that is born to you shall die."* ¹⁵ *Then Nathan went to his house. The Lord struck the child that Uriah's wife bore to David, and it became very ill.*

Already by the early 1960s, psychiatrist Karl Menninger wrote the classic *Whatever Became of Sin?* The word *sin* was beginning to disappear from Christian vocabulary, and Menninger sought to call a spade a spade. What kind of Christianity is there apart from sin? The Joel Osteen variety—entertaining, flashy, and gimmicky, with a simple, straightforward gospel: love God and you will prosper. This view of faith is appealing to millions of Americans. But is it really Christianity or something different? Theologian H. R. Niebuhr summed it up well: "A God without wrath brought men without sin into a kingdom without judgment through the ministrations of a Christ without a cross."

The hero of psychology, Sigmund Freud, criticized religion as an "illusion." What he meant by that is that religion is a sugar pill that people take to cope with the stressors of life. It's not grounded in reality. Quite frankly, Freud's critique of religion applies, in my book, to Joel Osteen religion. It is an illusion, not grounded in reality. But in contrast to that happy-clappy pseudo-"faith" is the prophetic stance of Nathan and his bold confrontation of David: *You are the man!*

I can't imagine Joel Osteen having the guts to ever speak to a leader like that. His view of faith makes few demands of anyone. It boils down to feeling good about yourself. But you could have heard that on an Oprah rerun. But does David really have any reason to feel good about himself? Isn't that just David's problem—his belief that he would get away with murdering Uriah and taking his wife, Bathsheba? He feels really good about himself, convinced he can pull it off. But God has different plans. There is something far better than feeling good about yourself: it's called coming clean. And that's what David needs to do: come clean, be honest, get right with God and the world.

We've come to trivialize sin—not just in American popular culture but even in church. My now-retired boss, who grew up in a Nordic Lutheran community in rural Wisconsin, liked to chuckle about how guilt-inflicting Lutherans are. I hardly think that that is true in today's world, but he certainly has a point about the past. Sure enough, decades and decades ago, preachers (whether Lutheran or not), were apt to preach a "turn or burn" sermon. No doubt, many preachers did their best to make people feel some guilt or remorse so that they would have a "come to Jesus" moment.

Today's world is completely different. Again, Joel Osteen: he is supposedly a "conservative" Christian, but you'll never find him preaching about hell and trying to scare people into heaven. Instead, his message is that God is the carrot at the end of a stick. Accept Jesus and you'll get a bigger car, a bigger house, a trophy spouse, and kids. It seems to me that neither way of manipulating people to bring them into the kingdom, whether through punishment or rewards, is true to the Bible. Instead, all Nathan does is *simply tell David the truth*— "You are the man." He doesn't have to shout it, condemn David, cuss him out, or anything like that. All he does is tell the truth—the truth speaks for itself. And the truth hits David like an arrow or a bullet. David said to Nathan, "I have sinned against the Lord."

I don't think we should trivialize sin. More than once, when I served in the parish, I heard deathbed confessions: good, upright, solid, salt-of-the-earth people who didn't want to go to their graves with the guilt of a grievous crime on their consciences that even their own children didn't know about. How should a preacher handle the deathbed confession of a ninety-year-old? Call the police? What I did in every case—since it was obvious that each one was sincere and seeking relief before their Maker—was to forgive them their sins for Jesus' sake. I didn't even think twice about it. It was to their credit that these people wanted to come clean. It would have been better if they had done that sixty years before—and either faced prison or jail time or somehow made amends. They carried a weight of guilt on their shoulders that Jesus doesn't want any of His own to have to suffer. After all, He is the Lamb of God who bears that muck and mire away.

I sometimes think that twelve-step groups do one thing better than we church folks—and that's confession. After all, if you know something about the twelve steps, you know that the fourth step is making a searching moral inventory of your life—how you've hurt other people—and the fifth step is confessing this to your "higher power" and another person. Why another person? I suppose to keep it real. Often we Lutherans have a public confessional service at the beginning of our service, but in principle, we have private confessions—the matter is that no one avails him or herself of it. But quite frankly, we perhaps ought to take advantage of it—why? To come clean. What we confess, in general, isn't bad, but confession one-on-one really puts our guilt out there. And why would that be good? Because if it is put out there, then we can see it for what it is, allow God to deal with it (forgive you for Jesus' sake), and no longer let it define our lives. No longer do we have to slump around feeling worthless because we feel guilty. No longer would we have to cover all our bases so we don't get caught in our sin. In other words—confession and absolution lead to freedom.

Pastor, you might tell me, you are making it sound like guilt is a good thing. So I need to be clear: guilt isn't a good thing, but freedom is. By hearing Nathan's words—you are the man (or woman)—and taking them to heart, we can repent of our sin, turn from our guilt, receive forgiveness, and live with clean hearts. In other words, we can be free. When we come clean, we live more and more lives of integrity—we live the way God wants us to live and the way that best accords with our own natures. It isn't even only our worst that puts us at odds with God but even our best. We can care so much for our children, want to support them so that they never get hurt or feel misfortune—be helicopter parents—that we fail to allow God to be the Father for our children that He has promised us to be for them. Not just our misdeeds but even our good deeds can hurt. That's why we need Jesus. That's why the phrase "Jesus plus nothing is equal to everything" makes sense.

"So?" you say. "David was a big sinner but I'm not." I've never committed adultery and never murdered another. No doubt, you are telling the truth. But also to be said is that you haven't loved God with all your heart, nor have you cared for others as you would want yourself to be cared for. You've never murdered anyone, but all of us have spoken ill of our neighbors. No one is scot-free. David's prayer after being confronted by Nathan was: "Create in me a clean heart, O God, and renew a right spirit within me. Cast me not away from your presence, and take not your Holy Spirit from me. Restore to me the joy of your salvation, and uphold me with a willing spirit" (Ps. 51:10–12).

God is in the business of creating new, clean hearts. God makes your life to be under new management. No longer are you manager, but God Himself is manager. That can be unsettling because we have a hard time believing God. But God is faithful to you. You are His child, and through Christ Jesus, He has a claim on you. He refused to let you go, and He refuses to let your sin come between Him and you or between you and yourself or even between you and others. God validates you in Jesus Christ. You have His stamp of approval written all over you. To confirm it all, you are baptized, and you receive the body and blood of the risen and glorified Lord Jesus Christ here at the Lord's Table. You are a privileged person—no mere sinner. That you are—yes, a sinner, but at the same time, a saint, a holy one, one of God's own.

CHAPTER 22

God's Time

Ecclesiastes 3:1-13

3:1   *For everything there is a season, and a time for every matter under heaven:*

3:2   *a time to be born, and a time to die; a time to plant, and a time to pluck up what is planted;*

3:3   *a time to kill, and a time to heal; a time to break down, and a time to build up;*

3:4   *a time to weep, and a time to laugh; a time to mourn, and a time to dance;*

3:5   *a time to throw away stones, and a time to gather stones together; a time to embrace, and a time to refrain from embracing;*

3:6   *a time to seek, and a time to lose; a time to keep, and a time to throw away;*

3:7   *a time to tear, and a time to sew; a time to keep silence, and a time to speak;*

3:8   *a time to love, and a time to hate; a time for war, and a time for peace.*

3:9   *What gain have the workers from their toil?*

3:10   *I have seen the business that God has given to everyone to be busy with.*

3:11   *He has made everything suitable for its time; moreover he has put a sense of past and future into their minds, yet they cannot find out what God has done from the beginning to the end.*

> *3:12   I know that there is nothing better for them than to be*
> *happy and enjoy themselves as long as they live;*
> *3:13   moreover, it is God's gift that all should eat and drink and*
> *take pleasure in all their toil.*

A young man planning to propose will try to get the timing right. He will figure out just where it is that he'll pop the question, where he'll kneel, how to package the ring, whether to have a special dinner as the context of this event, and so on. Most men aren't going to ask a woman who is likely to say no. But even so, the man wants the timing just right, not only so that he hears a yes, but so that a memory is made. Timing is so very important in many things: when a movie makes its debut, when a touchdown pass is snapped, when a test is assigned in the course of a semester, and so on.

But this is not the kind of timing that the Preacher, the author of Ecclesiastes, is talking about. He's looking at timing in a way that we mortals could never offer. The kind of timing he speaks of is God's timing. And his point is crystal clear: everything, even something bad, as surprising as that sounds, has its place in God's timing.

Did you see the bad things that the Preacher brings up: a time to die, to pluck up, to break down, to kill, to weep, to reject, to tear, to keep silence, to hate, and to make war. Really, can he be serious? I thought God was only about good things. But here it would seem that God is about everything, obviously the good but at times even the bad. In some way or other, God has a say in all things. Nothing happens apart from His involvement.

Now, I'd like to keep that on the back burner for a second. Because one obvious matter that gives all this evil perspective is that God gives it its "season." That is, in this life, both the good and the bad are limited. They each have their seasons. Just like fall turns to winter and winter turns to spring and spring turns to summer (remember the '60s song—"Turn! Turn! Turn!"?), so there is a constant shifting of fortune. Ancient people honored fortune as a goddess but also feared her too, since our luck constantly goes up and down. No matter how you slice it, the Preacher relativizes both good and bad, sees them like the classroom I teach in. One class comes, participates in learning for an hour, and then departs, whereupon another class comes into that very room and does the same thing.

There is a constant flow of classes, and there is a constant flow of experiences. The good comes and so then later the bad, but then, again, away they both go.

If I were in the thick of a storm, I might feel really afraid. But if I see a storm far off on the horizon, chances are I'm not afraid, it can't hurt me, but it can amaze me with wonder, blow me away with awe. The Preacher is giving us that more detached stance because it is wisdom that he has learned. But he wants you to learn it too.

Now, some classes I like, and others I don't like. Classes that have engaged students who can't stop from asking questions or sharing ideas allow me to feel that I don't even work to earn my living. But other classes where no students participate become a chore for me. I could get really angry with those classes where students don't participate, but that would do no good. Those students are only bringing to the table those skills that they have. If they don't know how to engage in the material, there is no use in me blaming them. Usually, I'll experiment with different strategies to try to whet their appetites. Often I succeed but not always. The last thing I should do is take student indifference personally. It is, after all, not personal.

Now, shockingly, most bad things you experience in life are not personal. That your tire went flat or your team didn't win or the bread machine broke or whatever is not a personal matter. No one is out to get you. But all so often, we take it personally and make our own lives miserable.

Remember in the movie *The Matrix*, Neo, the protagonist, is told that if he takes the blue pill, he will unhook from the Matrix and experience reality as it is and not how AI (artificial intelligence) has manufactured it for humans. If he takes the red pill, he will stay in the Matrix and live in unreality. Of course he takes the blue pill, bringing on lots of adventure for him.

In a sense, the Preacher wants us to unhook from the matrix of the illusion that we must always struggle to get our way in life. God has His timing, and His timing often doesn't correspond with ours. But if we can embrace it, not being attached just to the good but letting the good and the bad come and go and letting them each work their magic upon us, we will be happier.

This must really sound crazy. Now, I know many of us have the Outback Bowl on our minds and want the Hawkeyes to beat the

Gators. But for most Iowans, the stakes are highest when Iowa plays Iowa State (ISU). Most of us live life like its game day of the Iowa/ISU football match. You are for one team or the other. You can't support both teams, and the winner takes all. You identify as a Hawkeye or a Cyclone. But the Preacher would have us view the game not as one taking sides but instead as if we are from another state and don't have much attachment to who wins. Now, I'm not saying don't be a Hawkeye or Cyclone fan. Of course be one! But if I understand what wisdom means to the preacher (because, after all, Ecclesiastes is called Wisdom literature), it means that we can accept that God has His timing, God has His ways, and God brings both good and even bad into our lives so that we learn to trust Him more and more. Because God is good, He is trustworthy. But that trustworthiness is proven only when we face challenges, obstacles, and even bad things. If you've ever been in the Sears Tower or the Eiffel Tower or the Empire State Building or on the edge of the Grand Canyon, you know what a vista is. We as mortals are not capable of having a "God's-eye" view, but we can get some perspective in life. No matter what drama we are tempted to hook into, we can step outside of ourselves and watch ourselves and see how we not only are recipients of other peoples' issues but also contribute to painful things in our families, communities, and workplaces. When we live from that sense of perspective, we become free of the drama that is around us and become freer and less like pawns.

It was in the fullness of time that God sent His Son, born of a virgin, born under the law, to rescue us all who have been oppressed and hounded by God's law. God gives us a promise to live from. That promise is: if God is for us, who can be against us? With that strength, we can face anything that comes our way; we can see even bad things as having their place. This doesn't mean that we shouldn't stand up to bad things. Of course we should stand up to tyrants and the like. But bad things need not and will not take us down. All things work together for good for those who love God as Paul tells us. In all things, God is ever working to make you a person of faith.

God's time for you is so that He can give you Jesus Christ as your Savior and Lord. God adopts you as His child, and His promise to you is that you will come to your fulfillment and purpose for this life and enjoy eternal life as well. God "has put a sense of past and future" into your mind, a sense of eternity, as it says in older translations, all so that He might fill you, empower you, and protect you. This He does through His promise ever to be faithful to you. For this you can be thankful this New Year.

CHAPTER 23

God's Medicine

Numbers 21:4–9

21:4   *From Mount Hor they set out by the way to the Red Sea, to go around the land of Edom; but the people became impatient on the way.*

21:5   *The people spoke against God and against Moses, "Why have you brought us up out of Egypt to die in the wilderness? For there is no food and no water, and we detest this miserable food."*

21:6   *Then the LORD sent poisonous serpents among the people, and they bit the people, so that many Israelites died.*

21:7   *The people came to Moses and said, "We have sinned by speaking against the LORD and against you; pray to the LORD to take away the serpents from us." So Moses prayed for the people.*

21:8   *And the LORD said to Moses, "Make a poisonous serpent, and set it on a pole; and everyone who is bitten shall look at it and live."*

21:9   *So Moses made a serpent of bronze, and put it upon a pole; and whenever a serpent bit someone, that person would look at the serpent of bronze and live.*

I grew up in Seattle. Seattle is a far damper climate than Iowa, and homes are prone to getting mold. Lutheran homes are no exception, and when I was a teen, my bedroom got a mold infestation. I decided to clean that mold off the wall, and so I looked in the cabinet for cleansing agents that would do the trick. Ammonia. Now, that sounds like that would work—clear up that mold. But what about mixing it with another strong agent—like bleach? Ammonia and bleach—sounds like a perfect combination to defeat mold forever. What I didn't know—but you all probably know—was that I was creating a poison. I'm stubborn. I started coughing and wheezing after I had concocted that mixture, but I tried to keep at it. I wanted that mold removed. Eventually, I came to my senses that I didn't have to die in order to have a clean house.

Poison isn't always readily apparent. It certainly wasn't for me. Nor was it for the Hebrew children. The story of Israel in the desert, on the way to the promised land, is a history of complaints—whining. God has done a remarkable work: He delivered the people from slavery, destroyed the armies of Pharaoh, and provided the people sustenance in the desert. Now, those were things to be grateful for—actually even things to be downright happy about. But were they happy? No. Instead, what the Hebrew children were good at was complaining, complaining, and complaining. Their complaint: here in the desert, there is no food and no water, and we detest this miserable food (the manna and quail that God provided for them).

As a child, I remember stories my family would tell from the Great Depression. They were never complaint stories but gratitude stories: grateful for abundant game in Eastern Oregon and large gardens and livestock. It wasn't dining at a fancy steakhouse, but it was better than starving. That was not the attitude of the children of Israel. Instead of looking on the bright side, specifically how God had kept His promises to them, all they saw and heard was bad news and bad news all the time. Chronic complaining without constructive engagement in life is poisonous. To use another metaphor: it's like a virus that spreads. You've all been there, where one family member becomes sick and eventually everyone in the family is sick. The virus spreads. And poison spreads as well. Poison isn't just chemical toxins. It is also in how we treat one another. When we constantly snub others, ridicule leadership, and invite a culture of put-downs, we undermine the good health of the community; we undermine trust. Our whole culture becomes toxic.

Drugs, too, are poisons—if you take twenty aspirin instead of the two prescribed, you will discover that. The Greek word *pharmakos*, where we get the English word *pharmacy*, means "poison." The drug taken at the appropriate dosage doesn't poison us but instead counters the disease or pain. The poisonous snakes God inflicted upon the people are an indicator that their complaints were not innocent but deadly. We often let ourselves off the hook—but it is all so often the little snubs rather than the big shouts that hurt and wound others. In our lesson this morning, the snake infestation is simply the outward and visible manifestation of the peoples' lack of health—their culture of complaint, victimhood, and whining. Many people love to vent, but venting without seeking a constructive approach to life and the world only contributes to misery. We might feel that we get things off our chests, but all too often, we simply reinforce ill will in ourselves and others.

A drug is a poison in unprescribed doses. But in a prescription, it heals. The same with Jesus. He, too, as surprising as it sounds, is a poison. He was certainly a poison to the scribes, Pharisees, and Sadducees. Otherwise, why would they want him dead? He was also a poison to the Romans. Otherwise, why would they execute him? For the Jewish leaders, Jesus was blasphemous, and for the Romans, He was treasonous. He was a poison to their legal and religious systems. But we aren't let off the hook. In a way, He is a poison to us as well.

Like the Hebrew children, our whining, ingratitude, and spiritual indifference are grounded in the same circling of the wagons of the Jewish leaders and the Romans. Jesus comes along forgiving sinners, and we find Him a threat. We don't like His hospitality. After all, God is generous and blesses us, but surely God would never bless every sinner. The God we want is a God who would be choosey like us. God would choose the right people, and we have a mental list for Him to make sure He gets its right. But here comes Jesus, blessing the riff-raff, the losers, and all kinds of people we would never allow. No doubt, that gives us something to whine about. But more to the point, it really threatens us. Remember Jesus' Parable of the Prodigal Son: If God is that generous, pardoning the prodigal son, then maybe our complaint is just like the elder brother's: "Dad, what is the point of me being true and faithful when you up and embrace that deadbeat son of yours?" Now, we have issues with whether or not God is fair. But God wants to make it crystal clear that He is merciful.

Now our congregations are welcoming, embracing, and loving toward a wide variety of people. But all of us at our cores tend to believe we are in the right and never wrong. All of us side up with the others like us, who we are convinced are right (like ourselves). We all want to be right-wised by our own standard of right and wrong. We just can't let God justify us by faith alone—that would take our power away and threaten our door-keeping.

But God will have it no other way. Jesus is a poison for our self-righteousness just as He was to the Romans and the Jewish leaders. But that isn't all who He is. He is also the "poisonous snake" that heals. God directed Moses to make a bronze "poisonous serpent"—not some serpent without venom but precisely one that in principle could kill. God's message has a bite. All the afflicted needed to do was look upon that bronze serpent and live.

Jesus tells us that "as Moses lifted up the serpent in the wilderness, so must the Son of Man be lifted up, that whoever believes in him may have eternal life (John 3:14)." But our concern this morning isn't for any and every "whoever believes," but instead, we narrow it down to you. As Jesus was a threat or poison for the Jewish leaders and the Romans, Jesus is also a threat or poison to you and me in that He counters our self-righteousness. He wants to bring down those defenses and uncircle those wagons. He refashions us and makes us humble and concerned for others. In a word, He makes you a person of faith. In that way, He is life and salvation for you.

Reminding ourselves again of the Prodigal Son parable: It isn't just the prodigal son who needs grace (and no doubt, many of us have been prodigals, running off into riotous living)—but also and especially the elder brother. And God wants you to receive or embrace that grace. That's why Jesus Christ is not just the Savior of the world but, most specifically, *your* Savior. Jesus died to take away all your sins—whether they be those sins that you are ashamed of or, even more important, all those things for which you are proud and that you use to prove just how good and important you are. There is no other path to God that honors God other than faith. And faith doesn't just mean believing the truth, but instead it means that we trust God's promise in spite of all the worldly poisons that attack us or the deceptive lure that leads us to invest significance in all the stuff or awards that we use to prove our worth, value, or merit. Faith says that we have nothing other than God's love given to us in Jesus—given to us whether or not we are the prodigal or the elder brother, whether we have been lost in riotous living or lost in prudish self-righteousness.

Now, how do you get faith? The first part of faith is knowing that you've been bitten and need healing. The second is having no other recourse than to look to the one who can and does heal. And so for Jesus' sake, I remind you: you are forgiven; you are God's child. You are free from all the bondage and poisons that the world and even yourself heap upon you. And the only judgment that ever matters is the judgment God renders upon you: forgiven for Jesus' sake.

Clever atheists often describe religion as a "drug" that people use to cope with their pain. But faith means to confront painful reality—and to free men and women from that pain. One reason to nix God—as our atheist friends do—is just so to avoid such painful realities. But to look to the poisonous serpent—to look to Christ—is the end of the poison we inflict upon ourselves and others. It kills all our self-righteousness but leaves us free, clean, and open—all so that we don't have to be caught up in the trap of whining, like the ancient Israelites, and instead can be quite free to love God from the heart and love our neighbors as ourselves. Jesus, who is poison for the Pharisee and the Roman—poison for the elder brother and the prodigal son—is eternal life for you.

And so I want to leave you one word—chances are it's a word you've never heard before. That's the word *impute*. To impute is to validate. When I was a youngster, I couldn't get math. But I had a teacher in the seventh and eighth grades, Mr. Britt, a man originally from Alabama and who had a thick Southern accent. Mr. Britt would help me day after day for months on end and help me get math. I went from a D/C student to an A student. He validated me—saw past my seeming inabilities and instead imprinted the tagline "mathematician" on me. That faith empowered me to start doing my math work well. In a word, he "imputed" this ability to me. Mr. Britt put that confidence in me.

God gives you His righteousness—He imputes it to you. He claims you as His own. Our spiritual walk isn't based on what you do or fail to do—whether or not you ever get mathematics—or even the ability to calculate the proper dosage of self-regard to heal yourself; instead, it is based on His love for you given in Jesus Christ. In Christ you are God's child. He provides Jesus as His affirmation, His mercy toward you. In Jesus Christ, you are free from the poisonous snakes that can derail your life, and you are secure in your identity and destiny as a child of God.

Acknowledgments and Permissions

Many who write do so in a kind of solitary confinement. That is not me. I am happy to be dependent on and in constant collaboration with a cohort of friends and colleagues who are generous in providing me not only feedback but even pushback. Through their reactions, they have made an impact on me pastorally, confessionally, and intellectually and sculpted me as both a pastor and an academic. Among this cohort, first of all, I am grateful to John Pless for offering a foreword to this book. We not only come from the same spiritual DNA, but we are brothers in a common confession of the faith. Also, it has been my good fortune that New Reformation Publications generously offered to bring this book to publication. Much gratitude to Scott Keith for his willingness to include this project as a resource for gospel-centered theology. Steve Byrnes, who has shepherded this project from start to finish, has been diligent in all relevant details. To Rick Ritchie, who has carefully edited this book, many thanks are due. Since the essays presented here were written over a period of a decade and a half, several others connected with *Lutheran Quarterly* provided critical and insightful comments: Paul Rorem, Robert Kolb, Mary Jane Haemig, Oswald Bayer, Oliver Olson, Charles Arand, and Steve Paulson. Likewise, Ron Darge repeatedly has a hand in all my work, whether speaking or writing, if not always in an obvious way, then most assuredly in demeanor, disposition, and depth. I would not be who I am today apart from his generosity and collegiality. (He is also to be credited with the photo on the back cover!)

Thanks are especially to be offered to Ken Sundet Jones, who was often the first to read these essays and who, giving many hours, has generously and in detail commented on them. Similarly, thanks must be rendered to my Grand View University colleagues John Lyden, Kathryn Pohlmann Duffy, Alex Krumm, Kyle Fever, and Russell Lackey for their critique and fellowship. Librarian Sheri Roberts was ever diligent in securing interlibrary loan resources. Additionally, Roy Alvin Harrisville, Dennis Bielfeldt, Wade Johnston, Bror Erickson, Aaron Pederson, Gil Kracke, Jono Linebaugh, Jady Koch, Matthew McCormick, Jack Kilcrease, Curtis Leins, Johan Hinderlie, Gene Veith, Steve Shipman, Dennis Nelson, Kevin McClain, Roger Burdette, and Brent Kuhlman, each in their own ways, provided welcome relief through sound advice, cheerfulness, and support. Grand View alumni now serving in the parish, as either pastors or parish workers, Jamie Strickler, Ryan Cosgrove, Hannah Hanson Nichols, Angie Larson, and Roger Fears, were helpful in providing oral feedback to the convictions now in print here but first of all presented in the classroom. Finally, many thanks to my wife, Carol Marie Mattes, who from her childhood knew the ups and downs of academic life and has, in spite of my long delays in the office, always cheered me on in my work.

I am grateful to the following publications and institutions for granting permission for the works in this volume:

American Lutheran Publicity Bureau, *Lutheran Forum Letter*, "Rethinking Social Justice" (August 2017); "Retrieving a Confessional Identity" (October 2008).

American Lutheran Publicity Bureau, *Lutheran Forum*, "How to Cultivate Biblical, Confessional, Resilient, and Evangelistic Pastors" (Fall 2017).

Concordia Theological Quarterly, "A Confessional Response to North American Lutheran-Reformed Ecumenism" (2011) 3–24.

John D. Koch, ed., "Theology of the Cross Today," in *Comfortable Words: Essays in Honor of Paul Zahl* (Eugene, OR: Wipf and Stock, 2013).

The Luther Academy, "A Contemporary View of Faith and Reason in Luther," in *Propter Christum: Christ at the Center* (2013).

Logia: A Journal of Lutheran Theology, "Bioethics and Honoring Humanity: A Christian Perspective" (Holy Trinity 2011); "*A Brotherly Office*" (Easter 2009); "A Lutheran Case for Apologetics" (Holy Trinity 2015); "The Mystical-Political Luther and Public

Theology" (Eastertide 2007); "Revival Time" (Easter 2009); "Should Lutherans Be Mainline Protestants?" (Fall 2015); "Standing on Scripture, Part 1" (Epiphany 2010); "Standing on Scripture, Part 2" (Eastertide 2011); and "Theses on the Captivated and Liberated Will" (Holy Trinity 2007).

Lutheran Quarterly, "Discipleship in Lutheran Perspective" (Summer 2012); "The Thomistic Turn in Evangelical Catholic Ethics" (Spring 2002).

Sola Publishers, "Towards a More Robust Lutheran Theology: Response to Dennis Bielfeldt," in *Network News* 7, no. 6 (November–December 2006): 3–6.

In all things: *Soli Deo Gloria.*
Mark Christopher Mattes
Pentecost 2018

Abbreviations

AELC	Association of Evangelical Lutheran Churches
ALC	American Lutheran Church (1930)
ALS	Amyotrophic lateral sclerosis (a.k.a. Lou Gehrig's disease)
BC-K/W	*The Book of Concord: The Confessions of the Evangelical Lutheran Church*, ed. Robert Kolb and Timothy J. Wengert (Minneapolis, MN: Fortress, 2000)
BC-T	*The Book of Concord: The Confessions of the Evangelical Lutheran Church*, ed. Theodore G. Tappert (Philadelphia: Fortress Press, 1959)
BSLK	*Die Bekenntnisschriften der evangelisch-lutherischen Kirche* (Göttingen, Germany: Vandenhoeck and Ruprecht, 1952)
CWA	Churchwide Assembly (the primary decision-making body in the Evangelical Lutheran Church in America)
ECUSA	Episcopal Church in the United States of America
EKD	Evangelische Kirche in Deutschland
FA	Formula of Agreement
GOP	Grand Old Party (the Republican Party)

ISU	Iowa State University
LCMS	Lutheran Church–Missouri Synod
LW	*Luther's Works* [American edition], 55 vols. (Philadelphia: Fortress; and St. Louis, MO: Concordia, 1955–86)
TALC	The American Lutheran Church (1960)
WA	*Luthers Werke: Kritische Gesamtausgabe* [Schriften], 65 vols. (Weimar, Germany: H. Böhlau, 1883–1993)
WEIRD	Western, Educated, Industrialized, Rich, and Democratic

Notes

Introduction

1   John Pless, *Handling the Word of Truth: Law and Gospel in the Church Today* (St. Louis, MO: Concordia, 2015.) See also Mark Mattes, "Properly Distinguishing Law and Gospel as the Pastor's Calling," in *The Necessary Distinction: A Continuing Conversation on Law and Gospel*, ed. Albert Collver III, James Arne Nestingen, and John T. Pless (St. Louis, MO: Concordia, 2017), 109–33.

2   See Patrick J. Deneen, *Why Liberalism Failed* (New Haven, CT: Yale University Press, 2018), 47–63.

3   For a Lutheran critique of evangelicalism, see Bryan Wolfmueller, *Has American Christianity Failed?* (St. Louis, MO: Concordia, 2016).

4   Martin Luther, "Smalcald Articles," in *BC-K/W* 319:45, article 3, part 4.

5   John D. Koch and Todd H. W. Brewer, eds., *Comfortable Words: Essays in Honor of Paul F. M. Zahl* (Eugene, OR: Pickwick, 2013).

6   For more information, see http://www.mbird.com/.

7   See Gerhard Forde, *On Being a Theologian of the Cross: Reflections on Luther's Heidelberg Disputation, 1518* (Grand Rapids, MI: Eerdmans, 1997), 84.

8   See Rainer Rausch, ed., *Glaube und Vernunft: Wie vernünftig ist die Vernunft?*, trans. Oswald Bayer (Hannover, Germany: Lutherisches Verlagshaus, 2014).

9   See Mark Mattes, "A Contemporary View of Faith and Reason in Luther," in *Propter Christum: Christ at the Center*, ed. Scott Murray et al. (Ft. Wayne, IN: Luther Academy, 2013).

10   "Commentary on Jonah" (1526), in *LW* 19:53–55. Melanchthon develops the traditional proofs for God's existence. See Philip Melanchthon, *The Chief Theological Topics* (*Loci Praecipui Theologici* [1559]), trans. J. A. O. Preus (St. Louis, MO: Concordia, 2011), 43–45.

11   See Jennifer Roback Morse, *Love and Economics: Why the Laissez-Faire Family Doesn't Work* (Dallas: Spence, 2001) for a critique of how libertarian approaches to economics undermine traditional families.

12 Nancy R. Pearcey notes that the distinction between person and human is fraught with problems: "Personhood theory thus reflects the fact/ value divide, which says values have no grounding in facts but are subjective choice. . . . Ultimately, someone will have to draw the line defining who qualifies as a person. But without objective criteria, the concept will be defined by raw power. Whoever has the most power—namely, the state—will decide who qualifies as a person." See *Love Thy Body: Answering Hard Questions about Life and Sexuality* (Grand Rapids, MI: Baker, 2018), 59.

13 See Mark Mattes, *Die Leuenberger Konkordie im innerlutherischen Streit: Internationale Perspektiven aus drei Konfessionen*, ed. Werner Klän and Gilberto da Silva (Göttingen, Germany: Edition Ruprecht, 2012).

14 *Book of Concord*, ed. Robert Kolb and Timothy J. Wengert (Minneapolis, MN: Fortress, 2000), 41:1–4.

Chapter 1   Standing on Scripture

1 Richard Johnson, *Forum Letter*, November 2009.

2 Quotes from Benne are taken from Robert Benne, "How Did We Come to This?," *Concordia Theological Quarterly* 73, no. 4 (October 2009): 364–67. I follow Benne's language quite closely.

3 Ibid.

4 Again, I'm following Benne's language quite closely.

5 For information in this section, I've depended on Ryan Schwarz's address to the Lutheran Core Convention, "Reconfiguration," Fishers, Indiana, September 2009.

6 These statistics were valid at the time this essay was written in 2010.

7 The ELCA has 3.5 million members as of 2018. See https://en.wikipedia .org/wiki/Evangelical_Lutheran_Church_in_America.

8 Martin Luther, "A Brief Instruction on What to Look for and Expect in the Gospels" (1521), in *LW* 35:121.

9 Martin Luther, "Lectures on Galatians" (1519), in *LW* 26:387.

10 Epitome, summary 1, in *BC-T* 486.

11 See "The Small Catechism," in *BC-K/W* 348:11–349:13.

Chapter 2   Theology of the Cross Today

1 For the standard translation, see "Heidelberg Disputation," in *Luther's Works*, trans. Harold J. Grimm (Philadelphia: Muhlenberg Press, 1957) [hereafter abbreviated *LW*], 31:39–70. We will focus solely on the theological theses in this paper.

2 Martin Luther, *D. Martin Luthers Werke* (Weimar, Germany: Böhlau, 1883–1993), 5, 31, 179.

3 See Heiko Obermann, *Forerunners of the Reformation: The Shape of Late Medieval Thought Illustrated by Key Documents* (Philadelphia: Fortress, 1981), 123–44.

4 Luther, *LW* 31:40.

5 See Siegbert Becker's discussion on Luther's view of paradox in *The Foolishness of God* (Milwaukee, WI: Northwestern, 1982), 119–39.

6 Gerhard Forde, *On Being a Theologian of the Cross: Reflections on Luther's Heidelberg Disputation, 1518* (Grand Rapids, MI: Eerdmans, 1997), 21.

7 Theodor Dieter, "Why Does Luther's Doctrine of Justification Matter Today?," in *The Global Luther: A Theologian for Modern Times*, ed. Christine Helmer (Minneapolis, MN: Fortress, 2009), 191.

8 See Forde, *Theologian of the Cross*, 22.

9 Luther, *LW* 31:41.

10 "This is our theology, by which we teach a precise distinction between these two kinds of righteousness, the active and the passive, so that morality and faith, works and grace, secular society and religion may not be confused. Both are necessary, but both must be kept within their limits. Christian righteousness applies to the new man, and the righteousness of the law applies to the old man." See Martin Luther, "Lectures on Galatians" (1535), in *LW* 26:7.

11 See Robert Kolb, *Martin Luther: Confessor of the Faith* (Oxford: Oxford University Press, 2009), 126. Kolb builds on the work of Werner Elert. Elert notes, "When an accused person—in today's sense—justified himself we read that he 'proves his innocence,' or he 'exonerates himself,' or 'he is able to prove himself innocent of the misdeed of which he is accused.' The word 'justification,' on the other hand, which also occurred frequently, conveyed an entirely different meaning. It designated either the criminal law suit in which hide and hair or life and limb were at stake, or—and most frequently that—the execution of a sentence, especially a death sentence. For example, as late as the seventeenth century the Saxon penal code listed the hangman's fees and other expenses incidental to the execution of bodily punishment under the caption '*Unkosten der peinlichen Rechtfertigung*' (expenses incidental to penal justification). It speaks of the '*Körper der mit dem Schwert Gerechtfertigten*' (the body of the person justified by the sword). The same linguistic usage is found also in Hans Sachs. Thus it was not confined to the speech of jurists, which was foreign to the people in general. . . . Justification does not imply that man ex-culpates himself, but it means that the executioner 'must mete out justice to the transgressor.' Thus Luther conceives of it as the secular execution of punishment." See *The Christian Faith: An Outline of Lutheran*

Dogmatics, trans. Martin H. Bertram and Walter R. Bouman (Columbus, OH: Lutheran Theological Seminary, 1974), 299–300.

Elert concludes, "Justification by faith is judgment on 'the old man.' Justice has been done him. He receives death. That is the mortification carried out in repentance. And that is not to be understood figuratively, but very realistically. The man of faith is an other than the man of sin. To be sure, a final identity of the I remains. But it is the identity of the stalk of wheat with the seed-grain, which first had to be buried (John 12:24). As the sinner becomes a believing sinner, the enemy of God which he was but no longer is as soon as he receives forgiveness, dies. As our Confessions teach, justification is forgiveness of sin. However, forgiveness is not an exoneration for the 'old' man. It is, rather, his end. The declaration of righteousness is his justification because he is receiving justice. It is death for the sinner and resurrection for the believing sinner." Ibid., 305.

12 Forde, *Theologian of the Cross*, 1.

13 See *LW* 31:40–41.

14 Paul Zahl, *Grace in Practice: A Theology of Everyday Life* (Grand Rapids, MI: Eerdmans, 2007), 113.

15 Ibid. Zahl follows up this last sentence with: "St. Paul famously wrote, 'Faith, hope, and love abide, these three; and the greatest of these is love' (1 Corinthians 13:13). I would describe an obverse trio this way: original sin, total depravity, and the un-free will abide, these three; and the root of the thing is the un-free will," 114.

16 On *ephphatha*, see Oswald Bayer, *Martin Luther's Theology: A Contemporary Interpretation* (Grand Rapids, MI: Eerdmans, 2008), 106–12. See also Mark Mattes and Ron Darge, *Imaging the Journey: . . . Of Contemplation, Meditation, Reflection, and Adventure* (Minneapolis, MN: Lutheran University Press, 2006), 50–51.

17 For an excellent resource on the relation between justification and preaching, see Steven Paulson, "Categorical Preaching," *Lutheran Quarterly* 21 (Autumn 2007): 268–93.

18 Forde, *Theologian of the Cross*, 9.

19 Ibid., 17.

20 Following Theodor Dieter's interpretation of Luther, we can say that sin is nothing other than to seek one's own in all things. See Dieter, "Luther's Doctrine," 194.

21 Paul Althaus, *The Theology of Martin Luther*, trans. Robert C. Schultz (Philadelphia: Fortress, 1966), 34.

22 Marc Lienhard, *Luther: Witness to Jesus Christ—Stages and Themes of the Reformer's Christology*, trans. Edwin H. Robertson (Minneapolis, MN: Augsburg, 1982), 98.

23 *Ad deum contra deum confugere*—"to flee from (God) and find refuge in God against God." See Vítor Westhelle's discussion in *The Scandalous God: The Use and Abuse of the Cross* (Minneapolis, MN: Fortress, 2006), 155.

24 Alister E. McGrath, *Luther's Theology of the Cross* (Oxford: Basil Blackwell, 1985), 160.

25 See Walther von Loewenich, *Luther's Theology of the Cross*, trans. Herbert J. A. Bouman (Minneapolis, MN: Augsburg, 1976), 11.

26 Westhelle, *Scandalous God*, 45.

27 Ibid., 51–53.

28 Luther, "Lectures on Galatians" (1535), in *LW* 26:287.

29 Denis R. Janz, "Syllogism or Paradox: Aquinas and Luther on Theological Method" *Theological Studies* 59 (March 1998): 3–21.

30 See Eberhard Jüngel, *God as the Mystery of the World: On the Foundation of the Theology of the Crucified One in the Dispute between Theism and Atheism*, trans. Darrell L. Guder (Grand Rapids, MI: Eerdmans, 1983), section 18, 281–98.

31 Luther, "Lectures on Galatians" (1535), in *LW* 26:337. In spite of such contradiction between law and gospel, Luther says that they "are nevertheless very closely joined in experience."

32 See Richard Bernstein's discussion of comparability, compatibility, and commensurability in *Beyond Objectivism and Relativism: Science, Hermeneutics, and Praxis* (Philadelphia: University of Pennsylvania Press, 1983), 86ff.

33 Martin Luther, "Bondage of the Will," in *LW* 33:62.

This paragraph and the prior are also repeated in "A Contemporary View of Faith and Reason in Luther" since both essays evaluate the role of analogical reasoning in theology.

34 Helmut Richard Niebuhr, *The Responsible Self: An Essay in Moral Philosophy* (Louisville, KY: Westminster John Knox, 1999), 25.

35 See Gerhard Forde, "Luther's 'Ethics'" in *A More Radical Gospel*, ed. Mark Mattes and Steven Paulson (Grand Rapids, MI: Eerdmans, 2004), 137–55; William H. Lazareth, *Christians in Society: Luther, the Bible, and Social Ethics* (Minneapolis, MN: Fortress, 2001); Werner Elert, *The Christian Ethos: The Foundations of the Christian Way of Life*, trans. Carl J. Schindler (Philadelphia: Muhlenberg Press, 1957); and Thomas D. Pearson, "Luther's Pragmatic Appropriation of the Natural Law Tradition," in *Natural Law: A Lutheran Reappraisal* (St. Louis, MO: Concordia, 2011), 39–63.

36 Edna Hong, *The Downward Ascent* (Minneapolis, MN: Augsburg, 1979), 50–51.

37 "Man is by nature unable to want God to be God. Indeed, he himself wants to be God, and does not want God to be God." See Martin

Luther, "Disputation against Scholastic Theology" (1517), in *LW* 31:10, thesis 17.

38 See Gerhard Forde, "Speaking the Gospel Today," in *The Preached God: Proclamation in Word and Sacrament*, ed. Mark Mattes and Steven Paulson (Grand Rapids, MI: Eerdmans, 2007), 179.

39 See Harold Bloom, *The American Religion: The Emergence of the Post-Christian Nation* (New York: Simon and Schuster, 1992); and Philip J. Lee, *Against the Protestant Gnostics* (New York: Oxford University Press, 1987).

40 Ernest Becker, *The Denial of Death* (New York: Free Press, 1973), 3.

41 Edna Hong, *Bright Valley of Love* (Minneapolis, MN: Augsburg, 1976), 60–61.

42 Martin Luther, commentary on Galatians 3:13 in "Lectures on Galatians," in *LW* 26:277.

43 Oswald Bayer, *Theology the Lutheran Way*, trans. Jeff Silcock and Mark Mattes (Grand Rapids, MI: Eerdmans, 2007), 119.

44 "Thus also the desire for knowledge is not satisfied by the acquisition of wisdom but is stimulated that much more. Likewise the desire for glory is not satisfied by the acquisition of glory, nor is the desire to rule satisfied by power and authority, nor is the desire for praise satisfied by praise, and so on. . . . The remedy for curing desire does not lie in satisfying it, but in extinguishing it. It other words, he who wishes to become wise does not seek wisdom by progressing toward it but becomes a fool by retrogressing into seeing folly. Likewise he who wishes to have much power, honor, pleasure, satisfaction in all things must flee rather than seek power, honor, pleasure, and satisfaction in all things. This is the wisdom which is folly to the world." See "Heidelberg Disputation" in *LW* 31:54, thesis 22.

45 Rowan Williams, *The Wound of Knowledge* (Lanham, MD: Cowley, 1991), 152.

46 Gerhard Forde, *Justification by Faith: A Matter of Death and Life* (Philadelphia: Fortress, 1983), 33–34.

47 See the hymn by Danish bishop Hans A. Brorson, "God's Son Has Made Me Free," trans. Oscar R. Overby, put to music by Edvard Grieg (Minneapolis, MN: Augsburg Choral Library, 1945 and 1973). For a fine visual and audio rendition by the Luther College Norsemen Choir, see http://www.youtube.com/watch?v=zu-2cVgG6GM&feature=related.

Chapter 4   A Contemporary View of Faith and Reason in Luther

1 Particularly for those thinkers influenced by the radical orthodoxy movement, all Protestant reformers have been shaped by nominalist metaphysics, which affirms the univocity of being; that is, that both the infinite

being (God) and finite beings (creatures) can be understood on the basis of the concept of being as a shared property between both infinite and finite realities in contrast to the analogy of being affirmed, for instance, in Thomas Aquinas's approach to realism. These thinkers contend that the background of contemporary nihilism is in late medieval nominalistic univocity theory, since the univocity of being sidesteps being itself as the *telos* for all finite beings who participate in and instantiate being itself. With respect to Luther, radical orthodoxy fails to acknowledge the apophatic dimension of Luther's thinking, which excludes seeing him as a metaphysical nominalist but also makes it impossible for him to fit into the analogy-of-being schema. Given such apophaticism, God is nothing other and nothing less than the end of us and our quest for mystic oneness—only a preacher can raise us from such death. On Luther's apophaticism, see Knut Alfsvåg, *What No Mind Has Conceived: On the Significance of Christological Apophaticism* (Leuven, Belgium: Peeters, 2010).

2   Richard Dawkins, *The God Delusion* (New York: Mariner, 2006), 241. The context of Luther's own critique of reason cited by the atheist Dawkins is a defense of infant baptism against the Anabaptists. Luther's point is that even though children lack reason, that should not prohibit their baptism since reason does not contribute to faith. Dawkins, in being grossly unfair to Luther, pegged Luther as against reason based on this specific passage found in Luther's *Table Talk*.

3   The language of "policing" is of course taken from John Milbank's analysis of sociology as "policing the sublime." Sociology assumes a Kantian approach to religion as dealing with the "sublime" (as opposed to the Christian content-laden articles of faith), which it then keeps in check in public life. Luther's view of God in no way is tantamount to the sublime. Milbank writes, "For sociology, religion is a component of the protected 'human' sphere, although this sphere is sometimes (for Durkheim) made to coincide with the schematic possibility of theoretic understanding. But although religion is recognized and protected, it is also 'policed,' or kept rigorously behind the bounds of the possibility of empirical understanding. Hence sociology is inevitably at variance with the perspectives of many traditional religions, which make no separation between 'religious' and 'empirical' reality, and who do not distinguish their sense of value from the stratified arrangement of times, persons and places in their own society. Sociology's 'policing of the sublime' exactly coincides with the actual operations of secular society which excludes religion from the its modes of 'discipline and control,' while protecting it as a 'private' value, and sometimes involving it at the public level to overcome the antinomy of a purely instrumental and goalless rationality, which is yet made to

bear the burden of ultimate political purpose." See *Theology and Social Theory: Beyond Secular Reason* (Oxford: Blackwell, 1990), 105–6.

4 George W. Forell noted this some years ago: "It would take us too far afield to trace the development of the preoccupation with unreason in protestant thought and to attempt to identify the period when the respect for reason was lost to Protestantism. But it would seem that the increasing preemption of reason by the rising modern science, especially in the nineteenth century, forced the protestant defenders of religion, in whose environment its new world view was advancing, into a defensive position which rejected reason in favor of feeling. This resulted in a bifurcation of the theological enterprise. There have always been and there are now academic theologians of protestant background who use reason with great skill and devotion in order to articulate their idiosyncratic theological perspective. Their efforts, however, proceed independently of the protestant movement. Their books are only read by a small elite and have no discernible effect on the life of the protestant churches." See "Reason, Relevance, and a Radical Gospel," in *Martin Luther: Theologian of the Church*, ed. William R. Russell (St. Paul, MN: Word and World Supplement Series, 1994), 245.

5 See, for instance, Paul V. Mankowski, "What I Saw at the American Academy of Religion," *First Things*, March 1992, https://www.firstthings .com/article/1992/03/004-what-i-saw-at-the-american-academy-of -religion.

6 See Martin Luther, "The Disputation Concerning Man" (1536), in *LW* 34:137, thesis 4 (*WA* 39/1, 175, 9–10).

7 Martin Luther, "Against the Heavenly Prophets," in *LW* 40:175 (*WA* 18, 164, 24); Martin Luther, "Last Sermon in Wittenberg" (1546), in *LW* 51:374 (*WA* 51, 126, 29).

8 See Theodor Dieter, "Martin Luther's Understanding of 'Reason,'" trans. Mark C. Mattes and Ken Sundet Jones, *Lutheran Quarterly* 25, no. 3 (Autumn 2011): 249.

9 Ibid., 249–50.

10 The tendency of the Mannermaa School, unlike Ernst Troeltsch, is to see Luther as a medieval thinker and to assess that judgment in a thoroughly positive way. For a fine example of their interpretation of Luther through medieval theology and philosophy, among their many scholarly contributions, see Olli-Pekka Vainio, ed., *Engaging Luther: A (New) Theological Assessment* (Eugene, OR: Wipf and Stock, 2010). See also Carl E. Braaten and Robert W. Jensen, eds., *Union with Christ: The New Finnish Interpretation of Luther* (Grand Rapids, MI: Eerdmans, 1998). For the perspective of Luther as protomodern, see Heiko A. Obermann, "Luther and the *Via Moderna*: The Philosophical Backdrop of the Reformation

Breakthrough," *Journal of Ecclesiastical History* 54, no. 4 (October 2003): 641–70.

11 Dennis Janz, *The Westminster Handbook to Martin Luther* (Louisville, KY: Westminster John Knox, 2010), 112–16.

12 Martin Luther, "The Disputation Concerning the Passage: 'The Word Was Made Flesh'" (1539), in *LW* 38:249 (*WA* 39/11, 15, 9).

13 The definitive text is the massive book by Theodor Dieter, *Der junge Luther und Aristoteles: Eine historisch-systematische Untersuchung zum Verhältnis von Theologie und Philosophie* (Berlin: Walter de Gruyter, 2001).

14 Of many fine essays and books on this topic, one stands out: Thomas D. Pearson, "Luther's Pragmatic Appropriation of the Natural Law Tradition," in *Natural Law: A Lutheran Reappraisal* (St. Louis, MO: Concordia, 2011), 39–63.

15 See Martin Luther, "The Law of Identical Predication," in "Confession Concerning Christ's Supper," in *LW* 37:294–303 (*WA* 26, 437–45). For a sound commentary on this treatise, see Jörg Baur, "Luther und die Philosophie," *Neue Zeitschrift für systematische Theologie und Religionsphilosophie* 26 (1984): 13–28; and Enrico de Negri, *Offenbarung und Dialektik: Luthers Realtheologie* (Darmstadt, Germany: Wissenschaftliche Buchgesellschaft, 1973), 207–18.

16 Luther, "'The Word Was Made Flesh'" (1539), in *LW* 38:248 (*WA* 39/11, 13, 12).

17 Ibid., in *LW* 38:244 (*WA* 39/11, 8, 5).

18 Ibid., in *LW* 38:241 (*WA* 39/11, 5, 9–10), thesis 27.

19 Janz, *Westminster Handbook*, 112.

20 Martin Luther, "The Sacrament of the Body and Blood of Christ—against the Fanatics" (1526), in *LW* 36:335 (*WA* 19, 482, 17).

21 Luther, "Disputation Concerning Man" (1536), in *LW* 34:144 (*WA* 39/1, 180, 16).

22 Martin Luther, "Table Talk" (collected by Cordatus between January 26 and 29, 1533), in *LW* 54:2938b (*WA* Tr 3, 105, 11–106, 10; N 2938b; 26.1, 1533).

23 One reference in medieval thinking of philosophy as a handmaid can be found in Thomas Aquinas, *Summa Theologiae*, trans. Fathers of the English Dominican province (Westminster, MD: Christian Classics, 1948), 1.1.5. See also Kari Kopperi, "Theology of the Cross," in *Engaging Luther: A (New) Theological Assessment*, ed. Olli-Pekka Vainio (Eugene, OR: Cascade, 2010), 171: "Luther's theory of the relationship between theology and philosophy can be seen as a revised version of the classical concept of philosophy as a handmaid of theology. Essentially philosophy has, according to Luther, its own independent and beneficial function,

but it is always in danger of degenerating into a form of perverted human wisdom driven by the principles of *amor hominis*. In theological questions philosophy loses its relevance because it cannot adequately explain *paradoxical theological doctrines. In theological questions and doctrines, God's revelation in Christ defines the boundaries of the philosophical concepts*" (emphasis mine).

24 "It was easy for Aristotle to believe that the world was eternal since he believed that the human soul was mortal." See Martin Luther, "Heidelberg Disputation," in *LW* 31:41 (*WA* 1, 355), thesis 31.

25 See Alfred Freddoso, "Ockham on Faith and Reason," University of Notre Dame, accessed August 16, 2018, https://www3.nd.edu/~afreddos/papers/f&rcam.htm, for all references in this paragraph.

26 Hence Ingolf Dalferth notes, "Luther proposes, therefore, to replace the scholastic two-stage teleology with its emphasis on analogy and its mixing of philosophical and theological discourse with a two-relations eschatology worked out in strictly theological discourse, giving priority in its vision of reality to the dialectics between proctology and eschatology over the analogical ordering of finite and infinite reality. Thus theology neither includes nor merely adds to philosophical knowledge of human beings (and of everything else) but reworks it in terms of the eschatological contrast between sin and salvation. Its operative principle is the difference-in-unity of dialectics, not the unity-in-difference of analogy." See *Theology and Philosophy* (Eugene, OR: Wipf and Stock, 2002), 79.

27 Bayer, *Theology the Lutheran Way*, 104.

28 Note Augustine's famous passage in the *Soliloquies* (I, ii, 7), where Augustine and Reason are conversing, which indicates the strong rapport between philosophy and faith: "A. My prayer is finished. R. What then do you wish to know? A. All those things I have prayed to know. R. Sum them up briefly. A. I want to know God and the soul. R. Nothing more? A. Absolutely nothing." See Ralph M. McInerny, *A History of Western Philosophy* (South Bend, IN: University of Notre Dame Press, 1970). Philosophy, like faith, is concerned with the intelligible order. Of the Platonists, Augustine in *De civ. Dei* (VIII, 10) writes, "This, there, is the cause why we prefer these to all the others, because, whilst other philosophers have worn out their minds and powers in seeking the causes of things, and endeavoring to discover the right mode of learning and living, these, by knowing God, have found where resides the cause by which the universe has been constituted, and the light by which truth is to be discovered, and the fountain at which felicity is to be drunk." See *Nicene and Post-Nicene Fathers*, vol. 2, ed. Philip Schaff, trans. Marcus Dods (Grand Rapids, MI: Eerdmans, 1956), 151.

29 *Confessions*, III, 4.

30 Martin Luther, "Lectures on Genesis," in *LW* 1:63 (*WA* 42, 47, 33).

31 Ibid., in *LW* 1:63 (*WA* 42, 47, 33–38).

32 Luther, "Disputation Concerning Man" (1536), in *LW* 34:137 (*WA* 39/I:175, 10), thesis 4.

33 See Mark Mattes, "Luther's Use of Philosophy," in *Martin Luther's Theology of Beauty: A Reappraisal* (Grand Rapids, MI: Baker Academic, 2017), chap. 1, 15–42.

34 Luther, *WA* 10/1/1:531.

35 Luther, "Lectures on Galatians," in *LW* 26:88 (*WA* 40/1, 164, 21).

36 Ibid., in *LW* 26:174 (*WA* 40/I, 293, 29–33).

37 Luther, "A Sermon on Keeping Children in School" (1530), in *LW* 46:242 (*WA* 30/11, 562, 27–30).

38 Luther, "Lectures on Galatians," in *LW* 26:183 (*WA* 40/I, 305, 33).

39 "For if his righteousness were such that it could be judged to be righteous by human standards, it would clearly not be divine and world in no way differ from human righteousness. But since he is the one true God, and is wholly incomprehensible and inaccessible to human reason, it is proper and indeed necessary that his righteousness also should be incomprehensible." See Martin Luther, "The Bondage of the Will" (1525), in *LW* 33:290. Of apophaticism in Augustine, see Alfsvåg, *What No Mind Has Conceived*, 88–98.

40 Luther, "Lectures on Galatians," in *LW* 26:399 (*WA* 40/I, 607, 28–32).

41 Luther, *WA* 21, 509, 6–13 (translated by Siegbert Becker).

42 Luther, "Lectures on Genesis," in *LW* 2:208 (*WA* 42, 408, 34–409, 3).

43 Martin Luther, "Lectures on Jonah" (1525), in *LW* 19:53 (*WA* 19, 205, 27–206, 6).

44 Luther, "Heidelberg Disputation," in *LW* 31:42 (*WA* 1, 354), thesis 36: "Aristotle wrongly finds fault with and derides the ideas maintained by Pythagoras, but more ingenious is the interaction of ideas maintained by Plato."

45 Luther, *WA* 51, 150, 42–151, 3 (translated by Siegbert Becker).

46 Luther, "Lectures on Genesis," in *LW* 8:17 (*WA* 42, 591, 34–39).

47 Luther, "Sermons on the Second Epistle of St. Peter," in *LW* 30:152 (*WA* 14, 16, 11–17).

48 Luther, *WA* 5:163, 28–29 (translated by Siegbert Becker).

49 Luther, "Lectures on Jonah," in *LW* 19:54 (*WA* 19, 206, 15–17) and *LW* 19:55–56 (*WA* 19, 206–7).

50 Luther, *WA* 10, 1:1, 532, 1–12 (translated by Siegbert Becker).

51 Brian Gerrish notes that "the believer does not earn this divine imputation with his faith, neither is there any legal fiction: God counts the confidence of the heart as 'right' because that is what it is. Its rightness lives in the fact that faith, for its part, does not make God an idol but takes him for exactly

what *he* is: the author and giver of every good, the precise counterpart of the believer's confidence. In a sense faith, by believing, is the 'creator of divinity' in us: it lets God be God." See "By Faith Alone," in *The Old Protestantism and the New: Essays on the Reformation Heritage* (Edinburgh, UK: T. and T. Clark), 86.

52   Luther, "Lectures on Galatians," in *LW* 26:113 (*WA* 40/I, 204, 15–21).

53   Ibid., in *LW* 26:262 (*WA* 40/I, 411, 1).

54   Ibid., in *LW* 26:396 (*WA* 40/I, 603, 20–31).

55   Ibid., in *LW* 26:88 (*WA* 40/I, 164, 20).

56   Ibid., in *LW* 26:29 (*WA* 40/I, 77, 17).

57   Ibid., in *LW* 26:42 (*WA* 40/I, 99, 1–2).

58   Ibid., in *LW* 26:113 (*WA* 40/I, 204, 24–25).

59   "For if you ask a Christian what the work is by which he becomes worthy of the name 'Christian,' he will be able to give absolutely no other answer than that it is the hearing of the Word of God, that is, faith. Therefore the ears alone are the organs of a Christian man, for he is justified and declared to be a Christian, not because of the works of any member but because of faith." See Martin Luther, "Lectures on Hebrews," in *LW* 29:224 (*WA* 57/3).

60   Luther, "Lectures on Galatians," in *LW* 26:130 (*WA* 40/I, 229, 17–21).

61   Ibid., in *LW* 26:238 (*WA* 40/I, 376, 24).

62   Martin Luther, *Bondage of the Will* (1525), trans. J. I. Packer and O. R. Johnston (Grand Rapids, MI: Fleming H. Revell), 82; also in *WA* 18, 617, 16.

63   Luther, *Bondage of the Will*, 100 (*WA* 18, 632, 36–633, 1).

64   Ibid., 153 (*WA* 18, 674, 1–3).

65   Ibid., 158 (*WA* 18, 676, 38–677, 4).

66   Ibid., 168 (*WA* 18, 684, 6).

67   Ibid., 101 (*WA* 18, 633, 19–24).

68   Ibid., 176 (*WA* 18, 689, 22–25).

69   Ibid., 170 (*WA* 18, 685, 23–24).

70   Alister E. McGrath, *Luther's Theology of the Cross* (Oxford: Basil Blackwell, 1985), 160.

71   See Walther von Loewenich, *Luther's Theology of the Cross*, trans. Herbert J. A. Bouman (Minneapolis, MN: Augsburg, 1976), 11.

72   Vítor Westhelle, *The Scandalous God: The Use and Abuse of the Cross* (Minneapolis, MN: Fortress, 2006), 45.

73   See Helmar Junghans, "Die probationes zu den philosophische Thesen der Heidelberger Disputation Luthers im Jahre 1518," *Lutherjahrbuch* 46 (1979): especially 59. Junghans's article contains a German translation of the original Latin philosophical theses in the Heidelberg Disputation and their proofs. The proof for thesis 38, "The disputation of Aristotle

lashes out at Parmenides' idea of oneness (this is pardonable for a Christian) in a battle of air," demonstrates a firsthand knowledge of Plato's *Parmenides*.

74 Alfsvåg, *What No Mind Has Conceived*, 198ff.

75 Knut Alfsvåg, "Luther as a Reader of Dionysius the Areopagite," *Studia Theologica* 65 (January 2012): 105.

76 Ibid., 110–11. Alfsvåg concludes this section with: "By re-establishing trust in the unknowable One ('*sola fide*') as the only appropriate approach to reality, Luther again lets the world appeal as divine gift ('*sola gratia*')."

77 Westhelle, *Scandalous God*, 51–53.

78 Marc Lienhard, *Luther: Witness to Jesus Christ—Stages and Themes of the Reformer's Christology* (Minneapolis, MN: Fortress, 1982), 126 (reference is made to *WA* 6, 510).

79 On the happy exchange, see Luther, "The Freedom of a Christian," in *LW* 31:351–52 (*WA* 7, 25, 28-26, 1). With respect to knowledge, Olli-Pekka Vainio notes, "The intellectual and cognitive apprehension of the good news means knowing God who gives himself to and on behalf of sinners. This proclamation of the Gospel evokes faith in the sinner, which grasps and possess (*apprehendit*) Christ. The mode of this apprehension is to be understood in terms of Aristotelian epistemology, which Luther uses and develops further when he speaks of Christ as the form of faith. Aristotle claimed that in the act of knowing, the form of the object of knowledge is transferred into the knower. According to Aristotle, when we think about horses, for example, the object of the intellect is the form (*eidos, forma*) of the horse as the form is actualized in a particular horse. However, this entails the same form being actualized in the observer's mind, while the object retains its form; in other words, the horse does not lose its form (and consequently cease being a horse) when we perceive it. But how is this possible? . . . Without going into the details of the medieval discussion, the general view was that human thought and intellect re-enact the rational structure of the world and somehow become identical with the world, while objects in the world still retain their inherent structures." See "Faith," in *Engaging Luther: A (New) Theological Assessment* (Eugene, OR: Wipf and Stock, 2010), 141–42.

80 Luther, "Lectures on Galatians," in *LW* 26:287 (*WA* 40/1, 447, 15–17).

81 Denis R. Janz, "Syllogism or Paradox: Aquinas and Luther on Theological Method" *Theological Studies* 59 (March 1998): 3–21.

82 See Eberhard Jüngel, *God as the Mystery of the World: On the Foundation of the Theology of the Crucified One in the Dispute between Theism and Atheism*, trans. Darrell L. Guder (Grand Rapids, MI: Eerdmans, 1983), section 18, 281–98.

83 Stephen H. Webb, "The End of the Analogy of Being," January 27, 2015, https://www.firstthings.com/web-exclusives/2015/01/the-end-of-the -analogy-of-being.

84 This paragraph and the following are repeated prior in "Theology of the Cross Today" since both deal with the use of analogy in theology.

85 Overall, what is suggested here may not in principle rule out Jüngel's affirmation of theology as *nachdenken*, thought following those paths that God has already taken.

86 Luther, "Lectures on Galatians" (1535), in *LW* 26:337 (*WA* 40/I, 520, 25–27). In spite of such contradiction between law and gospel, Luther says that they "are nevertheless very closely joined in experience."

87 See Richard Bernstein's discussion of comparability, compatibility, and commensurability in *Beyond Objectivism and Relativism: Science, Hermeneutics, and Praxis* (Philadelphia: University of Pennsylvania Press, 1983), 86ff.

88 Luther, "Bondage of the Will" (1525), in *LW* 33:62 (*WA* 18, 633, 7–11).

89 Martin Luther, "Confession Concerning Christ's Supper" (1528), in *LW* 37:228 (*WA* 26, 339–40, 2).

90 See Kenneth Haynes, ed., "Aesthetica in nuce," in *Writings on Philosophy and Language* (Cambridge: Cambridge University Press, 2007), 65.

91 See Peter Gay, *The Enlightenment: The Rise of Modern Paganism* (New York: W. W. Norton, 1966).

92 Of modern Gnosticism, see Harold Bloom, *The American Religion: The Emergence of the Post-Christian Nation* (New York: Simon and Schuster, 1992), 49–52, 55–58, 256–58. Of Epicureanism, see Benjamin Wicker, *Moral Darwinism: How We Became Hedonists* (Downers Grove, IL: InterVarsity Christian Press, 2002).

93 Steven Smith, *The Disenchantment of Secular Discourse* (Cambridge, MA: Harvard University Press, 2010).

94 Ibid., 26–27.

95 Stanley Fish, "Are There Secular Reasons?," *New York Times*, February 22, 2010, http://opinionator.blogs.nytimes.com/2010/02/22/are-there-secular -reasons/?pagemode=print.

96 See James Hannam, *The Genesis of Science: How the Christian Middle Ages Launched the Scientific Revolution* (Washington, DC: Regnery, 2011).

Chapter 6   A Lutheran Case for Apologetics

1 Stanley Fish, "Are There Secular Reasons?," February 22, 2010, https://opinionator.blogs.nytimes.com/2010/02/22/are-there-secular-reasons/.

2 See Mark Mattes, *Martin Luther's Theology of Beauty: A Reappraisal* (Grand Rapids, MI: Baker Academic, 2017).

3   Media personality Tim Ferris even promotes Stoicism directly, offering
    Marcus Aurelius and Epictetus as trustworthy guides to modern life.

Chapter 7   The Thomistic Turn in Evangelical Catholic Ethics

1   See Robert Bellah, Richard Madsen, William M. Sullivan, Ann Swidler,
    and Stever M. Tipton, *Habits of the Heart: Individualism and Commitment
    in American Life* (Berkeley: University of California Press, 1985), 221.
2   See Alasdair MacIntyre, *After Virtue: A Study in Moral Theory*, 2nd ed.
    (Notre Dame, IN: University of Notre Dame Press, 1984), 11–12.
3   Hence MacIntryre wrote, "This provides us with an insight important for
    understanding the politics of modern societies. For what I described ear-
    lier as the culture of bureaucratic individualism results in their character-
    istic overt political debates being between an individualism which makes
    its claims in terms of rights and forms of bureaucratic organization which
    make their claims in terms of utility. But if the concept of rights and that
    of utility are a matching pair of incommensurable fictions, it will be the
    case that the moral idiom employed can at best provide a semblance
    of rationality for the modern political process, but not its reality. The
    mock rationality of the debate conceals the arbitrariness of the will and
    power at work in its resolution." See Ibid., 71.
4   To this day, Wayne Booth's book *Modern Dogma and the Rhetoric of
    Assent* (Chicago: University of Chicago Press, 1974) remains one of the
    best responses to the pervasive "fact/value" split. Milbank's discussion of
    scientific method as itself developing social codifications of a narrative-
    construed "reality" is also helpful. See John Milbank, *Theology and Social
    Theory: Beyond Secular Reason* (Oxford: Blackwell, 1990), 338.
5   For Immanuel Kant's ethical philosophy, see his *Groundwork of the
    Metaphysic of Morals*, trans. H. J. Paton (New York: Harper and Row, 1956);
    Critique of Practical Reason, trans. Lewis White Beck (Indianapolis, IN:
    Bobbs-Merrill, 1956); *Lectures on Ethics*, trans. Louis Infield (New York:
    Harper, 1963); *Religion within the Limits of Reason Alone*, trans. Theodore M.
    Greene and Hoyt H. Hudson (New York: Harper, 1960); and *Perpetual
    Peace and Other Essays*, trans. Ted Humphrey (Indianapolis, IN: Hackett,
    1983). For an important restatement of deontology from the Anglo-
    American tradition, see Alan Gewirth, *Reason and Morality* (Chicago:
    University of Chicago Press, 1978). For an appropriation of deontology
    from the stance of religious ethics, see Alan Donagan, *The Theory of
    Morality* (Chicago: University of Chicago Press, 1977).
6   Reinhard Hütter describes *autopoiesis* in the following way: "Moreover, if
    we want to grasp the sweeping theological invention of *Veritatis splendor*,

we need to understand the claim that is encapsulated in the modern
notion of freedom. It is the freedom of the self that demands a position
of sovereignty in relation to her or his body and the natural world—in
short, the freedom of the *Promethean self*. It is the self for whom freedom has ultimately come to mean autopoiesis, self-creation: I am genuinely free only if my identity is the creation of my own will. Everything
that might bind me, that might restrict me, that might direct me without myself having chosen the direction is regarded by the Promethean
self as estranging and oppressive—be it bodies, laws, traditions, conventions or something as simple as taxes." See "(Re-)Forming Freedom:
Reflections 'After *Veritatis splendor*' on Freedom's Fate in Modernity
and Protestantism's Antinomian Captivity," *Modern Theology* 17, no. 2
(2001): 120.

7 For the inroads of Gnosticism into mainline Protestantism, see Philip
   Lee, *Against the Protestant Gnostics* (New York: Oxford University Press,
   1983). Against the perspective that Protestantism unlike Catholicism
   is prone to Gnosticism, it will be argued in this paper that Gnosticism is
   particularly alien to Reformation Protestantism and unfortunately, due
   to many factors, much of Protestantism and Catholicism are infected
   with the Gnostic virus.

8 This designation is, of course, taken from Gerhard Forde's article "Radical
   Lutheranism," *Lutheran Quarterly* 1, no. 1 (Spring 1987): 5–18. I am also
   employing Forde's distinction of the law as *telos* and *finis*. With regard to
   this present essay, Forde's most important claim in "Radical Lutheranism"
   is: "We simply do not understand the pathos of the Reformer's utterances
   about faith doing the good spontaneously and naturally unless we see this
   (i.e., that it is only out of the radical unconditionally of the imputative justifying word that an appropriate understanding of the Christian life can
   be developed). Precisely because the declaration is unconditional we are
   turned around to go into the world of the neighbor to carry out our calling as Christians. The works of the Christian are to be done in the world,
   but not as conditions for salvation. The persistent and nagging debate
   about the two kingdoms among Lutherans arises mostly of a reluctance
   to be radical enough. Precisely because the gospel gives the Kingdom of
   God unconditionally to faith, this world opens up and is given back as
   the place to serve the other. Will it be so given? That depends, of course.
   It is not a static affair. To the degree that one is grasped and set free by
   the unconditional gospel, to that degree one can be turned from the sort
   of life created by the self (and its supposed free but actually bound will)
   to the world of the neighbor. To the degree that the theological use of the
   law comes to an end in Christ, to that degree a political use of the law for
   others becomes a possibility. If somehow this could be grasped, perhaps

we could cease the silly debates about whether the church's mission is proclamation *or* development, personal salvation *or* social justice, etc., and get on with the business of taking care of this world and the neighbor as lovingly, wisely, and pragmatically as our gifts enable" (16–17). For a strong critique of Yeago's work by Radical Lutherans, see James Nestingen and Gerhard O. Forde, "Beware of Greeks Bearing Gifts," *Dialog* 39, no. 4 (Winter 2000): 291–92. For a general discussion between Luther and the Neoplatonic-Augustinian-Thomistic tradition, see Anders Nygren, *Agape and Eros*, trans. Philip S. Watson (Chicago: University of Chicago Press, 1982).

9 In response to an earlier draft of this paper, Professor Gary Simpson of Luther Seminary rightfully and helpfully suggested that a more accurate designation for this position is "Neo-Aristotelian-Thomistic Turn." In this paper, "Neo-Aristotelian" will be omitted in the designation for the sake of convenience.

10 See David Yeago, "Gnosticism, Antinomianism, and Reformation Theology: Reflections on the Costs of a Construal," *Pro Ecclesia* 2, no. 1 (Winter 1993): 37–49; "The Catholic Luther," *First Things* 61 (March 1996): 37–41; "Martin Luther on Grace, Law, and Moral Life: Prolegomena to an Ecumenical Discussion of *Veritatis Splendor*," *The Thomist* 62 (1998): 163–91; "Gospel and Church: Twelve Articles of Theological Principle amid the Present Conflict in the ELCA," *Lutheran Forum* 34, no. 1 (Easter 2000): 14–21; "A Response to Bradley Hanson," *Currents in Theology and Mission* 27, no. 5 (October 2000): 359–68; "Ecclesia Sancta, Ecclesia Peccatrix: The Holiness of the Church in Martin Luther's Theology," *Pro Ecclesia* 9, no. 3 (Summer 2000): 331–54; "Interpreting the Roman Response to the Joint Declaration on Justification," *Pro Ecclesia* 7, no. 4 (Fall 1998): 404–14; "The Concordat, Ecumenism, and Evangelical-Catholic Politics," *Lutheran Forum* 32, no. 1 (Easter 1998): 422–46; "Sacramental Lutheranism at the End of the Modern Age," *Lutheran Forum* 34, no. 4 (Winter 2000): 6–16; and "The Church as Polity?: The Lutheran Context of Robert W. Jenson's Ecclesiology," in *Trinity, Time, and Church: A Response to the Theology of Robert W. Jenson* (Grand Rapids, MI: Eerdmans, 2000), 201–37.

11 See Reinhard Hütter, "The Twofold Center of Lutheran Ethics: Christian Freedom and God's Commandments," in *The Promise of Lutheran Ethics*, ed. Karen L. Bloomquist and John R. Stumme (Minneapolis, MN: Fortress, 1998), 31–54; "God's Law in *Veritatis Splendor*: Sic et Non," in *Ecumenical Ventures in Ethics: Protestants Engage Pope John Paul II's Moral Encyclicals*, ed. Reinhard Hütter and Theodore Dieter (Grand Rapids, MI: Eerdmans, 1998); and *Suffering Divine Things: Theology as Church Practice*, trans. Doug Stott (Grand Rapids, MI: Eerdmans, 2000).

For an insightful response to Hütter's theology, see Gary Simpson, "A Critical Conversation in *The Promise of Lutheran Ethics*," *Word and World* 19, no. 2 (Spring 1999): 189–94.

12 Hütter's thinking borrows the concept of *pathos* from Oswald Bayer's interpretation of Luther, a move that is currently absent or unthematized in Yeago's thinking. See Hütter, *Suffering Divine Things*, 39–94. However, for Hütter, the concept of *pathos* permits our participation in the energy of the triune God via practices and thus is reconfigured in terms of our pilgrimage toward God. For Bayer, by contrast, the concept of *pathos* serves to reinforce Luther's view of the centrality of justification by faith alone even in our doing of theology. See Bayer, *Theologie* (Gütersloh, Germany: Gütersloher, 1994). Also, in contrast to Yeago, Hütter emphasizes the importance of retrieving natural law, a position not rejected by but neither emphasized (yet) by Yeago. Hütter seems to disdain a "Constantinianism," while Yeago romanticizes the High Middle Ages. In a sense, Yeago has paved the way for important ideas that Hütter further elaborates.

13 See Yeago, "Sacramental Lutheranism," 7. For the role of Stahl in the development of Evangelical Catholic ecclesiologies, see Walter Sundberg, "Ministry in Nineteenth-Century European Lutheranism," in *Called and Ordained*, ed. Todd Nichol and Marc Kolden (Minneapolis, MN: Fortress, 1990), 83. While it would be misleading to imply that Yeago and Hütter are "MacIntyreans," it would be hard to imagine the force of their claims apart from the MacIntyrean quest to retrieve some form of an Aristotelian virtue ethics as an answer to the impasse of contemporary liberal views of ethics. With regard to ecumenism, one hears echoes of MacIntyre's concern that a *shared vision* of the good within a particular community is the only viable context for the healthy development of ethics. See MacIntyre, *After Virtue*, 258.

14 See Hütter, "Twofold Center," 47.

15 Thomas adopted many Aristotelian presuppositions of ethics, including the importance of teleology as the clue to human happiness. MacIntyre nicely presents the inner logic of teleology's impact upon human agency, the good, and community. He wrote, "Ethics therefore in this [Aristotle's] view presupposes some account of potentiality and act, some account of the essence of man as a rational animal and above all some account of the human *telos*. The precepts which enjoin the various virtues and prohibit the vices which are their counterparts instruct us how to move from potentiality to act, how to realize our true nature and to reach our true end. To defy them will be to be frustrated and incomplete, to fail to achieve that good of rational happiness which it is peculiarly ours as a species to pursue. The desires and emotions which we possess are to be

put in order and educated by the use of such precepts and by the cultivation of those habits of action which the study of ethics prescribes; reason instructs us both as to what our true end is and as to how to reach it." See *After Virtue*, 52–53. For an important, classic reassessment of antique virtue theory for the contemporary world, see Edmund Pincoffs, "Quandary Ethics," *Mind* 80 (1971): 522–71.

16   *Veritatis Splendor* defines morality thus: "the rational ordering of the human act to the good in its truth and the voluntary pursuit of that good, known by reason, constitute morality. Hence human activity cannot be judged as morally good merely because it is a means for attaining one or another of its goals, or simply because the subject's intention is good. Activity is morally good when it attests to and expresses the voluntary ordering of the person to his ultimate end and the conformity of a concrete action with the human good as it is acknowledged in its truth by reason. If the object of the concrete action is not in harmony with the true good of the person, the choice of that action makes our will and ourselves morally evil, thus putting us in conflict with our ultimate end, the supreme good, God himself." See Pope John Paul II, *The Splendor of Truth (Veritatis Splendor): Encyclical Letter of Pope John Paul II*, Vatican translation (Boston: St. Paul, n.d.), IV:72, 91–92.

17   Perhaps no one has articulated this distinction more clearly than John Milbank (another thinker heavily influenced by MacIntyre) in his *Theology and Social Theory*, 318, where he wrote, "Between nihilistic univocity and Catholic analogy there is no longer any third liberal path."

18   In this regard, Thomistic Turners appeal to Risto Saarinen, *Gottes Wirken auf Uns: Die Transzendentale Deutung des Gegenwart-Christi-Motivs in der Lutherforschung* (Stuttgart: Franz Steiner Verlag, 1989). See also Tuomo Mannermaa, "Why Is Luther So Fascinating?: Modern Finnish Luther Research," in *Union with Christ: The New Finnish Interpretation of Luther*, ed. Carl E. Braaten and Robert W. Jenson (Grand Rapids, MI: Eerdmans, 1998), 1–20.

19   See Karl Holl, introduction to *The Reconstruction of Morality*, ed. James Luther Adams and Walter F. Bense, trans. Fred W. Meuser and Walter Wietzke (Minneapolis, MN: Augsburg, 1979), 20–23. For Troeltsch's discussion, see Ernst Troeltsch, *Protestantism and Progress: The Significance of Protestantism for the Rise of the Modern World* (Philadelphia: Fortress, 1986), 56–57.

20   Yeago writes, "Therefore when Luther distinguishes between what the church is in her sinful personnel and what she is in Christ, this is not a distinction between hard reality and a 'legal fiction' contrived through bare imputation. It must be understood in terms of his account of salvation as shared life, our participation in the being of another by the

generosity of that other. Imputation itself is based on this sharing of the faithful in the being of Christ; the Father overlooks the sin which remains in the faithful precisely because they exist by faith as a single concrete whole with Christ. Union with Christ, not imputation, is the ontological rock-bottom in Luther's theology of salvation." See Yeago, "Ecclesia Sancta, Ecclesia Peccatrix," 353.

21 Again, it is hard not to be reminded of MacIntyre's definition of practices. He wrote, "By a 'practice' I am going to mean any coherent and complex form of socially established cooperative human activity through which goods internal to that form of activity are realized in the course of trying to achieve those standards of excellence which are appropriate to, and partially definitive of, that form of activity, with the result that human powers to achieve excellence, and human conceptions of the ends and goods involved, are systematically extended." See MacIntyre, *After Virtue*, 187.

22 See Yeago, "Church as Polity," 211–12.

23 Leif Grane offers a helpful interpretation of the relation between faith and love in Thomas's thought. He wrote, "In itself, faith is an act of the intellect, in which the intellect, moved by God, acknowledges the dogmas of the church as revealed truths. In this respect there is no difference between *fides informis* (unformed faith) and *fides caritate formata* (faith formed by love). The difference consists in the determination of the will. Seen from the side of the intellect, *fides informis* is just as complete as *fides formata*. Nevertheless, *fides informis* is a dead faith, because the will is not directed towards God. In *fides informis* the will is involved in the act of faith only as far as its assistance is necessary for the acceptance of revealed truths. That which perfects the will is love. Faith is the material, love is the form which gives faith its true character. As an intellectual act faith directs itself toward God as the first truth (*prima veritas*), but the act of the will, led by love, directs itself toward God himself. It is love, therefore, which is decisive in one's relationship to God. Faith, of course, must be there first, since the will cannot direct itself toward God until the intellect has presented it to the will as the good. Because love forms faith, faith itself is not altered, but rather its subject, the person who now receives a new quality through the infusion of love and is lifted up to a supernatural life." See Leif Grane, *The Augsburg Confession: A Commentary*, trans. John H. Rasmussen (Minneapolis, MN: Augsburg, 1987), 85.

24 As will be remembered, Thomas's understanding of justification analyzes it as a movement with a fourfold pattern. First, the believer experiences an infusion of grace, the gift of renewal in the Holy Spirit. Second, the believer is moved by means of free will toward God in faith. Third, the believer is moved by means of free will in recoil from sin.

Finally, the believer receives the remission of guilt. See Thomas Aquinas, *Summa Theologica*, trans. Fathers of the English Dominican province (Westminster, MD: Christian Classics, 1948), I–II, Q. 113.

25 Hütter, "God's Law in *Veritatis Splendor*," 95, 103. See also Simon Peura, "Christ as Favor and Gift (*donum*): The Challenge of Luther's Understanding of Justification," in *Union with Christ: The New Finnish Interpretation of Luther*, ed. Carl E. Braaten and Robert W. Jenson (Grand Rapids, MI: Eerdmans, 1998), 42–64.

26 See Yeago, "Martin Luther on Grace, Law, and Moral Life."

27 Ibid., 176.

28 Luther, *LW* 1:131 (*WA* 42:98).

29 Luther, *LW* 34:138, thesis 13 (*WA* 39/I:175).

30 Here there is a striking parallel with George Lindbeck's thinking. In "Luther on Law in Ecumenical Context," *Dialog* 22:4 (Fall 1983): 272, Lindbeck wrote, "Given these scriptural warrants, non-Lutherans see no reason why they should limit the function of the law in Christian life to its two harsh initial uses. They think it has both a gentler role and a more exalted content for Christians than for non-Christians. It does not simply restrain the flesh in the struggle against sin and drive to Christ, but it also provides guidance amidst chaos, delivers from anarchy, and frees from anomie. It is, in the psalmists' words, a guide to the feet, and a light to the path, sweeter than honey and the droppings of the honey comb. Perhaps it was impossible for rules and regulations to operate in this fashion in a penitential age such as that of the Reformation, but in normlessly permissive periods such as the present one, the third use of the law can be for Christians a liberating power rather than a repressive burden. We thus return to our starting point. When antinomianism is culturally dominant, Luther's neglect or denial of a specifically Christian law and use of the law does not seem unduly lax but excessively harsh."

31 Here the Thomistic Turn parallels Tuomo Mannermaa's Luther research. See Mannermaa's essay "Justification and *Theosis* in Lutheran-Orthodox Perspective," in *Union with Christ*, 41.

32 MacIntyre describes (rightfully) the contemporary vision of the world as "Weberian," meaning that it encourages an "irreducible plurality of values." See MacIntyre, *After Virtue*, 109.

33 See Yeago, "Sacramental Lutheranism," 9.

34 Ibid.

35 Hütter contrasts justification as the "floor" with it as the "ceiling," rejecting the latter position as the "Protestant Fallacy." See Hütter, "Twofold Center," 33.

36 For the Thomistic Turn, reason is "rational" when it participates mimetically in God as the highest good. Lutherans claim that reason is "rational,"

by contrast, when it stays limited to issues about human welfare without assuming a continuum between the divine and the human. When reason is construed in secular terms as "instrumental," then it is a device for self-serving humanity, leaving an *ambitio divinitatis* in place. One need not affirm "participatory" reason in order to avoid "secular" reason.

37 Hütter, "Twofold Center," 34–35.

38 This idea is shared by a number of different thinkers. See, for example, Richard M. Weaver, *Ideas Have Consequences* (Chicago: University of Chicago Press, 1948); Craig Gay, *The Way of the (Modern) World or, Why It's Tempting to Live as If God Doesn't Exist* (Grand Rapids, MI: Eerdmans, 1998), 166, 169–70, and especially 172; Leszek Kolakowski, *Modernity on Endless Trial* (Chicago: University of Chicago Press, 1990), 187; Milbank, *Theology and Social Theory*; and Charles Taylor, *Sources of the Self: The Making of the Modern Identity* (Cambridge, MA: Harvard University Press, 1989), 161. However, as Ulrich Asendorf claimed, it is more likely that a trajectory exists from Erasmus, not Luther, to Kant. See Ulrich Asendorf, *Luther und Hegel: Untersuchungen zur Grundlegung einer neuen Systematischen Theologie* (Wiesbaden, Germany: Franz Steiner Verlag, 1982), 78. If, as nominalism contended, reason is not participatory, then many thinkers claim that it defaults to a mode of self-interest and hence is instrumental, either analyzing matter-in-motion or promoting self-interest. Of course, Protestantism, it is said, did not "cause" modernity but paved the way for it. The relation between nominalism and the rise of modernity, however, is in dispute. Alfred Crosby, in *The Measure of Reality: Quantification and Western Society, 1250–1600* (Cambridge: Cambridge University Press, 1997), 228, noted that many forces were at work in the development of "instrumental" reason. He suggested that the role that visualization increasingly took in the late Middle Ages, which was heightened by the development of the printing press, was pivotal. Of course, for Luther, in contrast, hearing (not [Platonic] seeing) indicates the primary mode of human existence in the world, receptivity.

39 Of merit, Thomas wrote, "Man's meritorious work may be considered in two ways:—first, as it proceeds from free-will; secondly, as it proceeds from the grace of the Holy Ghost. If it is considered as regards the substance of the work, and inasmuch as it springs from free-will, there can be no condignity because of the very great inequality. But there is congruity, on account of an equality of proportion: for it would seem congruous that, if a man does what he can, God should reward him according to the excellence of his power. If, however, we speak of a meritorious work, inasmuch as it proceeds from the grace of the Holy Ghost moving us to life everlasting, it is meritorious of life everlasting condignly. For thus the value of its merit depends upon the power of the Holy Ghost moving us

to life everlasting according to Jo. iv.14. . . . And the worth of the work depends on the dignity of grace, whereby a man, being made a partaker of the Divine Nature, is adopted as a son of God, to whom the inheritance is due by right of adoption, according to Rom. viii.17." See Aquinas, *Summa Theologica*, Ia, IIae, 114, art. 3. For the context of the contemporary debate, see the statement on merit in Lutheran World Federation and Catholic Church, *Joint Declaration on the Doctrine of Justification* (Grand Rapids, MI: Eerdmans, 2000), 25. For an outstanding discussion of merit from the perspective of Lutheran theology, see Joseph Burgess, "Rewards, but in a Very Different Sense," in *Justification by Faith: Lutherans and Catholics in Dialogue VII*, ed. H. George Anderson, T. Austin Murphy, and Joseph A. Burgess (Minneapolis, MN: Augsburg, 1985), 94–110.

40 Furthermore, he notes that postmodernity has sufficiently undermined modern views of moral agency and autonomy. Hence neo-Darwinism unmasks modern agency as irrational forces of genetics; Freud unmasked it as irrational psychological conflict between the id, ego, and superego; and Marx unmasked it as scripted by class conflicts that ultimately will lead to the birth of a classless society. Clearly, modern attempts to justify ethics, for many, are exhausted or at least stand in need of improvement. It should be noted that Hütter's skepticism with regard to modern ethics has been influenced by Stanley Hauerwas's conviction that democracy isn't representative of all but rather is government "by the elite." See Stanley Hauerwas, *Christian Existence Today: Essays on Church, Word and Living in Between* (Durham, NC: Labyrinth Press, 1988), 183. However, in contrast to Hauerwas, Craig Gay's contention is important: "But what if this modern view is fundamentally mistaken? What if such things as freedom, dignity, and justice are *not* social in origin and *not* simply 'values' that have been socially constructed under certain local and historical circumstances? What if freedom, dignity, and justice are actually part and parcel of created moral order? And what if these things do *not* ultimately depend upon our political acumen and our ability to guarantee them? What if, on the contrary, social and political organization actually pose a profound threat to freedom, dignity, and justice precisely because of the tendency of power to corrupt and of political and social aspirations to eclipse all other human purposes? What if, instead, freedom, dignity, and justice are actually the consequences, as the Scriptures suggest that they ought to be, of each of us determining, before God, to love our neighbor as ourselves? This possibility—that modern social and political theory is fundamentally mistaken about the natures of freedom and dignity and, indeed, about the nature of human existence—is what we want to consider briefly in the light of a Christian understanding of hope." See Gay, *Way of the (Modern) World*, 74. It should be noted that

Yeago, Hütter, and Hauerwas are not to be understood as "conservatives" in the political sense. *Both* conservatism and liberalism affirm modern autonomy—which is exactly what they reject. Conservatives tend to think autonomy is served when order prevails in the "private" sphere while libertinism prevails in the "public" market, while liberals tend to think just the opposite. Both are wrong-headed for the Thomistic Turn (and perhaps for Radical Lutherans as well). This view is also nicely expressed by Jean Bethke Elshtain in *Democracy on Trial* (New York: Basic, 1995), 2–3.

41 See Gerhard Ebeling, *Luther: An Introduction to His Thought*, trans. R. A. Wilson (Philadelphia: Fortress, 1972), 192–96.

42 See ibid., 139.

43 See Gerhard Forde, "Christian Life," in *Christian Dogmatics*, vol. 2, ed. Carl E. Braaten and Robert W. Jenson (Philadelphia: Fortress, 1984), 416, 439–40.

44 Ibid., 435.

45 Ibid., 399, 403.

46 For Luther's stance in *The Bondage of the Will* as a reaction to Erasmus as a protomodern thinker, see John Carroll, *Humanism: The Wreck of Western Culture* (London: Fontana Press, 1993), 50–51.

47 Two key texts from Luther that Forde pointed to in *Justification by Faith: A Matter of Death and Life* (Philadelphia: Fortress, 1983), 16–17 are from (1) Martin Luther, "The Babylonian Captivity of the Church," in *LW* 36:67–68 (*WA* 6:534): "This death and resurrection we call the new creation, regeneration, and spiritual birth. This should not be understood only allegorically as the death of sin and the life of grace, as many understand it, but as actual death and resurrection. For baptism is not a false sign"; and (2) Martin Luther, *The Bondage of the Will*, trans. J. I. Packer and O. R. Johnston (Westwood, NJ: Fleming H. Revel, 1957), 101 (*WA* 18, 633): "When God quickens, he does so by killing; when He justifies, He does so by pronouncing guilty; when he carries up to heaven, He does so by bringing down to hell. . . . When God kills, faith in life is exercised in death."

48 In "Lectures on Galatians," in *LW* 26:260 (*WA* 40/I:407), Luther wrote, "Thus the 'doer of the Law' is not one who becomes a doer on the basis of his deeds; he is one who, having already become a person through faith, then becomes a doer. For in theology those who have been made righteous do righteous things, not as in philosophy, where those who do righteous things are made righteous."

49 See Bayer, *Theologie*, 400. Bayer noted that for Johann Georg Hamann, the sacrament of the altar was a clue to God's service to us in His creative work. Bayer wrote, "Im besonderen Gottesdienst ist zu hören, zu schmecken und—durch das Wort—zu sehen, daß das, was die Welt im

Innersten zusammenhält, nicht etwa der Kategorische Imperativ ist, sondern die Kategorische Gabe. *Der besondere Gottesdienst* kultiviert keine
religiöse Provinz, sondern *erschließt die Welt als Schöpfung.*"

50 See Wilfried Härle, "Zur Gegenwartsbedeutung der 'Rechtfertigungs':
Lehre. Eine Problemskizze," *Zeitschrift für Theologie und Kirche*, Beiheft
10 (December 1998): 108.

51 Luther in the "Disputation against Scholastic Theology" (1517), thesis 17,
in *LW* 31:10 (*WA* 1:225), wrote, "Man is by nature unable to want God to
be God. Indeed, he himself wants to be God, and does not want God
to be God." Also Luther noted that we are humanized by God's judgment
that evaluates us as sinners. Hence in his exposition of Psalm 5:3 (*WA*
4, 5, 39, 128–29), Luther wrote, "Through the kingdom of his humanity, or (as the apostle says) through the kingdom of his flesh, occurring
in faith, he conforms us to himself and crucifies us, by making out of
unhappy and arrogant gods true men, i.e., miserable ones and sinners."
For Luther (in the *Treatise on Good Works* [*LW* 44:32; *WA* 6:211]), one
makes oneself into one's own idol, if one looks to one's works and not
faith alone *coram deo*. Hence he wrote, "Now it may well be that if these
things are done with such faith that we believe that they please God, then
they are praiseworthy, not because of their virtue, but because of that
very faith by which all works are of equal value, as has been said. But
if we have any doubt about it, or do not believe that God is gracious to
us and pleased with us, or if we presume to please him first and fore-
most by good works, then it is all pure deception. To all appearances
God is honored, but in reality the *self has been set up as an idol.*" Also in
the "Lectures on Galatians" (1535, in LW 26:257–58 [WA 40/I:404–5]),
Luther wrote of those attempting to "keep the law" so that "they not only
do not keep it, but they also deny the first commandment, the promises of God, and the blessing promised to Abraham. They deny faith and
try to bless themselves by their own works; that is, to justify themselves,
to set themselves free from sin and death, to overcome the devil, and to
capture heaven by force—which is to deny God and *to set oneself up
in place of God.* All these are exclusively works of the Divine Majesty,
not of any creature, whether angelic or human. Therefore, Paul could
easily predict on the basis of the first commandment that abominations
would be established in the church by the antichrist. For those who teach
that some other worship is necessary for salvation than the worship set
down in the first commandment—which is fear, trust, and love toward
God—are antichrists and are setting themselves up in place of God
(2 Thess. 2:4). . . . Thus we today can say, both easily and surely: Whoever
seeks righteousness apart from faith and through works denies God and
makes himself into God. This is what he thinks: 'If I do this work, I shall

be righteous. I shall be the victor over sin, death, the devil, the wrath of God, and hell; and I shall attain eternal life.' Now what is this, I ask you, but to arrogate to oneself a work that belongs to God alone, and to show that one is God?" For a helpful discussion of Luther's understanding of anthropology with respect to many of the above passages, see Eberhard Jüngel, *The Freedom of a Christian: Luther's Significance for Contemporary Theology*, trans. Roy A. Harrisville (Minneapolis, MN: Augsburg, 1988), 24–25.

52 See Forde, "Christian Life," 468.

53 Ibid., 418.

54 See Jüngel's helpful discussion in *Freedom of a Christian*, 24.

55 See Gerhard Forde, "Fake Theology: Reflections on Antinomianism Past and Present," *Dialog* 22, no. 4 (Fall 1983): 246–51.

56 Forde, "Christian Life," 449. Luther emphasized in the "Lectures on Galatians" that the law is limited to the flesh and not appropriate for the conscience (*LW* 26:11 [*WA* 40/I:50–51]).

57 Jüngel, *Freedom of a Christian*, 70.

58 Hence one should be aware of the antiexistentialist thrust of Forde's thinking. See Gerhard Forde, "Bultmann: Where Did He Take Us?," *Dialog* 17, no. 1 (Winter 1978): 30; where he wrote, "For my own part, one thing seems certain. The basic difficulty with Bultmann's theological program, aside from the critical excesses, is that he did not go far enough. Like just about everybody before him, he thought we still had something going for us. In his case it was the possibility of 'authentic existence.' He thought he could translate the message into those terms, into that 'something' we still have going for us. In that he did nothing more or less than virtually every theology before—and since. But the truth lies, I think, in realizing at last that we haven't anything going for us. I expect that is what the *New* Testament is trying to tell us. It is *our* myth that needs finally to be excised so that Word can save us. Somehow we have to learn how to say that."

59 Luther, "Lectures on Galatians," in *LW* 26:171 (*WA* 40/I:289–90).

60 Ibid., in *LW* 26:376 (*WA* 40/I:573).

61 Forde, "Christian Life," 420.

62 Gerhard Forde, *Where God Meets Man: Luther's Down-to-Earth Approach to the Gospel* (Minneapolis, MN: Augsburg, 1972), 110.

63 Robert Benne referred to Luther's affirmation of the appropriateness of Aristotle for this-worldly affairs. See Robert Benne, *The Paradoxical Vision: A Public Theology for the Twenty-First Century* (Minneapolis, MN: Fortress, 1995), 78.

64 It should be noted that Bayer believes that there is a tension in conceiving the "theological" with the "civil," or providential use of law under the same term "law." See Bayer, *Theologie*, 417.

65 Luther, "Lectures on Galatians," in *LW* 26:167 (*WA* 40/I:283).

66 Interpreting *The Bondage of the Will*, George Forell wrote, "Christian freedom is not freedom of choice or freedom of the will, but rather it means to have been justified as a sinner. It means to be freed from the curse of sin, liberated from the obsessions with the self, from being turned into the self (*incurvatus in se*), and instead having become absolutely dependent on God. In Paul's terms it is having become 'a slave of Jesus Christ' (Rm 1, 1), a phrase utterly abhorrent to contemporary theology and religiosity." See George Forell, "Freedom as Love: Luther's Treatise on Good Works," in *Freiheit als Liebe bei Martin Luther*, ed. Dennis D. Bielfeldt and Klaus Schwarzwäller (Frankfurt, Germany: Peter Lang, 1995), 80.

67 And Platonism is by no means dead. See Iris Murdoch, *Metaphysics as a Guide to Morals* (London: Penguin, 1992), 507, where she wrote, "That we can and do love Good and are drawn towards it is something that we have to learn from our experience, as we move all the time in the continuum between good and bad. This is our everyday existence where spiritual energy, Eros, is all the time active at a variety of levels."

68 With the loss of a notion of a substantial self that has been so important for modernity since Descartes, many philosophers have been looking for a theory of "narrative identity." Perhaps the most devastating critique of the notion of a substantial self has been given by the utilitarian and Buddhist thinker Derek Parfit in *Reasons and Persons* (Oxford: Oxford University Press, 1986). Parfit attacked the notions of both a substantial self and reason defined as self-interest. He claimed that moral desire is no less rational than self-interest (131). With the loss of a substantial self, many argue for a narrative approach to personal continuity as the basis for a "self" in contrast to psychological categories. For instance, MacIntyre, *After Virtue*, 211, contended for a theory of narrative identity since human actions are "enacted narratives." Likewise, Paul Ricoeur, from the perspective of hermeneutics, argued in *Oneself as Another* (Chicago: University of Chicago Press, 1992), especially studies five and six, that narrative identity is a crucial component that unlocks the continuity of the self since it affirms that *ipse*, or similarity, and not *idem*, or sameness, is the key by which to decipher self-continuity over time. A "postmodern" thinker like Mark C. Taylor seems to miss the whole point of the loss of the substantial self in *Erring: A Postmodern A/theology* (Chicago: University of Chicago Press, 1984). Self "dies" for Taylor but not the carnival, comedy, or carnality of our current culture. For Taylor, are the idols of our current consumeristic economic system fixed or immortal? For more on Luther's antisubstantial view of the self, see Wilfried Joest's chapter, "Der eschatologische Charakter des Person-Seins," in *Die*

Ontologie der Person bei Luther (Göttingen: Vandenhoeck and Ruprecht, 1967), 320–32.

69 Forde, "Christian Life," 417.

70 Ibid., 418.

71 Hence Joachim Ringleben wrote, "Die Glaubensgewißheit ist also eine Prolepse eschatologischer Einheit mit Gott, auf die der Glaube also das endgültige Heil aus ist. Als solcher eschatologischer Vorgriff ist die Gewißheit, die der Glaube ist, naturgemäß nur zusammen mit Unsicherheit (sogar grundsätzlich), mit Anfechtung, Zweifel und Unglaube (Mk 9,24) 'empirisch' da, weil er eben als Glaube noch unter den Bedingungen von Welt, Sünde und göttlichem Zorn steht." See "Heilsgewißheit," *Zeitschrift für Theologie und Kirche*, Beiheft 10 (December 1998): 77.

72 See Forde, *On Being a Theologian of the Cross: Reflections on Luther's Heidelberg Disputation, 1518* (Grand Rapids, MI: Eerdmans, 1997), 15.

73 See Luther, "Lectures on Galatians" (1535), in *LW* 26:11 (*WA* 40/I:51).

74 Ibid., in *LW* 27:58 (*WA* 40/2:72).

75 Nominalism did not alter the essential Augustinian or Thomistic viator structure of the Christian *transitus* as progressive degrees of growth from vice to virtue. Instead, skeptical of our ability to know much with regard to our "participation" in God, it offered a "covenantal," *acceptatio* alternative in which God graciously chooses to accept our deeds as in some way meritorious. The Thomistic Turners and others have a tendency to overdraw the similarities between nominalism and Protestantism.

76 The *totus Christus* is the Augustinian view of Christ as the head conjoined in ministry with the body, the church,. In this view, the church is not primarily a witness to the coming kingdom but the first installment of it. See Robert Jenson, *Systematic Theology*, vol. 2 (New York: Oxford University Press, 1999), chap. 24.

77 John Locke, *A Letter Concerning Toleration* (Amherst, NY: Prometheus, 1990), 22.

78 See Ernest Becker, *The Denial of Death* (New York: Free Press, 1973), 5. Of course, the Thomistic Turn would recognize much of modernity as inherently religious as well.

79 Martin Luther, "Large Catechism," in *BC-K/W* 440:69 (*BC-T* 420:69 [*BSLK* 661:69]).

80 Martin Luther, "Treatise on Faith and Law," in *LW* 34:112, thesis 53 (*WA* 39/I:47),.

81 Luther in "The Freedom of the Christian" (1520) argued that the Christian lives in Christ in faith and in the neighbor in love. See Martin Luther, "The Freedom of the Christian" (1520), in *LW* 31:371 (*WA* 7:69).

82 Luther, "Large Catechism," in *BC-K/W* 389:26 (*BC-T* 368:26 [*BSLK* 56:26]).

83 Luther, "Lectures on Galatians," in *LW* 26:5 (*WA* 40/I:42).

84 Luther, "Large Catechism," in *BC-K/W* 388:15 (*BC-T* 366:15 [*BSLK* 563:15]); *BC-K/W* 389:25 (*BC-T* 368:25 [*BSLK* 56:25]).

85 Martin Luther, "Against Latomus," in *LW* 32:159 (*WA* 8:58).

86 Luther, *WA* 56:486.

87 Luther, "Disputation Concerning Man," in *LW* 34:139 (*WA* 39/I:176), thesis 32.

88 Ibid., in *LW* 34:139 (*WA* 39/I:177), thesis 35.

89 Luther, "Lectures on Galatians" (1535), in *LW* 26:96 (*WA* 40/I:177). See also Oswald Bayer, "Nature and Institution: Luther's Doctrine of the Three Orders," *Lutheran Quarterly* 7, no. 2 (Summer 1998): 125–59.

90 Such secularistic ideologies of salvation are more than willing to sacrifice the individual for their own survival. On the preciousness of the individual person in the view of Christianity, Glenn Tinder wrote, "Measured against empires and centuries, a human being is almost nothing. On the other hand, if the God who exalts individuals is superior to the world and to history, as eschatology implies, so are individuals. As creatures beloved by God, they have destinies. Even one insignificant person is more significant than a great historical movement, and one unworthy human being has more worth than a nation. Eschatology is a metaphorical rebuttal of human pretensions, a humbling of deified heroes and idolized masses; and it is a metaphorical defense of the individual, one of a numberless multitude, who is devoured by history. In history, very few are remembered; in Christ, none are forgotten. That, at any rate, is the eschatological faith of Christians." See Glenn Tinder, *The Political Meaning of Christianity* (Baton Rouge: Louisiana State University Press, 1989), 87.

91 Eberhard Jüngel, *God as the Mystery of the World*, trans. Darrell L. Guder (Grand Rapids, MI: Eerdmans, 1983), 41.

92 Gustaf Wingren, *Credo: The Christian View of Faith and Life*, trans. Edgar Carlson (Minneapolis, MN: Augsburg, 1981), 71.

93 See John Webster, "'The Grammar of Doing': Luther and Barth on Human Agency," in *Barth's Moral Theology: Human Action in Barth's Thought* (Grand Rapids, MI: Eerdmans, 1998), 159.

94 Luther, "Lectures on Galatians" (1535), in *LW* 26:261 (*WA* 40/I:410).

95 Ibid., in *LW* 26:266 (*WA* 40/I:417).

96 See Gustaf Wingren, *Luther on Vocation* (Philadelphia: Muhlenberg Press, 1957), 124.

97 Paul Althaus, *The Theology of Martin Luther*, trans. Robert C. Schulz (Philadelphia: Fortress, 1966), 17.

98 Luther, "Lectures on Galatians" (1535), in *LW* 27:352 (*WA* 40/2:74–78).

99 Ibid., in *LW* 27:353 (*WA* 40/2:72).

100 Ibid., in *LW* 27:58 (*WA* 40/2:73).
101 Carl Braaten, *Principles of Lutheran Theology* (Philadelphia: Fortress, 1983), 132.
102 Bayer, *Theologie*, 404.
103 See Robert H. Nelson, *Economics as Religion: From Samuelson to Chicago and Beyond* (University Park: Pennsylvania State University Press, 2001), 31.

Chapter 8 The Mystical-Political Luther and Public Theology

1 See Larry Rasmussen, "Luther and a Gospel of Earth," *Union Seminary Quarterly Review* 51, no. 1–2 (1997): 111–28.
2 See Cynthia D. Moe-Lobeda, *Public Church for the Life of the World* (Minneapolis, MN: Augsburg Fortress, 2004); and *Healing a Broken World: Globalization and God* (Minneapolis, MN: Fortress, 2002).
3 For a thoroughly developed notion of sustainability, see Herman Daly and John B. Cobb, *For the Common Good: Redirecting the Economy toward Community, the Environment, and a Sustainable Future* (Boston: Beacon Press, 1994).
4 See Jean-François Lyotard, *The Postmodern Condition: A Report on Knowledge*, trans. Geoff Bennington and Brian Massumi (Minneapolis: University of Minnesota Press, 1984). The first metanarrative that Lyotard examines is that of "the speculative spirit": "The great function to be fulfilled by the universities is to 'lay open the whole body of learning and expound both the principles and the foundations of all knowledge.' For 'there is no creative scientific capacity without the speculative spirit.' 'Speculation' is here the name given the discourse on the legitimation of scientific discourse. Schools are functional; the University is speculative, that is to say, philosophical" (33). The paradigm for this approach is Hegel's encyclopedic system. The alternative legitimation for scientific inquiry, the one impacting Moe-Lobeda's work, is the "narrative of emancipation": "According to this version, knowledge finds its validity not within itself, not in a subject that develops by actualizing its learning possibilities, but in a practical subject—humanity. The principle of the movement animating the people is not the self-legitimation of knowledge, but the self-grounding of freedom or, if preferred, its self-management. The subject is concrete, or supposedly so, and its epic is the story of its emancipation from everything that prevents it from governing itself. It is assumed that the laws it makes for itself are just, not because they conform to some outside nature, but because the legislators are, constitutionally, the very citizens who are subject to the laws" (35).

5 Globalization, Moe-Lobeda notes, has seven intimately related trends: (1) the rapid movement of goods and services, as well as trade and investment, across international borders; (2) the subordination of democratic political power to unaccountable economic power in order to ease that movement; (3) the unaccountability of the largest economies to the public as a whole; (4) the privatization of public goods and services (water, electricity, health care, and education) to corporations not accountable to communities; (5) the commodification of life, placing a monetary value on life forms (such as genetic material) and on life experiences (such as cultural practices); (6) the strategic marketing of Western consumer-oriented ways of life around the world; and (7) the commodification of money, the ascendance of "speculative" trade in money for short-term gain over trade in goods and services, and overinvestment in long-term production-oriented economic activity. See Moe-Lobeda, *Healing a Broken World*, 19–20. That for Moe-Lobeda, globalization is antithetical to the metanarrative of emancipation can easily be seen: "Globalization subordinates democratic political power to unaccountable economic power. This subordination undermines citizens' political capacity to shape alternative economic policies, structures, and lifestyles that contribute to social justice and sustainability. The moral significance of this claim is great: globalization removes, from more or less democratically constituted and accountable political bodies, significant power to influence decision that impact human and other well-being for generations to come and places that power into the hands of relatively few unaccountable economic players." See Moe-Lobeda, *Healing a Broken World*, 4. While everything about globalization is negative for Moe-Lobeda, is not the truth of the matter that its interrelated components are mixed: both life-sustaining features and problematic features?

6 See Jeffrey D. Sachs, *The End of Poverty: Economic Possibilities for Our time* (New York: Penguin, 2005). Sachs claims that "many people assume that the rich have gotten rich *because* the poor have gotten poor. In other words, they assume that Europe and the United States used military force and political strength during and after the era of colonialism to extract wealth from the poorest regions, and thereby to grow rich. This interpretation of events would be plausible if gross world product had remained roughly constant, with a rising share going to the powerful regions and a declining share going to the poorer regions. However, that is not at all what happened. Gross world product rose nearly fifty-fold. Every region of the world experienced some economic growth. . . . The key fact of modern times is not the *transfer* of income from one region to another, by force or otherwise, but rather the overall *increase* in world income, but at a different rate in different regions. . . . This is not to say that the rich

are innocent of the charge of having exploited the poor. They surely have. . . . However, the real story of modern economic growth has been the ability of some regions to achieve unprecedented long-term increases in total production to levels never before seen in the world, while other regions stagnated, at least by comparison. Technology has been the main force behind the long-term increases in income in the rich world, not exploitation of the poor. That news is very good indeed because it suggests that all of the world, including today's laggard regions, have a reasonable hope of reaping the benefits of technological advance" (31). See also Sach's critique of the antiglobalization movement, ibid., 353–58.

7   Moe-Lobeda, *Healing a Broken World*, 1.
8   Moe-Lobeda, *Public Church*, 8.
9   Ibid., 45.
10 See Tuomo Mannermaa, *Christ Present in Faith: Luther's View of Justification*, trans. Kirsi Stjerna (Minneapolis, MN: Fortress, 2005).
11 Martin Luther, *LW* 26:129. For a further critique of Mannermaa's work, see Mark C. Mattes, *The Role of Justification in Contemporary Theology* (Grand Rapids, MI: Eerdmans, 2004), 126–32; and "A Future for Lutheran Theology?," *Lutheran Quarterly* 19 (Winter 2005): 445–47.
12 Luther, *LW* 26:88–89.
13 Moe-Lobeda writes, "Historically, Lutherans have framed discussions of the church in public life around the two-fold rule of God, commonly referred to as 'two kingdoms.' It is a rich resource—especially in twentieth-century interpretations seeking to undo the dualism that characterized the theme in the nineteenth century—and could frame the discussion at hand fruitfully. However, I have chosen to relocate the discussion of church in public life in the incarnation of Christ as seen in cross, resurrection, and living presence." See Moe-Lobeda, *Public Church*, 5.
14 Of the mystical union, Heinrich Schmid notes that it "is not merely figurative, but literal and actual, so that it cannot be described otherwise than as the union of the substance of God with the substance of man, in consequence of which God pours out the fullness of His gracious gifts upon the regenerate." See Heinrich Schmid, *The Doctrinal Theology of the Evangelical Lutheran Church*, trans. Charles Hay and Henry Jacobs (Minneapolis, MN: Augsburg, 1961), 480. The orthodox fathers followed the *Formula of Concord*, Solid Declaration, article 3, against Andreas Osiander, teaching that the mystical union or the impartation of Christ is subsequent to God's imputation or forensic decree that the sinner is acquitted for Jesus' sake. See Solid Declaration, article 3: Righteousness in *The Book of Concord: The Confessions of the Evangelical Lutheran*

Church, ed. Robert Kolb and Timothy J. Wengert, trans. Charles Arand (Minneapolis, MN: Fortress, 2000), 573:61–63.

15 Mannermaa speaks of imputation and the *inhabitatio dei*, different sides of the same event; see Mannermaa, *Christ Present in Faith*, 22.

16 *Intuitu fidei* was the approach of Mathias Loy (1828–1915) and others, where God elects people to salvation in view of faith, against the view of C. F. W. Walther (1811–87), for whom God's election brings about faith in the believer. For a recent study, see David R. Liefeld, "Saved on Purpose: Luther, Lutheranism, and Election," *Logia* 15 (Eastertide 2006): 5–16.

17 Prophetic critiques of unjust social structures that violate the needs of the poor and downtrodden from the Old Testament assume a political scenario where the worship of Yahweh is supposed to be one with the state. Clearly, contemporary American civil religion is not tantamount to Christianity or even biblical faith per se. It is a form of Enlightenment faith with a variety of venues. All of which is to say, there is no direct trajectory between the biblical concern for the poor and contemporary American social policy. To the degree to which American ideals are rooted in biblical faith and/or to the degree that one can make a case that all humans ought to be concerned for the poor, whether here or abroad, is the degree to which scriptural social ethics can address today's context. Proof-texting from the Bible over social matters is persuasive only for the faithful Christian who actually trusts that the Bible is the word of God. It does not help them persuade non-Christians why they, too, should share such concerns or why public policy ought to be changed on the basis of biblical mandates.

18 See Ronald F. Thiemann, *Religion in Public Life: A Dilemma for Democracy* (Washington, DC: Georgetown University Press, 1996), 33–34.

19 See John Milbank, *Theology and Social Theory: Beyond Secular Reason* (Oxford: Blackwell, 1990), 37–40.

20 See George Marsden, *The Soul of the American University: From Protestant Establishment to Established Nonbelief* (New York: Oxford University Press, 1994). For the impact of secularization on Christian higher education, see James Tunstead Burtchaell, *The Dying of the Light: The Disengagement of Colleges and Universities from Their Christian Churches* (Grand Rapids, MI: Eerdmans, 1998); and Gavin D'Costa, *Theology in the Public Square: Church, Academy, and Nation* (Malden, MA: Blackwell, 2005).

21 See Moe-Lobeda, *Healing a Broken World*, chap. 3.

22 In discussing economist Paul Samuelson, Robert H. Nelson clues us into the hidden religious-mythical agendas of capitalism: "The goal of Economics, in short, is progress; the means is an efficient economic

system; the sinners are the special interests, the greatest danger posed for the world is cyclical instability and unemployment of resources that will lead to demagoguery, dictatorship, and war. If the economy can instead be put on a track of rapid economic growth, poverty in the United States can soon be eliminated and with it the social ills of crime, drug abuse, suicide, and many others. As more and more people reach a high standard of living themselves, they will increasingly be willing to support government plans to redistribute resources to the less fortunate and otherwise take the collective actions needed for the further progress of American society. Growth can also provide the resources to build an environmentally beautiful world. Economic growth thus creates a 'virtuous circle.' Within a few generations, all the old wars and other ills of human existence can be abolished forever after." See Robert H. Nelson, *Economics as Religion: From Samuelson to Chicago and Beyond* (University Park: Pennsylvania State University Press, 2001), 110. Nelson points out that for economics, "the state of material deprivation is the original sin of economic theology. Then, if this diagnosis is correct, the cure for evil in the world follows directly enough. If sin results from destructive forces brought into existence by material scarcity, a world without scarcity, a world of complete material abundance, will be a world without sin" (28). For similar views, see Harvey Cox, "The Market as God," *Atlantic Monthly*, March 1999, 18–23.

23 Hence Jean Bethke Elshtain, *Democracy on Trial* (New York: Basic, 1995), 2–3, notes, "Both liberals and conservatives are failing America. He [E. J. Dionne] laments the false polarization in American politics that has been cast in the form of a cultural civil war: Give no quarter! One mark of this divide is the irony of liberals seeking ways to tame the logic of the market in economic life even as they celebrate a nearly untrammeled laissez-faire in cultural and sexual life. Their mirror image is provided by conservatives, who argue for constraints and controls in the cultural and sexual sphere but embrace a nearly unconstrained market. Politicians and citizens get stuck in the *danse macabre* of these two logics and see no clear way out. Needless to say, it is far easier . . . for the media to reinforce the political and cultural divide than to explore ideas that cannot be captured so easily by one logical or the other."

24 See Roger W. Fjeld, "American Civil Religion: A De Facto Church," in *The Difficult but Indispensable Church*, ed. Norma Cook Everist (Minneapolis, MN: Fortress, 2002), 181–90.

25 Of "objective justification," J. Michael Reu writes, "There is an objective, or general, or world justification. It took place at the resurrection of Christ. By raising Christ from the dead God declared that the sin of the world was covered (1 John 2:2, HILASMOS) by Christ's suffering and

death. It was a declaration by an act, not by a word of God (Comp. Rom. 6:7, where DIKAIOUSTAI is a declaration performed by an act, the act of death). Consequently we can speak of an objective, or world justification, even if it should be wrong to supply in Rom. 5:18 a verb in the past tense ('There resulted a justification that brings life'). Beside this general justification Scripture, however, knows also a justification in the life of the individual that takes place in the moment when faith is wrought in his heart." See J. Michael Reu, *Lutheran Dogmatics* (Dubuque, IA: Wartburg Seminary Press, 1963), 346–47.

26 See H. Richard Niebuhr, *Christ and Culture* (New York: Harper and Row, 1975). Or, this might be termed "Christ of Counter-Culture." See Paul C. McGlasson, *Invitation to Dogmatic Theology: A Canonical Approach* (Grand Rapids, MI: Brazos, 2006), 25.

27 This is not said in opposition to the *Formula of Concord's* affirmation of the third use of the law. It is said, rather, against those overarching ethical perspectives that would transpose God's law into their own matrix of understanding.

28 See Moe-Lobeda, *Healing a Broken World*, 112–14. Undoubtedly, Moe-Lobeda is seeking to stem the tide of ecological violence by appealing to such apparent pantheism: "We are a species destroying the very life-support systems (for example, air, water, soil, and forests) upon which all life depends. Our society is so addicted to consumption-oriented ways that we close our hearts and minds to the death and destruction required to sustain them." See Moe-Lobeda, *Public Church*, 43. Quite accurate in her assessment of current ecological indifference, is this violence toward the earth not an expression of our *ambitio dei*, our inability to accept our creatureliness and allow God to provide for us?

29 Barth wrote, "Thus, we can certainly make the general and comprehensive statement that the Law is nothing else than the necessary form of the Gospel, whose content is grace. Precisely this content demands this form, the form which calls for is like, the Law's form." See Karl Barth, "Gospel and Law," in *Community, State, Church* (Gloucester, MA: Peter Smith, 1968), 80.

30 See Lowell C. Green, "The Question of *Theosis* in the Perspective of Lutheran Christology," in *All Theology Is Christology: Essays in Honor of David P. Scaer*, ed. Dean O. Wenthe et al. (Fort Wayne, IN: Concordia Theological Seminary Press, 2000), 168.

31 See Jennifer Roback Morse, *Love and Economics: Why the Laissez-Faire Family Doesn't Work* (Dallas: Spence, 2001). See also Family Scholars, *Why Marriage Matters: Twenty-One Conclusions from the Social Sciences* (New York: Institute for American Values, 2002).

32 "I say that the righteous God does not deplore the death of His people which He Himself works in them, but He deplores the death which He finds in His people and desires to remove from them. God preached works to the end that sin and death may be taken away, and we may be saved. . . . But God hidden in Majesty neither deplores nor takes away death, but works life, and death, and all in all; nor has He set bounds to Himself by His Word, but has kept Himself free over all things." See Martin Luther, *The Bondage of the Will*, trans. J. I. Packer and O. R. Johnston (New York: Revell, 1957), 170.

33 Gerhard Forde noted, "The Kingdom of God indeed comes by God's power alone, and thus one is turned back into the world for the time being to serve the neighbor. But such turning takes place only to the degree that one believes in the eschatological Kingdom of God, and is thus freed to do so. If we are to remain true to the gospel, we must realize that there are no levers here. If the movement is not one of freedom, all is lost. Moralists, social reformers, ideologues, revolutionaries, and even just plain zealous religious people may no doubt find this frustrating and maddening, but it is of the very essence of the matter. Wherever a cause is exempted from the negation, so as to exert a pressure which destroys this freedom we come to a serious parting of the ways. At this cross-roads the church has seriously to ask itself what it is here for. Is it here to ratify the world's causes or to foster the freedom and spontaneity of faith? That, of course, is not an absolute either/or since the freedom of faith can only exercise itself in worldly causes for the time being. But at the very least it does raise the question of priority and order. When such causes are espoused, it cannot be at the *expense* of freedom, but rather the means through which freedom expresses itself." See "The Viability of Luther Today: A North American Perspective," *Word and World* 7 (Winter 1987): 29. Similarly, consider Edward Schroeder: "Christ's king-dom is a Good-News promise in God-relations. It's coram deo stuff. The word 'eternally' in the last line above (Luther, Large Catechism, Lord's Prayer, Second Petition) signals both the kingdom's turf (vis-à-vis the Eternal One) and its durability (forever and ever). Partial para-dises in human relations, even extensive world-peace and equity-justice among peoples, are not 'what is the Kingdom of God.' For one thing, they cannot pass the 'eternal' durability test. In Jesus' words, the still 'pass away.' They are part of heaven-and-earth. They are never death-proof. Death-proofing is a coram deo agenda." See "'Peace and Justice Mantra,'" *Thursday Theology* 339 (December 13, 2004), https://crossings.org/the-peace-justice-mantra/.

34 Vítor Westhelle, "Luther and Liberation," *Dialog* 25 (Winter 1986): 51–57. The Luther reference is to *WA* 51:412.

35 "As a 'theology,' the theology of the cross turns very easily into a negative theology of glory. Our occasional pain becomes our good work. If we can't make it by escaping suffering, perhaps we can by entering into it. So we hear a good bit of sentimental talk these days about entering into solidarity with those who suffer, as though it were something we might do on weekends." See Gerhard O. Forde, *On Being a Theologian of the Cross: Reflections on Luther's Heidelberg Disputation, 1518* (Grand Rapids, MI: Eerdmans, 1997), 84.

36 Luther, *The Bondage of the Will*, 317–18.

37 See Immanuel Kant, *Groundwork of the Metaphysic of Morals*, trans. H. J. Paton (New York: Harper and Row, 1964), 100–102.

38 See Oswald Bayer, *Theologie* (Gütersloh, Germany: Gütersloher, 1994), 458.

39 George Forell noted that "the pope who clashed with Luther was a Medici banker and that the indulgence salesmen were always accompanied by a representative of the Fugger banking house." See *Faith Active in Love* (Minneapolis, MN: Augsburg, 1954), 29.

40 See Carter Lindberg, *Beyond Charity: Reformation Initiatives for the Poor* (Minneapolis, MN: Fortress, 1993), 111.

41 As Carter Lindberg points out in *Beyond Charity*, Clement of Alexandria's (150–215) answer to the question "How is the rich man to be saved?" is: "by giving alms to the needy" (22). Likewise, for Hincmar (806–82): "God could have made all persons rich but he willed that there be poor in the world so that the rich would have an opportunity to atone for their sins" (32–33).

42 See *Economics as Religion*, where Nelson notes that with respect to eschatology, Marxist economics is codified in terms of a premillennialism from which, beyond the conflict that arises from the fundamental depravity of the proletariat, an apocalyptic transformation of the human condition will arise. Keynesian capitalism, by contrast, is framed as a postmillennialism. Millennial progress has already begun and, through the increase of material abundance, will eventual lead to a heaven on earth (31).

43 Johann Michael Reu and Paul H. Buehring, *Christian Ethics* (Columbus, OH: Lutheran Book Concern, 1935), 378.

44 Lindberg, *Beyond Charity*, 113.

45 See Ernest G. Schwiebert, "The Reformation and the Capitalistic Revolution," in *God and Caesar: A Christian Approach to Social Ethics*, ed. Walter Bauer and Warren Quanbeck (Minneapolis, MN: Augsburg, 1959), 143.

46 Schwiebert, "Reformation," 150–51.

47 Ibid.

48 Lindberg, *Beyond Charity*, 89.

49 Wilhelm Mauer, *Historical Commentary on the Augsburg Confession*, trans. H. George Anderson (Philadelphia: Fortress, 1986), 153.
50 Luther, "Psalm 101," in *LW* 13:193.
51 Luther, "A Sermon on Keeping Children in School," in *LW* 46:237.
52 See, for example, John R. Stumme and Robert W. Tuttle, eds., *Church and State: Lutheran Perspectives* (Minneapolis, MN: Fortress, 2003); and Craig Nessan, "Reappropriating Luther's Two Kingdoms," *Lutheran Quarterly* 19 (Autumn 2005): 302–11. The single best current discussion of the two kingdoms is in Vítor Westhelle, "The Word and the Mask: Revisiting the Two-Kingdoms Doctrine," in *The Gift of Grace: The Future of Lutheran Theology*, ed. Niels Henrik Gregersen et al. (Minneapolis, MN: Fortress, 2005), 167–78. For a presentation of the impact of the two-kingdoms thinking on the social statements of the former Lutheran Church in America, see Christa R. Klein and Christian D. von Dehsen, *Politics and Policy: The Genesis and Theology of Social Statements in the Lutheran Church in America* (Minneapolis, MN: Fortress, 1989).
53 As quoted by A. D. Mattson, "The Church and Society," in *What Lutherans Are Thinking* (Columbus, OH: Wartburg Press, 1947), 110.
54 See Ernst Troeltsch, *The Social Teaching of the Christian Churches*, vol. 2, trans. Olive Wyon (Chicago: University of Chicago Press, 1981), 472, 508, 510–11. For a critical response, see Brent Sockness, "Luther's Two Kingdoms Revisited: A Response to Reinhold Niebuhr's Criticism of Luther," *Journal of Religious Ethics* 20 (1992): 93–110.
55 See this helpful summary in William Lazareth, *Christians in Society: Luther, the Bible, and Social Ethics* (Minneapolis, MN: Fortress, 2001), 5.
56 Lindberg, *Beyond Charity*, 29.
57 In fact, Lutheran resistance to tyrannical authority was best expressed in the Magdeburg Confession of 1550. David Whitford notes that "Luther did not advocate a general theory of resistance. Yet the success of Magdeburg in 1550-1 demonstrates that it is historically inaccurate to attribute political quietism to Luther, either negatively as in Troeltsch (Luther did not have a theory of resistance) or positively as in Barth (Luther's two kingdoms necessitated quietism). The resistance affirmed by the Magdeburg pastors was clearly based in Luther. Luther's political legacy is not, and cannot, be the cause of much 20th-century tragedy. Luther's legacy, more properly, belongs to the city of Magdeburg and all those who found in these faithful pastors and laypersons an example of conviction and courage for the sake of the gospel." See *Tyranny and Resistance: The Magdeburg Confession and the Lutheran Tradition* (St. Louis, MO: Concordia, 2001), 105.
58 John Witte, *Law and Protestantism* (Cambridge: Cambridge University Press, 2002), 107.

59 Heinrich Bornkamm, *Luther's Doctrine of the Two Kingdoms in the Context of His Theology*, trans. Karl H. Hertz (Philadelphia: Fortress, 1966), 6.

60 Robert Benne, *The Paradoxical Vision: A Public Theology for the Twenty-First Century* (Minneapolis, MN: Fortress, 1995), 177.

61 Richard Niebanck, *Economic Justice: An Evangelical Perspective* (New York: Lutheran Church in America, 1980), 108.

62 John Stumme, "Interpreting the Doctrine of the Two Kingdoms," *Dialog* 27 (Fall 1988): 278.

63 Luther, *WA* 11, 249–50.

64 Whitford, *Tyranny and Resistance*, 97.

65 Uwe Simon-Netto, *The Fabricated Luther: The Rise and Fall of the Shirer Myth* (St. Louis, MO: Concordia, 1995), 78–79.

66 See Alfred W. Crosby, *The Measure of Reality: Quantification and Western Society, 1250–1600* (Cambridge: Cambridge University Press, 1997).

67 See George Schner, "Metaphors for Theology," in *Theology after Liberalism: A Reader*, ed. John Webster and George P. Schner (Oxford: Blackwell, 2000), 10–12.

68 Francis Bacon, *Meditationes Sacræ. De Hæresibus* (1597).

69 See James K. A. Smith, *Who's Afraid of Postmodernism?* (Grand Rapids, MI: Baker Academic, 2006), 81–107.

70 Lyotard, *Postmodern Condition*, 35.

71 Ibid., 36.

72 Reinhard Hütter, *Bound to Be Free: Evangelical Catholic Engagements in Ecclesiology, Ethics, and Ecumenism* (Grand Rapids, MI: Eerdmans, 2004), 32.

73 George Lindbeck, *The Church in a Postliberal Age*, ed. James J. Buckley (Grand Rapids, MI: Eerdmans, 2002), 185.

74 "What matters at this stage is the construction of local forms of community within which civility and the intellectual and moral life can be sustained through the new dark ages which are already upon us. And if the tradition of the virtues was able to survive the horrors of the last dark ages, we are not entirely without grounds for hope. This time however the barbarians are not waiting beyond the frontiers; they have already been governing us for quite some time. And it is our lack of consciousness of this that constitutes part of our predicament. We are waiting not for a Godot, but for another—doubtless very different—St. Benedict." See Alasdair MacIntyre, *After Virtue* (Notre Dame, IN: University of Notre Dame Press, 1984), 263. Undoubtedly, fostering local communities of virtue is a must. However, insularity will never be sufficient for the Christian who is impelled by a message that is of its very nature outreaching—to the Jew, first, but also to the Greek (and the barbarian!).

75 See Gerhard Forde, *Where God Meets Man: Luther's Down-to-Earth Approach to the Gospel* (Minneapolis, MN: Augsburg, 1972), 117.

76 As quoted by Lindbeck, see *The Church in a Postliberal Age*, 160.

77 Oswald Bayer, "Luther as an Interpreter of Holy Scripture," in *The Cambridge Companion to Martin Luther*, ed. Donald K. McKim (Cambridge: Cambridge University Press, 2003), 80.

78 Luther, "A Brief Instruction on What to Look for and Expect in the Gospels," in *LW* 35:119.

79 Luther, "Table Talk Recorded by John Schlaginhaufen," in *LW* 54:127.

Chapter 9   Discipleship in Lutheran Perspective

1   See Robert H. Nelson, *Economics as Religion: From Samuelson to Chicago and Beyond* (University Park: Pennsylvania State University Press, 2001), especially page 110.

2   "The Augsburg Confession," article 7, in *The Book of Concord*, ed. Robert Kolb and Timothy Wengert (Minneapolis, MN: Fortress, 2000), 42.2–4.

3 . For a helpful summary of this teaching, see John Stumme, "Interpreting the Doctrine of the Two Kingdoms," in *Dialog* 27, no. 4 (Winter 1988): 277–89. The doctrine helpfully distinguishes politics from salvation without sacrificing one for the other. For further reading, see Mary Jane Haemig, "The Confessional Basis of Lutheran Thinking on Church–State Issues," in *Church and State: Lutheran Perspectives*, ed. John R. Stumme and Robert W. Tuttle (Minneapolis, MN: Fortress, 2003).

4   For one of the best treatments of Luther's view of the simultaneity of the Christian's sinfulness and saintliness, see Carter Lindberg, "Justice and Injustice in Luther's Judgment of 'Holiness Movements,'" in *Luther's Ecumenical Significance: An Interconfessional Consultation*, ed. Peter Manns and Harding Meyer (Philadelphia: Fortress, 1984), 161–81.

5   See Gilbert Meilaender, "The Place of Ethics in the Theological Task," *Currents in Theology and Mission* 6 (1979): 199.

6   In his "Commentary on the Sermon on the Mount," Luther identified twelve "evangelical counsels." See Martin Luther, *LW* 21:132.

7   The affirmation of ordinary life does not come without critique. See Risto Saarinen, "Finnish Luther Studies," in *Engaging Luther: A (New) Theological Assessment*, ed. Olli-Pekka Vainio (Eugene, OR: Cascade, 2010), 2.

8   Lindberg, "Justice and Injustice," 162.

9   Ibid., 163.

10 Luther, "Commentary on Galatians" (1519), in *LW* 27:238.

11 Ibid., in *LW* 27:263.

12 Oswald Bayer, "Nature and Institution: Luther's Doctrine of the Three Estates," trans. Christine Helmer, *Lutheran Quarterly* 12, no. 2 (Summer 1998): 104.

13 Martin Luther, "The Blessed Sacrament of the Holy and True Body of Christ, and the Brotherhoods," in *LW* 35:58.

14 Bernhard Lohse, *Martin Luther's Theology: Its Historical and Systematic Development*, trans. Roy Harrisville (Minneapolis, MN: Fortress, 1999), 48.

15 Of course, Christ's death is an atoning sacrifice and not merely a prophetic, martyriological witness. See Robert W. Bertram, *A Time for Confessing*, ed. Michael Hoy (Grand Rapids, MI: Eerdmans, 2008).

16 The first six are, in order: (1) possession of the holy word of God; (2) the sacrament of baptism; (3) the sacrament of the altar; (4) the offices of the keys exercised publicly; (5) the possession of consecrated ministers; and (6) the offering of prayer, public praise, and thanksgiving to God. See Martin Luther, "On the Councils and the Church," in *LW* 41:148ff. See William J. Abraham, "Discipleship: On Making Disciples of the Lord Jesus Christ," in *Marks of the Body of Christ*, ed. Carl E. Braaten and Robert W. Jenson (Grand Rapids, MI: Eerdmans, 1999), 154.

17 Luther, "On the Councils and the Church," in *LW* 41:164–65.

18 See Marc Lienhard, *Luther: Witness to Jesus Christ* (Minneapolis, MN: Augsburg, 1982), 120–21.

19 "As long as we live in the flesh we only begin to make some progress in that which shall be perfected in the future life." See Martin Luther, "The Freedom of a Christian," in *LW* 31:358.

20 Gerhard Forde, "The Lutheran View of Sanctification," in *The Preached God: Proclamation in Word and Sacrament*, ed. Mark Mattes and Steven Paulson (Grand Rapids, MI: Eerdmans, 2007), 240.

21 Alasdair MacIntyre, "Virtues, Unity of a Human Life, and Tradition," in *Why Narrative?: Readings in Narrative Theology* (Grand Rapids, MI: Eerdmans, 1989), 106.

22 See Martin Kähler, *The So-Called Historical Jesus and the Historic, Biblical Christ* (Philadelphia: Fortress, 1960), 80n11.

23 Werner Elert, *The Christian Ethos*, trans. Carl J. Schindler (Philadelphia: Muhlenberg Press, 1957), 201.

24 Martin Luther, "The Small Catechism," in *BC-K/W* 363:2.

25 Gerhard Ebeling, "The Necessity of the Doctrine of the Two Kingdoms," *Word and Faith*, trans. James W. Leitch (London: SCM, 1963), 404.

26 Hans Hillerbrand, "'Christ Has Nothing to Do with Politics': Martin Luther and the Societal Order," in *Seminary Ridge Review* 13, no. 2 (Spring 2011): 20.

27   See Carter Lindberg, *Beyond Charity: Reformation Initiatives for the Poor* (Minneapolis, MN: Fortress, 1993); and Samuel Torvend, *Luther and the Hungry Poor: Gathered Fragments* (Minneapolis, MN: Fortress, 2008).

28   See Martin Luther, *The Bondage of the Will*, trans., J. I. Packer and O. R. Johnston (New York: Fleming H. Revell, 1957), 268–69.

29   See Michael W. Foss, *The Disciple's Joy: Six Practices for Spiritual Growth* (Minneapolis, MN: Augsburg, 2007); and *Power Surge: Six Marks of Discipleship for a Changing Church* (Minneapolis, MN: Fortress, 2000).

30   Foss, *Power Surge*, 21.

31   Ibid., 14.

32   See Philipp Jacob Spener, *Pia Desideria*, trans. Theodore G. Tappert (Philadelphia: Fortress, 1964), 117.

33   Charles G. Finney, *Lectures on the Revival of Religion* (New York: Leavitt, Lord, and Co., 1835), 91.

34   Dietrich Bonhoeffer, "Protestantism without the Reformation," in *No Rusty Swords: Letters, Lectures and Notes, 1928–1936*, ed. Edwin H. Robertson, trans. Edwin H. Robertson and John Bowden (London: Collins, 1965), 92–118.

35   See Frederick Schmidt, "The Issue-Driven Church," *Patheos*, November 7, 2011, http://www.patheos.com/Resources/Additional-Resources/Issue -Driven-Church-Frederick-Schmidt-11-07-2011.html.

36   The 1991 ELCA social statement, "Church in Society: A Lutheran Perspective," claims that the church is a community of moral deliberation. While it is hard to trace the encapsulating of the phrase "congregations as communities of moral deliberation," we are reminded of James Gustafson, "Moral Discernment in the Christian Life," in *Moral Discernment in the Christian Life: Essays in Theological Ethics*, ed. Theo A. Boer and Paul E. Capetz (Louisville, KY: Westminster John Knox, 2007), 25–40.

37   Immanuel Kant, *Religion within the Limits of Reason Alone*, trans. John Silber (New York: Harper and Row, 1960), 92.

38   In order to assess the millennial aspirations in economics, see Nelson, *Economics as Religion*.

39   See Jacob S. Hacker and Paul Pierson, *Winner-Take-All Politics: How Washington Made the Rich Richer—and Turned Its Back on the Middle Class* (New York: Simon and Schuster, 2010).

40   Nathan Hilkert, "Searching for Wisdom in the ELCA's Genetics Statement," *Lutheran Forum* 45, no. 2 (Summer 2011): 56–57.

41   Eric Metaxas, *Bonhoeffer: Pastor, Martyr, Prophet, Spy* (Nashville, TN: Thomas Nelson, 2010), 153.

42   See Mark Mattes, *The Role of Justification in Contemporary Theology* (Grand Rapids, MI: Eerdmans, 2004), 105.

43 "The primary social task of the church is to be itself—that is, a people who have been formed by a story that provides them with the skills for negotiating the danger of this existence, trusting in God's promise of redemption." See Stanley Hauerwas, *The Hauerwas Reader*, ed. John Berkman and Michael Cartwright (Durham, NC: Duke University Press, 2001), 113.

44 See Mark Nygard, *The Missiological Implications of the Theology of Gerhard Forde* (Minneapolis, MN: Lutheran University Press, 2011), 169.

45 "The church does not exist to provide an ethos for democracy or any other form of social organization, but stands as a political alternative to every nation, witnessing to the kind of social life possible for those that have been formed by the story of Jesus Christ." See Hauerwas, *Hauerwas Reader*, 115. My comments are directed likewise against the positive political teachings of radical Orthodoxy. See Mark Mattes, "A Lutheran Critique of Radical Orthodoxy," in *Lutheran Quarterly* 25, no. 3 (Autumn 2001).

46 "Thus no program is called for, but instead a *necessity* which grows out of the gospel of the cross and resurrection of Jesus Christ. The gospel demands that *from now on*, on the basis of prayer (kneeling) and scholarship (sitting), we *stand* and accept responsibility for it in the world in which we live. When we no longer approach the gospel from a trailblazing stance or as a simple demonstrable witness of the proof of Spirit and power, we find ourselves instead included within it and come to recognize ourselves as part of it. At that point both prayer and humility can break out of the confines of the form and structure of our work within the church, with its private chambers of study and struggle, and can discover its place and form in the world we live. Thus, we can find a substantive theological scholarship and, not for the last time, win back the Bible. Then instead of using and standing in judgment over the Bible, we allow ourselves to be led by it into God's wonder and mystery and thereby attain the language of truth." See Klaus Schwarzwäller, *Cross and Resurrection: God's Wonder and Mystery*, trans. Ken Sundet Jones and Mark Mattes (Minneapolis, MN: Fortress, 2012), 101.

Chapter 10   Bioethics and Honoring Humanity

1 Gregory Stock, quoted by Paul Jersild, *The Nature of Our Humanity: A Christian Response to Evolution and Biotechnology* (Minneapolis, MN: Fortress, 2009), 118.

2 Jersild, *Nature of Our Humanity*, 91.

3 Ibid.

  4 Ibid., 115.
  5 Ibid.
  6 Ted Peters, *The Stem Cell Debate* (Minneapolis, MN: Fortress, 2007), 17.
  7 Ibid., 2.
  8 Ibid., 44.
  9 Jersild, *Nature of Our Humanity*, 112.
 10 Ibid., 110.
 11 Gregory E. Pence, *Medical Ethics: Accounts of the Cases That Shaped and Define Medical Ethics* (New York: McGraw-Hill, 2008), 125.
 12 Ibid.
 13 Ibid.
 14 Ibid., 126–27.
 15 Peters, *Stem Cell Debate*, 37.
 16 Ibid., 44.
 17 Ibid., 77.
 18 Ibid., 79.
 19 Ted Peters, "Framing Stem Cell Arguments," *Journal of Lutheran Ethics Online* 9, no. 8 (August 1, 2009), http://63.236.234.41/JLE/Articles/364.
 20 Peters, *Stem Cell Debate*, 67.
 21 Ibid., 97.
 22 Peters, "Framing Stem Cell Arguments."
 23 Jersild, *Nature of Our Humanity*, 124.
 24 Ibid., 125.
 25 Leon R. Kass, *Life, Liberty and the Defense of Dignity: The Challenge for Bioethics* (San Francisco: Encounter, 2002), 10.
 26 Ibid., 14.
 27 Ibid., 124.
 28 Ibid., 131.
 29 Gilbert Meilaender, *Bioethics: A Primer for Christians* (Grand Rapids, MI: Eerdmans, 1996), 32.
 30 Ibid., 43.
 31 Stephen Schwarz, *The Moral Question of Abortion* (Chicago: Loyola University Press, 1990), 56.
 32 Ibid., 74.

Chapter 12   Should Lutherans Be Mainline Protestants?

  1 For a recent history of the development of mainline Protestantism, see Elesha J. Coffman, *The Christian Century and the Rise of the Protestant Mainline* (Oxford: Oxford University Press, 2013).
  2 Roy A. Harrisville and Walter Sundberg distinguish an Enlightenment approach to historical criticism from an "Augustinian" approach, which they

accept. Streng, it would appear, represents the "Enlightenment" approach, while Harrisville and Sundberg represent the "Augustinian" approach. Of the Enlightenment approach, these authors note, "The chronic hostility of the Enlightenment tradition toward religious communities and their creeds and its need to impose its own faith in place of them is, in our view, the key factor that is responsible for the continuing suspicion of historical-critical method in the church, even among mainline denominations that train their clergy in its use." Roy A. Harrisville and Walter Sundberg, *The Bible in Modern Culture: Baruch Spinoza to Brevard Childs*, 2nd ed. (Grand Rapids, MI: Eerdmans, 2002), 268. The authors note that an Augustinian approach to the historical-critical method can be found in a thinker like Rudolf Bultmann: "For all the criticism that Bultmann receives for his use of Heidegger, it must be remembered that what finally attracts Bultmann to existential philosophy is its articulation of the desperate plight of the human being who faces the reality of death without protection. This is Augustinian to the core. That is to say, it stands within the dominant religious tradition of Western Christendom. And his greatest student, Ernst Käsemann, is imbued with the same urgent sense of the wretchedness of the human condition. The answer to this wretchedness is the gospel of Jesus Christ. . . . What we learn from Bultmann (at least on occasion) and Käsemann (on all occasions) is that, when all is said and done, historical criticism of the Bible is never able to go beyond establishing the Easter faith of the first disciples. The 'science' of historical-critical method establishes the 'fact' that *the disciples* believed that Christ had been raised from the dead and that, therefore, *in their eyes*, his ministry of preaching and the sacrifice of his life was validated by the Lord almighty, creator of heaven and earth. Whatever our view of the resurrection, historical criticism tells us where the initiative in the biblical narrative is laid and where, therefore, it *ought to be laid*" (272). Finally, the authors note, "What this Augustinian tradition of historical criticism teaches is that, in principle, the rigorous, scientific examination of the bible can neither destroy nor support faith. It is obligated, however, to point to faith" (272).

My own way of thinking resonates with that of Brevard Childs, who seeks a "canonical approach" to Scripture where the focus is less on matters behind the text—the historical context to which the text refers—and more on the interrelationships between signs, symbols, and figures within the text and the future to which the text invites us. Childs notes, "The canonical approach recognizes the need of a 'second naiveté' (Ricoeur) to acknowledge the complexity of the shaping of Scripture, and yet it also to see the Bible from a different and unified perspective: that of the community of faith who bore witness by its transmission to the continuing

redemptive intervention of the one divine reality, whom the church confesses to be the God and Father of Jesus Christ." See Brevard Childs, "On
Reclaiming the Bible for Christian Theology," in *Reclaiming the Bible
for the Church*, ed. Carl Braaten and Robert Jenson (Grand Rapids, MI:
Eerdmans, 1995), 9.

3 For further discussion, see Oswald Bayer, *Theology the Lutheran Way*,
trans. Jeffrey Silcock and Mark Mattes (Grand Rapids, MI: Eerdmans,
2007), 139–71.

4 See Oswald Bayer, *A Contemporary in Dissent: Johann Georg Hamann
as a Radical Enlightener*, trans. Roy Harrisville and Mark Mattes (Grand
Rapids, MI: Eerdmans, 2012), 117–27.

5 "Act as if the maxim of your action were to become through your will a universal law of nature." See Immanuel Kant, *Groundwork of the Metaphysic of
Morals*, trans. H. J. Paton (New York: Harper and Row, 1956), 89.

6 "The *death* of the divine Man, *as death*, is *abstract* negativity, the
immediate result of the movement which ends only in *natural* universality. Death loses this natural meaning in spiritual self-consciousness,
i.e., it comes to be its just stated Notion; death becomes transfigured
from its immediate meaning, viz. the non-being of this *particular* individual, into the *universality* of the Spirit who dwells in His community, dies in it every day, and is daily resurrected." See G. W. F. Hegel,
Phenomenology of Spirit, trans. A. V. Miller (Oxford: Oxford University
Press, 1957), 475.

7 "The common element in all howsoever diverse expressions of piety, by
which these are conjointly distinguished from all other feelings, or, in other
words, the self-identical essence of piety, is this: the consciousness of being
absolutely dependent, or, which is the same thing, of being in relation
with God." See Friedrich Schleiermacher, *The Christian Faith*, trans. H. R.
Mackintosh and J. S. Stewart (Philadelphia: Fortress, 1976), 12.

8 See Klaus Schwarzwäller, *Cross and Resurrection: God's Wonder and
Mystery*, trans. Ken Sundet Jones and Mark Mattes (Minneapolis, MN:
Fortress, 2012), 25–39.

9 See William Streng, *In Search of Ultimates* (Minneapolis, MN: Augsburg,
1969).

10 The American Lutheran Church united the American Lutheran Church
(1930), a German background group, with the Evangelical Lutheran
Church (1917), a Norwegian background group, and the United
Evangelical Lutheran Church, a Danish background group.

11 "The Augsburg Confession," article 7, in *The Book of Concord*, ed. Robert
Kolb and Timothy Wengert (Minneapolis, MN: Fortress, 2000), 42.1.

12 For a laudatory history of the Iowa Synod, see G. J. Zeilinger, *A Missionary
Synod with a Mission* (Chicago: Wartburg, 1929).

13 See J. Michael Reu, *Lutheran Dogmatics* (Dubuque, IA: Wartburg Seminary Press, 1963).

14 See Eric Metaxas, *Bonhoeffer: Pastor, Martyr, Spy* (New York: Thomas Nelson, 2010).

15 "A scriptural world is thus able to absorb the universe. It supplies the interpretive framework within which believers seek to live their lives and understand reality. . . . It is the text, so to speak, which absorbs the world, rather than the world the text." See George Lindbeck, *The Nature of Doctrine* (Philadelphia: Westminster, 1984), 117–18.

16 See James Hannam, *The Genesis of Science: How the Christian Middle Ages Launched the Scientific Revolution* (Washington, DC: Regnery, 2011).

17 See Jonathan Haidt, *The Righteous Mind: Why Good People Are Divided by Politics and Religion* (London: Penguin, 2012), 112–14. My discussion here and throughout the paper is quite dependent on Haidt.

Chapter 13   A Confessional Response to North American Lutheran-Reformed Ecumenism

1 The most extensive study of the research involved in the development of the *Leuenberg Agreement* is found in Elisabeth Schieffer, *Von Schauenburg nach Leuenberg: Entstehung und Bedeutung der Kondordie reformatorischer Kirchen in Europa* (Paderborn, Germany: Verlag Bonifatius-Druckerei, 1983).

2 See, for example, Philip Melanchthon, "Apology of the Augsburg Confession," in *The Book of Concord*, ed. Robert Kolb and Timothy Wengert (Minneapolis, MN: Fortress, 2000), 130:62.

3 "We believe, teach, and confess that the assumed human nature in Christ not only has and retains its natural, essential characteristics but also that through the personal union with the deity and, afterward, through the exaltation or glorification, this nature was elevated to the right hand of majesty, power, and might over all things that can be named, not only in this world, but also in the world to come [Eph. 1:20–21]." See the *Formula of Concord*, Solid Declaration, article 8, in *BC-K/W* 618:12. One inference of the *genus maiestaticum* is drawn later in the article in the Solid Declaration: "The union between the divine and human natures in the person of Christ is a much different, higher, indescribable communion. Because of this union and communion God is a human being and a human being is God. Nevertheless, through this union and communion neither the natures nor their characteristics are mixed together with the other, but each nature retains its own essence and characteristics" (619:19).

4 Criticism of the Calvinistic view of Christ's presence in the Supper as "spiritual," since His body is limited to heaven as a locus, can be found in the *Formula of Concord*, Solid Declaration, article 7, 592:2–615:128.

5 Speaking colloquially, Steve Paulson notes, "Luther completely reversed normal descriptions of 'assumption' found in so-called Logos Christologies, where an incarnate God somehow subsumes humanity and makes it more perfectly 'divine.' Luther's assumption theory is not preoccupied with how humans get up into the divine but how the divine goes so deep into our flesh that he gives his weight to sinful human flesh (our desire to escape into 'spiritual' matters that we think are 'higher' than body). When God sits his corpulent mercy down in this world, no spiritual diet or holy crane will ever get him out again. Sinners 'go up' to being real human beings for the first time because he 'came down' like an enormous divine weight that won't move. Consequently for Luther, salvation is not taking leave of humanity and becoming like God; it is becoming really and fully human as God's own trusting creature in Christ's new kingdom." See *Luther for Armchair Theologians* (Louisville, KY: Westminster John Knox, 2004), 144.

6 The *locus classicus* for the *extra-Calvinisticum* is: "For even if the Word in his immeasurable essence united with the nature of man into one person, we do not imagine that he was confined therein. Here is something marvelous: the Son of God descended from heaven in such a way that, without leaving heaven, he willed to be borne in the virgin's womb, to go about earth, and to hang upon the cross; yet he continuously filled the world even as he had done from the beginning." See John Calvin, *Institutes of the Christian Religion*, ed. John T. McNeill, trans. Ford Lewis Battles (Philadelphia, PA: Westminster, 1960), II.13.4.

7 Commenting on Luther's critique of Nestorius (with parallels to the Reformed), Paulson notes that "if the preacher says, 'There goes *God* down the street fetching water,' Nestorius would get all flustered because this wasn't the sort of thing God did—more to the point, it wouldn't leave any water for *humans* to fetch. That is why Luther called Nestorius proud and stubbornly stupid. He did not want God sullied by bodily things, and he wanted to save room for humans to do the works of the law. He did not want to preach that 'God died,' nor did he want to preach that 'this man Jesus created the world.'" See *Luther for Armchair Theologians*, 140–41.

8 While informed by Reformed theology at several points, the Episcopal theologian Paul Zahl through his own deep refection on grace has helpfully grasped the pastoral significance of a bound will: "The point for theology is that we are not subjects; we are objects. We do not live; we are lived. To put it another way, our archaeology is our teleology. We are typically operating from drives and aspirations generated by our past.

What ought to be free decisions in relation to love and service become un-free decisions anchored in retrospective deficits and grievances. This is the message of tragic literature. . . . Free entities are subjects. Un-free entities are objects. Christ Jesus, the body of God on earth, was free. The world to which he came was un-free. It is un-free still. There is therefore only one Subject in the world today, and he is surrounded by countless beleaguered objects. St. Paul famously wrote, 'Faith, hope, and love abide, these three; and the greatest of these is love' (1 Corinthians 13:13). I would describe an obverse trio this way: original sin, total depravity, and the un-free will abide, these three; and the root of the thing is the un-free will." See Paul Zahl, *Grace in Practice: A Theology of Everyday Life* (Grand Rapids, MI: Eerdmans, 2007), 113–14.

9   "For if God is to make a testament, as he promises, then he must die; and if he is to die, then he must be a man. And so that little word 'testament' is a short summary of all God's wonders and grace, fulfilled in Christ" See Martin Luther, "A Treatise on the New Testament, That Is, the Holy Mass" (1520), in *LW* 35:84.

10 James E. Andrews and Joseph A. Burgess, eds., *An Invitation to Action: The Lutheran-Reformed Dialogue Series III 1981–1983* (Philadelphia: Fortress, 1984), 2.

11 Ibid.

12 Marc Lienhard notes that *Leuenberg*'s view of the Lord's Supper is beyond Zwingli's, since the Lord's Supper is not commemorative but conveys Christ's presence (either through the Spirit or through bodily presence) but differs from Calvin in that double predestination is denied. See "The Leuenberg Agreement: Origins and Aims," in *The Leuenberg Agreement and Lutheran-Reformed Relationships: Evaluations by North American and European Theologians*, ed. William G. Rusch and Daniel F. Martensen (Minneapolis, MN: Augsburg, 1989), 29. Conservative reactions to *Leuenberg* were published in the LCMS journal, *The Springfielder* 36, no. 3 (December 1972). There, Hans-Lutz Poetsch noted that Jacob Preus "called attention to the dangerous lack of distinction between the Law and the Gospel which would call into question any proposed concept of the church" (186). And, similar to my claim in this essay, Gerhard Rost criticized *Leuenberg* for "a soft-pedaling of the Holy Trinity and of Christ's nature as true Son of God; a *suppression of God's wrath*, with the attendant danger of covering up the mystery of God's love; a suppression of the apocalyptic return of Christ and in connection with that a reinterpretation of the Kingdom of God into a development of peace and justice within this world" (191, emphasis added). He went on to say that "all recognized that this Concord is not a document making for true unity between the Lutheran and the Reformed churches, but it is the artificial

product of current liberal theology. It actually expresses infinitely less than the genuine ecumenical unity that is already present now in the Christian churches" (191). Finally, Eugene Klug noted, "Surely there must be an awareness that much of European theology at this time, Lutheran and Reformed, moves with an aversion to the blood atonement and vicarious satisfaction for sins, that Christ bears, satisfied, placates the avenging wrath of God against sin and sinners" (195). Likewise, Lowell Green, four years later in *The Springfielder* 40, no. 2 (April 1976): 106, outlining the roots of the *extra-Calvinisticum* in Neoplatonic philosophy, as mediated for Zwingli via Erasmus, asked, "Have today's Reformed theologians declared their readiness to surrender the maxim of their forefathers that the finite cannot be grasped by the infinite (*finitutum infiniti non capax*)? Until such a concession is made, 'agreement' on the sacrament is meaningless, since the sacramental teaching of the Reformed fathers was but the application of their philosophy and their Christology. Whenever clarity on this point is lacking, not only the doctrine of the sacrament is in jeopardy, but also the doctrine of Christ and human salvation. On this matter there can be no yielding."

13 Friedrich Schleiermacher, quoted in Steven Paulson, "The Wrath of God," *Dialog* 33, no. 4 (Fall 1994): 246.

14 Paulson, "Wrath of God," 250. Paulson identifies the problem of mainline Protestantism's issue with God's wrath in this way: "If there is a God who operates outside his own law *ex lex*, Ritschl argued, there is no basis for certainty or a standard of justice. God must not operate outside the revelation of his will in law or in Christ if faith is to make any sense. Therefore, Luther's tendency to talk about God (and especially God's wrath) outside God's own word, and even outside Christ, must be exorcized" (247). Paulson argues that this contention also actually distances Luther from nominalism: "We can conclude that Luther's distinction between God preached and not preached is not meant to 'protect' God's freedom, as a Nominalist might attempt, but is rather the protection of the preaching office entrusted to the church. God's wrath is not an attribute that needs protection, but is the necessary presupposition of the church's work on earth" (250–51). In this light, our interest in ecumenism waxes to the degree our interest in evangelism wanes.

15 See Edgar Trexler, *High Expectations: Understanding the ELCA's Early Years, 1988–2002* (Minneapolis, MN: Fortress, 2003), 113.

16 These bodies were the Lutheran Church in American (LCA; 1962), The American Lutheran Church (TALC; 1960), and the American Evangelical Lutheran Church (AELC; 1976). The LCA was composed of East Coast Lutherans of German ancestry, many of whom settled in the United States before the revolution, others of old Swedish background from

the Augustana Synod, and much smaller groups of Finns (the Suomi Synod), and Grundtvigian Danes. TALC was composed of largely Upper Midwest and West Coast Lutherans, including a German-background synod, the American Lutheran Church, a Norwegian-background synod, the Evangelical Lutheran Church, and the United Evangelical Lutheran Church, which had a Danish background indebted to the "Inner Mission." In 1963, another Norwegian American group, the Lutheran Free Church, joined TALC. The AELC was a breakaway group from the Lutheran Church–Missouri Synod, stemming from the time of the dispute over Seminex, the historical-critical method, and "gospel-reductionism."

A summary of the ecumenical ventures of these church bodies can be found in chapters 14–17 of *Lutherans in Ecumenical Dialogue: A Reappraisal*, ed. Joseph Burgess (Minneapolis, MN: Augsburg, 1990). In the late 1960s, TALC theologian Eugene M. Skibbe presented a study of the Arnoldshain Thesis that affirmed its ecumenical role and encouraged its impact in North America: *Protestant Agreement on the Lord's Supper* (Minneapolis, MN: Augsburg, 1968). Commenting on thesis 8.2 and thesis 4 of Arnoldshain, Skibbe, departing from the historic practice of closed communion in TALC, advocated for open communion: "The Lord calls to his Supper not just certain people, but all men. This sentence does not say that all people are saved by Christ, as though it did not matter whether a person believed in Christ or not. Nor does it say that all who come to the Lord's Supper come worthily, for some among them might come hypocritically or with evil intentions. But it does say that he calls all—regardless of their past sins, their lack of understanding, or even their wrong theories—that he calls all in his church to his Supper, and that to all who long for God's righteousness he gives the forgiveness of sins" (116).

17 See William G. Rusch, *A Commentary on "Ecumenism: The Vision of the ELCA"* (Minneapolis, MN: Augsburg, 1990), 151–52.

18 Trexler, *High Expectations*, 105.

19 Ibid., 115–16.

20 Ibid., 117.

21 Keith F. Nickle and Timothy F. Lull, ed., *A Common Calling: The Witness of Our Reformation Churches in North America Today* (Minneapolis, MN: Augsburg, 1993), 32.

22 Trexler, *High Expectations*, 154.

23 Ibid. TALC had established pulpit and altar fellowship with the Presbyterian Church USA and the Reformed Church of America in 1986.

24 Rusch and Martensen, *The Leuenberg Agreement and Lutheran Reformed Relationships*, 95. A representative voice of this party is the late James Kittelson. See James Kittelson, "Enough Is Enough!: The Confusion over

the Augsburg Confession and Its *Satis Est*," *Lutheran Quarterly* 12, no. 3 (Autumn 1998): 249–70.

25 Robert Jenson, "The Leuenberg Agreement in the North American Context," in *The Leuenberg Agreement and Lutheran-Reformed Relationships*, 100–101.

26 See Trexler's discussion, *High Expectations*, 145ff.

27 Rusch, *Commentary on "Ecumenism*," 32.

28 For an overview, see Keith Bridston and Samuel Nafzger, "Lutheran-Reformed Dialogue," in *Lutherans in Ecumenical Dialogue: A Reappraisal*, ed. Joseph Burgess (Minneapolis, MN: Augsburg, 1990), 33ff. See also John Reumann's discussion about the influence of *Leuenberg* in the North American context in *The Supper of the Lord: The New Testament, Ecumenical Dialogues, and Faith and Order on Eucharist* (Philadelphia: Fortress, 1985), 99–100.

29 Trexler, *High Expectations*, 110. The *Study Guide* developed for TALC members to help them examine Lutheran-Reformed ecumenism noted, "In the past Lutheran pulpits and altars were restricted to Lutherans, perhaps for good and sufficient historical reasons. Now practice has changed. This is not because of unionism or theological relativism. To the contrary, this is a sign of theological health. No longer are we a settled people. We wander to and fro, and any attempt to fence the altar is misunderstood as snobbery rather than as a concern for truth and holiness. Only the one who denies the real presence of the risen Christ who forgives sins should be excluded from the altar. Other than this we can safely leave it to the Lord to fence his table. Nor do Lutherans hold strictly any longer to 'Lutheran pulpits for Lutheran pastors.' Guest preachers are common. Pulpit exchange is common. But guests are not invited if there is any question about the clarity of the gospel that is going to be preached" (Office of the Presiding Bishop, The American Lutheran Church [Minneapolis, MN: TALC, 1986], 10). The statement here indicates that our doctrine follows our practice. But isn't this the tail wagging the dog? Additionally, why single out the Reformed for pulpit and altar fellowship when, de facto, the Table has become open to all confessional groups?

There can be no doubt that the ancient church practiced "closed communion," as Werner Elert has shown in *Eucharist and Church Fellowship in the First Four Centuries*, trans. N. E. Nagel (St. Louis, MO: Concordia, 1966). To translate this practice into a more contemporary idiom, the Lord's Supper is to be seen not as a service to the public but as a ministry of the Lord for the assembled congregation. Admittance to the Lord's Table is a privilege, not a right, and should not be construed as a right. No doubt, closure at the Lord's Table comes across as offensive to democratic sensibilities—as well it should. God's kingdom is not a democracy. Commenting on Joakim Jeremias' interpretation of the Supper as akin to and grounded in Jesus' table fellowship with outcasts, John Pless notes, "Jeremias makes the move from Jesus' meals with those deemed outcasts and unrighteous to the Lord's Supper. He sees a continuum between these meals and the sacrament. The contrast between the meals where Jesus sits at table with sinners and the Last Supper is overlooked by Jeremias. In the Last Supper, Jesus gathers only the twelve. It is not an open meal but a supper with those called to the life of discipleship; they had followed Jesus throughout his public ministry. It is no ordinary meal that Jesus partakes of with his followers but the last supper where he institutes the sacrament of the New Testament—the meal of his body and blood." See "Can We Participate Liturgically in the Atonement?," in *Logia* 19, no. 2 (Eastertide 2010): 40.

What TALC *Study Guide* did indicate accurately is the fact that we are a mobile society whose members are interlocked with others of many confessional traditions. Given that fact, we may wish to reflect upon the statement on communion practices of The American Association of Lutheran Churches, a small group that broke away from TALC at the time of the formation of the ELCA in 1988. Their position states, "A faithful steward of the mysteries of God sees that each communicant has the tools to examine himself or herself, whether he or she be in the faith (1 Cor 11:28; with 2 Cor 13:5). The faithful steward knows who among his flock has been catechized in the faith, who has transferred their membership from elsewhere, and who is living in open and unrepentant sin. Visitors are handled in the same way as any other communicant; the faithful steward sees that they share the confession of the church within which they wish to commune, knows whether they are engaged in open and unrepentant sin, and ensures they have the tools with which to examine himself or herself. Nevertheless, exigent circumstances exist; we do not bind a man's conscience in such matters. We call this, our practice, 'Responsible Communion.'" See Kristofer Carlson, "We Proclaim and Celebrate: The Position of the AALC on the Lord's Supper," April 2006, http://www.krisandsusanna.com/Documents/We%20Proclaim%20and %20Celebrate.pdf.

On a different note, I cannot help but wonder if the openness to pulpit and altar fellowship with the Reformed in TALC was not due at least in part to the fact that many of the denomination's teaching theologians had received their doctorates from historically Reformed institutions, such as Harvard, Yale, Princeton, and Chicago. Likewise, North Americans tend not to like doctrinal differences that separate them from their fellow Americans. I will never forget a pastoral visit in which a retired

parishioner, a veteran of the Second World War, after showing me shrap-
nel wounds to his leg received at the Battle of the Bulge, said, "Pastor, you
can say what you want, but I fought beside Catholics, Jews, and Baptists,
and when it comes right down to it, there are no real differences between
us." This man represents a sentiment quite common in the USA. Hence
American Christians tend to see themselves as belonging not to different confessional traditions but instead to different *denominations*, a
term taken from currency implying that you receive *the same* amount of
change back per each dollar given.

30 Johannes Friedrich, "The Significance of Lutheranism for Fellowship
    among Churches," trans. Kristian T. Baudler, 2006, http://crossalone.us/
    2006/HeavyLifting/CCM/SignificanceOfLutheranismForFellowship.pdf.

31 Jenson, "Leuenberg Agreement," 100–101.

32 I hesitate to use the term *born-again religiosity* since being "born-again"
    or "born from above" are Jesus' own words (John 3:3). The basic problem
    is that unlike Jesus' teachings in John's gospel, such religiosity assumes
    the freedom of the will. We should have a campaign about the proper
    understanding of regeneration.

33 See Charles Porterfield Krauth, *The Conservative Reformation and Its
    Theology* (Minneapolis, MN: Augsburg, 1963). Commenting on Colossians
    2:9, Krauth notes, "If all the fullness of the Godhead in the second per-
    son of the Trinity dwells in Christ bodily, then there is no fullness of that
    Godhead where it is not so dwelling in Christ; and as the human in Christ
    cannot limit the divine, which is essentially, and of necessity, omnipresent,
    the divine in Christ must exalt the human. The Godhead of Christ is every-
    where present, and wherever present, dwells in the human personally, and,
    therefore, of necessity renders it present with itself" (507).

34 See E. Clifford Nelson, ed., *The Lutherans in North America* (Philadelphia:
    Fortress, 1975), 217–27.

35 Nickle and Lull, *Common Calling*, 31.

36 Talk of the "mode" of Christ's presence in the Supper is misleading. John
    Pless notes that "it was from the Formula that [Hermann] Sasse would
    argue that the difference between the Lutherans and the Reformed on the
    doctrine of the Lord's Supper is as lively today as it was in the sixteenth
    century. It is not merely a debate over the *how* of Christ's presence but
    rather *what* is present. No Christian believes in a *real absence*. That was
    not the issue at the time of the Reformation, nor is it the issue now. Thus
    communion announcements that ask that those who come to the altar
    'believe in the real presence of Christ in the sacrament' are meaning-
    less. As Albert Collver has demonstrated, the language of the real pres-
    ence is not yet a confession of Christ's body and blood." See "Can We
    Participate?," 41.

37 Nickle and Lull, *Common Calling*, 43.

38 In *Marburg Revisited*, Presbyterian theologian Joseph C. McLelland notes the Reformed objection to the Lutheran view of Christ's presence in the Supper, "The Calvinists were not convinced that the Lutherans had not divinized the glorified humanity. For them it was the ascension and descent of the Spirit that provided the proper 'moment' in Christological-Eucharistic discussion. They took them as two sides of the one event; ascension means that the living Christ is not essentially discontinuous with the divine-human One who presence was circumscribed; Pentecost means that the dynamic of Christ's presence is not a question in the abilities of his new body but in the peculiar power of the Spirit" (50). Hence in Calvinism, the role of the Holy Spirit is crucial in how Christ is present in the Supper: "It is in this context that the distinctive reformed doctrine of the Holy Spirit is to be understood. The Spirit fulfils his office by bringing us into contact with Christ's substance, which Calvin interprets in terms of a *virtus*, a power judged by its effects in the human realm. Just as much as Luther he wished to preserve objectivity in the Sacrament, the objective presence of the personal Lord" (48). As helpful as this is, the *non capax* approach to Christology is best expressed by Calvin himself: "There is a commonplace distinction of the schools to which I am not ashamed to refer: although the whole Christ is everywhere, still the whole of that which is in him is not everywhere. And would that the Schoolmen themselves had honestly weighed the force of this statement. For thus would the absurd fiction of Christ's carnal presence have been obviated. Therefore, since the whole Christ is everywhere, our Mediator is ever present with his own people, and in the Supper reveals himself in a special way, yet in such a way that the whole Christ is present, but not in his wholeness. For, as has been said, in his flesh he is contained in heaven until he appears in judgment." See John Calvin, *Institutes of the Christian Religion*, ed. John T. McNeill, trans. Ford Lewis Battles (Philadelphia, PA: Westminster, 1960), 4, 17, 30; and Joseph C. McLelland, *Marburg Revisited*, ed. Paul C. Empie and James McCord (Minneapolis, MN: Augsburg, 1966).

The contrast between this Reformed perspective on Christology and the Lord's Supper and that of a Lutheran like J. Michael Reu's view of the ascended Christ as filling all cosmic reality is significant. Reu writes, "The first generation of Christians was definitely convinced that the Lord after the resurrection spent a number of days in physically perceptible communion with his own. If such fellowship has been terminated and superseded by a different sort of communion, and if the believers now address their Lord—who is at the right hand of God—as king and high priest, then they thereby affirm that the risen Lord has ascended to

heaven some time after his resurrection. In keeping with common scriptural usage 'heaven' is here used in contrast not only with the earth but
with the universe, the sense being that Christ has entered into a state
of supramundaneness, a state of existence which makes it possible for
him to be present everywhere; not only have 'the heavens received him,'
Acts 3:21, but he ascended far above the heavens that he might fill all
things (Eph. 4:8–10). His resurrection changed his relation to the human
nature; his ascension changed his relation to the whole created universe,
it marks the transition from a mundane to a transcendent mode of existence." See *Lutheran Dogmatics* (Dubuque, IA: Wartburg Seminary Press,
1963), 234. As a follow up to this Christology, Reu concludes his *Two
Treatises on the Means of Grace* (Minneapolis, MN: Augsburg, 1952) with
this stance about Holy Communion: "If the possibility of the real presence of Christ's body and blood is questioned, we answer that our exalted
Lord is omnipresent also according to his human nature and therefore
able to offer His body and His blood where- and whenever He desires to
do so. His marvelous power is unlimited. If the dogma of the *unio sacra-
mentalis* is stigmatized as unreasonable or contra-rational, we reply that,
measured by this criterion, every mystery of faith would ultimately have
to be surrendered. . . . If it is objected that bread and wine, being earthly
and transitory substances, could not serve as vehicles for the body and
the blood of Christ, we would refer to the incarnation of Christ as the
plainest proof that the finite may comprehend the infinite. If we are told
that it is unworthy of God that we orally receive His body and blood, we
praise Him who in grace has condescended to our level in order to assure
us of our salvation" (117–18).

39 Nickle and Lull, *Common Calling*, 49.

40 Ibid., 66.

41 *A Formula of Agreement* also quotes the *LA*, III.I.19: "We cannot separate
communion with Jesus Christ in his body and blood from the act of eating and drinking. To be concerned about the manner of Christ's presence
in the Lord's Supper in abstraction from this act is to run the risk of
obscuring the meaning of the Lord's Supper."

42 McLelland, *Marburg Revisited*, 51.

43 James E. Andrews and Joseph A. Burgess, ed., *An Invitation to Action: A
Study of Ministry, Sacraments, and Recognition* (Philadelphia: Fortress,
1984.), 111.

44 "Since the Reformed traditions have neither agreed on a single common confession nor codified an authorized book of confessions, none of
their historical statements of faith have equivalent status to documents
gathered together in the Lutherans' Book of Concord. Since Lutherans
have effectively elevated the ecumenical creeds and the confessions of

the sixteenth century above later statements of faith, they have declined to add new documents to their confessional corpus. Thus they continue to assert the sufficiency of the historical creeds and confessions for the contemporary faith and life of the church. By contrast, the Reformed communities have shown a greater willingness to develop new confessions in response to contemporary problems and issues. By asserting the principle *reformata simper reformanda*, the Reformed churches seek to preserve a dynamic relation between the churches' confessions and the living Christ to whom these confessions witness." See Nickle and Lull, *Common Calling*, 29.

45 Quote from Notger Slenczka in Werner Klän, "Aspects of Lutheran Identity: A Confessional Perspective," International Lutheran Council, 2005, http://ilc-online.org/files/2011/10/Berlin-Aspects-of-Luth-Identity -Klan.pdf, 14.

46 Karl Rahner, *On the Theology of Death* (New York: Herder & Herder, 1961), 49.

47 See Martin Luther, "Lectures on Galatians" (1535), in *LW* 26:277.

48 See Wayne Booth, *Modern Dogma and the Rhetoric of Assent* (Chicago: University of Chicago Press, 1974).

49 Harold Bloom notes, "President Eisenhower is notorious for remarking that the United States was and had to be a religious nation, and that he didn't care what religion it had, as long as it had one. I take a sadder view; we are, alas, the most religious of countries, and only varieties of the American Religion finally will flourish among us, whether its devotees call it Mormonism, Protestantism, Catholicism, Islam, Judaism, or what-you-will. And the American Religion, for its two centuries of existence, seems to me irretrievably Gnostic. It is a knowing, by and of an uncreated self, or self-within-the-self, and the knowledge leads to freedom, a dangerous and doom-eager freedom: from nature, time, history, community, other selves. I shake my head in unhappy wonderment at the politically correct younger intellectuals, who hope to subvert what they cannot begin to understand, an obsessed society wholly in the grip of a dominant Gnosticism." See *The American Religion: The Emergence of the Post-Christian Nation* (New York: Simon and Schuster, 1992), 49. While Europe is the most secularized region of the planet, my hunch, given what Bloom says, is that it is no less Gnostic. The secularism wishes to mask its religiosity; I think we can appreciate the late Ernest Becker's comment in *The Denial of Death*: "Every society thus is a 'religion' whether it thinks so or not: Soviet 'religion' and Maoist 'religion' are as truly religious as are scientific and consumer 'religion,' no matter how much they may try to disguise themselves by omitting religious and spiritual ideas from their lives" (New York: Free Press, 1973), 7.

Chapter 14   Revival Time

1   This is no new idea but was done by Aimee Semple McPherson almost one hundred years ago.

Chapter 17   How to Cultivate Biblical, Confessional, Resilient, and Evangelistic Pastors

1   For a table of Lutheran membership growth in the nineteenth century from 25,000 members to 2,175,000 members, and in the twentieth century from 2,175,000 to 7,705,000, see Mark Granquist, *Lutherans in America: A New History* (Minneapolis, MN: Fortress, 2015), 115 and 203, respectively. For tables detailing dramatic losses in the ELCA, see Mark Granquist, "The ELCA by the Numbers," *Lutheran Forum* 50, no. 3 (2016): 17–21.

2   Theodore Tappert, "The Church Must Be Planted," *Lutheran Quarterly* 12 (1998): 181–84.

3   These statistics are from Mark Granquist, email correspondence, January 20, 2017.

4   Mark Granquist notes that beginning in the late 1960s, "Some Lutherans had come to the conclusion that it was not appropriate to attempt to make new Christians" in an increasingly pluralistic America, with its huge variety of different religious groups. See "Exploding the Myth of the Boat," *Lutheran Forum* 44, no. 4 (2010): 15–17.

5   Fred W. Meuser, *The Formation of the American Lutheran Church* (Columbus, OH: Wartburg Press, 1958), 27, fig. 10.

6   G. J. Zeilinger, *A Missionary Synod with a Mission: A Memoir for the Seventy-Fifth Anniversary of the Evangelical Lutheran Synod of Iowa and Other States* (Chicago: Wartburg, 1929), 48.

7   Leo Rosten, *Religions of America* (New York: Simon and Schuster, 1975), 165.

8   In part, this critique of the Enlightenment was due to the pioneering work of Johann Georg Hamann. See Oswald Bayer, *A Contemporary in Dissent: Johann Georg Hamann as a Radical Enlightener*, trans. Roy Harrisville and Mark Mattes (Grand Rapids, MI: Eerdmans, 2012).

9   See Mary Jane Haemig, "Coming In or Going Out?," *Dialog* 53, no. 4 (2014): 312–18.

10 According to Oxfam International, eight individual people own as much as the poorest half of the world's population, which amounts to 3.6 billion people. See "Just 8 Men Own Same Wealth as Half the World," Oxfam International, January 16, 2017, http://www.oxfam.org/en/pressroom/pressreleases/2017-01-16/just-8-men-own-same-wealth-half-world. That Luther opposed nascent capitalism is well known: "In the end, Luther considered early capitalism to constitute a *status confessionis* (a condition

requiring a particular confessing of Christian faith) for the church, in spite of the fact that many of his contemporaries began to think he was tilting at windmills." See Carter Lindberg, *Beyond Charity: Reformation Initiatives for the Poor* (Minneapolis, MN: Fortress, 1993), 114.

11 As the world grows increasingly secular, the Lutheran "two kingdoms" doctrine must, at some level, be expanded in order to appropriate the ancient church's teaching that Christians are "resident aliens." The reader is commended to seek out the early church writing *Letter to Diognetus* 5.1–10.

12 The language of "matrix" is taken from Jonathan Haidt, *The Righteous Mind: Why Good People Are Divided by Politics and Religion* (London: Penguin, 2012), 319–66. Haidt seeks ways for conservatives and liberals to find a common ground in public discourse, surely a praiseworthy endeavor in today's politically charged environment. He argues that both sides have insights necessary for social health that the other side lacks.

13 George Lindbeck, *The Nature of Doctrine: Religion and Theology in a Postliberal Age* (Philadelphia: Westminster, 1984), 118.

14 See Johann Michael Reu and Paul Henry Buehring, *Christian Ethics* (Columbus, OH: Lutheran Book Concern, 1935), 378, for insightful commentary on economic matters and secularism.

15 See Robert H. Nelson, *Economics as Religion: From Samuelson to Chicago and Beyond* (University Park: Pennsylvania State University Press, 2001), 101–13.

16 Robert Benne defends the need to protect "the radicality and universality of the gospel" in *The Paradoxical Vision: A Public Theology for the Twenty-First Century* (Minneapolis, MN: Fortress, 1995), 120.

17 Steve Paulson, "The Augustinian Imperfection," in *The Gospel of Justification in Christ: Where Does the Church Stand Today?*, ed. Wayne Stumme (Grand Rapids, MI: Eerdmans, 2006), 113.

18 See Jean Bethke Elshtain, *Democracy on Trial* (New York: Basic, 1995).

19 See, for instance, Reu's defense of traditional Christian doctrines such as the Trinity, the virgin birth, the deity of Christ, vicarious satisfaction, and the inspiration of Scripture in "Unambiguous Clarification in Matters of the National Lutheran Council," in *Anthology of the Theological Writings of J. Michael Reu* (Lewiston, ME: Edwin Mellen, 1997), 16. See also his critique of the theology of Nathan Söderblom in the same volume in the essay "Hallesby and Söderblom," 61–76.

20 Of course, many other great theologians could be named. I single out these two because of their work in social ethics. For the fruits of some of their work, see Christa R. Klein and Christian D. von Dehsen, *Politics and Policy: The Genesis and Theology of Social Statements in the Lutheran Church in America* (Minneapolis, MN: Fortress, 1989).

21 See Mark Mattes, "Should Lutherans Be Mainline Protestants?," *Logia* 24, no. 4 (2015): 29–40.

22 The language of "purification" is from Jonathan Haidt's TED Talk, "The
    Moral Roots of Liberals and Conservatives," *YouTube*, September 18,
    2008, https://www.youtube.com/watch?v=vs41JrnGaxc. "Purification"
    conveys the fact that pro-life Democrats are marginalized in their party
    while the same is true of moderates in the Republican Party.

23 "Left-wing theological liberalism has built few, if any, great theological
    institutions. Left-wing theological liberalism as well as left-wing bureau-
    cratic leadership has maintained itself by appropriating what far more
    traditional Christian believers have built and endowed." See John Leith,
    Crises in the Church: The Plight of Theological Education (Louisville, KY:
    Westminster John Knox, 1997), 34.

24 "The plethora of theologies now current in seminaries and in the life of
    the church leave ministers and church members with no clear sense
    of identity and no comprehensive framework of theology in the context
    of which they can understand the world and their own lives." Ibid., 46.

25 Roger Finke and Rodney Stark, *The Churching of America, 1776–1990:
    Winners and Losers in Our Religious Economy* (New Brunswick, NJ:
    Rutgers University Press, 1992), 255.

26 Charles Austin, "Get Set for Clergy Retirement Wave," *The Lutheran*
    (November 2014): 19–22.

27 Toward that end, see the Nexus Institute for Theology and Leadership
    in Ministry at Grand View University, http://www.grandview.edu/aspx/
    audience/content.aspx?aid=0&pageid=2191.

28 Paul Ricoeur, "The Hermeneutical Function of Distanciation," in
    *Hermeneutics and the Human Sciences: Essays on Language, Action and
    Interpretation*, ed. John B. Thompson (Cambridge: Cambridge University
    Press, 1981), 131–40.

29 See Brevard Childs, *Reclaiming the Bible for the Church*, ed. Carl E.
    Braaten and Robert W. Jenson (Grand Rapids, MI: Eerdmans, 1995).

30 Thomas Reeves, *The Empty Church* (New York: Free Press, 1996), 67.

Chapter 19   Fear and Love of God

1   All Bible verses used in the following sermons are taken from the New
    Revised Standard Version (NRSV).

2   Martin Luther, "The Small Catechism," in *BC-K/W* 354:22.

Chapter 20   Treasured Possession

1   "Rock of Ages, Cleft for Me," *Lutheran Book of Worship* (Minneapolis,
    MN: Augsburg, 1979), no. 327, stanza 3.

Index of Scripture References

Index of Names

Index of Subjects

9 781948 969239